Washertown:
An American
Masterpiece!

Washertown: An American Masterpiece!

Where It All Began
And
How I Got To Be This Way

Ernest Arlington Twain

To order additional copies of this book, contact:
Xlibris Corporation
1-888-795-4274
www.Xlibris.com
Orders@Xlibris.com
44657

Contents

Dedication

WASHERTOWN: AN AMERICAN MASTERPIECE! is dedicated to Washertown, an American masterpiece—to the wonderful place it was, and the even more wonderful people I knew. Thank you (I think) for being "where it all began for me," and (probably anyway) for contributing so definitively to "how I got to be this way."
                                        Love,
                                        Ernie

ACKNOWLEDGEMENTS

I wish to acknowledge and thank myself (and as a matter of fact rather profusely) for all that it took to make this book a reality. I mean tired as the expression may be, there simply are not words to express (at least adequately anyway) the extent to which I am in awe of what I have accomplished. Or, to put it another way, it is absolutely impossible to describe the immense amount of talent and determination that I have so obviously demonstrated in writing *WASHERTOWN: AN AMERICAN MASTERPIECE!* And I won't even try to recall for you the endless number of hours that I gave to this project. Just keep in mind that there are a lot of other things I could have been doing for the last twenty years.

Had I chosen not to write, however, much of the world would never have known Washertown, my hometown, and as far as that goes, the author of this stellar masterpiece of American literature. And that would be unfortunate indeed. Perhaps even tragic. Whatever. My abilities to write, rewrite, edit, and proof-read turned out to be truly astounding; so much so, as a matter of fact, that it is incredibly difficult for me to fully own the several and diverse literary skills with which I so obviously have been endowed. "Thanks be to God!" (as a rather common expression goes . . . an expression, by the way, that I have never particularly appreciated). Or, as others might say, "Praise Jesus!" (as goes another such expression . . . and one that I appreciate even less). Simply put, I am happy with one big *"WOW!"* Anyway, it is little wonder that I decided to add to the original title, which was to have been only *WASHERTOWN,* the additional title, *AN AMERICAN MASTERPIECE!* (although I still haven't decided whether it is Washertown itself, the book itself, or perhaps even *my* self—although I do not wish to appear immodest—that is the true masterpiece). Perhaps all three. Stranger things have happened I guess. Maybe anyway.

I also wish to thank those of you (great as your numbers surely must be) who have chosen to read my book. Especially those who have actually purchased a copy. This is not to say that I don't appreciate the many readers who were too cheap to actually pay for the experience; but only that when you borrow a copy from a friend or neighbor, or perhaps the public library even, you are obviously making a statement about yourself (and especially your priorities) that is not particularly flattering.

Finally, I wish to thank the people who assisted me in mastering (somewhat anyway) the eccentricities of my Hewlett-Packard computer. Each of these persons, in his or her own way, contributed to my being able to write WASHERTOWN with less effort (I think), and also perhaps with less frustration (although I seriously doubted it at times). Whatever. These people are individuals who were always there for me, and willing to help out. They are (in some kind of order I guess): Dan (who also gave me an Erector Set last Christmas), currently residing in Rockville, Maryland; Will (my "hang-out" buddy and neighbor), two doors down; Mary (especially Mary), a mile away; and the guy at the computer store (I suppose) who sold me the goddamn thing, although he seemed more than somewhat disappointed, perplexed, and just plain pissed off when I made my final selection based on the color of the brushed aluminum "surround" on the flat screen, and not on one of the many technological advances he at least considered to be of such remarkable, if not earth-shattering importance. That, however, was his problem, not mine.

THE CRITICS RAVE . . . (You won't want to miss this part!)

"THIS IS A REALLY GOOD BOOK ABOUT A LOT OF REALLY GOOD STUFF THAT HAPPENED TO A PRETTY GOOD KID IN A MOSTLY GOOD PLACE!"
The Washertown Daily News (anticipated).

"YOU'RE GOING TO LOVE THIS BOOK! GUT-WRENCHINGLY FUNNY. AT TIMES I LAUGHED SO HARD I THOUGHT I COULDN'T STAND IT . . . ALMOST PEED MY PANTS . . . AND I DON'T EVEN LAUGH VERY MUCH!"
Comment from a typical intelligent reader
(also anticipated).

"WHERE DID THIS GUY COME FROM?"
A curious person's question
(even after having read the book).

"STUPENDOUS!" . . . "A MUST READ SELECTION OF SORT OF STRANGE BUT MOSTLY HAPPY AND REALLY FUNNY EVENTS" . . . "DESTINED TO BE THE ALL-TIME *MASTERPIECE* IT ALREADY CLAIMS TO BE" . . . "THE KIND OF BOOK THAT COMES ALONG ONLY VERY OCCASIONALLY" . . . "THE UNDISPUTED 'LOONY TUNES' OF ALL TIME!" . . . "YOU'VE JUST GOTTA READ THIS BOOK!"
Some of the many comments from the
nation's greatest critics (anticipated).

"SENSATIONAL! THE ONLY WORD THAT CAPTURES THIS BOOK IS *SENSATIONAL* . . . JUST *SENSATIONAL* . . . I MEAN I ABSOLUTELY LOVE IT! GOOD JOB, SON!"
Author's mother (deceased).

PROLOGUE

Tales From the 1940s (Mostly)

A real long time ago, and I mean *really* long, like eight hundred or nine hundred or maybe even a thousand years ago long, a man named Chaucer, Geoffrey Chaucer to be exact (although I suspect his friends just called him Jeff), wrote what he called a "Prologue" to a book that he also wrote called *The Canterbury Tales*. Well, since I kind of liked the way it went (although now that I think about it more, not a lot), I thought I would begin my book with one (a prologue) also. Some of Mr. Chaucer's so-called "tales," as I recall, were actually sort of risqué, as they say; but that doesn't matter, since I won't be telling you any of them anyway. I have my own tales to tell, tales from the 1940s, and besides that we all know what can happen to you if you plagiarize someone else's stuff (and I'm not looking for trouble). Also, if you should think that calling what I'm starting out with a prologue sounds too pretentious (how's that for a pretty big word?), you can call it something else. I really don't care. I just happen to like the way the word sounds, and you do have to say it puts me in rather good company. I guess, anyway. At least if you like dead authors and strange people. But to tell you the truth, you don't even have to read this part of my book if you don't want to. You can just go right to the "Preface," or even to the first chapter, which I called the same thing as the title of the whole book. Whatever. It's your choice. I would read it though (the "Prologue"), if I were you (which however and of course I'm not), partly because it isn't very long, but mostly because it just might tell you something you need to know. Anyway, here it is . . . prologue or not.

PROLOGUE
(Like I already explained up above.)

Sometimes I think I might be somewhat strange. But not totally. I mean I don't think I'm crazy or anything, like certifiably nuts, or completely wacko (or totally "fucked-up," as a somewhat less than eloquent expression goes), because I'm not. It's just that I've always had this nagging feeling that there might be something just sort of a little bit wrong with my mind. Not a *lot* wrong, but just a little. (Like more than not at all, but a lot less than there could be.) Take this next sentence for example (it's almost what I was going to make the first sentence of my whole prologue say, but then I began to think about it more and changed it). So anyway, here it is (the "almost" first sentence): "Sometimes I think I'm crazy." I mean I just thought it was only fair to begin by telling you that. But then, and at the very same time, it kind of scared me, partly because of where they (i.e. psychologists, psychiatrists, and other often "not so stable themselves" kinds of people) could put me, and partly because of what they might "give" me, or actually do to me. Although, now that I think about it, and to tell you the very truth, what they might give me could be sort of fun (I mean who doesn't like to get "buzzed up" once in awhile?).

Anyway, then I started thinking that by changing just one little syllable, or maybe just one word, I could change the meaning of the whole sentence. Well, maybe not the *whole* sentence, but kind of. Like, "*Some*times I think I'm crazy," would tell you that I don't think I'm crazy all the time, but just part of it. Or if I wrote, "Sometimes *I* think I'm crazy," it could maybe mean that *I* might think I'm crazy (but only sometimes), but that other people don't (i.e. don't think I'm crazy). At least not very many. I hope anyway. Or, if I said, "Sometimes I think I'm *crazy*," it sounds like I really do think I am (crazy). Like certifiably nuts (although I denied that up above). Or totally wacked out. Or bonkers even. Jesus! That would be scary. Anyway, although it gets kind of confusing sometimes, you can see what I mean. And it's because I get this way sometimes (there's that word *sometimes* again . . . I use it a lot) that I think there might be something wrong with me. But I don't mean *morally*. I'm not a reprobate or a "sicko," or anything like that. God knows, I'm probably moral enough for two people. It's just my goddamn mind. Oh well (and this is the *really* crazy part I guess), none of this shit actually matters. *None* of it! Except I guess that it tells you I'm trying to be honest. So anyway (I use the word *anyway* a lot too), if it doesn't bother you, it doesn't bother me! Well, maybe a little bit. But not much. Anyway (there it is again), so much for the "Prologue." Maybe it wasn't such a good idea after all. Maybe. Whatever (another word I use a lot), it's a start. The "Preface" comes next, and you might like it better. I know I do. At least most of the time anyway. So even though mine is a pretty long one (meaning my "Preface"), stick with me. You not only should get a few laughs, but might also even learn some things.

PREFACE

(A long one. But it's really the beginning of
my whole story; so read it.)

I wet my pants three times when I was in elementary school (a "gradeschooler"). But I'll bet you think it's kind of strange that I would say that. In fact, I would also bet that you probably think that wetting ones pants doesn't have much to do with anything, or that it's a pretty dumb thing to write about, or that it's maybe just plain disgusting even. And you could be right. But I'm not so sure. You'll have to decide for yourself, as you learn more about Washertown and how I got to be this way. But you might want to keep in mind that it just could be that some other people who became famous writers did it too (i.e. wet their pants), only maybe they just didn't have the courage to tell anyone. I know for sure that a fourth grade friend of mine, Sharon Walker, wet her pants (although to the best of my knowledge she never became a famous author or anything). Unless maybe she had a pen name that I never knew about. Anyway, Sharon only did it once (at least once is all I know about). It was really sad though when it happened.

As I said, it was in fourth grade (homeroom), and she, Sharon, peed this enormous puddle right under her desk and then just sat there, frozen-like, with this awful sort of shitty and totally pathetic kind of "Oh my God" look on her face. Then she cried real hard. You know, like when you sort of choke up and make spit bubbles and then gasp for air, and your nose gets all snotty and runny and everything. Whatever. Anyway, I really felt sorry for her, but then I was *always* feeling sorry for someone (you'll find this out as you read more of my book). I mean clear back to when I was really little, like before "kindygarden" even (that's the way I spell *kindergarten*), I always seemed to know someone to feel sorry for. Or if not someone, then someone's dog or something. So anyway, I guess maybe it was just Sharon's turn (i.e. her turn to be the one I felt sorry for). But to tell you the very truth, I think maybe some pretty bad things were happening at her house; like her parents weren't getting along very well, or maybe the dog died or something. Or perhaps her grandmother. I don't know. I just know that she (Sharon, not her grandmother . . . although her grandmother may have had a pee problem too), unfortunately wet all over the floor in fourth grade, got really, *really* upset, and that I felt sorry for her. But this isn't supposed to be about Sharon. And as I already said, she didn't grow up to become a famous author anyway. So I won't tell you any more about her. She just happened to come to mind.

As I started to say a lot of lines ago, I wet *my* pants *three* times. Once was when my best buddy and I sneaked off to the movies to see *Frankenstein*. Or maybe it was called *Dr. Frankenstein's Monster,* or perhaps *The Return of Frankenstein*. Or *Frankenstein Forever* or something; I can't remember. But what I do remember is that we weren't supposed to be there, so I guess we eventually got just about what was coming to us. But maybe I shouldn't even be telling you this. However, I guess if you can trust me with stuff, I can trust you. So anyway, to begin with, our parents thought we were too young to go to a Frankenstein movie (third grade), and that we would get nightmares and everything if we did. And you know, as it worked out, it was one of those times (which of course we thought were petty rare when we were little) when they were right. I guess everyone is right once in a while. Even parents. To tell the truth though, I didn't actually wet my pants at the Frankenstein movie; but I would have if I hadn't peed on the floor, so I guess it's kind of the same thing.

What happened is that I had to go real bad (I mean really, *really* bad), but I didn't want to miss any of the scary stuff that was happening. You know, like when Dr. Frankenstein's monster (can you believe that guy was a doctor?) takes it in the neck through that metal electrode plug, or whatever it was, that stuck out of it, and then everything buzzes and sparks and gets crazy, and he (the monster) starts coming at you—"clomp, clomp, clomp"—and everything. Remember those big black boots he wore? I mean they must have been size 20 or something. Well anyway, that's what was happening, and so I got "scareder and scareder," and had to go "badder and badder," and therefore dropped down on my knees (although I did kind of look around first), pulled out my little nine-year-old "tool," and peed on the floor of Washertown's very finest movie theatre. I mean what was I supposed to do?

I can still remember watching the little river of urine ("Pee Creek"?) that I had made, as it slowly meandered down the slope of the theatre floor. (It kind of like glistened from the light of the screen, as it emerged from under the next row of seats.) Thank God no one was sitting right in front of us though. That could have really been embarrassing. Anyway, there wasn't anything I could do. It was already too late to head for the bathroom (which was like about two miles away in the balcony), so the only remaining options were to pee down the floor or pee down my leg, and I chose the floor. I would have done just about anything (maybe even tried to pee in a popcorn bag or something) to avoid that "warmy-wet" feeling you get when you do it in your pants (or in your bed sometimes, when you're real little and drink too much and then forget to go to the bathroom first . . . or maybe have a scary dream or something). I don't know. But I bet you remember how it felt without my telling you. At least if you're honest you do. And if you're a boy. Well . . . maybe a girl. I really can't say.

Actually, now that I think about it more, I was probably too scared at that Frankenstein movie to be making *any* decisions, what with that crazed, goddamn monster coming right out of the screen at us. Really. He was! I sometimes think about him (Dr. Frankenstein's wacko monster), even to this very day. And I can still remember the way his head was sawed off, totally flat-like, and that he had really stupid-looking "bangs," and great big blocky feet and boots (as I said up above). Then there was that real jerky-like walk that he had; I still remember that. I mean he actually "thumped" when he tried to move ("clomp, clomp, clomp," as I also said before). Whatever. He was one weird and scary guy! And one person I *didn't* feel sorry for.

Well, as fate would have it, my buddy (the one who had gone to the forbidden movie with me) had to go real bad too. I guess he was as scared as I was, and so right after I did it, he did it. Dropped right down next to me, took it out, and peed on the floor. Just like me. Now *that* tells you something about what being best buddies is all about! And also what small town America is about, or used to be anyway. At least when we were little. Everything had to do with loyalty, and the flag, and keeping secrets, and stuff like that. I mean peeing on the floor of the finest theatre in Washertown, and right alongside your best buddy (like almost shoulder-to-shoulder even), was just one example of how guys stuck together and kept secrets. Maybe not the best example. But a pretty good one I think.

The second time I wet my pants was even worse. This time I peed my pockets on a really cold day in December (just before Christmas), right next to the exhaust pipe that came out of the back wall of one of Washertown's local dry cleaning establishments (Cozad's). It was brand new too (the dry cleaning building), and maybe stuck out (meaning the whole building did, not just the pipe) toward the street too much. At least I thought so, and I always noticed stuff like that; kind of like I was a little architect-in-the-making or a city planner or something. Fortunately, however, the exhaust pipe, as I just told you, was at the back end of the building, so it wasn't as if what I'm going to tell you happened right out on the street side or anything. I think the pipe itself was connected to one or two steam pressers or something. But I don't know for sure. Anyway, my "laugh at everything until you go nuts and your stomach hurts" buddy and I (the same best buddy who peed on the theatre floor with me) were playing this really neat game that we had invented and called "jump in the clouds." We could have called it something else I guess, but strange as it may have sounded, we both kind of liked the name we chose. Whatever. (I use that word a lot too.) Anyway, we only did it (played the game) when we were alone and playing with just each other. Don't get me wrong though; I don't mean that we were "playing with each other," in a bad way, like some guys might do. We never did anything like that. What I mean is we would never let anyone else play with us (meaning play *the game* with us). Man, this is getting all messed up!

Anyway, here's how it worked. The really hot, "blowy" air that shot out of the exhaust/presser pipe, and the cold December air that blasted out of the North (once in a while from other directions too . . . but it doesn't really matter), combined just right on some days to make great big billowy clouds of steam that kind of rolled around and then rose up high into the air. Like "roiled" even, if you know what that word means (and of course I didn't when I was little). Whatever. Every so many minutes, and always with a totally unpredictable roar (which only added to the excitement), the dry cleaning building would blow a big blast out of the pipe and my buddy and I would jump up and down in it, kind of like wild horses in a lightning storm or something (I guess anyway), and then start to laugh ourselves sick. Like we'd get real out of control and crazy and everything. But let's take "time out" for just a moment so I can tell you something I learned, and then we'll get back to the game.

A lot later, when I went to college (this is what I learned, and sort of like a digression), I read about a pretty smart, but also sort of weird and sometimes drugged-up doctor (really) named Sigmund Freud. He called himself a psychoanalyst, although some of us just call him "psycho." He, I found out from one of my professors (who was also kind of strange . . . in fact *very* strange), even had some kind of fascination with eels. No kidding. I mean what was *that* all about? Anyway, from what I learned when I went to college, Dr. Sigmund Freud would have made something erotic (meaning like real sexual, or dirty even) out of the steam pipe with the stuff coming out of the end of it, and what my buddy and I did in it and everything. He (Freud, not my buddy) always wrote about sex and sex *organs* even ("swear to God"), and probably would have wanted people to think that that's what the exhaust pipe was (meaning it was a sex organ). You can probably figure out which one. But to us ("swear to God" again), to my pure and innocent buddy and me, that exhaust pipe was just a great big thing that stuck way out and once in a while shot out a mess (I mean mass) of really thick white steam. And besides, back then when my buddy and I were playing with each other we didn't even know who that psycho/psychoanalyst guy was, or, as I said up above, what the word "erotic" even meant. I mean we were only like nine or ten at the time. Man, that Freud guy had some strange ideas! Trust me. But we need to get back on track here.

So this one time when we were playing with each other ("jump in the clouds"), we started to laugh really hard. I mean really, *really* hard. Harder and harder. (And don't even think about that Freud person anymore; we were just playing our little game.) So anyway, this one time, although it took a little longer, an extra sudden and really big blast came shooting out of the pipe. The problem was that when it happened (the big blast) we were already laughing (probably about some feeble ten-year-old kid's joke with the word *tits* in it or something). We did that a lot. Or maybe we hadn't gotten over the last blast. Whatever, in the laughter and excitement of the steam that was now shooting out of the pipe, I totally "lost it," meaning I almost laughed myself dead. *And,* I peed my pants. Went right through my winter underwear and straight down my leg. I think it was my left one, but I guess it doesn't really matter. And then (of course) my friend and all-time best buddy cracked up and peed his pants too. I thought that was pretty neat. I mean it was just one more example of that 1940s loyalty stuff I was telling you about. And a good one too!

Actually, now that I think about it more, I guess maybe what happened was sort of like when religious people say, "those who pray together stay together" (or something like that). Anyway, for us, for my buddy and me, it was like since we had peed our pants together we had to keep it a secret together. At least I think that's what we thought. I don't know for sure though; it was a long time ago. But this kind of stuff just sort of comes to my mind sometimes. Anyway, if you wanted to, and if you had a really good imagination, you could probably even think of our behavior, meaning our "pee pact," as such a good example of loyalty and everything that people could maybe even hear "The Star Spangled Banner" playing, only you wouldn't be able to figure out from where. Or maybe Kate Smith singing "God Bless America." She was *always* singing "God Bless America." I guess it was her favorite song. And you could hear her every week on the radio.

When I got bigger though (but not a lot . . . like maybe when I was ten or twelve), I remember learning that another Kate Smith song, a song called "When the Moon Comes Over the Mountain," had something to do with a place called Lake Placid in New York, and I thought that was pretty impressive. I mean Lake Placid, and New York, and New York City were a long way from Washertown, Iowa (Iowa is where Washertown was, in case I haven't told you yet). And Washertown didn't have any lakes or mountains. And not only that, but our very tallest building was only five stories high. And that isn't nearly as tall as the ones in New York City (especially the Empire State Building). I hadn't been there of course, but I knew all this from what I had heard. Anyway, I just started talking about this stuff having to do with Kate Smith and New York and everything to let you know that I was pretty smart even when I was just little (although I don't mean to sound "stuck up" or anything). Of course Kate Smith didn't have anything to do with my buddy and me wetting our pants by an exhaust pipe sticking out of the back end of a dry cleaning store. But since I was really patriotic, even when I was little, we (Kate Smith and I) did have that in common. She probably never even heard of Washertown though. And I guess I'm really pretty far off track again.

So anyway, to get back to my story, the fact is that my buddy and I were laughing so hard (as I already told you) that we just couldn't hold it. I mean I thought I was going to go crazy or something, and my side even started to ache. Maybe you've laughed that hard too. I don't know. But I can tell you this: peed-in pants (especially "Levi 501s," the kind with the metal buttons) get really, *really* cold in December. Like icy, slushy cold (the cold sets in right after they stop steaming). Yeah, I know, you're probably thinking that "steaming Levi's" sounds kind of strange. But that's what they do. *Then* (and I'm not lying either) they actually begin to freeze up on you, and get really stiff and hard, and start to rub the inside of your legs raw (mainly your thighs, and clear up to where they fit onto your body too). But remember once again (I just felt I should say this) that Freud was a lot more weird than he was right; so don't make too much out of this "stiff and hard" and "raw thighs" stuff. Anyway, what happens next (after the freeze-up) is that even if you try as hard (much) as you can to walk "normal-like" (your Levi's have now become frost-covered), only with your legs almost straight and as far apart as you can keep them (kind of like the bottom half of you is an upside down "V" or something), it still hurts. Really bad. Almost as bad, but not quite, as when you're in a bicycle crash and your nuts hit the goddamn cross bar. (That *really* hurts.)

Whatever. As if things weren't already messed up enough, it just so happened that we were wearing rubbers (on our *feet* . . . remember this is fourth grade stuff), and the pee therefore kind of puddled up in them and "squished," sort of strange like, with each careful step we took. They (meaning the rubbers) didn't steam or actually get slushy inside, but almost. Let's just say it wasn't very pleasant. So anyway, *that* was the second time I wet my pants. You of course can think what you want, and you're probably already thinking I'm a little strange to have told you these things. Nevertheless, you can always learn something from stuff like this. And as I think I pretty much said before (although maybe in a sort of different way), this is America, and you can say anything you want to in America. Even foreigners can. So whatever you think, it won't bother me. At least not very much. But do us both a favor, although this doesn't actually have anything to do with wet pants or slushy rubbers. Never *ever* forget the way Kate Smith sang "God Bless America." I mean that lady was the absolute best!

The *third* time I wet my pants was really bad. And I do mean *really* bad. "God-awful" bad. Like worse than anything even. It happened right in front of my fourth grade teacher and my Frankenstein/blow-pipe buddy, with whom (my teacher, not my buddy) I thought I was in love and everything. I mean I used to get some pretty funny feelings about her sometimes. Like maybe even sex feelings, although I didn't know much about that stuff then. She (my fourth grade love object) had blonde hair, just like a movie star, and shiny-red fingernails and lips and everything. Maybe even big tits. I can't remember for sure, and it doesn't really matter. As I said, I wasn't thinking a whole lot about those kinds of things yet, and besides that, I don't mean to talk dirty or be disrespectful or anything. And anyway, you're only ten when you're in fourth grade. (Compared to all the fourth grade girls though, her tits were obviously pretty big . . . except maybe for JoAnn Feinberg's.) I'm not real sure. But maybe.

Her (my teacher's) name was Miss Dimons (almost like diamonds), and she was the most special teacher a little boy could ever have. I guess that's why I was pretty much if not totally in love with her. I even bought her a small, flat bottle of "Evening in Paris" perfume for Christmas that year. Not only was the bottle pretty flat, like real thin (I don't know why I remember this kind of stuff), but it was also sort of "shoulder-shaped" on the top, real dark blue, and had a silver cap and label on it. Since it was from Paris and everything I figured she would really like it. What I did to get it was to save extra quarters from my paper route so I could buy it for her all by myself. Later on though I found out that the perfume she usually wore was "White Shoulders." But she was nice and said she really liked what I got her, and never even mentioned the other stuff. (Maybe she at least noticed that the "Evening in Paris" bottle was shaped sort of like shoulders.) *And* Miss Dimons also told me she thought I was pretty special for giving it to her. I didn't know for sure, but maybe, just *maybe* I thought that she might be trying to tell me she was in love with me too. I do know that she kissed me on my tenth birthday, and I'm telling you *that* was one pretty special kiss. Good thing she didn't try anything like that today though; she'd be in jail.

But we need to get back to the main subject (I always seem to get off track, and anyway I'll tell you more about Miss Dimons in a little while, when I let you know about school in general). So, this really terrible, third and final "pee event" happened ("strike three and you're out," I guess) right after school one day when we (my buddy and I) were in Miss Dimon's room, and she was at her desk writing something, and I was just standing there doing I don't know what, and my buddy and I got laughing real hard again, and I just couldn't hold it, and so it happened. I don't remember what we were laughing about. It probably had something to do with another one of our sick little fourth grade jokes or something. Or maybe we were thinking about Miss Merriman's (our Washertown Elementary School principal) funny looking black shoes, and her weird, "you couldn't see through them," shitty-looking, brown stockings that she wore all the time. Sorry about the "shit" part, but that's what they were—shitty-looking. Her first name (i.e. the principal's) rhymed with Beaver (or something like that, and we thought that was kind of weird too). Anyway, she was nice and everything, but some of the stuff she wore was pretty bad, and I doubt that any of the fourth grade boys was in love with her. I can't say for sure, of course. But I don't think so. *Anyway* (sometimes I can't believe how easily I get off track), what I do remember is that I was laughing real hard and just couldn't hold it any longer, and therefore peed my pants (probably corduroys . . . I think maroon ones as a matter of fact, although they could have been brown . . . or tan . . . I had all three colors). Whatever. It went all down my goddam leg again! The left one, I think (as in the "blow-pipe" incident), but again I can't be sure. It's hard to remember this stuff.

Well, all I can say is that it helped a whole lot that my buddy wet his pants too. I mean once more it wasn't as though I was the only one. He was "right there" for me. And at least it wasn't a real cold day (and we were inside of course), so our pants didn't steam or freeze up and get stiff or anything like they did the second time I told you about (again, the time having to do with the "blow-pipe" and the thick, white, creamy-looking steam and everything). So what I'm trying to do right now, meaning what I'm trying to do by talking about the fact that this time our pants didn't freeze up, is give you an example of what I was taught a long time ago, i.e. to "look on the bright side." When I was little, you were *always* supposed to look on the bright side. My Sunday school teacher first taught me that when I was really, really little. It kind of went along with other stuff I learned later, like you should always "look for the silver lining," and "its always darkest before the dawn," and "into every life a little rain must fall," and all that other shit that you heard old people and teachers say when things went wrong. Anyway, although I can't think of her name (and it really doesn't matter), I think the Sunday school teacher who first taught me to think about the bright side was the same lady who provided the crackers and juice for Vacation Bible School. And if that's true, she would also have been the teacher who first taught me that Jesus loved me and wanted me to be a sunbeam and everything (which still doesn't make much sense to me). It does make me think though of another Sunday school teacher (a few years later), who told my buddies and me that he (Jesus) didn't want us to "play with ourselves," whatever that was supposed to mean. I think he meant we weren't supposed to "jack off." (I never did figure out how teachers, and Jesus even, always seemed to know so much about what we were doing.) Kind of scary.

But anyway, to get back on track (one more time), I guess maybe there was something that was kind of OK about wetting my pants in front of Miss Dimons: Miss Dimons with the blonde hair and red fingernails and lips and maybe even big tits that I was in love with. And as I hope I made pretty clear before, I don't mean that I was in love with just her tits either. I was in love with *all* of her, kind of like in the song, "All of Me . . . Why Not Take All of Me." Remember that one? I mean I wasn't some "nut-case," sex freak or anything. Whatever. As I started to say, what was maybe OK (again, to get back on the goddamn track) might have been that even peeing in your pants in front of the person you're in love with can have a bright side; meaning that since it was indeed a warm day, and we were inside and everything, and our pants didn't steam (as I told you up above), Miss Dimons maybe didn't even notice that anything had happened. And so thinking about "not steaming" was the bright side. I guess anyway. At least if I understand what people were trying to teach me. But I also have to admit that it's probably kind of a stretch to believe that. I don't know; maybe I should never have gone to Sunday school and learned all that stuff. But anyway, I probably can't make the "bright side" any brighter, and I guess it's one of those "who cares?" things anyway. I'm just glad I'm not in fourth grade anymore. But I have to say that I sure would like to be in love with Miss Dimons again! Only this time I'd remember to buy "White Shoulders."

Well, I guess that's about it regarding my wetting my pants (three times) and everything. And even if you don't think that talking about it made any sense (and I said at first that you might not), or that peeing in your pants is what should be in the preface to a book that is obviously destined to become an American masterpiece (and again you might not), at least it was a way to let you know right off that what I'm telling you about is true stuff. And besides, when I first started to do it (meaning to write this whole book, not just tell you about wetting my pants), I happened to remember some of the other things that I also just told you about, and something deep inside of me (well, sort of deep anyway) made me feel that I was supposed to talk about that stuff too. Whatever. Even if you thought that what I just wrote about was a little off base, you're still going to really like knowing about what went on in Washertown, the place where it all began for me, and the events that led to how I got to be this way. I promise. And I still think my little talk about wet pants should make it more "truer" and meaningful for you. Maybe anyway. You'll just have to find out. But remember, when you read true masterpieces of literature, you're supposed to look for subtle meanings and hidden messages, and even other things (although right now I can't remember what). That's something else I learned in college.

However (wouldn't you know there would be one), before I actually go on to the first chapter and start telling you about the main things that happened to me in Washertown, and to make sure you understand enough about me to keep everything in perspective, there is just a little more that I think I should tell you about the way my mind works (or perhaps doesn't). You may recall that I started to tell you about some of my mind problems in the "Prologue," meaning (just to make sure you've got it right) the part of my book that came just before this part, and that was inspired by another great writer and extremely deep thinker, Geoffrey Chaucer, who wrote dirty stories and everything. Well, as I just kind of said, you probably still need to know a few more things. (I didn't want to say too much right at first, since I was afraid you wouldn't want to keep reading, or maybe wouldn't like me even.) Therefore I'll just tell you a little, *little* bit more, and then, I promise, we'll be on our way to Washertown. OK? And besides, you're already learning stuff about Washertown and me anyway. At least it seems to me you are. So here's what I want to say now.

Once, or maybe even two or three or four or five times, when I was real little and ate Campbell's Cream of Mushroom soup (either in a bowl on a cold day, like in January, or in the tuna casserole that I really liked that my mom made with it), I would sometimes think that I actually saw some (i.e. mushrooms). My grandpa ate cream of mushroom soup too, because there was something wrong with his stomach (I think he had ulcers), and creamy stuff was supposed to make it better (which we learned later of course doesn't). He also swallowed little cod liver oil capsules, and man were those things nasty! I know, because I ate one once (he kept them in little trays in the refrigerator). You're supposed to swallow them whole, only I didn't know that then.

But to get back to the main topic (which I guess is seeing mushrooms), I don't know if my grandpa saw any in his soup or not. But I did, and I thought that was somewhat noteworthy, given that those things (the mushrooms) were so chopped up that you had to read the label and then really be paying attention to even know they were there. And then, especially when I was sick sometimes, like with the flu or a sore throat maybe, my mom would make me Campbell's Chicken Noodle soup (because of the Jews or something like that . . . I can't exactly remember), and the same thing would happen. I would sometimes think I could see some chicken parts in it. (By saying "parts" I mean just little pieces . . . not like a whole head or a foot or anything like that.) If I had seen an actual head or foot in it, I can tell you it would have made me sicker (a lot) than I was even. And *then* ("swear to God"), when I was eating some Campbell's Pork and Beans one day (just because I liked it, not because I was sick or because it was Jewish or anything), I saw not one but *two* pieces of pork. You know, that white, greasy, fat mass that floats on the top of the syrupy, clear stuff that they float the beans in. Two pieces of that shit in the same goddamn can! Can you believe it?

But now I'm thinking I don't even know why I'm telling you this. It's not like I have something against the Campbell soup people or anything (although now that I think about it, it seems that all the stuff they made was too salty and had something missing). I guess it's that I just seem to remember these kinds of things and then have to talk about them. But anyway, see what I mean? There's definitely something just a little bit strange, maybe goofy even, about my mind. I mean, who should give a rat's ass about the presence (or absence) of pieces of mushrooms or chicken parts or pork fat in a bowl or a can? I don't know. I guess for some reason I just thought I should tell you about it. And now I'm wondering if my grandpa maybe *did* see some mushrooms in his soup, and just chose not to talk about it. Whoa! This is getting really bad.

Sometimes though, and to be perfectly honest and not leave anything out, I think that some of what goes on in my mind, like these thoughts about mushrooms and chicken parts and greasy pork and stuff, is because again when I was real little (and this time I mean really *really* little, like when I was still almost a baby even) my big brother beat me up in the sandbox. (Who remembers this kind of stuff?) Actually, my brother tried to beat me up lots of times. I think maybe he didn't like me very much. In fact I know he didn't. Anyway, the sandbox attack might have been why I started to have trouble with my mind or brain or whatever it is. But remember, it's only *sometimes* that I think there's something wrong. Not all the time. And it's not that I'm really crazy or totally nuts or anything. At least I don't think I am.

One other time (before the sandbox incident even) my brother pounded on my head real hard and for a real long time (or at least he hit me anyway) with a wooden mixing spoon. My mother told me that, so I know it's true. Just like I know Jesus loves me because "the *Bible* tells me so," which I told you I learned in Sunday school. (Remember?) Anyway, I was in my baby buggy one day, helplessly stretched out on my little back, like real vulnerable and everything, and just trying I suppose to be happy—even though the tensions and momentum were building up for World War II (which of course and to be honest I couldn't have known anything about). *Anyway,* when I was trying to be happy my brother hit me right on the head . . . maybe in the face even. Whatever. It was a horrendous blow to the head with a gigantic wooden mixing spoon! For all I know he maybe even hit my "soft spot." Probably not though, since (thank God) I was lying on my back, as I already told you. But that means (as I also told you, or at least suggested) that it really *was* in the face that he hit me! I guess that probably means that he didn't like me for sure. But anyway, maybe *that's* when they (my mind problems) started. The "buggy incident" might have made me a little bit funny in the head or something. Which is to say my problems might not have had anything to do with mushroom soup. Or chicken parts. Or pork fat.

But again, I don't know for sure. And, as I said up above, it could have been the sandbox beating that I endured later. Anyway, this is only going to get worse if I try to explain it all, so perhaps I should just pray about it. Or maybe not. Or maybe I should just forget it. I can't decide. Jesus, this is getting bad! I hope you still love me.

Whatever. It's clearly time to move on; which is another one of the things I've learned about life. Sometimes you just have to keep going. I mean life isn't always what you want it to be. But you probably already know that. I remember when I got a lot, lot older and everything, like in college, there was a poem that I had to read that said something about keeping going. I think, anyway. There was a line in it that went, "Hurry up please, its time." I remember the poem writer (I guess I should say poet) kept having this guy say it over and over. And I think the guy he had say it was a bartender, so it must have meant something pretty important. I mean bartenders always seem to pretty much know what's going on. "Hurry up, please, its time." I think, by the way, his name (the poet's, not the bartender's) was Mr. Eliot. I can't remember if the bartender had a name, but he probably did. I mean everyone has a name. "T.S." sticks in my mind for some reason too. And "wasted" places. *Anyway* (I get *so* off track sometimes), everyone said he was a really good poet (although most of the time I could never understand what the hell he was trying to say), so therefore he probably knew what he was talking about, even though I didn't. I do agree however that it's time to "hurry up" ("please"). So I will.

Therefore, "without further to do" (or something like that), I shall begin to tell you about Washertown and what happened there and everything. Well . . . not everything of course, since a lot of the stuff is pretty personal, and some of it might even kind of gross you out. But I *will* tell you enough to let you know how really good (mostly) it was in Washertown. I mean that's not to say there weren't some bad times too. But bad times are just examples of that saying I already mentioned to you about "into every life a little rain must fall." Anyway, you can just forget all this crap/shit about my mind if you want to (I couldn't decide which word to use). I mean my mental issues aren't so bad that I can't still tell you stuff. OK? So then, "get ready . . . get set," and it's "over the river and through the woods" (sort of) to Washertown we go! ("The horse knows the way . . . etc. etc.")

Pause

"Notes to the Reader"

(This is pretty important for you to know; so don't skip over it.)
(*Then* start reading Chapter One.)

OK. So now that all this introductory stuff is over with, although you may have noticed that there actually is no "Introduction," but only the "Prologue" and the "Preface," even though some other authors who are also unusually talented might have called my preface an introduction, and then perhaps my prologue a preface. (It just happens that I like to do things my way.) Whatever. With these early sections over with, but before continuing with the even more important issues about growing up in Washertown, there are just a few things I need to note for you. (I don't mean to be dragging my feet, and I would have written this part earlier, except that I knew it probably wouldn't have meant as much.) Anyway, the first chapter is only a few paragraphs away.

First, about my name. It isn't really Ernest Arlington Twain. (But you probably already figured that out.) My real name is something else. I chose the name Ernest Arlington Twain because I was originally going to say my name was E. Andrew Thomas (for very personal reasons). But when I decided not to do that, I still kind of wanted to stick with the letters *E, A,* and *T,* so I decided to name myself Ernest Arlington Twain (as I just said and did). First of all, i.e. my first reason for choosing this name, is that as I grew older (and I like to think *matured)* I learned that a man named Ernest Hemingway had written some pretty good books (even though he eventually shot himself). So there (Ernest) was the "E." Then I remembered how much Edward Arlington Robinson's poem, "Richard Cory," had totally scared the shit out of me when I was in junior high school. So there was the "A." (I of course had already used Ernest for the "E," as I just told you, so I obviously couldn't use the "E" in Edward for the "E" in my new pen name, and therefore I used his middle name, Arlington, for the "A.") Next I decided that since everyone seemed to like Mark Twain a lot (most people anyway, although there seems to have been a little trouble with his calling some people bad names), and then because I also knew that he was a pretty famous American writer (and I always pretty much wanted people to like me too, and *aspired* to be a famous American writer, which this book should make me I think . . . although that will be up to you), I decided I would use Mr. Twain's name for my last name. And of course it also began with "T," which made it a perfect choice. So that's about as much as I can say about my pen name (and probably more than you needed or wanted to know anyway). Also, although I already told you this, I chose to have the word *masterpiece* as part of the title of my book so it would already be there when people decided that it was.

Second, as you already may have noticed, sometimes I seem to sort of go in and out of my present and past "voice," which is to say that sometimes I probably sound like a little boy (which I was when most of this stuff was going on), and at other times I kind of slip into being the older guy that I am now. Or maybe an "in between" guy. So anyway, I hope that doesn't bother you too much. (It doesn't bother me.) Although it sometimes creates "tense" problems for me (meaning not "tension," but just "tense" in the way I write things). And then I have to admit that (sometimes anyway) I can get sort of moody; and if I'm in a good one (mood) I use nice words, but if I'm in a bad one (mood) the words can once in a while get pretty bad too. Real bad sometimes. So try not to let that bother you either.

Also, ever so often I know I can get sort of carried away with some pretty serious stuff, maybe even real serious stuff (and therefore can get *really* carried away), so I'll try hard not to do that too much. It can be both distracting and depressing. And also annoying. But otherwise, most things will probably go just fine.

Third (I mean fourth), I want to note that writing about Washertown has truly been an endearing experience for me. It has allowed me to reminisce and have a lot of fun with both people and places. Most of all, however, it has reminded me of just what wonderful and caring people the folks in my hometown of Washertown were. Know for sure then that in writing *WASHERTOWN: AN AMERICAN MASTERPIECE!* I have meant to offend no one, nor to lessen the importance of any of the places or events that follow. I only wish to celebrate, and with a modicum of humor, the lives of some very ordinary, extraordinary, and *special* people.

And just two other and kind of related things. First, you will find that this book isn't perfect; meaning not that what I have written isn't perfect (or pretty near), but that there may be a "typo" or two . . . or three, or four, or fifty (only kidding), and maybe an occasional misspelled word or something. Like you might find an "it's" for "its" maybe, and a few other things kind of similar (like the absence of a comma, or maybe a period outside that belongs inside a parenthesis mark). Anyway, the reason the book isn't perfect is because I didn't want to pay some unknown and maybe not even very bright editor or copyreader person (or whatever they're called) several hundred dollars to proofread it. (They might have tried to change some stuff and therefore ruined it too.) And besides, as "they" say, "nothing is perfect" (although some of us come close). So don't worry about a few editorial or proofing problems. I don't. Also, I can write some pretty long and kind of convoluted sentences (just to "test" you sometimes). Like the one near the very end of Chapter Two, "School Daze," or, and probably even more hard to get through (but give it your best), the fourth from the last sentence in Chapter Four, "Of Swimming Pools and Popsicles." And some of my sentences might not even come out quite right. But anyway, don't worry about those things either. There's a big puzzle to life, and it all fits. Oh yeah . . . and I like to use parentheses a *lot* (it seems sort of "protective" of the words or something). Whatever. Someone once said, "The essence of genius is knowing what to ignore." (I can't remember right now who that was, but it was a good thing to say.) So be a genius, and just ignore the small stuff.

And then (finally) I think I used the name of the Lord in vain a time or two (maybe more). Yeah, more I'm afraid. You know, like some "goddamns" and stuff. So anyway, I would appreciate it if you don't go "ooooh . . . he's going to be punished for that," or "wow . . . that's really bad." I mean I know all about *The Ten Commandments,* and Moses, and Jesus, and other things about the *Bible* and God and everything. And besides, I've already talked this out with Him (God). He says it's OK (or at least forgivable, since it was mostly just for literary effect), and that He pretty much understands. So you needn't worry about these things either. I mean Jesus! Just enjoy the book. You might also have to kind of over look some other bad words though, like an occasional *fuck* even, and maybe also some rather twisted and not very nice interpretations of how some stuff actually happened. But again, don't worry about it. I'm betting you can handle it! OK then. Here it is . . .

CHAPTER ONE

WASHERTOWN: AN AMERICAN MASTERPIECE!

Of People, Pigs, and Some Other Basic and Pretty Important Stuff

Washertown is where it all began—for me, anyway. I mean not like in the *Bible* or anything, where *everything* began. Like where Adam and Eve began: who, as you may recall, got evicted from their fruit farm, or someplace like that, for bad behavior (I think Eve got into trouble in the apple business or something), and whose son, Cain, for some reason beat the shit out of his brother Abel (who died, by the way). Or like where Moses began: a little Jewish baby that someone found floating downstream in a wicker basket somewhere, and then when he got older (a lot older), went up a mountain, talked to God (really), and came back down with a list of pretty hard-to-follow rules that had been burned into some stone tablets. Or like where Noah began: another Jewish guy, who built a "couples only," flood-proof boat (he called the thing his ark) to save just his own family (which I always thought was sort of selfish) and a lot of other animals from getting drowned in a really big (and I mean *really* big) flood. Or where a few years later another Jewish kid, this one named Jesus, began: who grew up to be a really good teacher and everything (*really* good), and then was crucified, died, and eventually got turned into a Catholic (I think that's what happened to him anyway). And finally, not like where all the animals and the fish and the flowers and the trees and a whole lot of other stuff began, and earlier even than all these people I just told you about. *Anyway*, that's not what I mean. What I mean is just that Washertown was where *my* own little life began. And I'm not even Jewish; although someone must have thought so at one time, since I apparently got held down and circumcised (i.e. had the end of my little wee-wee cut off) when I was just a baby. But so what, right?

Anyway, where it all began and how I got to be this way was mostly in and because of this place called Washertown: Washertown, Iowa, U.S.A. It didn't have any zip, which isn't to say that there wasn't any excitement there; only that the postal service hadn't started using those codes yet. (And when they did, it seemed to me that it just confused a lot of people.) Anyway, and as a matter of fact (and I've learned it's best to stick with the facts whenever you can), for a midwestern town with a population of only about 10,000 residents *total*, big and little people combined, it had quite a lot of it (zip). Maybe in some ways too much even. Or perhaps just the wrong kind sometimes. Whatever. You'll just have to wait until you've read more about the place, and then decide for yourself.

Washertown is located in the very heartland of America, where the dirt is a real dark black color (especially when it gets wet), the cornfields emerald green (the corn itself being a yellowy, almost gold color), and the pigs (the "state animal") are just plain big and ugly (and mostly black and white with pink snouts). Regardless of what color they were, they were simply god-awful ugly. If people had been using the term when I was little, they would have said "butt-ugly." The pig thing, however, disgusting and "grunty" as it may have been, was only a problem if you had to be around them a lot, like if you were a farmer or something and had to feed ("slop") them all the time.

Pigs, by the way, were pretty important to the rural areas that surrounded small-town Washertown, which of course (i.e. rural areas) were all that was out there, except for two or three even smaller towns that you went through on your way to Des Moines or maybe Colorado even. If you can believe it, and I'm not lying to you either, the pigs were probably even more important than corn (which is what most people think of when they think about Iowa . . . if of course they think about it at all). Anyway, at the state university in Iowa City (although it was really more like just a town), they even sang a song that went, "On Iowa/On forever more," and then ended a lot of words later with, "That's where the tall corn grows!" But a lot of people didn't like it very much (the song), since they thought it made Iowa sound like a place where dumb people (like "hicks" and everything) lived. And Iowans, enlightened as we were, knew that hicks were people who lived in Arkansas (wherever that was). Anyway, Washertown was a pretty little place, meaning both pretty and little, not just small; and pork and corn (to get back to the basics) were really important to it. (I'll tell you some stuff about life in Iowa's *big* city when I talk about Des Moines.) Pork, by the way, was even important right *in* Washertown too, not just in the country around it. You'd know what I mean if you ever ate a deep-fried pork tenderloin sandwich at one of the local restaurants (Snoops Inn made the best one). The pork was all hammered out real flat and thin-like, and came on a really good, tasteless, soft, white bread bun, with mustard and pickles on it. *And* (if you didn't care what you smelled like and didn't have a date or anything), you could even get it with chopped onions sprinkled on top of the mustard. Man, were those things ever good!

Not to get too carried away with "butt-ugly" stuff (I realize we've been talking a lot about pigs), but at the county fairs there were even celebrations and blue ribbons and other prizes set aside just for the pigs (really). State Fair too. And later on (although not in Washertown, I don't think, but in other places) they even had beauty queens for the pigs. Well, not actually *for* them, of course, but *because* of them. You know what I mean. Like they would elect a Queen of the Pork Festival, or Fair, or whatever was going on. And then, as you might suspect, there were always a few guys (thinking of course that they were the very first ones to ever come up with this) who would call some pig the queen, and the queen herself a pig. But they didn't really mean it (at least probably they didn't anyway). In fact, they most likely would have gotten all excited and been proud and everything if their own girlfriend (especially if they were "going steady" and maybe even "doing it") had been chosen to be the Pig Queen. But we need to get on to some other stuff. Actually though, now that I think about it, it may be that some of those queens *were* pigs. I mean you have to kind of wonder what kind of girl would want to be chosen as "Queen of the Butt-uglies." I mean, don't you? But I can't really say, since I actually wasn't too inclined to pay a lot of attention to stuff that had to do with pig contests anyway. I just know they (the real pigs, i.e. the "state animal" pigs) were pretty important to people who lived in Iowa and Washertown.

Speaking of people (we're done with the pigs), the ones who lived in Washertown were really good (mostly anyhow), and people are a lot more important than pigs. Washertown folks were the kinds of individuals who would mostly do just about anything for you. In fact, some of them would do things for you, meaning help you out a lot, even if you maybe didn't even want them to. And some of them would insist on doing it to you "in the name of the Lord," and that kind of crap. But that's OK. Annoying as it could be, it's just kind of the way it was then, and they really did mean well. (I'll tell you more about religion and churches and doing good deeds and shit like that later.) Just remember though, Washertown people were really nice. And God-fearing. They took care of themselves and each other, worked hard, went to church (a lot of them anyway), and always stood up to salute the flag (or put their hands on their hearts). Especially when it went by during a Fourth of July parade. So as you can see, almost like in "O say can you see," from "The Star Spangled Banner" itself (I just happened to think of that), Washertown was a pretty good place to "begin," and especially in the 1940s. Things were simple then. I mean, when I was a boy you didn't even know about being "politically correct" or anything like that. Patriotic, yes. Politically correct (whatever that even meant), no. People in Washertown were just simple, and honest, and kind of special. At least that's the way it seemed to me when I was little.

Like take for example (to explain what I just said about being simple and not political or correct or anything) the little song that we sang, when we were in about second or third grade (you probably sang it too). It was when we were learning about the Indians and John Smith and Pocahontas and everyone. I think maybe, if I remember right, Pocahontas and John Smith got married and then went to England, and then she became a queen or someone like that. I'm not sure though. Anyway, third grade (or maybe fourth), just before Thanksgiving, was about the time at the grade school I went to (Washington Elementary) when we learned about Pilgrims and all the problems they had with bad weather and no food and everything, and also about how the Indians helped them by showing them how to plant corn and stuff (so they wouldn't have such a bad time the next year). And here is the little song we sang about them (meaning about the Indians). As I said up above, you probably did too; so sing it with me now, real fast, since that was part of what made it so much fun (before the "politically correct" people came along and ruined it). Ready? "One little two little three little Indians/Four little five little six little Indians/Seven little eight little nine little Indians/Ten little Indian boys"! And then you'd sing it backwards from ten to one (which was kind of hard for some kids). But anyway, that's the way it was sung when things were simple and the way they're supposed to be. Now, because of that politically correct bullshit I just told you about (pretty dumb, if you ask me), here's how it would have to be: "One little two little three little Native American children (boys *and* girls)/Four little five little six little Native American children/Seven little eight little nine little Native American children/Ten little Native American children" (you have to kind of hold the "dren" part of "children" in the last line or the song seems to stop too soon). It's all kind of sad if you ask me.

So anyway, back when I was little you could just sing about Indians and boys. But now, as I just explained to you, the Indians have to be called Native Americans and include girls and everything. (There are even clubs called the ACLU and NOW, and other names like that, that actually fight for this kind of shit.) Sometimes I think the "LU" in ACLU stands for "Lunatics" or something. And then the "AC" part for "All Communist" maybe. Anyway, because of this kind of stuff, *now* we're even supposed to believe that some of our little grade school "song friends" (the ten little Indian boys) not only have to be girls, but also foreigners—and maybe even homosexuals (whatever *that* was supposed to mean to a third grader), and probably maybe some other things too. So anyway, nothing is simple anymore, since as I said, you have to be political and correct and mess up the rhythm and everything. And, by the way, I won't even *try* to explain what might happen to you if you wanted to read *Little Black Sambo* today (remember him?). You'd probably be called a racist, or maybe even a child molester or some other kind of wacko. You might even get locked up somewhere. I don't know. All I can say is I just hope that that black Sambo kid is doing all right, since my friends and I really liked him. And he was fast too. Man, could that kid run! But I guess that's enough about Indians and Sambo the sprinter.

When I first began to think about writing this book (if you don't mind kind of a brief digression here), I thought of calling Washertown

"Mayville," or maybe even "Tagtown," since both of those names would be quaintly reminiscent and, although kind of odd sounding, rather representative of the place. I'll tell you why in a minute or two. But anyway, just as I've changed the names of the people I'm writing about (at least most of them, although some not very much), "to protect the innocent" and everything, I thought I should also change the name of the town a little bit too (although actually I changed it completely). Or maybe I did it thinking that I could keep it (Washertown itself) innocent too. I guess that's what I was thinking. But maybe not. I don't know. *Anyway,* that's kind of why I came up with the name Washertown. I want you to remember though, that the whole place was there mostly because of one family, and that's why I thought for a while about somehow trying to use their name and everything. (Meaning that's what I was just talking about when I said I had thought about calling Washertown Mayville or maybe Tagtown.) But this is getting too complicated. Just remember that the family who did so much to make Washertown the "American Masterpiece" that it became, were a modest, hard-working, generous, and self-effacing group of folks (i.e. for the most part . . . although now that I think about it more I suppose one or two of them was a little bit strange maybe). Which brings to mind that when I was in third grade (and singing about Indian boys), one member of the "First Family" of Washertown stole the heart of our exceptionally pretty music teacher (on whom every little boy had a crush . . . at least if they were normal anyway), and within months drove her off into the sunset in his powder blue Cadillac convertible. Pretty selfish, if you ask me. And then they got married. And then they got divorced (at a time when it wasn't a very good idea to do that). Well, I can tell you this: no third-grader would have divorced her! I mean she was really, really beautiful. But anyway (back to the subject), Washertown won out in my little "name that town" contest, so Washertown it is! And since (as you might have figured out already) it was a town where they made washing machines, I guess that name actually makes a lot of sense anyway. So I'll just go on with my story. Before I do, however, let me remind you that if you think some of my paragraphs are kind of long (like this one), and my sentences are sometimes sort of convoluted and stuff, they are (I already told they would be in the "Notes" section). Bear with me though, since I really do kind of like things that way (i.e. long and convoluted, if not totally drawn out and twisted). You might learn to like it that way too.

The local pronunciation of Washertown, by the way, was *Warsher*town, as in *warsh* your face (which, when I was little, I was told to do often), *warsh* the car (which, as I grew older, I was expected to help with sometimes), and "you're all *warshed* up" (which, as you probably know, meant that you had really screwed up what you were supposed to be doing, or had lost all your money or something). One of our neighbors did that (lost all his money) when he was doing some illegal gambling, although no one was supposed to know about it. But anyway, to say "warsh" instead of "wash" wasn't just Washertown talk. At least I don't think it was. A lot of other people in Iowa (maybe even the whole Midwest) said warsh too. Even teachers, I guess. At least I think so, because saying warsh for wash got started when I was pretty little (like maybe in first grade) and listened to stories about General George *Warsh*ington and his Revolutionary War. And then about *President Warsh*ington (who, as I'm sure you probably remember, was the same person as the General was). And then about his dad (i.e. Warshington's), who had one of his cherry trees cut down by him (meaning this time George, his son) when it shouldn't have been. But anyway, he (meaning George the son again, not his father) was real honest and everything (although his father probably was too), and told his dad what he had done.

Also, although George Washington may not have been the best general we ever had, at least not when he first got started, he must have been pretty good (and honest) as President, since he got a whole town named for him. And then later on (although with a few delays) a really big monument and everything. But you probably know all this stuff. Anyway, as a good American, I learned even more things about the juvenile tree-chopper, then General, then President, and all the really good things he did for our country; and then I even learned about the really important principles he said he wanted to be remembered for when he died (although I can't remember now what any of them were). It was pretty impressive though. Whatever it was. It seems we just kept learning more and more about him (even that something was wrong with his teeth), and *Warsh*ington, D.C. and everything too. I guess we learned so much because we had such really good schools in Washertown. One of them, by the way, the second one I went to, was actually named after him. But he never went there. He died before they built it. But how about that? I mean it isn't everyone who gets a school named for him.

*Warsh*ington, D.C. (to digress just a little bit more . . . but you might find this kind of interesting) was actually a place that most Washertown folks thought about very little, and about which, for the most part, they probably cared even less. It was just too far away. They thought about it during election years though. And election time in Washertown could get pretty nasty, since that was when the bankers, business men and company "big-shots" became deadly serious about getting (or keeping) the goddamn Democrats *out* of the place (*Warsh*ington, D.C.), whereas a few of Washertown's perhaps smarter folks (relatively speaking anyway), and the vast majority of the washing machine company's workers (Earth's "salt," if you will), wanted to keep the goddamn Democrats *in,* but were equally serious about getting (or keeping) the goddamn Republicans *out.* Some of the less sophisticated folks probably even changed the "o" in big-shots to an "i."

Anyway, I hope you followed all that. It was a pretty long sentence, but then keep in mind that I eventually went to college and everything (the State University of Iowa, as it was then called), and writing long sentences is the kind of thing that sometimes happens to you when you go to college and try too hard. (And, as I said before, I just sort of can't help it.) Anyway, in Washertown Democrats were thought (but only of course by the incredibly and forever virtuous Republicans) to be absolute sons-of-bitches; whereas Republicans (according to the Democratic, just smart people) were simply bastards, or, even worse, total assholes. (Asshole was a *really* bad word when I was little, so I guess I'm kind of sorry I said it.) Anyway, Democrats were sons-of-bitches, and Republicans were bastards (if indeed not assholes)—"rich" bastards perhaps, but bastards nevertheless. Now that I think about all this name-calling and stuff, it seems there was a lot of illegitimacy in Washertown. When I was little anyway. And at least during election years.

Whatever. As I was saying, for the most part, and for most of the time, *Warsh*ington and Capitol Hill were simply too far away to make much of a difference to the people of Washertown. And besides, a select few of the politicians at the state capitol in Des

Moines (that's *Dez Moinze* to the less well taught . . . as in Illi*noize*) were considerably more accessible and at least somewhat more concerned about Washertown's priorities than were "the big boys" in Warshington, D.C. Washertown itself, by the way, was not exactly "no where" politically (at least not when I was a boy). We had our very own state senator, Senator Ross, who just happened to live right across the street from my grandpa's house (on my mother's side of the family, although I guess you don't really need to know that). Senator Ross was a vintage 1940s politician: a portly man, who was usually seen with a wet and well-chewed cigar stuck in his face. The "cigar in the face look" was pretty much "in" at the time, along with pinstripe suits, suspenders, and spats (for special occasions). So anyway, Senator Ross looked just about how an important state senator was supposed to look (although a very similar look was also owned by Al Capone). I can assure you however that Senator Ross was not a gangster (at least I think I can). He probably didn't even know any Italians. And probably very few Jews, Catholics, or "coloreds" either. Rather, the people Senator Ross knew and associated with, at least I think anyway, were clearly patriotic (although maybe in a self-serving way), principled (as he would have defined the term), white, Protestant, and portly (like himself) politicians. Remember, this was Washertown. "Middle America." And vintage 1940s.

Moving right along, not only did Washertown have its own rotund and somewhat imposing (underscore "somewhat") senator in the state house in Des Moines (complete with a gold-plated dome), we also had our own county workers and politicians housed under a dome right here at home. And a rather grand edifice it was too: the Casper County Courthouse (grand at least to a little person). It had a big but maybe kind of too tall dome on the top (it seemed that all government buildings were supposed to have domes), and it sat "smack dab" in the middle of the Washertown Square. You see, Washertown was not only the washing machine capital of the world; it was also the "seat" of Casper County! How's that for status? The state capitol in Des Moines had a bigger one (dome) of course, but that was OK. I learned later in life that size doesn't matter. At least that's what *some* people said. (Starting in about junior high school, however, I wasn't so sure.) Anyway, the state capitol dome in Des Moines was for the whole state to behold, and as I said before, it had real gold on it (although thinner than the foil in a pack of cigarettes, I was told). Our dome, on Washertown's Casper County Courthouse, was just for us, and had on its concrete surface whatever may have been blowing around and got stuck, or perhaps had been dropped during a flyover by a squadron of pigeons or something.

Speaking of domes (although I promise I won't digress too much), there was even another domed building in Washertown. I think maybe Washertown had been intended to be sort of a "Greek Revival" place, although we had only four or five Greeks in the whole town (and they were all from the same family). One of them, by the way, (i.e. one of the Greeks) was really pretty, and a high school cheerleader and everything. But to tell you more about her right now would really be a digression. So anyway, and to kind of get back to the subject (which is?), I'll save what I have to say about both domed buildings for later on (and there's a *lot* more to say). The only point I'm trying to make now is that when I was little domes were synonymous with grand and important places (as were other buildings that were made to look Greek-like), and Washertown was indeed a grand and important place. As a matter of fact, I suspect most of us thought it was about the most grand and important place anywhere. And most of Washertown's really important buildings (a little more detail here), because of their being a part of the way the Greeks did things, also had a whole lot of columns in front of them. Usually, at least in Washertown anyway, the columns (unfortunately) were just concrete that was trying to look like something else. Granite perhaps, or maybe marble even.

Whatever. There were lots of columns in Washertown. About six in front of the Washertown National Bank, four in front of the Casper County Bank, about sixteen or so on the sides of the courthouse (over the entrances), and maybe eight or ten in front of Washertown's First Methodist Church. They were stately and everything, so it isn't that people didn't like them. And they made the places where they stood look mighty important. However (it seems there's always a "however" to everything), and unfortunately (*really* unfortunately), all those columns also meant lots of pigeons, which (and even more unfortunately), meant lots of pigeon shit (if you will pardon the expression). This was especially true (the abundance of pigeon shit) on the steps at the bottoms of the Ionic style columns in front of Washertown's First Methodist Church. (The columns in front of the Washertown National Bank, the Casper County Bank, and the Casper County Courthouse were Doric, which allowed less space on which the pigeons could roost, and therefore less an area from which they also could shit.) Not that I knew (I was too little) that those columns had names like Doric or Ionic or whatever. I only learned that kind of stuff later on in college . . . or maybe it was in Miss Phoebe Wilcox's Latin class in ninth grade (which isn't worth a further digression, although she herself was really nice).

Anyway, it (the way the columns were named) had to do with the presence or absence of fancy, "scrolly" stuff on the top of them. As I already said, the Ionic ones simply provided more area for the pigeons to sit and shit from (except for maybe Corinthian ones, of which Washertown had none). At least I don't think we did. So anyway, there was in fact a lot of shit in Washertown. But then I guess there is a lot of shit everywhere. Probably even in Des Moines, at least as far as I could tell. Whatever. I'll have more to say about this (the pigeon shit problem) later, and I'm sorry about using bad words while telling you about Washertown. It seemed to me however that to say pigeon feces, or excrement, or something like that (and of course I didn't even know those words anyway) would sound sort of pretentious (another word I didn't know then). At least for Washertown. Maybe even for Des Moines. And pigeon "poop" is something only a sissy would say. Like dog poop. Or cat poop. So anyway, I decided to say shit. Just plain shit. Pigeon shit (although now that I think about it, there was sometimes more than a little shit from some other big birds too, like blue jays, and maybe some crows or doves). I don't like to think about dove shit though, since doves are supposed to be really nice and are thought to be lovebirds and everything.

By the way, it once occurred to me (but not for very long actually) that since Washertown people thought Washertown was so grand and important that I should maybe be just a little grandiose myself and call the place Washer *City*. Not like Kansas City of course, or New York City, or anything like that. I mean I knew better, although I had never actually seen those places, and so just had to take other people's word for it. "City" does sound a lot more important than "town" though. ("Village" sounds sort of more important too, or at least somehow more sophisticated, but village would have been too eastern for Iowa in the 1940s.) And anyway, as my account of Washertown continues to unfold, you would probably know better. Washertown really isn't a city (or village). It's a town: it's just plain Washertown. But *wonderful* Washertown, nevertheless. As I've said before (and especially in the title to this whole book), the place was truly an American masterpiece. Anyway, I learned a long time ago, and know it to be true to this very day, that being "just plain" anything is a good thing. Sometimes even a *really* good thing. Good, as in "a rose is a rose is a rose," or something like that. Maybe anyway. Or it could be that the rose thing might not be quite right. I think it is though. But I can't, to be totally honest, say for sure (I was never really good at poetry and stuff like that . . . at least not when I was little). Whatever. You decide. I've got too much to tell you about to get stuck here, and besides that I don't want my mind to start getting goofy or wacked out or anything. *However,* just mentioning the word *city* makes me think of a place in Washertown that I simply have to tell you about (although it doesn't have anything to do with being a real city). It deserves its own little section though, so that's what's next. And if I don't tell you now, I might not find another time to talk about it, which would be a real loss. Well . . . kind of a loss anyway. At least I think so. It's another one of those things you'll have to decide for yourself. So next is a separate section about a place called The Washer City Café.

The Washer City Café

So, as I just said, telling you that I thought about calling Washertown Washer City makes me think of a place you really should know about. You might even wish you could have gone there once (or maybe even more times). I often wished that, but I wasn't even supposed to walk by the place unless I had to. That's what my mom and dad said. I guess they were pretty sure it wasn't a good place for kids my age to know much about.

Anyway, in the Washertown of my early youth and total innocence (well . . . early youth anyway), there was an establishment of sorts called The Washer City Café. (Restaurant would be city stuff again; café is Washertown.) The Washer City was part of *real* Washertown, meaning that it was sort of gritty, and almost as though you didn't dare mess around with it. You know, like an institution or something, or a place where bullies might hang out. Not the kind of institution where you put crazy people or anything, but a place where people could just smoke cigarettes and drink and act crazy and "play around" and stuff (if you know what I mean, and you probably do). As I said though, I had been told by my parents never to go there (the owner's wouldn't have let a little kid like me in anyway), so in a sense there's not a lot I can say about the place first hand. The reason was (i.e. the reason that I was told not to go there), mostly I guess, had to do with the cigarettes and beer and maybe even some other stuff you could get there. You see, when I was a boy in Washertown and (as I suggested above) pure and innocent and in Sunday school and everything, beer was mostly something nice people weren't supposed to drink. At least not very often. Unless of course you belonged to one of the local animal clubs, like the "Moose" or "Elks" or something. Then they could. At least I think that's the way it worked. And you could do it (drink beer and stuff) at places called Banes and The Lombardi, and at The Washertown Country Club too, only if you did it (meaning drank beer, not like actually "did" someone or anything) at the Country Club you were supposed to pour it into a glass first . . . especially if you were a woman (we called them ladies when I was little). It was pretty much OK to smoke though (except for women who were ladies, and teachers, and of course if you were little), and no one even thought about cancer or anything like that. You just smoked and enjoyed it (Camels, Chesterfields, Lucky Strikes, and Old Gold's mostly). And no sissy filters either.

To stay with the beer issue, however (although I'm not sure that we need to for very long), some of the real "churched-up" people in Washertown, like mostly the Methodists and Baptists (especially the "Southern" Baptists, whatever that was supposed to mean) and "Four Square" people (again, whatever that meant), wouldn't let their people drink beer at all. I think they thought it was actually immoral or maybe something worse even (meaning really, really, *really* bad). But you probably already knew that. And so they didn't (i.e. drink beer), unless they were willing to take the chance of being kicked out of their church in this life and going to hell in the next. And according to these same people (the real "churchy" ones), if you went to hell Satan (whoever that was) would set you on fire and do some other really bad stuff to you. Maybe even sexual stuff (if you were lucky I guess). And all this punishment for having a beer would go on forever. So how's that for a pretty scary thought? But anyway, and to stay on the subject (beer drinking), I guess they (the church people) had read somewhere, probably in the *Bible* I guess, that Jesus didn't drink beer, and so they maybe decided that meant that he didn't want other people to drink it either. But it could be that he just didn't like it. I don't know. But that would be pretty hard to believe, since he lived in the desert and everything, and a cold one would probably have tasted pretty good sometimes. Maybe the problem was that you just couldn't get good beer in those days. Again, however, not having been there, I really can't say.

I *do* know, however, that these same church people said that he, Jesus, their "Lord and Savior," (I was never quite sure what that meant either) had changed water into wine once. No kidding. It was at some big outdoor desert party or a wedding or something. So I guess you can't say that he was totally against drinking. For all I know he might even have changed some of that same water into beer. I mean a lot of people don't like wine, and when you have a party and everything you usually try to please all your guests, not just some of them. Anyway (and to try once more to get back on some kind of "track") these same "church-heads" (especially the ones who looked like they had their underwear up their cracks or something) really bought into the wine story. Curiously, however, when they "took communion," meaning the drinking wine and eating bread ritual that they believed Jesus had told them to do a long time ago (although you probably already knew that), they, meaning the Methodists and the Baptists for sure (and maybe the others too) used Welch's grape juice instead of wine. I remember I thought that was kind of dumb. I mean Jesus and his friends drank wine. But the "churched-up," "church-head," underwear up their cracks people drank Welch's. I guess, in their strange way of thinking (at least it always struck me as strange), they thought that drinking wine for communion was like drinking beer at the Washer City. I don't know. I mean it's not as though someone was going to get buzzed on a single sip of communion wine.

All church people didn't think that way, however. Episcopalians drank wine for communion; and, as I later learned, for just about any other occasion they could arrange too. And they also drank martinis and manhattans and everything. Not for communion though. They just drank wine for that. Whatever. The Episcopalians, I decided, really knew what they were doing, so eventually I became one. Washertown Catholics (actually Catholics everywhere) I found out, only let their priests drink it (the communion wine), which struck me as kind of a selfish way of doing things. I mean I always thought religious people were supposed to share and "do unto others" the stuff they wanted other people to do to them (which also raised some issues in my at times somewhat twisted little mind). At least sharing and doing stuff with (to) other people is what I was taught in Sunday school. But I'll tell you more about that later. The Catholics got to eat communion bread though (crispy little wafers, actually . . . sort of like thick paper), even though they didn't get any wine. Whatever. Anyway, the Methodists and Baptists (as I was saying before) only drank Welch's grape juice for communion. And they all got some bread (but with no peanut butter or jelly or anything).

But I need to get back to Jesus (perhaps in more ways than one), and to part of how this digression of sorts got started. See, I always liked to think, contrary to what a lot of Methodists tried to teach me, that Jesus' wine trick (when he made it out of water) meant that he wasn't against everything that made you feel good (although it seemed to me that the Methodists often were . . . at least that's what I thought). I mean it just made sense to me, even when I was still pretty little, that you ought to be able to love Jesus and enjoy a cold one (or two or three) also. But then I wasn't a theologian or anything. I was just a kid, a Methodist kid, but a little boy who was trying pretty hard to make sense out of things nevertheless. Later on I became a Presbyterian for a few years, then an Episcopalian (as I already said), then a Lutheran (but not for very long), and then an Episcopalian again. I guess I got a little confused there for a while. I don't know what I am now. Probably not much of anything. But that's another story. And, as I'm sure you will agree, we have been off track long enough. (I'm not sure why, but these occasional and rather strange digressions somehow seem important to me.) However, this part of my story is supposed to be about the Washer City Café, and I'll therefore try to get us back there for a while. Sometimes though, digressions like this kind of help me keep my mind from getting funny on me. I told you before that once in a while the way my mind works can be a problem, so just understand that I'm doing the best I can.

So anyway, when I was little, I wasn't supposed to go to the Washer City Café, although I did make it a point to sometimes kind of walk by on my way to somewhere else. But I heard a lot of stuff about it. I mean *lots* of stuff. And I pretty much got the impression that most of the guys who hung out there sometimes got in trouble, and maybe even got kind of roughed up there. And sometimes really bad too. They drank their beer in brown, recycled, chipped up and scratched around the middle, long-necked bottles. (I knew that because you could see the "empties" stacked up on the sidewalk sometimes.) Beer at the Washer City (meaning the bottles) always seemed to be beat up looking. That was because (I decided anyway) the truck drivers saved the newer and nicer bottles for the animal clubs I already mentioned, and especially for the Country Club crowd. But anyway, the beer bottles at the Washer City were pretty beat up, like some of the guys I guess. I also learned that the Washer City Café was for just "blue collar" guys, although when I was little and first heard of the place I didn't know what that meant. Eventually though I learned that it meant guys who were *real* guys and had *real* jobs. *Men*, if you know what I mean. No sissy-shit white-collar stuff. I also know that whenever I saw anyone go in there (almost always a guy, but sometimes not), he was wearing either a blue work shirt (maybe tan) or a dirty t-shirt with a pack of cigarettes rolled up in one sleeve. I guess that would indicate that they wore just about whatever they wanted to. But there's nothing wrong with that. I mean it was their business not mine. Whatever. Blue, tan, or "T" with cigarettes rolled up, they were all considered to be the blue-collar crowd. And real *men,* as if maybe the "T" in t-shirt stood for testosterone or something (although I didn't know what that was then). Anyway, what the guys wore was nothing compared to what I heard some of the women who went there wore (or didn't).

I thought I should tell you that about the Washer City women, since when I was a lot older (pretty much anyway) a kind of strange acting guy once told me that some of the women ("gals") who went to the Washer City (although as I said, there weren't very many who did) sometimes didn't wear any underpants. Really. That's what he told me. That seemed kind of strange to me. And of course I never found out for sure. I mean I only heard that from the weird guy. And I don't even know how he knew (now that I think about it I do, but I didn't know then), or why he would have singled me out to say this to. Kind of scary. Anyway, the strange guy told me (I think) that it was mostly on Saturday nights that some of them didn't (i.e. when some of the women didn't wear any underpants). Or maybe he said that they wore them when they went in, but not for very long. Or maybe what he said was that they took them off when they came out. I really don't know. You've got to remember that I was still just a little kid when he told me this stuff, and it was pretty confusing. I do know though, as I said before, that when I was little I would have thought not wearing underpants was pretty strange. Unless maybe you got really, *really* hot or something. So maybe that was it; in fact I bet it was. They got hot. But I don't think the weird guy was just talking about summer. As I said, it was all pretty confusing. *Anyway*, it really doesn't matter. At least I don't think it does. And I know for sure that I'm thinking about it too much, and I don't want to take the chance of letting it make my mind get goofy again or anything. That, as I just reminded you, is sometimes a problem. And besides, Washertown's Washer City Café wasn't just about beer and underpants. There's other stuff to tell you too.

First though, and to get back to what the Washer City Café was really all about, you need to hear a little more about the blue collar guys who went there. But don't misunderstand me. As I said before, there wasn't anything wrong with wearing blue collars. Anyone should know that. I mean Washertown had a high regard for the work ethic, and rightly so; it was the work ethic (and these guys were the ones who did most of the work) that made the place what it was. There would have been no washing machines and no Washertown without them. (The town's feeling about the work ethic of the women with no underpants would probably have been another story.) However, there was in fact a bit of a problem with some of these guys, and it was (as I figured out much later) that the necks of a lot (if not most) of the men who hung out at the Washer City were red. *Really* red. And rednecks often meant trouble (along with a lot of other stuff, if you know what I mean, and I'm sure you do). That's "trouble with a capital T" (to borrow an expression), and therefore trouble in Washertown itself. I mean those guys had some pretty strong opinions about stuff, and you didn't want to mess with them. The bottles (long neck) may have been brown, and the shirt collars blue, but their necks were red. Believe me.

Here's an example, I think anyway, although this might get kind of complex, and some parts be hard to remember. Whatever. At the edge of Washertown, on the way to the public park pool where I went swimming with my buddies (I'll tell you more about that later), there was this sort of peculiar and "who knew what the hell it meant" sign (at least my buddies and I thought it was peculiar) that read something like "God Save the World With the Townsend Plan." We of course didn't have a clue as to what The Townsend Plan was (although many years later I learned that it was a left-over from the "Great Depression" . . . something having to do with a doctor named Townsend wanting to give everyone money). I guess he was a Democrat. Whatever. I'm not even sure that anyone else really knew what "the plan" was about either. But that didn't matter. What *did* matter was how something like this could solidify the attitude of the guys at the Washer City Café. If they believed (and let's say some union "insider" had told them to) that this so-called plan of Dr. Townsend's was going to put more money in their pockets (and less in the wallets of the white-collar guys), whether it was true or not, then they damned well were going to support it! It then became like God himself was going to save the world with this plan. And in the eyes of a lot of the blue-collared, brown bottled, rednecks, the world was pretty much centered on (perhaps had even been created for) the Washer City crowd.

So anyway, believing in stuff like The Townsend Plan (at least I think so) was most likely and pretty much part of believing in the general Washer City "Credo," which you probably should know about too. They didn't call it that, of course; it was just kind of a "given." Like part of the rules or something. (I only figured this out when I got a lot older, like in junior high maybe.) Anyway, the Credo (pretty much at least) went sort of like this: "I. All Republicans are rich, phony, blow-hard, sons-of-bitches (I kind of explained that to you earlier); II. White people, especially white people who wear blue collars and have red necks (actually that sounds rather patriotic when you think about it) are *better* than, *smarter* than, and *more equal* than, 'Coloreds' (i.e. 'Niggers'), Germans, Japs, and Jews." Homosexuals, i.e. "fucking queers" (pardon my language again, but that's how they talked) would have made the list too, except for the fact that fucking queers (even non-fucking queers, I suppose) were thought to be pretty much if not totally non-existent in Washertown. And it was for sure, if indeed there were any, they would never have even thought about crossing the threshold of the Washer City Café (as if I had to tell you that). Finally, although this last part of the infamous credo was only relevant about every three or four years (when union contracts were up for negotiation), there was this final point: "III. If there ain't more money comin' from the Company soon, *real* soon, the Union takes over, and it's 'fuck those guys' (again, that's what they said), and we go out on strike!" So, and to sort of sum things up, according to the Washer City credo committee, people who were not totally American and patriotic—which meant any male who was not *red*-necked, *white*-skinned, *blue*-collared (and of course screamingly heterosexual and constantly horny)—were well advised to not even *think* about drinking at the Washer City Café. After all, a credo is a credo. It's the 1940s. And these are the guys (*men*) of the Washer City Café. It's just that simple. "You wanna be an American? Then be one!" "You wanna be one of the boys and drink at the Washer City? Then believe what we stand for . . . or shut the fuck up"! (I don't know where those guys went to Sunday school, but I can tell you for sure that it wasn't Washertown First Methodist.)

One other thing about the Washer City Café, and then we'll be done with it. It was rumored that you could buy "dirty" pictures there, but only of course if you had the money and knew the right people. You could even get a whole magazine or "deck" of them (dirty pictures). At least that's what someone told me. Someone also told me that the pictures were from France, which I guess made them even better. Maybe it was that same sort of weird guy I mentioned before. I can't remember. But anyway, I guess the assumed availability of dirty pictures was another reason I wasn't supposed to go there. You could also get "rubbers" at the Washer City (the word *prophylactic* was way beyond their and my vocabulary); they were sold in machines that were attached to the wall in the men's room. At least that's another thing I heard. And although I don't mean to digress (again), you might like to know (although maybe not) that I learned all about rubbers and everything from my friend Mike in second grade. Or it might have been third grade. I guess it doesn't matter.

Anyway, he (Mike) was really smart and everything, and taught me how to kind of like masturbate (although we didn't know that word either . . . we just said "jack-off," and knew that it felt really good), by sliding down one of the support poles that held up the big sliding board on our grade school playground. It (the slide) was just next to the steel jungle gym. But that's another story. And I really don't want to get too far off track. So anyway, to finish off then (i.e. about the Washer City Café, not what we did on the playground), I kind of figured out that the dirty pictures and rubbers and stuff all had something to do with the occasional presence of the women who didn't wear any underpants (which I already told you about). But again, I can't be sure. And I could be wrong. As I said, I was pretty little then, and actually only figured this stuff out a lot later. But anyway, it sort of seems to me that the fact that rubbers, and dirty pictures from France, and the people who went to the Washer City Café were all a part of Washertown means that it really is true that there's something (and someone) in this world for just about everybody (if you know where to look for it). That's what I was taught anyway. Even way back in Sunday school, only in Sunday school what you were looking for wasn't supposed to be rubbers, dirty pictures, and hot women. But I was probably pretty too much influenced by Sunday school. Whatever. I'm getting a little bit strange in the head again, and since as I said, I wasn't even supposed to go there (the Washer City), I should probably just get back to some of the other really important stuff about Washertown. (Some of the guys at the Washer City were real assholes anyway.) So what I need to get back to are the other people who lived in Washertown. All of them. I already told you they were mostly good and everything, but it wasn't quite that simple, and I really need to tell you more. In fact, I'll give the people their own little section too, just like I did for the Washer City Café. OK?

The Washertown Chosen

To start with the facts, the Washertown of my childhood was home to about ten thousand of God's finest, most hard-working, healthiest-looking, and maybe even actually "chosen" people. I first heard about chosen people (although I think they were just Jews then) in Sunday school (always Sunday school), and it seemed to me that I wouldn't have wanted to be one (a chosen person), if that meant that I had to live the way they did and get pushed around and everything. But the guys who wrote the *Bible* weren't talking about Washertown. Anyway, among them (the Washertown chosen), were about three Jews and their families, maybe twenty to thirty Jehovah's Witnesses and their *Watchtowers,* and around five hundred or so Catholics (*Roman* Catholics) and their statues. The remaining folks, and the majority of the Washertown chosen, were Protestants, or nothing at all. Well, not really *nothing,* of course; I mean everyone is someone or something. But you know what I mean. The "nothings" were simply not very public about their religious convictions (if they had any). So as you can see, religion was really big in Washertown. And bigotry, although of a relatively benign variety, was pretty big also. You have to remember though that this was the 1940s, and things were a lot different then. To entertain a certain amount of bigotry was almost a duty, especially in small towns, and people held on to it for the most part to protect (they thought) the community from real and imagined evils (especially imagined). And anyway, it was pretty much understood and accepted that there was business enough for the Jews, corners enough for the Jehovah's Witnesses (and their *Watchtowers*), fish enough for the Catholics to eat on Fridays (which in Iowa meant a lot of catfish), and issues enough for the Protestants to protest. As for the Washertown nothings, they were allowed (I think so anyway) to just move about and do as they pleased.

Also among Washertown's ten thousand or so residents were *two* Black men and their families (a less than overwhelming percentage of Washertown's citizens, I know, but there were more in Des Moines). A daughter of one of these men, by the way, June Anne, became a good homeroom friend of mine in junior high school, and was a really good singer. And I mean *really* good. (I learned later that she went on to have a successful career in the jazz and nightclub world.) Anyway, her father, who was a good guy and pretty well known around town, was referred to (and appropriately for the 1940s) as a Negro by the more educated people of Washertown, as a "colored man" (like a black or brown crayon with legs or something) by the less well educated and perhaps just a little more prejudiced folks, and (and most unfortunately) as a Nigger or "boy" by some of the more "patriotic" inhabitants of the Washer City Café (the guys with the red necks), and other local assholes of similar and limited brains and sensibilities. It was thought at the time, by the way, (but again of course by those of less smarts) that Black men tended to father a lot of children (some in wedlock, most not), to eat great quantities of watermelon (and chicken's intestines), to smile a lot, and to have really big ones (if you know what I mean . . . and again you probably do). Bigger in fact, much bigger I suspect, than most white men could even dream of (or pray for).

In truth, however, Mr. Jackman, as I previously suggested, was one of the nicest, friendliest, most deserving of respect, and, by necessity I would guess, most forgiving persons in all of Washertown. Again, however (as with the bigotry issue that I already mentioned), I should point out that regarding racial and other "differences" attitudes, you need to remember that in Washertown in the 1940s "Niggers," as well as "Kikes" and "Wops" (I think there was only one Wop family) were for the most part just carelessly and "matter-of-factly" referred to by those particular names. There was actually very little thought involved, or real malice intended (at least by the majority of Washington folks). This was just the way it was. Some people were "ordinary" people (meaning traditional white, Anglo-Saxon, Protestant, and "basic" Americans), and others were Niggers, Kikes, or Wops. I'm not saying that there weren't some truly prejudiced, even hateful people in Washertown (as I suggested up above, I'm sure there were), although I always wished it had been otherwise. I really think, however (or maybe it's just that I really, really *want* to think), that they were a *very* small minority, like perhaps just ten or twelve of the boys at the Washer City Café and perhaps a few other stragglers. In their hearts though (which of course they probably wouldn't have opened to anybody), some of these people may have been pretty good guys too.

There was another "lone ranger" living in Washertown when I was little. At least he was trying to live there. (Remember the "real" Lone Ranger . . . the one you listened to on the radio and who had a buddy named "Tonto" and a horse he called "Silver"?) Well, he's not the one I'm talking about. But I think I should tell you about Washertown's own lone ranger, or you might think I'm just writing about the "easy" parts of Washertown. So to begin with, this man's very presence (trust me) was not easy for the folks of Washertown, and unfortunately the whole situation got worse when he became the focus of one of Washertown's scandals (partly because there weren't really that many scandals in Washertown to focus on). Anyway, he,

Mr. Lewis by name, was homosexual. A "homo," or "queer," or even worse, a "*fucking* queer," to again use some of the language of a few of Washertown's less enlightened citizens. (And one more time, I apologize for the language; but that's what they said.) Later on I'll tell you more about the *fuck* word and why I keep thinking I should apologize when I use it. Anyway, to stay on track, the majority of people in Washertown were in truth either unaware of Mr. Lewis, were indeed aware of him but chose to ignore him, or simply wanted to pretend that he didn't live there at all. But to be perfectly honest about the situation, again I suspect the reactions to Mr. Lewis were "in that strange 1940s sense" rather benign (kind of like living next door to a Jew, but not talking to him very much), and were based mostly on people simply not knowing how to react. It was maybe sort of like if you saw a person in a wheel chair or something and didn't know what to say, when in fact all you needed to say was "hello." I mean as I've already told you, Washertown people, for the most part, wanted to be good citizens, to do only the right thing, and thereby protect their community. There was no questioning that. It's just that they had some problems doing it sometimes.

So anyway, Mr. Lewis, believe it or not, was thought by many of the folks in Washertown (although as I said, most of them probably didn't think about him at all) to be the only queer in town (again to use their language). Maybe even the only one in all of Iowa (although they might have thought there could be another one in Des Moines maybe, or one just passing through on his way to Chicago or somewhere). Whatever. There was actually of course no great threat in Washertown. Just a small amount of discomfort. Nevertheless, and unfortunately (as was the case for some of the other minorities in town), Mr. Lewis was considered to be "a not very nice person" by at least a few people, and especially (wouldn't you know) to some of Washertown's finer religious folk. To those people, i.e. to the members of Washertown's ever vigilant "Society of All Things Sacred and Loving," Mr. Lewis was not only an aberration, but an *abomination* as well. That's right. A bona fide abomination. And an abomination (I figured this out when I got a lot older and actually learned the word) was really bad . . . worse even than being a vampire, or cross-eyed, or having the "clap," or syphilis or something. I mean you were better off just being a total asshole. These religious folks of course got the abomination idea (you guessed it) right out of the *Bible*, and therefore probably thought the guy shouldn't even be allowed to get near a church (or go anywhere else as far as that goes), unless perhaps he wanted to become a Jew or a Jehovah's Witness maybe, and go to the temple or Kingdom Hall, or wherever it was they went. It was for sure he was never going to be a Baptist or some other kind of really sacred and saintly person. (It kind of makes you sick, doesn't it?)

But a little clarification here. As you may recall, so-called religious people in the 1940s, and especially in places like Iowa (although Arkansas and Alabama and other "hillbilly" and "hick infested" places were thought to have been worse), were more concerned about judgment than compassion. Understanding another person's plight (especially a person less fortunate), or filial love, or things like that didn't always count for much. And to this day, I don't "for the life of me" (old expression) know how they managed to over look such basic Biblical ideas as loving ones neighbor, or "doing unto him" what you would like him to "do unto you." I mean correct me if I'm wrong, but I'm sure that's pretty much what Jesus told us to do. The Washer City Café people probably even knew that. So anyway, as a result of some of this religious shit, when I grew older I became absolutely convinced that if Jesus had known about how those people acted (and I mean the "church people," not the Mr. Lewis's of the world), he would probably have puked. In fact, the older I get the more convinced I become that Jesus would have puked at a lot of the stuff that went on (and still does) because of some of the stupid, sadistic, and otherwise sick assholes who populate some so-called "Houses of God." Well, I guess I got that out of my system for a while. Anyway, try to *understand* Mr. Lewis? Show some *compassion* for Mr. Lewis? *Love* Mr. Lewis? I mean love a homo? A *fucking* queer? Are you kidding? So, because of such fine, religious, *Bible*-based attitudes (and before continuing one line further), I want to set the record straight and let you know that Mr. Lewis was of fine family, and, I suspect, a person of simple, but significant religious faith. He was also somewhat (actually, I'm sorry to have to say, quite a bit) mentally retarded, and physically handicapped as well. Talk about bad breaks. Remember that old Sunday school song, "Jesus loves me/This I know"? Well, it was written for the Mr. Lewis's of this world. Trust me on this one.

But now, about the scandal that I mentioned not too long ago (you might as well know the whole story). Mr. Lewis, "Hard Luck Lewie," was of course right in the middle of it. Which is to say that even though many people wanted to pretend Mr. Lewis didn't exist, the reality of the scandal made that pretty hard to do. First then, a little background information. Not infrequently, Mr. Lewis could be found in Washertown's theatre district (how's that for giving the place some sophistication?), hanging out (unfortunately in more ways than one) in the men's room at the very finest of the town's three theatres (movie theatres, of course). Therefore, if you were a movie-goer (and almost everyone in the 1940s was), and if you were at all observant (and it was hard not to be), it was pretty difficult to deny Mr. Lewis's existence (and sexual orientation)—unless of course you never had to go to the bathroom (even during a "double feature"), or were a girl or something. But anyway, here's what happened regarding the scandal. And I'm determined to try to stay on track for a change.

One night, three or four of Washertown High School's finest young men (they were all athletes of course . . . you had to be an athlete to be a "finest") met up with Mr. Lewis (probably in the men's room of the movie theatre), and shortly thereafter proceeded to go down an alley with him where he, Mr. Lewis, then "went down" (as the expression goes) on them, all of which eventually was to lead to making things considerably worse for the naïve, retarded, handicapped, and homosexual Mr. Lewis ("Hard Luck Lewie"). All this "good time Charley" stuff, as I just said, took place in an alley, but *not* (I guess it's important that you know this) in the alley next to Washertown's *finest* theatre (it is not my intention to tarnish the theatre district's image more than I have to), although the initial "connection" (if you know what I mean) may have been in that particular theatre's men's room. There is, however, such a thing as good taste, and I'm sure that at least one of the participants in this scandal-in-the-making must have had some. So, in fact, the major event took place in an alley next to Washertown's *least* fine theatre, a theatre right next door to a bar (not the Washer City, but in the same general category and vicinity, and with a similar reputation).

Whatever. Everyone in that alley was apparently being good to everyone else, which is to say that everybody pretty much got what he wanted (i.e. both "Hard Luck Lewie" *and* "the good time

Charley's"). They also, however, got caught (a not insignificant event involving the Washertown Police Department), since as I already said, there weren't a lot of scandals to be had in Washertown. Anyway, as fate would have it, they (a couple of Washertown's police officers) apparently walked down (not to be confused with "went down") that particular alley at just the right (or wrong) time, depending on your feelings about this sort of thing, and crashed the party (so to speak), ending whatever "connection" (or "connections") there may have been between the boys and Mr. Lewis. Eventually, of course, the story got out. When it did, it was made clear (of course) that it was Mr. Lewis who had committed the "crime" (and certainly not Washertown High School's "finest"). I guess the moral of the story (if it has to have one) is that in the Washertown of my youth it was much more acceptable to be a reasonably bright (or maybe even stupid) young athlete looking for a quick "blowjob," than to be an aging and unfortunate, dumb-fucking queer (however disadvantaged and disabled the dumb-fucking queer may have been). So, with that you now know the circumstances surrounding Washertown's scandal of the decade. As I said before, everything that went on in Washertown wasn't necessarily good (although most stuff was). Also, once again, I apologize for some of the language I used in telling you about this, and especially for the *blowjob* word; but that was the only term I knew at the time (except for *cocksucker,* and I thought I would spare you that one). Clearly, however, I need to get away from this (these?) unfortunate affair (affairs?), and go on to other, acceptable, and more ordinary events in the Washertown of my youth.

To several of Washertown's citizens, and probably more than you would like to think, the three or so Jews, the twenty Jehovah's Witnesses, five-hundred Catholics, the "nothings," Nigger or two, Wop or two, and dumb fucking queer were all considered to be suspicious in one way or another. At least by someone (and most likely by a pious Protestant). The degree of suspiciousness was not necessarily in the above order, however. As a matter of fact, the Catholics were probably considered to be the most "suspect" of all, since as most people knew (and as I sort of started to say before) they, the *Roman* Catholics, prayed to statues and worshipped the Pope and shit like that. Almost everyone knew it too. And the local priest, Father McJar, drank too much. (I think I learned later that drinking too much just kind of went with the territory.) He wasn't *my* father, of course, or actually anybody's (unless he had gotten carried away with some nun maybe and had sent the kid to a secret "school" or something). They just called him that: Father McJar.

The Catholics even lighted incense fires and put them in swinging pots. And, *and* (and this was a really tough one for the Protestants to handle), they, the *Roman* Catholics (as in "Roooman Catholics") even ate Jesus' body! Swear to God. They *ate* his body. And, as if that wasn't enough to make a Protestant puke (and a Jehovah's Witness wince), the priests even drank his blood! No kidding. They did! They drank his blood, and from silver cups. I remember that the Baptists and Methodists and people like that talked about this all the time. And all this barbaric eating and drinking and shit wasn't just make-believe or symbolic either. They actually did it! (The priests said it had to do with the doctrine of a "train-substation," or "transobliteration," or something like that.) But anyway, they ate Jesus' body. And the priests drank Jesus' blood. I mean it was awful. Just *awful*! At least that's what some people said, and what I was told. It's no wonder people were suspicious of them. I mean if anyone else had done stuff like that they'd have been locked up somewhere. Like if not in a jail or a penitentiary, then in some goddamn loony bin or something.

And then to get back to the Pope and people like that (although now that I think about it, I guess there weren't any other people like the Pope), I can remember that when I was little, but already a member in good standing at Washertown's First Methodist Church, his (the Pope's) name was Pius. Really. Pius. Pius Number 12, I think. Kind of like the number on a bottle of really expensive perfume, only higher. The perfume was only a number 5 (if I remember correctly). Yeah, I do. It was called "Chanel Number 5." I think anyway. But I guess it really doesn't matter. Anyway, I never knew what the Pope's number really meant, but I think some of the kind of really nasty and sarcastic Protestants probably joked about it being his "mental age" or something. Of course I didn't even know what mental age was when I was little. (Again, it was only when I got older and went to college that I learned about that kind of stuff.) But Protestants actually didn't joke about the Pope *too* much, since in the 1940s it was almost like everyone was sort of afraid of him. I mean the possibility existed that he (Pious Number 12) just may have been right sometimes (about something at least . . . your guess is as good as mine). And some people even thought he could send about anyone to hell that he wanted to—Catholic or not. But I always thought, at least as I got a little bit older I did, that that was bullshit.

Anyway, I remember that Mr. Pope Pius Number 12 was real skinny, wore a dress (with a kind of fancy and lacy little sweater over it), and that he always had a funny looking hat on his head. Sometimes it was kind of like a red "beanie;" then at other times it was white, and totally different, and looked a lot like the kind of cup you got when you bought a snow cone at the State Fair, only it (i.e. the Pope's "cone head" hat) was a lot bigger and was turned upside down. So anyway, this was the guy who supposedly gave the OK to all the "train-substation" and "transobliteration" stuff I told you about. But you know what? When I look back, given how kind of "birdy-eyed" (like a mentally ill sparrow or something) and generally sick-like he looked all the time (I remember this from seeing him in the "RKO Pathfinder News" at the movies, and on magazine covers), I don't know why people were afraid of him. Suspicious, yes. But afraid, no. I mean there were a lot weirder and scarier (and healthier) looking guys out there than Number 12. Like try Hitler, for example. Or Mussolini. Or ToJo (my buddies and I always called him "Toe Jam"). Think about *those* guys. They were really nasty. The Pope was just sick looking. Whatever. Just trust me; I mean that guy even had really dark brown circles around his eyes, as though he was not only a nut-case sparrow, but also had end-stage cancer or something. But anyway, a lot of Washertown folks were suspicious of the Pope (and afraid at times) and most other Catholic stuff; and therefore I remember being really glad that I wasn't one (a Catholic . . . i.e. a Rooooman Catholic). Frankly, I was having enough trouble just trying to be a good little Methodist. But more on that part of my story later.

So, to not get too carried away with or spend too much time talking about various groups in Washertown that were suspicious of other various groups in Washertown (that were probably suspicious of still other various groups in Washertown), you might just want to keep in mind that people like for example the Jehovah's Witnesses (few as they were in number) were considered by most Washertown folks to be just plain deranged. And a real pain in the butt of course, because of their *Watchtower* and *Awake* magazines, and their knocking on your door all the time and everything. I mean Jesus! You never knew sometimes when you opened the door how many of them would be there. But you know, now that I think about it more, people weren't suspicious of Jehovah's Witnesses at all (partly maybe because their ministers didn't drink blood and wear dresses or goofy hats or anything). In fact, as I said before, I think most people in Washertown just thought they were nuts. Not suspicious. Nuts. So there really isn't a lot more to say about them. (It simply occurred to me that since I gave so much space to the Catholics, I should be fair and give at least some to smaller groups like the Jehovah's Witnesses as well.)

I guess this means that I owe the Jews a word or two also. (In addition to the Catholic crap, I've already said a few things about Negroes and homosexuals, so we can just pass over them for now.) Isn't it interesting though that I just said "pass over" when I started to talk about Jews? I guess that's maybe part of why a lot of people think everything is kind of connected. You know, like in a sort of weird but true sense. Or maybe not. Whatever. Anyway, to kind of bring this part my discussion to a close, I can recall only one real issue having to do with people being suspicious of the Jews, although in fact it was probably more a matter of anti-Semitism than suspiciousness (I of course didn't know what anti-Semitism meant when I was little.) The issue, or "problem," had to do with the time that one of them, i.e. one of Washertown's limited number of Jews, a man named Melvin (or was it Irving?), who played a good game of golf, wanted to play it (golf) at The Washertown Country Club. That's right, *The Washertown Country Club* (that ever-present reminder that Washertown did indeed have an "upper crust").

Well, and to stay on track here, it wasn't that Melvin/Irving wasn't a nice guy or a good golfer or anything. He was at least those things. And he was also an unusually successful businessman. So in truth there really wasn't anything wrong with him; and, therefore, there was absolutely no real reason to be suspicious of him. That is, of course, unless you weren't real happy with the idea of having a Christ killer driving his balls from the same tee and putting on the same green from or on which *you* drove and putted. And (and most unfortunately), according to more than a few of Washertown's Protestant subsets (and of course the flesh-eating Catholics), that is precisely what a Jew was: a Christ killer! Some two thousand years ago, their forefathers had shouted for the wrong person to die (as the sub-setters and flesh-eaters interpreted the story anyway).

Forefathers, or foreskins (but that's another sort of Jewish story), or whatever, the Jews had killed Jesus, the "Lord and Savior" of the always charitable, supposedly forgiving, "filled with the spirit," God-fearing, Washertown Country Club Christians. All this of course had to do with some rather perverse theology, but that too is another story. And (as though reason could possibly prevail), if you were naive enough to try to remind them (i.e. the sub-setters, flesh-eaters, and Country Clubbers) that Jesus himself was a Jew (surrounded by natural sand traps, although not a golfer), they of course would have told you, and as the expression goes, "in no uncertain terms," that you simply didn't know what the hell you were talking about. What they would have *wanted* to say (although they of course would "never in the world" have said it this way) was that you were full of theological bullshit! And probably up to your eyeballs.

Anyway, regarding Melvin/Irving (or was his name Max?), in addition to the theological shit, it was thought that should they (the governing Board of *The* Washertown Country Club) go against their best instincts and let Melvin/Irving/Max drive and putt there, he might then bring all his "Jew friends" down from Des Moines to shoot a round or two with him. Like Nates, and Abes, and probably even more Melvins, Irvings, and Max's too. And what a fucking (sorry) catastrophe that would be! Probably as catastrophic (almost anyway) as was Cain killing his brother or the great flood or something . . . both of which I already mentioned earlier. And should it actually occur, i.e. should Melvin/Irving/Max actually be allowed to join, who was to say what other evils might follow? Tony the wop maybe (and the entire goddamn Mafia)! Well, it just wasn't going to happen. So, as fate and The Washertown Country Club Board would have it, Melvin/Irving/Max was "not allowed in" (i.e. not granted an esteemed membership at The Washertown Country Club). In no way could this happen. He was, for all practical purposes banished; and destined therefore to play golf only at the Washertown Municipal Course. (Or of course he could go to Des Moines, where most of his friends were.) Anyway, with that issue resolved, the concerned and truly righteous could now turn their attention (and suspicions) from the imminent threat posed by a Jew with a golf ball (and flawed forefathers, and of course no foreskin), to issues of even greater concern. The Washertown Country Club was safe. And so, my friends, it's probably a good time for us to move on.

The Highway

The highway, again a topic important enough for its own little section, "ran right through it" (i.e. Washertown) when I was little, neatly dividing my hometown into two halves, one north and one south. Neither half was necessarily "better" than the other, although the factories were north, and the nicest houses south. The north part included the Casper County Courthouse though, so that was a "just" compensation I guess (no pun intended). Especially at Christmas, when the place was all decorated up (which I'll tell you about later). On the other hand, the south side had Washertown's (and all of Iowa's, I thought anyway) finest park. So maybe the south side was better. But it doesn't really matter, and besides, this part of my story is about the highway itself, not whether you lived north or south.

So anyway, the highway that went through the middle of Washertown was (at least when it was built) one of the best in the nation: U.S. Highway 6—all two lanes of it—and some stretches of it (believe it or not) actually even had curbs (which it was rumored had cost the State Highway Commissioner his job). Anyway, not only did Highway 6 cross the entire nation, from New York to L.A., and pass along the south side of the Casper County Courthouse (as I sort of suggested before), it also ran right in front of the Washertown Public Library (Carnegie), Walgreen's Drug Store, the Thriftway Supermarket (although such markets were not so "super" in the 1940s), and countless other shops, businesses, restaurants, gas ("filling") stations, *and* some pretty big and fancy houses. The highway even went right past the A and W Root Beer Stand at the east end of town, and within five feet or less of the front door of Huxford's Grocery Store, where my buddies and I bought our cigarettes when we were in high school. Anyway, that's how important U.S. Highway 6 was.

Before I tell you more about the highway itself though, let me explain something kind of strange about how it also figured into the way all our street addresses were "spelled" out. As I already told you, the highway divided Washertown into two halves, one north, and one south. OK? And then all the streets that ran east to west (whether north or south of the highway) were called avenues, and all the streets that ran north and south were just called streets (perhaps that was a little redundant, but you know what I mean). However, unlike any other town or city I ever heard about, in Washertown if you lived in the southwest part of town (although I could just as easily have said the southeast, northwest, or northeast part), and let's say on an avenue, your address would be like 627 South Fourth Avenue West. Not 627 Fourth Avenue SW, as in other places. I think maybe this was so that new people and visitors didn't have to handle too much information all at once. In other words, if you lived there (627 South Fourth Avenue West), and wanted to tell someone to come and see you, they were supposed to know to first go south (of First avenue, i.e. Highway 6) to Fourth Avenue, and then to go west to the 600 block (which meant six blocks west of First *Street*), and then to go on across Sixth Street to the house numbered 627. OK? And that was where you lived.

Or, to give you one more example (in case you didn't get it the first time), if you lived on a street, like say your address was 627 Fourth Street SW (as it would have been in other towns), your address in Washertown would be 627 West Fourth Street South. That was so people knew (again, without having to handle too many directions at once I guess) to go west to Fourth Street (from First Street), and then to turn south to the 600 block, i.e. to go six blocks south of the highway (which was in fact First *Avenue,* as I mentioned already . . . but was mostly just referred to as Highway 6), and then look for the house numbered 627 (where you wanted to be). OK? Notice also that if you lived on a street (and that street was anywhere except Washertown, as I also said up above), you would say you lived on Fourth Street SW, whereas in Washertown, if you followed all the rules (and could understand the whole goddamn system *logically*), the same Fourth Street would be designated Fourth Street WS, and you would therefore tell people you lived at 627 Fourth Street, West-South which, however true, would probably really have been confusing. But something tells me this is more information than you might need. Or want. So just remember, Washertown had its own way of designating addresses. (And if you got lost tying to find someone's house, you had to just call them.) But back to the highway.

From one end of Washertown to the other, east to west, there was a grand total of twelve "stop and go" lights. That's right. Twelve. That was about one for every thousand of Washertown's citizens, with two lights left over (maybe because the town was expected to grow). Also, these red, yellow, and green monsters were of course totally non-synchronized.

They all worked OK (most of the time), all day *and* all night even; it's just that they didn't work together. So anyway, these twelve ill-timed (and thought by many people to be totally unnecessary) lights had led to Washertown becoming well known, i.e. infamous, *really* infamous, to the vast and burly fraternity of tractor trailer drivers ("semi truck" drivers), who had no choice but to obey them, as they drove their big rigs across the mighty Midwest and on into Washertown. And as I told you already, to make things even worse, there were only *two* lanes, and absolutely no "turn lanes" on any part of that road. Furthermore, this of course, the 1940s, was a long time before "by-passes" (highway or heart) were available. So . . . the truckers had no choice but to drive this "goddamn stretch of lights," as they called it, right through Washertown on route to (or from) such major transportation hubs as Denver, Des Moines (well, sort of major), Rock Island, and Chicago. I can still recall the hissing sound of the air brakes, and the squeal of the "dualies" (double sets of tires), as the really big ones (trucks) lurched and shook from one "goddamn stop" to another.

A really good place to watch all this happen, by the way (i.e. the lurching and shaking), and especially on an already hot, boring, and really humid summer morning (the kind of August morning when everything smelled kind of funny—like wet, freshly cut grass, hot road tar, and maybe even someone's toast burning, all mixed together), was from in front of the Washertown Public Library, with (as I already kind of mentioned) the name Carnegie boldly carved into the stone work over the front doors. Actually, it was along about the second to third week of August that provided the best "truck" show in town, at least for a gradeschooler who was getting pretty tired of summer, and would rather be outside the library than in. (The "first of the summer" reading programs were over by then, although they never were anything I was especially interested in.) So anyway, all I'm trying to say is that the front of the library in August was a good time and place to watch the trucks from.

Right across the street, i.e. across "goddamn Highway 6," was a Conoco gas station, green and white (and sleek and modern looking too), with gas pumps that were squared off at the top. "Kitty corner" was Skelley Oil, a station that had not yet opted for the newer look, and instead still had a sort of whitish-tan brick look to it, with classic, *red* gas pumps that gurgled and swished the gasoline up into glass cylinders that were on the tops of the pump fixtures themselves. I'm not sure that the gurgling was necessary, but it did kind of get your attention, especially when you were little. It was sort of like watching enormous "bubble lights" (if you remember those things, and the Christmas trees of the late forties and early fifties that displayed them). My parents wouldn't buy bubble lights for our tree though, because my mom didn't think they were traditional enough. But that's another story (and a sort of sad and regretful one for me), so I'll just leave it alone. At least for a while. Besides, it's August now, not December.

Anyway, just north of the Washertown Public Library (Carnegie), and across from Skelley Oil, was yet another gas station, a Phillips 66, painted blue and orange, and with a great big circular "66" sign in front. Sometimes, given the presence of all these gas stations, and especially on August mornings that were really, really, *really* hot (and humid), you could actually smell the gasoline in the air (as well as the cut grass, tar, and burnt toast). You know, the kind of morning that was so hot that the flies were already buzzing around your head, sort of like they were on some kind of goddamn crusade to drive you crazy or something. Especially if you were sort of sweaty, or trying to eat a donut or something. Actually, I really liked the gasoline smell. Not as much as the smell of wilting, fresh-cut grass though, or the roasted coffee beans at the A & P Grocery Store on down the street (Highway 6). But almost.

Whatever. Back to the library. Having so far made about five or six traffic light stops on their journey through metropolitan Washertown (remember, these lights were not synchronized), and especially if they had been driving a long time and the morning was god-awful hot and they were already (or still) really sweaty and everything, some of the truckers got pretty upset (as in "really pissed"). And that was when, in addition to the hissing of brakes, lurching, and squealing of tires, the drivers of those beauties, especially the really big ones (meaning really big trucks, not drivers . . . you couldn't usually tell if the drivers were big or not), downshifted their language right along with their gears. First, they shifted from *goddamn* to *shit* (that's "sheeitt" in truck talk). But that was probably only when they had had to stop one or two times. Then (after the third or fourth stop), it went from "sheeit" to *son-of-a-bitch* (they always seemed to emphasize the "bitch" word). And then, *then* (give them one or two more stops), they shifted way down (and I mean *way* down) to a screaming *FUCK!* That's right, *FUCK.* A screaming, yowling *FUCK!* I know, since as I said, I would be sitting in front of the library (where about the sixth stop took place) with the goddamn flies buzzing around or sitting on my maple iced "long John" (if I was lucky enough to have one . . . I really liked those things). Anyway, I loved it (the language, not the flies). Absolutely loved it! Probably because that was the one word I was never *ever* supposed to say. And I guess that's probably why I have already apologized several times for writing it. But that's what they said. And right in front of Mr. Carnegie's library too. I guess I could try to use a different word, except that if I'm supposed to be telling you how it really was in Washertown, I have to be honest. It was *FUCK*. No doubt about it: *FUCK!*

Just so you know how really bad it was for me to say that word (when I was little anyway), and also to be kind of done with it then (so I don't have to keep apologizing, unless I maybe slip once in a while), I can tell you that if I ever said fuck in front of my mom or anyone, I'd get my mouth washed out with soap. Really (this was before "time out" and all that shit was invented). Probably "Ivory" (like when I once in while might have said some other bad stuff). Although if I had been dumb enough to say fuck in front of the wrong person, it might even have been "Lava." And that stuff (although you probably wouldn't remember) had sand or something in it. I think it was to help factory workers and other real guys get the grease and shit off their hands. Whatever. It was pretty gritty.

Anyway, what I'm trying to say is that what I just told you about up above is the way the truckers talked when they went through Washertown; and, as a recorder of historic events of considerable importance, I felt I owed it to you to present the story in as totally objective and dispassionate a manner as I possibly could (well, objective anyway). Of course I wouldn't have known what either of those words meant when I was little (i.e. *objective* and *dispassionate*), but I'm not anymore (little), and therefore I do now (i.e. know). And besides, if I were to tell you that these guys had said "doggone it," or "oh golly," or "gosh darn it," or "dang" even (an "almost" bad and very Midwestern word), or maybe "screw it" or something (or someone), you would know better, and then you wouldn't believe what else I said. So, as I told you (regarding the truckers), what they said after having to stop at too many goddamn lights was a great big and real loud *FUCK!* That's what they said. And as I also already said, they probably said it more than once, especially since they didn't have their mothers riding with them (at least I don't think they did, although I do remember seeing some pretty strange looking ladies in some of those big rigs). But anyway, the likelihood that those "mothers" would have had any Ivory soap with them would have been pretty slim. (They might however have had some Lava.) But you know, the more I think about it, the ladies I saw with the truckers were *anything* but mother types.

So anyway (I guess I really do say that a lot), and to be *absolutely* and *finally* done with this "fuck shit" (at least for now), I wish to declare right now (meaning tell you real loud and strong and formal-like) that being a little boy of respectable Washertown breeding, and having eventually acquired very good taste, heightened sensibilities (whatever that meant), and a fair degree of sophistication (I have a Ph.D. and a pretty good collection of classical CDs, although of course I didn't have that stuff then), *and* having never even owned a truck (although I have borrowed one a couple of times when I needed it) . . . man, can I ever get off track . . . *anyway,* I wish to declare that from here on out I shall make every effort to refrain from (i.e. not say it anymore) any and all unnecessary uses of the word *fuck.* I mean whether it's just plain fuck, or like when the word is used in various expressions I was later to come to know, such as "fuck this," or "fuck that," or "fuck you" (or me too, I guess), or "fuck 'em all," or even worse, *"MOTHERFUCKER"* (and trust me, that would have been a two-bar Lava washout), *fuck* is not, is *not* a nice word, and *I* am simply not going to use it anymore (unless maybe I forget, or as I said before, slip . . . or maybe find that there simply isn't any other word that really works).

Actually, now that I think more about the word *Motherfucker,* the subsequent two-bar Lava experience might even have been followed with a cup or two of "Duz" granules (remember the old commercial, "Duz Does Everything"?). But enough of this shit (stuff). Man, I mean it's so hard sometimes to talk nice. Whatever. I have reported enough on (i.e. told you enough about) how the truckers talked, and besides, there are other and more acceptable ways to express ones displeasure and frustrations (unless maybe you *are* a trucker and have already stopped at six or more goddamn lights . . . I mean I have to be fair here). Anyway, the word fuck, F-U-C-K *fuck*, is henceforth (to the best of my ability) banned. And I will not, therefore, be apologizing anymore either.

Some Other Stuff

(Before we go on to even bigger stuff.)

Next I'm going to tell you (briefly, and again in this separate section) just a few more things about Washertown itself (starting with domes), and then I'll tell you even more about what happened to me there, and about school and things, and about how I really got to be this way, i.e. soaped up, fucked up (don't expect perfection), or perhaps just somewhat "twisted." I'm a happy guy, however. At least now I am. And I was never institutionalized or anything like that. At least if I was, I don't remember it, and no one has ever told me I was. So I guess that would suggest that whatever happened to me in Washertown was for the most part good.

Domes

Washertown, not unlike many other Midwestern communities of its time and size, was built around a town square, and in the very center of that square, since Washertown was the "county seat" of Casper County, stood The Casper County Courthouse. (I already said some stuff about this up above, but you need more detail; so that's what you're going to get now.) Anyway, it (the courthouse) was kind of a neo-classical structure (probably mostly "neo"), and therefore sort of a bastard of a building, I guess. It was constructed of gray, stone-like blocks (made of real smooth cement), all of which had been cut into square or oblong pieces, "puffed up" a little by being rounded on the edges, and stacked irregularly, one on top of the other. The building therefore looked like kind of a giant pile of concrete breadboxes that formed a rather massive, dirty gray (but not *real* dirty), two or three story pedestal of sorts, on top of which was a rather awkwardly shaped dome. (You may recall from what I said before that I have always had a certain fascination with domes.) Whatever.

The dome part of the Courthouse was, to tell you the truth (and I told you I always would), more than somewhat "phallic" in shape (although when I was little I of course didn't know anything about phalluses and stuff like that, or even what the word meant). It was only *somewhat* phallic, however (I learned later), since it was actually a little bit too thick (given its height) to be *really* phallic. Well, maybe not. I don't know. Anyway, I do know that it appeared to have the right kind of "head" on it, or I guess I should say "top" to it (top probably sounds better). And since Washertown was so in touch with its Judeo-Christian heritage (underscore Christian, of course), it (the dome) had been sort of architecturally circumcised; at least it looked that way to me (when I got older). As I learned later though, although you probably already know this, the Jews did that to little boys (i.e. circumcised them) because of their religious beliefs. And then later on, maybe to compete for members or something (I'm not sure), the Christians started doing it too. Actually, the Christians did it, mostly anyway, because the medical experts of the time (meaning a number of "know it all" doctors, who eventually always seem to change their minds about things like this) said that it made little gentile boy's "wee-wees" cleaner (or at least easier to take care of). And cleanliness, as you probably also already know (although I'm really getting off track again), was considered to be right next to Godliness. At least Protestants thought so. To tell you the truth, I always thought it was a pretty dumb expression, even when I was a little person, but I'm pretty sure most people thought it (meaning the cleanliness and Godliness thing) was true. So anyway, Washertown (actually just the architects and the builders) probably did it to the Courthouse dome (i.e. structurally circumcised it), I suspect (although I don't know for sure since it happened even before I was born), because they not only believed it was the thing to do, but also because they thought it would look nicer. Maybe anyway. It's really hard to say. But to keep telling you the truth, I don't even know why I'm talking about this. A circumcised *dome?* I mean that's pretty strange talk.

Anyway, that thing (the big, phallic-shaped, custom-clipped dome of The Casper County Courthouse) stood straight up in the air, proud as it could be, towering over all of Washertown. But you know, now that I think about it more, the courthouse dome could also be described, and perhaps more simply, as just sort of silo-shaped; and therefore (I guess anyway), a perfectly appropriate (and sexless) symbol for a Midwestern town. But then if you think about it even more than just more, I mean if you think of that courthouse dome being a silo, and then add the hundreds of real silos spread across the whole state of Iowa (for grain storage and stuff), all of them standing up real straight and stiff-like, Freudian-oriented literary critics (about which, of course, I knew nothing at the time, and of whom, to be sure, there were none in Washertown) could, with some legitimacy, have had a real "field day" (to use another Midwestern expression). Think about it: hundreds of phalluses rising up out of the ground (probably one for every five-hundred people or so). I mean like here are all these huge male sex organs standing at attention across the whole goddamn state of Iowa, with yet another one (cast in concrete mind you) right in the very center of Washertown itself. But whoa there! This is getting out of hand (no pun intended). OK. I'll leave it alone. Just remember that there was a dome on top of the Casper County Courthouse that looked like sort of a stubby but hygienically altered penis (and notice I didn't use any bad words, like *cock,* or *dick,* or *joy-stick* or anything). At least I think it might have looked that way to *some* people. (To the "weirdos" anyway.) Just kidding. But I guess it's pretty obvious that I need to get back on track here. My mind could get really wacked again thinking about any more of this kind of stuff! And besides, I don't even know how (or why) I got started on it in the first place. I'm just trying to tell you about my hometown.

There was, however, one other domed structure in Washertown that you maybe should know a little bit about (I just don't seem to be able to get away from talking about domes). I already mentioned this one too, but only briefly, and I didn't tell you this part. Anyway, this dome was on top of The Methodist church. Washertown's *First* Methodist Church. Actually, there was no "second" Methodist, but I guess the First Methodists felt it made them sound more important to say that. There was, however, when I was really *really* little, a "Free" Methodist Church, where kind of strange things went on, and where the members thought they were more "fundamental" than other Methodists. Something like that anyway. Fundamentally *what*, I don't know; I always thought there was something pretty fundamental about The *First* Methodist Church. Whatever. At The Free Methodist Church the people sometimes got up, and then fell down, and then sort of rolled around on the floor, and then got up again (usually with someone helping them). And I remember they shouted a lot too, like "Praise Jesus" and "Praise God" and everything, which kind of scared me at times. If those people (or anyone else, as far as that goes) had tried to do that stuff at The First Methodist Church, they probably would have been thrown out, or sent to a loony bin or something. Anyway, the rest of what the Free Methodists did (it was just the shouting that bothered me) I thought was pretty funny. I know all this stuff, by the way, because The Free Methodist Church was right by my grandmother's house, which in the summer had really pretty hollyhocks all around it, and in the spring little flowers that my mother liked a lot called "lilies of the valley" (I just added the part about the flowers to kind of "break things up" and make this part of my story nicer). Whatever. I obviously need to get back on track (once again), since I'm trying to tell you about the dome on The First Methodist Church. And besides that, The Free Church building didn't even have a dome; and if it had, I don't think they would have wanted to say much to their people about it. I mean, having a big "dick" on top of your church (if their dome had been shaped like the one on the Courthouse) just wouldn't have been what they would have wanted folks to focus on. Trust me.

So anyway, back to the dome on The First Methodist Church. It wasn't phallic at all. A good thing too, since as I said up above, the First Methodists were more than a little "fundamental" about things also, and I don't think they would have wanted people to think that they had a dick on their roof either. (I'm using the word *dick* now, instead of *penis,* because I decided penis, although I used it before, sounded a little bit too "clinical.") And in fact, as I just suggested, they didn't (i.e. the First Methodists didn't) have a dick on their roof anyway. The dome that crowned The First Methodist Church looked more like a diaphragm (another word I didn't know at the time). It was a somewhat "inflated" diaphragm, but a diaphragm nevertheless. It wasn't inflated too much though. Anyway, as I already told you, I belonged to it (i.e. to the whole First Methodist Church, not just to the diaphragm), and shall have more to say (again, about the whole church) when I tell you about one or two of the outstanding members of the congregation and their organs, i.e. the churches *pipe* organs (they had two when I was growing up), not of course the member's organs or anything like that. Once again, I would not want you to think I'm a "sicko." But those stories will be in another chapter; in fact, they will make up a whole chapter of their own. One other thing for now though. The First Methodist Church had fancy, "fluted" Ionic columns in front of it, and although those fancy columns weren't of course "genuine," the tops nevertheless provided a really good place for pigeons to roost (as I think I may have explained to you before), and from which therefore to shit (another bad word, as I admitted earlier). But to talk about pigeons having bowel movements, or dropping feces ("do-do") on the steps and the sidewalk and stuff, would sound just a little bit pretentious (how's that for a big word?) Anyway, I really don't mean to be drifting away from the glory of The Casper County Courthouse (with its mighty dome), about which there is yet more to be said.

The Courthouse sat on a lovely green lawn, which (years before I was little even) had been planted with an abundance of beautiful shade trees: mostly giant Oaks and even taller and more graceful Elms. And there were just enough Maples to create wonderful color in the fall. On this lawn were also several gently curved, green, painted wooden benches, perfect for all who would pause there to rest, and especially well-suited for Washertown's fraternity of retired guys with little else to do. The lawn was, quite simply, a vintage 1940s Midwestern community gathering place. Also, on each approach to the courthouse itself, there was a drinking fountain, one of which even had a thoughtfully placed cement step, so that little people could get a drink too. This was of course before the time of refrigerated drinking fountains, but I can assure you that the courthouse fountain water tasted pretty cold and really good, especially on one of our too-frequent and really hot summer days. And the fountain was always bubbling. I mean you didn't even have to turn it on. It just was there, bubbling away on its own. You did have to be careful not to put your lips right on the spout though, since if you did you might get polio or something. My mother told me that. Or maybe if not polio, just a bad cough or something. Or maybe measles . . . or mumps . . . or chickenpox. I don't know. I had all that stuff, and believe me, chickenpox was the worst. I mean you should have seen my blisters (not that you would have wanted to). And itch? Anyway, you were supposed to be careful when you drank out of the fountain.

Such is the way it was then at Washertown's Casper County Courthouse. Until I grew older that is, and some inept committee (a society of fools it seemed to me) decided to cut down the trees and remove the water fountains to make way for parking spaces. Actually, I think the arguments for the destruction of the beautiful old trees were two. First, and to be fair, there indeed was at least the beginning of a parking problem in "downtown" Washertown, and second (and even more indeed), there was the ubiquitous (how's that for another big word I learned later?) Washertown pigeon population to deal with. I mean it sometimes seemed as though there were thousands of them (Alfred Hitchcock could have made his movie, *The Birds,* at the Casper County Courthouse), and of course (just like at The First Methodist Church, only more so) that meant thousands of pretty gooey globs of pigeon shit everywhere. I would say *feces,* but again that would be trying too hard. And besides, *shit* isn't nearly as bad as *fuck,* and for the sake of honesty and accuracy I've already had to use that word (*fuck*) a lot (because of the truckers and stuff). *Anyway,* the pigeons dropped (shit/shat) stuff all over the sidewalks that led to and from the Casper County Courthouse. They were probably some of the very same pigeons that seemed to worship at, or at least fly around and shit at, The First Methodist Church (diaphragm and all). Whatever, the pigeon problem, I'm quite sure, did in fact contribute to the demise of the courthouse trees, a sad and truly unfortunate happening to befall beautiful and green downtown Washertown (but a "happening" that was later to be corrected).

Before going on, I want to be sure that you understand that I don't mean to imply that the Washertown Methodists were bad people for harboring so many of the pigeons (that eventually contributed to the demise of the courthouse trees). I mean they didn't "ask" or provide for the pigeons to live on top of their columns or anything like that. They may have tried sometimes (as a defensive maneuver) to get them to fly towards the Courthouse (only a block away from the church), but I doubt even that. So don't blame the Methodists. And the actual truth is that the Methodists, although their columns may have been "home base," were not the only God-fearing people on whom the Washertown pigeons liked to shit. It's just, as I already kind of said, that all those almost militaristic-looking, fake Doric columns in front of First Methodist made for a prime nesting place. Anyway, the "Doric soldiers" (talk about phallic symbols) simply provided a better place from which the pigeons could propel their droppings than any of the other and perhaps less architecturally distinguished churches in town. The Episcopalians didn't have any columns, but they of course would probably have been "immune" anyway. I mean can you imagine it? A pigeon shitting on an Episcopalian? Are you kidding? As the expression goes, "it just isn't done." (Defecating, maybe, but not shitting . . . and then it would have been only a very occasional and misdirected occurrence.) Presbyterians? Shit on the Presbyterians? Maybe. (But *not* on Episcopalians.) And then of course there were the Baptists, who probably wouldn't have seen or said "shit" if they had had a mouthful of it. Or perhaps had even been totally inundated by the stuff during a major "flyover."

And the Catholics (the *Roooman* Catholics) and the pigeons? I suspect they may have had some kind of localized, divine protection built into their organizational structure (or maybe it was just their location). Whatever. They didn't seem to be suffering too much. And anyway, and again from what I had seen in another of those *RKO Pathfinder* newsreels at the movies (which as I think I already told you always preceded the main feature . . . just before the cartoon, and the "follow the bouncing ball" sing-along) . . . *anyway,* most Catholic pigeons seemed happy to shit at the Vatican. A lot, too. Trust me. There's a *lot* of shit at the Vatican. And probably always has been. I'll bet you've seen it too. I mean those Roman Catholic pigeons are always there, scratching and pecking away on the ground, and then swooping up to shit on everything they can. Especially it seems at the very moment the Pope comes out, or the bells ring too long or something. Whatever. To wrap this pigeon shit stuff up, I can't remember much about the Lutherans in Washertown, although I do recall that the Methodists thought the Lutherans remained entirely too close to their Roman Catholic parents. I suppose, therefore, that Lutheran pigeons wouldn't have known for sure exactly where, how much, or on whom (or with just how much decorum) to shit. The Washertown Jews (all three or four families), and the Jehovah's Witnesses (twenty to thirty) were the lucky ones. No temple. No church. No shit! But I don't know *why* I got off on all this talk about pigeons. If it upset you I'm sorry. And I know, as I said a couple of times before now, that *shit* isn't a very nice word. Keep in mind though that I'm just trying to do the best I can to explain about Washertown. Nevertheless, I probably really ought to change the subject, since it's also making me feel a little strange in the head again. Meaning like in my mind. I mean what kind of person spends this much time talking about pigeon shit, for God's sake? It's pretty much time to stop this crap!

But just one thing else about The Casper County Courthouse (and then we can move on for sure). Strange as it may seem to talk about it (I guess I just want to make certain that you have a real "feel," which I guess actually means "smell," for the place), inside the Courthouse, on the entire first floor, it always, *always* smelled sort of unclean. Some days maybe even *really* unclean. At least I thought so. Kind of damp and musty-like. And it was really, *really* bad when it got extra hot and humid in August. It also smelled (although I kind of hate to have to tell you this), and sometimes not just faintly, of urine from the public men's room, which, I suspect, was because it was so frequently used and so infrequently cleaned. Sometimes this urine smell (and I'm not saying some of it couldn't have come from the women's room too) would actually waft out of the bathroom door, flow over the floor (in a kind of misty, swamp-like, science fiction movie sort of way), and pour out onto the lawns and sidewalks. Like some kind of eerie, supernatural fog or something. And you could really notice it (the smell) if you happened to be bending over the outside drinking fountains that I told you about earlier. Especially if you had your mouth full of water and had to kind of suck your breath in through your nose. Then you could almost taste it (the urine smell). But as I said, this was mostly (thank God) just during the heat and humidity of August (actually sometimes in July too) when you were like really hot and thirsty and stayed bent over the fountain too long.

All this was OK though (meaning the heat and humidity, not the urine smell at the courthouse), because that's what helped ripen the corn. (We're going to talk about corn now.) July and August were when out in the country, far from courthouses and public men's rooms (the one in the Methodist church basement didn't smell so good either), and miles away from phallic symbols, diaphragms, and the pigeon shit of the civilized world, you could almost see, and for sure taste, the scent of ripening sweet corn. It so filled the hot, hazy August air that you wouldn't have been surprised if it had even formed little droplets. The Iowa, August haze, by the way, was *not* pollution. At least not when I was a boy. It was perfection! Pure perfection. And August in Iowa, in addition to the corn smell, was also the time for "lightning bugs," some of which (and this is kind of hard for me to say), I murdered in order to make really neat, "glow-in-the-dark" rings for my fingers, and "water lanterns" out of fruit jars. See (but maybe you did this too), if you pinched the tails off the lightning bug bodies, and you did it just right (which wasn't real easy, by the way), they would keep glowing (and sort of pulsating) for a long time. Actually, the pulsating part sort of bothered me. Whatever. On your fingers, everywhere you placed them, they looked gold-like, and although sometimes sort of sticky, they were also really pretty (at least my friends and I thought so). In the fruit jars for the lanterns (which I first prepared by filling the jars with water), if I had enough lightning bug "tails" to put a whole lot of them in all at once, and then "stirred" them up real well (carefully, but well), they would turn the water into a sort of mysterious, magic-like green color, kind of the color of Luna moths (although I didn't know that that was what those gentle and "floaty" green moths were called then).

Speaking of bugs and stuff, August was also the time of the year when in the evening you had to listen to the incessant, and I do mean *incessant* whining and droning of the goddamn late summer Cicadas (we just called them locusts or "katy-dids"), which reminded me that school was about to start again. That's why I said *goddamn*: see, when school started was when I always got real nervous and stuff, and that's why I hated that goddamn sound. But I'll tell you about school later. By the way (I know I use "by the way" too much), not only did the Methodist church men's room smell bad, it also had old, cracked wooden toilet seats that could really get you if you had to do serious "business" before church, and weren't really careful when you sat down. Anyway, we need to move on. And besides, I'll tell you more about the lightning bug lanterns later too.

Actually though, there is still one more thing to tell you about The Casper County Courthouse. In fact, it's the very most important, and even *grandest* thing about it. But I'll wait to tell it to you until later, when I talk just about Christmas in Washertown (a whole other chapter). It'll give you something to look forward to. I mean, everyone looks forward to Christmas (at least all the kids in Washertown did). But you just won't believe what it was like when I was a boy. I mean "wow"! Just "wow"! But now (it seems there are a lot of "buts" in the world of writing too), following that little "tease" about Christmas, I want to change the subject and tell you about one or two (or three or four maybe) early experiences of mine having to do with the neighborhood and some other OK but sometimes sort of shitty stuff. Then I'll take you to school with me. And then we'll go back downtown for a fun-filled walk around the Washertown Square. (All that will be more stuff for you to look forward to.) First, however, I'll tell you about some of the OK but sometimes shitty stuff. "OK" stuff, by the way, is like what you could tell your mother about; "shitty" stuff is kind of like the lightning bug murders I just confessed to. So shitty isn't really meant to be a bad word (although just "shit" is); it's simply a word I use sometimes to sound kind of reckless and tough. And lots of times when I was little (and even when I got bigger) I had to work pretty hard at being tough. But that's another story also.

Fires, Tadpoles, and a Dead Robin
(and other dead stuff . . . like all my dogs.)

So anyway, guess what I did on special summer days and sometimes after school when I was real little? Well, maybe not *real* little, but pretty little anyway. What I did was that we had a brick fireplace in our back yard, with a real chimney and everything. This was where my dad (rarely though, except when it was first built) and maybe my mom sometimes (but not very often) cooked hot dogs and stuff before people had portable charcoal grills. The reason my dad cooked mostly, although as I just said he didn't do it very often, was because when we were out in the back yard and stuff it was kind of supposed to be "time off" for my mother (although it wasn't). Whatever. Anyway, I used the fireplace more than anyone. That's because I liked to collect old cardboard boxes (lots of them), and when I had a really whole lot, and different sizes and everything, I would build a great big cardboard "skyscraper" on top of the fireplace grill. (The skyscraper was supposed to be kind of like the ones my grandparents had told me they saw when they went to New York City to see the 1936 World's Fair.) That was the World's Fair, by the way, that had a "Unisphere" and "Pylon" (I learned that later) for its signature attraction. And all the stuff there (at the 1936 fair) was real modern and was supposed to make everyone think that everything was OK in the world, only it wasn't of course, because of Hitler and stuff.

Anyway, when no one was at home, I would build a great big skyscraper out of my cardboard boxes, maybe almost six feet tall even, and then light it (from the bottom) and pretend that everyone was screaming and burning up and dying in it and everything (especially really pretty girls), and then I would imagine that I rescued them. All by myself. I was a really good rescuer too; I mean *really* good, almost like Superman or someone like that. Maybe the Green Hornet or Batman even. Anyway, I saved a lot of people, and never even got scared either. Except once. That was the time when my skyscraper toppled over too soon (before the top floors had burned up enough), and I almost set fire to the back of our garage. Actually, a lot of those pretty girls I just told you about (and probably some other people too) died in that fire. I mean it was a real tragedy. I think maybe it was during that fire though that I managed to rescue Lana Turner (or was it Dorothy Lamour?). No, now I remember; it was Rita Hayworth. Yeah. Rita Hayworth. Anyway, bad as it was, had our garage also gone up in smoke it would have been even worse, at least for me. (I don't think it would have particularly enhanced my relationship with my father very much, that's for sure, or probably with anybody else either.) I mean I could have burned down the whole goddamn neighborhood. But anyway, except for that one scary time, these Superman (or Green Hornet or Batman) rescue missions made me think I was a really good person, and strong everything too, and that everyone liked and admired me a lot. Actually, I *was* a good person. Only, as I've said before, maybe just a little bit twisted. Oh . . . and I think I rescued Betty Grable too. But that was in a different fire.

I wasn't always good though. I mean basically I was, but I had my lapses. For instance, I wasn't so good sometimes when I made my clandestine (sneaky) visits to Dr. Campbell's fishpond (he was our dentist). Little ponds for goldfish (and sometimes big ones) were a pretty fashionable thing to have when I was a boy; however, I always wished they were even larger so you could maybe swim in them (after dark). Anyway, I would go there (to Dr. Campbell's fishpond) and catch tadpoles and then put them in an old Mason jar (the kind with a dull-gray, lead, screw-on lid). What I actually did was that I would wait to catch them (I've always been a very patient person) until they were just beginning to grow their thin, wiggly, itty-bitty legs and feet (although looking at their little baby feet sometimes kind of made me feel bad for what I was doing . . . even though I did it anyway). Eventually, as you may already know, the tadpoles were supposed to grow into frogs or toads (I can't remember which). Frogs I think. Whatever. It really doesn't matter. Anyway, I'd put the tadpoles in the jar, add some gravel and pond water (which, by the way, often smelled really bad), and then shake them to death. Sometimes almost in a frenzy. I guess that was pretty sick, now that I think about it. But I did it. Not real often, but kind of, I guess, especially during the summer between second and third grades (I think anyway), when I ran out of other things to do. Like if there weren't any green apples to steal, and no one to play "Kick the Can" with.

At night, again when there wasn't much else to do (this is just to see if you remember part of what I told you about just a little while ago) I would sometimes go to a secret place and empty the tadpole bodies and gravel, rinse out the jar (at least I was trying to practice good hygiene), and then go out and catch the lightning bugs to drown in it. Remember? What I think I didn't tell you before, however, was that when you pinched the tails off the lightning bugs you had to be real careful, and I mean *real* careful, or some kind of brownish stuff might squirt out on you. I guess maybe that was their insides. Anyway, it could be pretty messy (gross even), if you weren't careful. One time the stuff actually squirted right in my face. And as you can imagine, that was pretty icky. Sometimes you could even hear a sort of "cracking" sound when you pinched them (it was maybe like you broke one of their wings or something). By the way, I hope you know I really trust you, or I wouldn't be telling you some of this stuff. And frankly, it's kind of making me sick. One good thing though was that the tadpoles never squirted like the lightning bugs did (maybe because I never pulled their legs off or anything).

But anyway, when the lightning bug tails were in the jar (as you can see, this really fascinated me), and it was all filled up with water (from the garden hose at the back of our house), it glowed (as I told you before) a beautiful but sort of weird, yellowy-green color (as I also told you). Kind of like a lantern from China or someplace. Maybe anyway. Since I had never been to China, I can't say for sure. And now that I'm thinking about it more, I probably should have been happy just making the lightning bug rings. Other kids made rings (and they didn't seem to be too bothered by it), but I don't remember that they made lanterns too. Whatever. Don't forget that this was the same little boy who rescued all the people from the burning skyscrapers (including Rita Hayworth and the other beauties). I mean, as I already told you, I wasn't *all* bad. I just did some pretty shitty things to lightning bugs and tadpoles. But, and I'm pretty proud of this, I also screwed (drilled) holes through the middle of buckeyes that I collected (from Dr. Campbell's buckeye tree . . . only the tree was in the front yard, whereas the fishpond was in the back), and made necklaces out of them to give to special people for presents. Like maybe my girlfriend or someone else that was important. So that was good. Don't you think?

And then I suppose I might as well tell you this too. Once I killed a robin. I shot it with my BB gun (a "Red Ryder" that my uncle gave me when I was four). It had a real wooden stock, with the words *Red Ryder* burned right into it! My mom said she didn't think he (my uncle) had exercised very good judgment in giving my brother and me those guns when we were so young; but my brother was already five, so he (my uncle) was probably thinking more about him. Anyway, after I shot it (the robin), the little fucker (whoops) wouldn't die, so I had to chase him all over the place and then club him to death, I'm sorry to say, with the butt of the gun. I didn't want to, I mean I *really* didn't want to, but I had no choice. It was against the law to shoot robins (sparrows were OK, but not robins), so I had to silence him and them hide him or I would have been sent to The State Penitentiary at Fort Madison or somewhere. Or if I was lucky, just to the "reformatory" at Eldora (which, now that I think about it, sounds just a little too much like "crematory"). So I guess it could have been even worse. Anyway, that's what I thought might happen to me. And I was real scared, and so, as I said, I beat it to death with the butt of the "Red Ryder." Having to do that made me feel real sick inside. *Real* sick. Shitty sick even. And sorry too. Maybe like I was in fact the sinner the folks at Washertown First Methodist Church had been telling me I was. Not just me though; everyone, they said, was one (a sinner).

And then later once, when I was maybe in about sixth grade, I went hunting with my brother and my cousin on my grandfather's farm and shot a rabbit with a borrowed "22" (although I didn't know what that meant). I was just trying to be like the other guys—tough and shitty—instead of like a sissy or something. Well, the goddamn rabbit wouldn't die either (just like the robin, only maybe even worse), so I had to run after him and shoot him again. He just kept flopping around all over the fucking place (shit, I slipped and said it again). And he was bleeding and everything too, and also kind of quivering. And it wasn't even cold outside. So anyway, by the time I got to him (the pathetic and totally helpless little Peter Cottontail bunny that I had just brutally murdered with a borrowed "22"), I was far enough away from the other guys (fortunately), so that they couldn't see me crying. Really hard too. Just like when I saw Bambi's mother get killed in the movies. I mean that kind of stuff really made me feel bad. I guess the point is that the whole hunting expedition was really sad and shitty. I hated it; and I never went hunting again. By the way, what the hell do you think those people who made that movie about Bambi were thinking? I mean Jesus! Why show that kind of stuff to little kids? And then in another movie they actually had Snow White die for a while. I mean *what the hell were they thinking?*

But anyway (and to kind of "lighten things up"), when I was still little, in about third grade maybe, my dad and mom took my brother (who as I told you before didn't like me very much) and me to The Iowa State Fair in Des Moines (only one of my numerous big city experiences). Well, I don't know if you've ever heard of the Iowa State Fair, but it was a really good one, and pretty exciting for a third grader. The original *State Fair* movie was made there even. And that's the truth too. So anyway, during the day we got to go on lots of rides (the "Tilt-a-Whirl" was my favorite, and next "The Old Mill" water ride); then at night we went to the big "Variety Show" that was held in the Grandstand, where they had fireworks and everything. Like "stars" of country western music. Once I think maybe even Gene Awtry was there. No kidding. I'm talking *stars!* Then at the very end of the evening (it would be really late, like nine or ten o'clock), they set off a great big American flag display that took shape from bursts of red, white, and blue "skyrockets" and stuff (I think that's what they were anyway). And this was right after another one (display) had just gone off that looked just like Niagara Falls (at least I *thought* it did . . . at the time I hadn't been there . . . but I had seen pictures of it). Niagara Falls was made out of an enormous string of white "Roman Candles" (I think that's what they were called) that had been turned upside down or something. I mean think about it; all these big displays were made totally out of fireworks! Can you believe it? And then not only was there that stuff, but huge rockets and "bombs" were going up and off and exploding in the air and everything. And we're not talking "cherry bombs" and "sparklers" either. None of that sissy shit. I mean this show was big. *Really* big. I'm just lucky I lived in Iowa and got to go see it.

One other thing about the State Fair (although this gets pretty sad again), and maybe even the very best thing about it (not spectacular like the fireworks, but best at first . . . but then not so best), was that I got to buy a real, live chameleon. So did my brother. I can't remember how much it cost, but I'll bet it wasn't cheap. Anyway, this State Fair man had a booth with a sign over it that read, "The Magic Lizard that Turns Color" (or something like that), and he had the little suckers stuck to and crawling all over his shirt. Each one, i.e. each chameleon, came complete with a string around its neck and a brass safety pin. (The pin wasn't stuck in the chameleon or anything, so don't think it was some kind of cruelty to animals issue.) The safety pin was simply tied to the other end of the string that was around the Magic Lizard's neck (sort of noose-like), so you could pin him on your own shirt somewhere. Like right on your shoulder maybe, so he could look around and see everything. Speaking of seeing, although I don't mean to be unkind, his eyes were sort of goofy-looking. But anyway, my mom and dad let my brother and me each buy one, and we pinned them to our shirts, and then walked around feeling pretty important. You know, as though everyone we passed was looking at us with our magic lizards.

A long time later when we got home (and it was a real *real* lot later, like after midnight even, since as I told you the fireworks didn't get over until after maybe ten o'clock or so, and then my dad had to drive us home at thirty-five miles an hour because of World War II and gas rationing and everything) . . . *anyway*, a lot, lot, lot later when we got home, I pinned my new little friend (the chameleon) to the curtain on my bedroom window, so that it would have someplace to sleep and not be lonely or anything. (I didn't want to leave him on my shirt, since the shirt was going on a hook in my closet.) And not only did I not want him to feel lonely, I was thinking he also might be afraid of the dark, and a little bit of light always came in through the window curtains from the streetlight outside. And, besides all those concerns, tired as I was, I knew better than to try to sleep with him pinned to my pillow, or especially to my pajamas (I mean I might have rolled over on him or something). Anyway, where my chameleon finally slept is not the point. What *is* the point, and it's pretty painful to have to tell you this (this is the sad part), is that when I woke up the next morning my chameleon had hanged himself. That's right. The little sucker had hanged himself! My poor little magic lizard guy was off the curtain and just dangling there, real limp-like, with the string around his neck and the safety pin still stuck to the curtain.

And trust me. He was dead. *Real* dead. I don't have any idea how many colors he may have turned before he died, but it was probably a lot (when he was alive he just went from sort of a light green to kind of shit brown). Now he was gray. Really gray. Almost white. And nothing was moving. Nothing. Anyway, it was pretty sad. Then, as the minutes passed and I thought more about the untimely and tragic death of my many-colored friend (sort of like in the song, "Love is a Many Splendored Thing," I guess, although probably not, and I didn't even know that song then) . . . *anyway* (I'm really having trouble keeping on track again), I realized that I had to confront the facts (or at least consider the evidence) and make a pretty major decision. Do I admit that I was stupid, really stupid (at least neglectful anyway), to have pinned him to the curtain, thus setting the stage for what could have been an "accidental" hanging (like maybe he fell from the curtain and couldn't get back on), *or* am I forced to entertain the idea ("God forbid," as the expression goes) that "Mr. Many Colors" *intentionally* jumped from the curtain and killed himself (by "dangling to death" I guess)? That was my dilemma. Was it a careless although unintentional act of negligence on my part, or a suicide? Did I do it, or did he "dangle" himself? One thing was for sure: the way the string had been tied around his neck was indeed "noose-like," as I mentioned up above.

Well, needing to reach some resolution (meaning I just wanted to get over it and move on), *I* chose to believe that *he* had chosen to hang ("dangle") himself. And that being the case, I also concluded that it really couldn't have had anything to do with me, since we had hardly known each other (although I was already referring to him as "my little friend"). Of course I have no way of knowing for sure just how he felt about me. The fact was, however, that we, having had so little time together, had never really gotten to know each other *at all*. Furthermore, I could honestly say that I had attempted to make his first night in his new home a pleasant one. Anyway, this is what I wanted, and chose, to believe. And although it was something I had to consider (but only momentarily), I also concluded that his death was not because I had taken him away from the other chameleons. That *may* have contributed to a form of separation anxiety, or perhaps to a brief depressive episode (I learned all this stuff later when I became a psychologist), but certainly this brief period of "adjustment" could not have been enough to push him over the edge (or as one might say, "off the curtain"). Neither did I conclude that his death had anything to do with my room, or, and in particular, the color of or amount of light coming through the curtains. No, I think the poor guy had more likely been clinically depressed for a long time. A long, *long* time (had he lived decades later, he may have benefited from medication). And, I decided, he just happened to choose that night to end it all. Whatever, it was not a pretty sight for a barebacked third grader in his jockey briefs to wake up to (it had gotten hot that night, and I had taken my "jammys" off). I mean the thing was just dangling there—his gray, lifeless body silhouetted against the morning sun that, regardless of the death scene it illuminated, streamed through the curtained window. Anyway, the aforementioned explanation was enough for me to be able to get on with my life. However, don't think I didn't first follow through with my responsibilities, because I did. I unpinned him, carefully removed the lethal piece of rope (string) from his tiny little neck, kept the safety pin, dropped him in the toilet, put the seat down (saying goodbye is not easy), and flushed the little fucker away, vowing never, *ever* to buy a chameleon again. At least not a depressed one with a string around its neck. ("Little fucker," by the way, is a term of endearment, and does not therefore classify as a "slip-up.")

Speaking of not very pretty sights and other sad stuff, and before I go on to tell you about some better things that happened to me in Washertown, you probably should know that all my dogs died. That's right. All five of them. Once in a while I wonder if it might have been something about me. I hope not though, and I don't think so; but you can never be sure about those things. Anyway, our first dog, Tippy, (black spot on the end of his otherwise white tail) just died I guess. I was too young to remember. He was our Christmas dog, and as I just suggested, I think he died of "natural causes," as they say. Then we got Snippy (I guess we weren't quite ready to give up the "ippy" sound) who was sort of kidnapped (dognapped?), although I think my dad might have been involved in the plot. I know for sure that he was taken on a "last ride," and I fear that he (the dog, not my dad) might have died of a broken heart. (Snippy actually found his way back home, but was then taken on yet another ride, which took place, rather curiously I thought, just before my brother and I were presented with a really old, beat up, swaybacked Shetland pony.) Maybe as compensation. Or sort of anyway. The horse didn't even have a name, for God's sake, and lived (if you can call it that) out on my grandfather's farm. My friends thought he (the horse) was a real piece of shit.

Then Butch (third dog) got eaten (chewed up pretty bad) by a predator Pit Bull (gruesome), and I had to help hold him down while the vet tried to sew him back together. Next, Ike got run over by a car, which was especially unfortunate, since my dad liked Ike more than any of our other dogs. That was because he, Ike, was named after President Eisenhower, and although his perky little lop-eared head didn't appear on any of the "I like Ike" campaign buttons, it was as though he (the dog as well as my dad) supported him nevertheless. Then, after Ike got run over, another one got run over (different dog, different car . . . same result). This ones name was Tuffy. (I know, with a name like Tuffy you'd think he would have survived.) But to back up one dog (I left this part out), after Ike got run over he actually bled all over the living room carpet in the new house my mom and dad had just had built. Therefore, although my dad liked him for some reasons, he didn't appreciate him (Ike) a whole lot for doing that. And to back up even further, when Butch died (having been cannibalized), although I guess I don't have to keep saying *died,* since they *all* died, he got real stiff in the basement overnight (right in the little bed where we had put him to get well . . . although he obviously didn't), and I was the one who found him the next morning. That wasn't much fun either.

But let's get back to the final hours of my fifth and last dog, Tuffy. When he died (there's that word again) he actually had a little doggy girlfriend from next door sit by him all night (really). Tuffy, having also been run over (and given the bloody living room incident having to do with the earlier demise of Ike), had been left out on the porch. That was good though, since that's how his girlfriend could be with him. And, given the way things transpired, i.e. given that Tuffy expired, we thought it was all pretty special. Painful, but special. I mean it was almost as though Tuffy had been "laid out" as well as left out (on the porch), and there had been some kind of calling hours or something. I'm not sure if any other neighborhood dogs came by though. And I don't remember Tuffy's girlfriend's name, or I would have mentioned it, since she was so loyal and everything. It was probably Puffy, or maybe Snuffy, or Sniffy even, or something like that (probably not Sniffy). Or Pansy maybe. Pearl? Taffy would have been *really* nice; you know, as in Tuffy and Taffy, but that would probably be stretching things. Anyway, I guess I wasn't very lucky with dogs. I'm not sure what that says about anything, but it sure was sad. A lot sadder than my chameleon's suicide, that's for sure. I mean to be totally honest it was pretty hard to get real attached to a lizard. Especially, as I said up above, in just a matter of hours. Whatever. As I grew older I had to conclude that *everything* in Washertown couldn't always be the way I wanted it to be. But most stuff was.

CHAPTER TWO

SCHOOL DAZE

Special Dedication

There is absolutely no way I can tell you about my school days in Washertown, without first dedicating the entire chapter to my "kindygarden" teacher (and I still think that's the way it should be spelled), my grade school homeroom teachers, and our school principal. So, and in the order in which I encountered them, they were: Nettie, my kindygarden teacher at Lincoln Elementary; (and, having then moved across town) Bertha, first grade; Ora, second grade; Crystal, third grade; Myra, fourth grade; Alice, fifth grade; Alvina, sixth grade; and Reva (the principal); all of Washington Elementary. These absolutely phenomenal ladies of learning (they would have liked that word "phenomenal") probably shaped and changed my life in more ways than one could "shake a stick at" (although as often as I heard that expression, I never understood it). Whatever. To these strident educators, I dedicate this chapter, "School Daze." Each one, I truly believe, in her own and singular manner (although sometimes "the manner" was kind of peculiar, painful, or just plain shitty), had a great deal to do with how I got to be this way. Really.

School Daze (Part I)

Well, everyone has to go to school, of course, and so did I. First to Lincoln Elementary, and then (you guessed it) to Washington, i.e. *Warsh*ington Elementary. That was because we moved across town just after my kindygarden year. So . . . kindygarden at Lincoln Elementary? I *hated* it! First of all, I saw no reason to leave my mother and the safe, easy days of having someone do everything for me. She and her sister, my aunt Velma, and my grandfather's housekeeper (more about her later) all had been doing a perfectly fine job of taking care of me; meaning they bought me stuff, took me places, and made me feel important. And I didn't see why any of that had to change. Whatever. There was one thing for sure though; I was *not* ready for the experience that awaited me with Miss Nettie Tally and her kindygarden class at Lincoln Elementary. And that's putting it mildly. In fact, I was so "unready," meaning I was so shy, so attached to my mother, so happy with the way things were (like eating maple "long johns" from the local bakery in the middle of the morning when my mom and my grandpa's housekeeper had "coffee time"), and so uncomfortable with anything that was not familiar to me (like *everything* at Lincoln Elementary), that in reality I was a towheaded (hated that term), five-year-old "train wreck" ready to happen. And this was even before my mom took me shopping for school clothes. *And* before the goddamn locusts had started to make that dreadful, late-summer droning sound (which, as I told you before, made me really nervous). Did you ever notice how those things (the goddamn bugs) could suddenly just "shut off," and everything would get sort of mysteriously still? I mean this "nervousy" feeling started even before I went to the Rialto Barber Shop to get my "ready for school to start" haircut. It was like I could just feel something bad was about to happen to me—like a whole truck full of shit was about to hit some enormous fan. And it did too.

Anyway it started (school), and it was awful. If I hadn't been so little, and if I hadn't told you I was going to try to be careful about using some bad words, I would say *fucking* awful. And as if the whole thing about just going to school didn't already seem scary enough, from my very first week in kindygarden (maybe the very first *day* even) I, along with having what seemed like an acute and incurable case of separation anxiety (another college expression), began to stutter. And really bad too. I mean like *hopelessly,* or so I thought anyway. Even on simple words like ch-ch-ch-chicken. In fact I especially remember ch-ch-ch-chicken, because when I couldn't say it once (it was my turn to tell the class what the picture was that we were looking at, and it was a chicken), I called it a duck (I could usually say "d" sounds) . . . and then a few tries later a turkey, and maybe I called it a pigeon even . . . when it was obviously a goddamn ch-ch-ch-chicken. Well, Miss Tally got really mad at me. I mean *really* mad. I think she thought I was trying to be funny or something. I thought she might even hit me; that's how mad she was. So anyway, this ch-ch-ch-chicken shit meant that all the kids laughed at me. *They* laughed. *I* cried. And the teacher, insensitive old "sh-sh-sh-shitbag" that she was, came off as totally unwilling to deviate (in the least way even) from the prescribed procedures of early twentieth century discipline. So that didn't help much either. I mean, couldn't she have f-f-f-felt sorry for me or tried to h-h-h-help me or something? (And now, as you can see, I'm stuttering all over again just thinking about it.) But oh no! Miss Tally, the old "sh-sh-sh-shithead" that she was (I had decided already that she was *both* a shit *bag* and a shit *head*) . . . anyway, the old "shitbag/shithead" just kept telling me to say my words the way they were supposed to be said, without showing any understanding at all that sometimes I just plain c-c-c-couldn't! Well f-f-f-fuck her! (Sorry.)

Maybe, now that I think about it more, her being so cruel and heartless could have been because her hair was too tight or something. I can't say for sure of course; but she did wear her hair pulled back, kind of real severe-like, and she wore one of those fake-looking clumps on the back of her head. I think they were called "buns" or something like that. So maybe her hair hurt. But that's still no excuse. At least not if you ask me. I mean who was the adult here? I also remember that everyday she wore real plain-looking, gray, or maybe navy blue dresses, and black, low-healed "oxford" shoes with little holes in them. And her shoelaces had fringe on the ends of them (I guess that was supposed to be fancy). Anyway, although I didn't know what the word meant then (or of course caused it even), an older person might have said that she was a little less than orgasmic-looking. Whatever. As I continue to look back on all this (although maybe I should just let it go), I'm not sure whether Miss Tally she was simply insensitive or just plain sadistic (another word I didn't know then).

Anyway, it's for sure that Miss Tally was "just plain" *something*, and right now I'm thinking I would vote for sadistic. Whatever, she sure as hell didn't do much to help me feel b-b-b-better. But I should be fair, I guess; maybe it was like she just didn't know what to do. And besides, "my little problem" (I'm trying to act as though it wasn't as bad as it really was . . . so you don't feel too sorry for me) *was* a bit of a disruption for the rest of the class, in that it always created a sort of "laugh time" for everyone (except me, of course), and probably therefore a not very good time for her. For all I know, she may even have been doing her best. I mean the woman wasn't *all* bad (I probably got a little bit carried away there for awhile). In fact in some ways Miss Tally was probably pretty good, and sometimes maybe even nice (although I have a hard time remembering when). Sometimes I guess a person might even have wanted to feel sorry for her. Especially me of course, since as I told you a long time ago, I was always feeling sorry for someone (like I did for Sharon Walker when she wet her pants, although that was later on when, as I also already told you, I went to Washington Elementary). Anyway, I was not, was *not* liking Lincoln Elementary and my kindygarden year at all. As a matter of fact, I just plain h-h-h-hated it!

And then, *then,* as if the stuttering problem wasn't bad enough (and in fact driving my daily anxiety level sky high), there were those g-g-g-goddamn air raid drills that scared the very shit out of me! I mean I realize it was 1942, and that we had a problem with the Japs (pardon me, Japanese) and the Germans and the whole war and everything, but it seemed to me that it should have occurred to at least someone in Washertown that if the Japs (or the Germans) and their airplanes ever got as far inland as Iowa, there would be a hell of a lot more to think about than scaring the shit out of a bunch of hapless, snot-nosed little kindygardners at Lincoln Elementary. And what were they going to blow up anyway? Pigs? Whatever, two or three times during my kindygarden year some local whiz of a dumb-ass, called the "Air Raid Warden" (or something like that), would "rev up" a set of screamy, g-g-g-goddamn sirens, and we would have an air raid drill. First there would be this awful, eerie, kind of distant, "moany-drony" sound (the siren was downtown on top of the water tower), and then, as if that wasn't scary enough, the Lincoln Elementary "tardy" bells would explode with this h-h-h-hideous, m-m-m-metallic, h-h-h-head-rattling sound that would shake the whole g-g-g-godamn building. Maybe even every building in Washertown. I don't know. I do know, however, that it wasn't necessary. But anyway, there I was, the shy, nervous, self-conscious, might-start-to-stutter-at-anytime little kindygardner living in absolute terror because of a stupid, f-f-f-fucking air raid drill. (And so I slipped yet again. Who cares?) But that's what it was: a stupid, f-f-f-fucking drill. As I already told you, I *h-h-h-hated* the place anyway, except maybe for my girlfriend Ruella, whose mother was in charge of the hot lunch program, which of course is totally beside the point (meaning the hot lunch program, not Ruella). And then to have to endure those drills. It's no wonder I have a few problems. I mean it was g-g-g-goddamn awful!

So I guess you might as well hear the rest of it. When those sirens and brain-rattling bells would go off, all the kindygardners (in a kind of mock military ceremony) would immediately be lined up and led forward, single file (like in a parade or something), up the stairs (*up* mind you) into the large, central, open part of the building. (Lincoln Elementary, except for the kindygarden room which was a later addition and down lower, was one of those old kinds of two-story schools with the classrooms and offices all built around a big, common, wasted empty space.) Whatever. Once we got upstairs we were told to sit on the floor, Indian style, to put our hands over our heads, and then to lean way forward. Way, *way* forward until it almost hurt. I guess the point was that when the J-J-J-Japs dropped their g-g-g-goddamn bombs on us (and the p-p-p-pigs and everything a few miles away), and the roof therefore started to fall in, the collapsing rafters and bricks and other shit would instantly break our backs, thereby preventing our having to suffer too much. Two hundred innocent little Lincoln Elementary School kids would thus perish instantly. Or almost anyway; it probably would have been just my l-l-l-luck to l-l-l-live a l-l-l-little l-l-l-longer. (See how bad it could be when I was really nervous?) But at least we would have died together, and our suffering, as I already suggested, would have been relatively short-lived. Think about it though. Two hundred, once smiling, now huddled up, bent-over little kids, each with their heads in their hands (and hopefully still attached to their bodies), all dead! Crushed. I mean h-h-h-holy shit! What the h-h-h-hell did those air raid people have in mind? I don't think our teacher, old "bunhead" (i.e. "shitbag/shithead"), ever even thought about it, and p-p-p-probably not even the p-p-p-principal either. They just let it happen.

Oh. One more thing. And wait until you hear this. *My* place in the dreaded second floor "hall of death" was right under the base of the pedestal (a fine, Doric-style column of plaster) on which the school's very own bust of its namesake, President Lincoln, sat. So this way, if the J-J-J-Japs did bomb us, I would have had the dubious (although of course I didn't know what that word meant then), but honorable (I guess) distinction of having been momentarily stunned, and then instantly killed, by a blow to my backside from the p-p-p-plummeting h-h-h-head of the greatest Re-p-p-p-publican p-p-p-president ever to have occupied the White house. Shit! I just h-h-h-hated that f-f-f-fucking place! I can only hope they re-thought their air raid procedures for the next year. *And* that the kindygarden teacher, old "bunhead" Tally, (although she wasn't *all* bad) was nicer. Especially if she had another shy (but adorable of course) little blonde-haired kid in the class who couldn't talk right. But again, I don't mean to be so hard on Miss Tally. I mean I guess she was pretty nice at times, and calling her names is making me feel bad. Besides, for all I know she might have had some pretty serious problems of her own.

After my kindygarden year, we moved across town. So it was "Goodbye Lincoln," and "Hello Washington." My dad bought a house on the west side of town (we were just renting the one near Lincoln Elementary), and that's where Washington was (meaning the school, not Washington's body or anything like that). His body and stuff were mostly at a place called Mount Vernon (as I learned later, like maybe in third grade), where he lived with his wife, Martha, and a whole lot of slaves ("darkies," I think they called them . . . at least that's what they called them in the movie about Uncle Remus and everyone . . . *Song of the South*?). But I don't want to get off track here. So anyway, to move from east to west in those days was usually considered to be a good move, although west was not quite as good as southwest, and *far* southwest was better yet (we won't revisit the kind of strange address system which I already told you about . . . once is enough). But get this. If we had moved to southwest Washertown, instead of just west Washertown (although of course as I just told you we didn't), it would have been (believe it or not) "Goodbye Lincoln" and "Hello Woodrow Wilson." Can you believe it? Perhaps moving there would have meant "peace at last." Maybe even for me, as well as the rest of the world. But all that was just wishful thinking. Anyway, you can see that Washertown, when I was a boy, was a pretty patriotic place. (I know I already said that when I was telling you about the Washer City Café, but this naming of the schools stuff was a better kind of patriotism.) Anyway, when I was little all four of the elementary schools in Washertown were named for our nation's Presidents, except for one (and that one was named for a writer of some renown). However, as the expression goes, "Three out of four ain't bad."

Actually, and to get back to where you lived and went to school and everything, any real difference between west and southwest Washertown was not as pronounced as the names of the elementary schools might suggest. Although more rich people lived in the southwest part of town (in fact, I think all of them did), the politics and other stuff of the west and southwest folks were pretty much mixed together. So even though the southwest school carried the name of a Princeton man, whereas the just west school only bore the name of a *good* man and our very first President—despite the cherry tree incident and his having messed up pretty bad as a young general, he was still good—it really didn't matter much. I mean some of the southwest people may have known more about Wilson and Princeton and "The League of Nations" (which of course never actually happened, causing President Wilson to get really depressed . . . or so I read somewhere) than the just west people (given the Republican propensities of the southwest people . . . and how do you like that big word?), but they didn't talk about it very much. (Remember at the very beginning when I told you I sometimes wrote some pretty convoluted sentences? Well, that last one was one of them . . . sorry.) As a matter of fact, few people in Washertown in the 1940s had even heard of Princeton. Whatever. Just as Washington had crossed the Delaware, my mom and my dad and my brother (the one who didn't like me very much) and I crossed Washertown itself (I don't think Woodrow Wilson ever crossed anything), and there I was, the new kid on the block. Still shy, scared, nervous, and kind of self-conscious, but nevertheless a first grader at Washington Elementary!

So, let me tell you how things went for me there (I trust you are enjoying this school part.) "Things" at Washington were probably maybe a little better than at Lincoln. But not much. I still stuttered.

And now (as if I needed this), I was sporting round, gold-colored, wire-rimmed glasses. I thought they made me look kind of like a frail owl or something. Had I worn them thirty years later, I would have looked just like a "hippie" in San Francisco. As it was, the glasses looked kind of old-fashioned; they were the only ones that would stay on my face, however, since my nose was so skinny. Whatever. They just seemed to add one more element to my sense of being kind of different. Therefore, problem solver that I was learning to be, I "relieved" myself one day (of the little round glasses), by placing them very carefully into the very depths of the right front pocket of my Levi's (probably on a Sunday night, since Monday was wash day), and then put the Levi's down at the very bottom of the dirty clothes basket. Later, when it was time for my mom to do the "dark load," those little round glasses, wire rims and all, not only got sloshed around in the wash water, but also got smashed flat (there is a God after all) by the wringer of one of Washertown's very own "multi-motor" washing machines (the "automatic" was still a few years off). And so, with that particular mission accomplished, the frail little owl was on his way (he thought at least) toward becoming a mighty eagle. Or maybe just a screaming blue jay. Well . . . at least a big sparrow or something. Anyway, the glasses were history.

I learned later, just to let you know that a person has to be somewhat wary about life, that those little gold glasses, and as a matter of fact two other pairs of glasses that I got later on, hadn't really been necessary. It seems the optometrist (and so-called "friend of the family") needed business more than he needed a sense of integrity. He, as you might suspect, had rather expensive tastes, and therefore drove a Packard (the ugly, mid-forties model that led to the company's demise) and lived in a pretty big house. My dad, on the other hand, had integrity, lots of it, lived within his means, and drove a Ford (it was a "Custom" though, not just the basic "Mainline"). I think being the custom model meant that it came with an extra strip of chrome on the side, a radio, and a heater. Anyway (I'm beginning to drift), just remember that when the glasses needed to be gone, they were. I don't know why it never occurred to me to try putting my head (at least my tongue) in the wringer; perhaps it could have helped take care of my stuttering problem. Well, actually I guess I do (know why I didn't put my tongue in the wringer). It's because when I was real little (way before I destroyed my glasses), and trying to help my mom, I accidentally ran my arm half way through it (the wringer) one rainy Monday morning. It went all the way up to my elbow too, before my mom heard me yelling really hard and came and turned the thing off. *That* hurt. And bad too. And of course my mom was really scared. I guess it just shows what can sometimes happen to you even when you try to be good and do something nice for your mother. I mean even when you're doing something good it doesn't mean something bad can't happen too. (My mom by the way, like my dad, was a pretty special person too, only in a more lady-like sort of way.) But to stay on track, I have to say that I did learn something from my little "wringer accident," so I can't say all was lost. What I learned (although its not like some great big "moral of the story" or anything) was that when you try to stick a wet sheet into a washing machine wringer, you're supposed to let go of it, even if it's going through all bunched up and crooked-like.

But anyway, more about Washington Elementary. First grade was not too bad. Not too good . . . but not too bad. The teacher, Miss Volts (Bertha from the dedication list), was a lot nicer to me than that Victorian bitch at Lincoln, although I really should stop calling her names (I mean, as I already said, she wasn't really *that* bad). I learned to make "dashes" and "O"s on the blackboard which, when I was a boy, was in fact black, the way blackboard's are supposed to be. I mean why do you think they called them blackboards? They weren't green, as they became in the 50s, or white and shiny, like the felt marker boards you might see today. Oh well. I also learned to print in my very own lined writing tablet (which had a red cover, with a black Indian chief on it). Maybe I don't need to say this, but the Indian wasn't a Negro or anything (I mean Indians were supposed to be sort of red); it's just that the picture of his head was colored black, sort of like a silhouette (just wanted to make myself clear). And anyway, since the cover was already red, it had to be something else. Better black than green or something, I guess.

Anyway, we not only learned to do this writing stuff, and more about how to read and everything, but also got to play "house" in Miss Volts' class too. The house was a small, three room (with bath), half-a-wall-high bungalow (with no roof on it), which had been assembled in the northwest corner of the room. The place was even wallpapered, except for the kitchen I think, and had real furniture and stuff (scaled down for little people, of course). And when you went into the kitchen it had a sink, and little pots and pans . . . even an eggbeater (I'm not sure why I remember the eggbeater, but I do). Anyway, the whole layout was pretty progressive for the 1940s. The best thing about it was that I got to go in there to play with Marcia Stringfinger (meaning to play *house* with Marcia Stringfinger, not of course to "play with" Marcia Stringfinger herself). I should remind you that we were only in first grade. Whatever. Marcia Stringfinger was a pretty little blonde-haired girl that I had a really big "crush" on (actually she was a little bit chubby, but I didn't mind). Unfortunately however (if indeed not tragically), I found out that she liked my friend Mike better than me. (Mike, as I think I said a lot earlier, was the same little friend who told me about rubbers, and also about how to kind of like masturbate—i.e. make yourself feel really good—while sliding down one of the poles that supported the big slide on the school playground, and other stuff like that.) But that, I think, wasn't until we were in third grade . . . or was it second? I guess it doesn't matter. It was just kind of a disappointment though to lose out with chubby little Marcia Stringfinger.

We also colored pigs (as I already told you, Iowa was big on pigs) and other animals in first grade, on smelly, "ditto" sheets. The pigs, or whatever, were outlined in purple, and we colored the insides (meaning the insides of the outlines, not the actual insides of the pigs). That would have been pretty disgusting. Actually, we got to color lots of animals, but I always remembered this one pig. That's because when I took it home (I always took stuff like this home, since someone, usually my mother of course, always said nice things about how good my pictures were, and even if they weren't) . . . anyway, when I took it home my aunt Mag (Margaret was her real name) was visiting our house and she told me it was a really *really* good pig. Not to hurt her feelings or anything, but I always thought the name Mag sounded kind of "icky." Oh well. We also learned to spell a few words in first grade. I of course was the conscientious, "good little boy," and learned to spell all of the required ones and then some others. Too bad, however (meaning it was too bad I was too good, not too bad I did extra credit spelling words), since I think I would have been better off (eventually anyway) had I not been so conscientious about this kind of stuff. And (but man, I hate to say this), although I tried really hard not to, I st-st-st-still st-st-st-stuttered a lot in first grade. But n-n-n-not quite as much as when I was in k-k-k-kindygarden. Not usually anyway (just now is sort of an exception I guess . . . probably because I started to th-th-th-think about it again). Stuttering always gets worse when you think about it, by the way. And when you have to answer the telephone. Or worse even, tell the operator what number you want (remember this was the 1940s, and you had real live operators to place your calls). That could r-r-r-really be hard. Like if she said, "Number please," and you said "f-f-f-four" too many times (without even getting to the next number), she would hang up on you. Most numbers then were like "f-f-f-four O th-th-th-three R" (you always said "O" for zero, and the "R" meant which house on the "party line." Only rich people had their own number.

I also changed my name when I was in Miss Volts' class. I wanted to be called by my first name, which I had gotten from my uncle who was in the Army Air Corps during World War II (that was before they called it the Air Force). He was an "ace" top-turret gunner (I put in the "ace" part, which meant he was really good gunner, because he was *my* uncle). In fact, he was probably one of the best guys in the whole army. This was the same uncle, by the way, who gave me my Red Ryder BB gun when I was four years old (eventually launching the murderous career that culminated in the death of that robin I told you about a few pages ago . . . remember? The one I had to club him to death, since the little bastard wouldn't die?). My uncle also drove a 1941 Buick convertible, in which (in the glove box actually) he had stowed away a "45 automatic revolver" that my brother and I found one day (when I was only about five years old, or maybe six). That wasn't such a good thing, I guess, although my brother and I thought it was pretty neat. And no one got shot with it or anything. Not even a robin or a rabbit. I never knew why he had the gun in the glove box, just that he was a really exciting kind of uncle to have. And he liked me so much (partly I guess since I had his name) that he gave my mother a big gold and silver ring that he always wore, and told her to see that I got it when I grew up. (I learned later from my grandpa that he had won it in a crap game in Mexico or somewhere.) Maybe that's why he had the revolver in the glove box. I don't know. But maybe.

Anyway, when my uncle was leaving the last time to go back to the war in Europe, he gave the gold and silver ring to my mom at the train station, and told her to give it to me, "in case I don't come back." She told me that when I got older. "If I don't come back," was what soldiers said when they thought they might get killed before the war ended. It was really sad I guess. I was actually there at the train station with my mom and my grandpa and everyone when he gave the ring to her. I didn't see it though. I just remember everyone was crying. Especially my grandpa (my grandma had died the year before, or I'll bet she would have been crying even harder). Or just as much anyway. My grandma and grandpa were pretty special people too. Everyone in my family was (well, almost).

So to get back to changing my name, what happened was that one day I told my mother that Miss Volts wanted to know if she could call me by my first name (i.e. the name I shared with my uncle, although Miss Volts of course didn't know that), because there were so many other kids in the class with my middle name. The whole thing of course was a lie (meaning that what *I* said was a lie, not anything Miss Volts said), so you can imagine how really pretty disgraceful it was, given that I told it (the lie) when I was going to the very school that was named for the President who didn't. I mean everyone knows that President Washington himself didn't lie, even when he got caught chopping down his father's cherry tree (which I already told you about), and here I was telling a lie just to get my name changed. Actually though, I think my mother knew all the time that it was really just my idea, and that Miss Volts had nothing to do with it. But whatever she really thought, I began the next day to carry the name of a great soldier and turret gunner and "ace" and hero and everything else of World War II! And no one had better question that either. And so, I decided, I had just become pretty special (if indeed not heroic) myself. By the way, my uncle *did* come back. In 1945. And you can be sure that that made everyone happy! So anyway, not very much else happened at Washingon Elementary that year. Except, as I already told you, the st-st-st-stuttering problem was st-st-st-still with me, and Marcia Stringfinger stayed with Mike.

Second grade was a lot like first grade . . . only worse. It was a mixed blessing, to say the least. I traded M-M-M-Miss Volts for M-M-M-Mrs. Doofus. Mrs. Ora Doofus to be precise (you can check the dedication list). Pretty discouraging, since I had mostly stopped stuttering during the summer, except sometimes when I had to talk on the telephone or something. Anyway, I remember how I dreaded it in second grade when it was my turn to lead "The Pledge of Allegiance." The teacher, Mrs. Doofus (my only "Mrs." teacher in all of grade school, by the way), had this system of going around the room in alphabetical order (the "kiss of death" for a stutterer), so that everyone could have a turn to stand up and lead the Pledge. Maybe so as not to deprive anyone of their civil rights or something. I don't know. (Actually, no one thought about stuff like that when I was in second grade, so that couldn't have been it.) Or maybe Mrs. Doofus just sort of saw it as democracy at work. But as I said, I really don't know. What I *do* know, however, is that this really awful "nervousy" feeling would start to build up in me as I anxiously, and I do mean anxiously, awaited my turn to have to lead. My turn (alphabetically) was right after some kid whose name I can't remember, and just before a girl named Marilyn (I'll tell you more about her later), and maybe also before a kid named Raymond Mouschkoff too (who I won't tell you about, since he was a total asshole).

Actually I think I will tell you about Raymond, since what happened makes me sound pretty tough. Raymond was the first (and only) kid I ever punched in the face on the school playground. I don't remember why; but I do remember that I was totally surprised (and relieved) when he didn't hit me back or "rat me out" to the teacher. He must have been picking on me . . . yeah, that's it, I think . . . always picking on me. But to get back to the pledge and then other stuff in second grade (and this was enough to make me think there truly was no god), "P" sounds were especially hard for me to say. So there I would be, this really nervous, self-conscious, skinny little second grade shithead, standing in front of the whole g-g-g-goddamn class (it seemed to me like everyone in the whole g-g-g-goddamn *world* actually), hand over my heart (which was kind of a lie, since my heart was actually stuck up in my throat somewhere), trying to lead the class. I mean this is what it was like on a really bad stutter day: "I p-p-p-pledge allegiance to the f-f-f-flag of the United St-St-St-States of America, and t-t-t-to the R-R-R-Republic for which it st-st-st-stands" (I'll spare you the rest; it's making me sick just thinking about it again). Shit! Just plain shit! Suffice it to say that leading "The Pledge of

Allegiance" didn't do much to help with my now rapidly disintegrating, seven-year-old ego (whatever the hell that was). One more "shit" might make me feel better though; so "SHIT."

And then there was second grade "art time." I got my feelings hurt pretty bad then too, when Mrs. Doofus (who was usually real nice, even though she didn't volunteer to help me much regarding the pledge stuff . . . which would have meant excusing me from doing it at all) didn't like a painting that I thought was a true masterpiece in tempera. Really. A masterpiece! Anyway, what happened was that everyone got a monthly turn (kind of like a "period," I guess, although at the time I didn't know much about girls, and nothing of course about periods) to paint at the one easel we had in the back of our classroom. So once when it was my turn I soaked up my brush with lots of extra thick tempera and painted some really neat mountains. I mean I put every bit of my artistic skill into those mountains, and I was convinced that they were award-winning. At least, really good. She, however, Mrs. Doofus, just kind of stood behind me looking like she was thinking too much or something; so I just kind of stood there too, waiting for her to recognize my genius. I don't mean of course that I thought I was as good as those guys from a long time ago who painted pictures of the baby Jesus, or Mary the virgin (so they said anyway), or the Moaning Lisa, or anything like that, but maybe that I was at least a younger version of them or something, like a *developing* artist. And to tell you the truth, although I of course didn't claim to be a big time art critic (like the guy at *The Des Moines Register* newspaper or anything), I always thought most Jesus pictures made him look too big. I mean, when I learned about how babies were actually born and everything (maybe like in third grade, and from Mike), it made me hurt just thinking about a kid that big coming out of anyone. Especially out of Mary the virgin (but of course I didn't really know much about what virgins could really do). I don't know; maybe Mary the virgin was really big too. She didn't look like it in those pictures though. In fact I always thought she looked kind of little. But maybe she was (big). They might have "air-brushed" her down or something. The virgin thing, by the way, continues to baffle me, but that's another subject, and perhaps (probably even) a story best left to the Pope (I've already talked about him), and other mystics.

Anyway, when Mrs. Doofus finally spoke, she simply said, "Why don't you try to paint mountains the way they really look?" Well screw her! I mean I don't know who the hell she thought she was to even be asking me that. She lived in Iowa too, so she couldn't have known any more about mountains than I did. It just so happened that my mountains were real "pointy" and plain on the sides, kind of like dark brown triangles, because I *liked* them that way. And I had also painted a few really neat looking, stick-like pine trees (although the trees were maybe a little bit too big for the mountains, and kind of fake looking). I would have maybe admitted that part. But then to make it (my whole picture) really good, I had also painted this almost perfectly round, somewhat smeary-looking, yellowy-white moon coming over them (the mountains). Clearly, the whole piece provided ample evidence that I had a natural talent for doing modern, impressionistic art (whatever that was). It's too bad Kate Smith (the really good singer I already told you about) wasn't my teacher *She* would have been impressed. Maybe inspired even. Especially with "the moon coming over the mountains" part of my picture (she used to sing a song entitled "When the Moon Comes Over the Mountains," which I also already told you . . . remember?). Actually, now that I think about it more, she (Kate Smith) maybe could have helped me a lot with "The Pledge of Allegiance" too. I mean she was real patriotic. And also she sang that Jewish song, "God Bless America" (meaning a Jewish guy wrote it . . . someone named Irving, I think, although I may have already told you that too). And she never stuttered or anything either. At least I never heard her do it (meaning st-st-st-stutter). Goddamnit! There I go again. Anyway, I don't think Mrs. Doofus could even sing. But I don't know for sure. She never sang for me though, I know that; although I also know that Mrs. Doofus was good at "playing" the water glasses (and I'll tell you some stuff about that in just a little while). Whatever. I'm beginning to feel a little bit like my wandering mind problem is beginning again, so let's just keep going.

The point is that Mrs. Doofus, Mrs. Ora Doofus, really hurt my feelings because she didn't tell me how good I was (as a painter). And that was when I therefore got really angry and confused and everything, and decided "right then and there" (as the expression goes), although I should have fought back, *not* to be an artist. (I've always had a bit of a problem with criticism.) Of course the world is a lesser place because of the decision I made regarding my artwork, but I hadn't yet figured out that what you sometimes have to do in life is "keep at it," and "stick by your guns," and other stuff like that, until you prove the other person wrong. But do you know what else? Not only did I eventually figure out that Mrs. Doofus didn't know very much about mountains, and therefore of course was totally wrong about my picture (which as I said led to the world being deprived of my talent), but also I figured that she probably didn't even know Kate Smith (although you may wonder what that has to do with anything). But anyway, that (i.e. Ora Doofus not knowing Kate Smith) was because she (meaning Kate, not Ora) lived in New York, as I already told you. (I didn't know that in second grade, but I learned it later.) To be precise, although I think I may have told you this too, she (Kate Smith) lived in Lake Placid (well, not in the lake itself, but you know what I mean). And that's where she saw the moon coming over the mountains. *And*, and you can trust me on this one, those mountains were real pointy, and had pine trees on them (and the moon was kind of smeary yellowy-white too). I know, because when I got pretty much to be a lot older I moved to New York and saw it all myself! Really. So anyway, too bad for the art world. It missed a good impressionist. At least that's what I think.

Moving right along, have you ever heard of Handel's *Water Music?* Well, I hadn't either of course, at least not in second grade, but you might like to know that even though I didn't know about Handel's water itself, I nevertheless once played another kind of water music. It was probably kind of a sissy thing, but I was absolutely fascinated by the fact that you could make up a whole musical scale just by varying the amount of water in each of eight glasses. So get this (another rather traumatic event in my then brief experience in the world of the fine arts). In recognition of my clearly burgeoning, perhaps even glorious, and although not yet flourishing, nevertheless obvious God-given talent for music (not to brag or anything, but by second grade I had already taken my first accordion lesson) . . . *anyway* (and to kind of start that sentence over), what I'm trying to say is that because I was pretty good at music, I was chosen by Mrs. Doofus (obviously a better music than art critic) to "play the glasses" for the upcoming Parent Teacher Association meeting. As it turned out, it was too bad it wasn't the accordion I was asked to play (I mean I could already play "Red River Valley" really well, *and* "by memory" no less). Anyway, it was quite an honor, at least I thought, to have been chosen to play the water glasses for the local P.T.A., since the other kids in the class just got to sing as a group and stuff like that. What happened, however (the traumatic event I mentioned above), was that during my solo on the glasses I hit one of them too hard (you used a little, metal, spoon-like thing to hit them with), probably because I got nervous or something, and the whole goddamn side of the glass fell out. Well, there went that "note," which of course made the rest of my little performance not sound very good. And it seemed of course that water was going everywhere. (A real "dog and pony show.") I mean I suddenly felt really shitty, and was just trying as hard as I could not to "jump ship" and drown myself or something.

So anyway, I thought I could hear people sort of laughing (but not Mrs. Doofus, of course, or my mother, for sure, and probably not the principal, Miss Merriman, either). And given my embarrassment and everything I almost started to cry (I maybe even did, just a little). Anyway, there I was, standing on the stage in the smelly gymnasium (where all our cultural programs were held at the time), with a busted goddamn glass. I mean what are you supposed to do when the whole side of the fucking "g" glass falls out right in front of everyone, and the water pours out, and you can't even go on with the song. I mean think of something like the song "Row, Row, Row Your Boat," only with the "boat" note busted all to hell. I mean it just doesn't work. And for all I know, that may have been the very piece I was playing (I can't remember for sure . . . probably because of the trauma and everything). Whatever. You can be sure that with even the principal watching (although as I said, she at least, probably anyway, wasn't laughing), along with the other thousands of people in attendance, this was *not* one of my better performances.

She, by the way, the principal, didn't think I was so hot anyway, since once I had lied to her about a snake I had in my pocket. I mean I was afraid she would hit me, or give me "the rubber hose" (a curious medieval torture device she supposedly had in her office closet), if I had told the truth about the snake being there and everything. (I had also made a pretty big scene outside her office one day when I fought real hard to avoid getting my smallpox shot.) But anyway, because of all the shit that happened during my debut as a water music player, I decided not to pursue a career in music either. At least not with the goddamn water glasses. I did in fact recover from this incident, however devastating it was at the time, and went on with my accordion lessons (more about that later). However, this whole mess, I decided, could have been avoided. Mrs. Doofus should have chosen a girl to play the glasses, since girls don't hit stuff as hard as boys do. And then maybe I could have been the star soloist and played (from memory) "Red River Valley" or maybe something even more advanced, on my accordion. (Or maybe I could have just not been there at all.)

Second grade was also the year of my first big love affair (another topic I'll tell you more about later). Otherwise, except for a brief, erroneously ego-inflating and really fun Valentine's Day party, not much else happened. But before we go on to third grade, let me tell you about the party. Mrs. Doofus, whiz of a teacher that she was (although not in art and music), required that a valentine be given *from* everyone in the class *to* everyone in the class. So we all brought them to school that fanciful day in February (remember, the little "press-out" cards?). That's what we always bought. Then, we put them (the valentines) in a great big cardboard "mailbox" decorated with red construction paper that was pasted to it (remember the gooey, sort of smelly, flour paste kids made?), and white, sissy-looking "doily things" (heart-shaped, mostly, with each one having lots of holes in it) that were glued (not pasted) on top of the construction paper. I can't remember the name of the glue (we didn't make it), but it came in a little bottle with a sort-of-like slanted rubber nipple on it. (*Nipple,* by the way, had already become a dirty word in second grade . . . at least for my friends and me it had.) Anyway, now that I think about it (the construction paper mailbox, not the slanted nipple on the glue bottle), and even though in its way it was sort of neat, the whole mailbox was in fact pretty much of a mess. But that didn't matter. It still looked pretty to us.

So anyway, on Valentine's Day, one person got chosen by Mrs. Doofus to be the "mailman" (it may even have been me even, but I don't want to brag about it since I can't remember for sure), and the mailman then handed out the individual valentines to everyone at their desks, one card at a time. Well! I became totally engrossed in what appeared to me to be my overwhelming popularity (as evidenced by all the valentines that were rapidly stacking up on my desk). It seemed as though everyone, I mean *everyone,* wanted to be *my* valentine. It never occurred to me that everyone else had the same size stack, since that of course was the way Mrs. Doofus had set the whole thing up. Actually though (but again I don't mean to brag), had it been different I still think I just might have gotten the most valentines. I mean, what can I say? I was a really nice little boy (too nice, as I already told you), and I think most people would have said pretty handsome for a second grader, and people simply liked me. I mean, what can I say? They just couldn't help it!

Next, it was refreshment (meaning food) time at our little party, and we all got those very small candy hearts that tasted like chalk and said "I Love You," or "Be Mine," and stuff like that. Of course we didn't mean *really* love, or *really* be mine (like *"do it"* with me or anything). I mean this was only second grade, for God's sake, and we didn't even know about those things. Well, not very much anyway. Whatever. We also had heart-shaped sugar cookies at our party, with red icing on them (like Christmas cookies, only Christmas cookies were of course shaped like stars and Santa Claus's and reindeer and stuff). Moms made the cookies (they actually did things like that when I was little). And no one got poisoned or anything either. The only thing that I thought wasn't so good about the party was the sissy-shit doily (like the ones on the mailbox) that we had to stack our candy and cookies on. Entirely too "girly" I thought. Maybe if the ones for the boys had at least been brown or something it would have been OK. I don't know though. I just know that it kind of bothered me. We also had juice at our party, to sort of wash down the cookies and candy, I guess, and maybe even some other stuff that I can't remember. We ate so much of this shit that some of the kids probably got sick when they went home, and maybe threw up even. But I didn't. So anyway, apart from the p-p-p-pledge stuff and the b-b-b-broken "g" glass, I guess second grade really wasn't all that bad. And M-M-M-Mrs. Doofus was a pretty nice teacher. Actually, to tell you the truth, she was *really* nice. She just didn't have the proper training to recognize true artistic talent.

Third grade. Well, first of all, I fell in love with my teacher (but not as much as I was going to fall in love with my fourth grade teacher).

My third grade teacher had kind of a magical name I thought: Crystal. Like snowflakes or something. And although I of course would never have called her by her first name (except in dreams about her, which I prayed I would have but never did), she was pretty special. See, there was this sort of erotic-like thing (although I of course didn't know that word then . . . just that what I felt sometimes was kind of strange and everything) that got hold of me even when I was pretty little. Maybe I was a freak or something. Anyway, Miss Landeer (Chrystal) came to my house for my ninth birthday party, and that made me feel really important. Kind of like maybe she liked me too. Of course since my mother had invited her she really didn't have much choice. Mothers and teachers did things like that when I was little. Sort of like a trade off for baking cookies maybe. I was still stuttering of course, but not quite as much. Maybe it was because Miss Landeer was the first teacher who let me feel more relaxed and think that I didn't have to be good all the time. And she didn't call on me to answer lots of questions the way my other teachers had. She just seemed to let me be whatever I was, and as I already said, I think she might have liked me a lot. Actually (and this is kind of "in general," and not just a Miss Landeer thing), I think most teachers liked me; although now that I look back I sometimes think that what they liked most about me was probably my blonde hair and shy, sort of sick puppy ways. But I was the teacher's pet (I guess maybe saying the word "puppy" made me think of this) at least a couple of times. I think anyway. Maybe even more. (That's kind of like being "teacher's sex object" today, I guess. Or "boy toy.") But I hope not. I mean I wasn't just some dumb blonde or anything. And I wasn't shy *all* the time.

In third grade we learned about Christopher Columbus, the European sailor who discovered us and then gave the Indians syphilis, and some other stuff. Miss Landeer didn't teach us about the syphilis part, but I learned that later (from liberals, whatever they were). And we also learned about Pilgrims and some other really important things, like President Washington and President Lincoln being real honest and everything, and President Lincoln getting shot at the movies. Actually I felt really important when we were learning about President Lincoln, since as I told you I had gone to Lincoln Elementary before coming over to Washington, and therefore kind of had some background knowledge that the other kids didn't have. Of course I felt good about Washington too (but I already said some things about him). And for some reason (going back to the Pilgrims . . . which is one of those words that if you repeat it a lot I think begins to sound kind of funny) I especially remember learning that Pilgrim kids had these little paddle-like things that they used for books. In fact, I think they called them "hornbooks." Yeah, that's it, "hornbooks" (I just looked it up in the dictionary; that's how I know).

Also, it was in third grade that I first remember singing the song "Over the River and Through the Woods to Grandmother's House We Go" at Thanksgiving time. Even though my family never did that, at least not in a sleigh the way they did in the song, I kind of liked the idea. It seemed really nice, and kind of exciting, and historic and everything (although I never believed the "the horse knows the way" bullshit). And anyway, all we had to do to go to *my* grandmother's house was just remember to take the right street. You can see though, that by third grade (based on the nicer part of what I just said), I had already begun to become kind of a romantic. I wanted to believe that life and whatever happened to everyone was really good and special. Like in the "Over the River" song the woods would have been all pretty, and the sleigh real fancy, and the horse great big and snorting steam out of its nostrils. And there would have been sleigh bells, and swirling snow, and smoke curling up real gentle-like from a chimney. After all, Thanksgiving was second only to Christmas in terms of make-believe and everything. Anyway, you weren't supposed to think about how awful cold it would have been in that sleigh, or about the horse taking a shit right in front of you, or about freezing your ass of in the outdoor toilet at grandma's house, and then fighting with your brother for who got to sit in the front seat and steer the goddamn horse and stuff like that. And for sure you didn't want to think about who had chopped the head off of the big turkey you were about to eat. I mean what a bloody, barbaric mess that must have been.

However, and on a more pleasant note, there is one other thing that comes to mind about third grade. That was the grade I was in when I wrote my first poem for my mother to give to her on Mother's Day, which I thought was really good but probably wasn't (my poem, not the day itself). I even colored a little rabbit on the same page as the poem to make it special. Or maybe because I was still thinking about Easter. I don't know. I do know that she really liked it though, since years later (like maybe fifty even) I found it in a folder with some other "treasures" she had kept. Anyway, not much else comes to mind about third grade. Except for lingering thoughts about Crystal of course. And, that it was in third grade when I became a Cub Scout (I think it was third grade anyway). But trust me, you don't want to hear about my abortive venture into scouting. I was for sure no Eagle; as a matter of fact, embarrassing as it is to say this, I quit Cubs when I got my Bear badge. The whole thing just bored the shit out of me. So in some ways I guess third grade ended up being kind of a "time out" period for me. Or maybe a warm-up time for things yet to come.

Fourth grade. I threw up in fourth grade, right after eating "hot lunch" (tomatoes, potatoes, and hamburger all cooked together), although there wasn't much hamburger in it because the war was still on (meat was one of the things that were rationed during World War II). Or maybe the school cooks ate all the meat. I don't know. But I doubt it, and. it really doesn't matter. Anyway, it came on me real sudden-like, and I threw up all over the floor around my desk (we didn't have a real lunch room then, so we had to bring our plates back to our desks). It was really gross looking too, so I won't tell you very much about it. Just that the stuff looked about the same on the floor as it did when I was eating it, only some pieces were maybe just a little bit smaller. It smelled about the same too, although probably a little worse. Not much though. I mean that stuff, meaning our tomatoes, potatoes, and hamburger treat, *never* smelled very good (you could smell it cooking during recess), and we had it really often, so I had become pretty tired of it. Anyway, I remember I thought it was all a little bit strange, since I never felt real sick or anything. It just happened. And of course I was embarrassed. Really embarrassed. Kind of like when the glass broke out of the goddamn "g" glass during the second grade music extravaganza I told you about, only different in some ways. But at least I didn't get diarrhea. *That* would have been even worse. Well, I'll start a new paragraph now, so we can get away from the mess on the floor. This is making me sick all over again.

So . . . as I told you a long time ago (when I was talking about wetting my pants the third time), I was petty much in love with my fourth grade teacher (even more than my third grade teacher, Crystal). With my fourth grade teacher it was kind of like in the songs "I Love You Truly" and "Always" all put together and everything, as though it was just one song, so that had made throwing up in her classroom really *really* embarrassing. But forget all that. I don't even know why I mentioned it again. I just want to tell you more about the fantastic Miss Myra Dimons. So first of all (as I also already told you, but could say a hundred times), Miss Dimons had blonde hair, and really red fingernail polish and lips and everything. I mean she was Hollywood beautiful, kind of like Lana Turner. I think maybe, in fact probably even, that the other teachers didn't like her very much, since she was so beautiful. Miss Dimons actually lived in a room she rented at my grandfather's house (no lie), with her sister Birdie (that wasn't her real name, but that's what everyone called her). In the 1940s a lot of teachers rented rooms in homes; I think because they weren't supposed to have a normal life with a private place where they could have fun or anything.

Anyway, I guess I also already told you even more stuff about how Miss Dimons looked, so I won't keep repeating it (although I could, at least a hundred *thousand* times). I think I even told you about the "Evening in Paris" perfume I bought her. Anyway, fourth grade turned out to be a really good year. And I stuttered only just a little bit. In fact, almost not at all. That was because (at least I think it was) I felt so good and "at home" (as well as in love) with Miss Dimons. I mean she was soooo special! She even went on a hike with two of my friends and me once. And to tell you the truth (and as I said a long time ago, I always will), I think I still love her, even though she moved out of my grandfather's house the next year, and I went on to fifth grade, and then she moved away, and so I didn't get to see her for a long time. But then, years later, believe it or not, I did get to see her ("Love is a Many Splendored Thing" to like refer to another song). It was after she was married and wanted her new husband to know "the boys" from her fourth grade class. So she called my mom (I think that's the way it happened anyway), and invited the three of us (then sixteen) to drive over to see her one evening—all the way to Des Moines. I knew, by the way, as soon as she opened the door and saw me again, that although she had found a really nice (I guess anyway) guy to marry, that she once (and maybe still even) loved only me. I just knew it (although I didn't tell her husband, since I didn't want any trouble). I figured he didn't need to know that she had kissed me on the cheek (in the stairway that went down to our basement) the evening of my tenth birthday, and that she had stayed at my house for dinner. And that all this was before she had even met him. Anyway, Miss Dimons was really special! It had been nice to have Miss Landeer over on my ninth birthday, but Miss Dimons on my tenth? And that kiss? I mean it doesn't get any better than that! (I was going to tell you that it was a really passionate kiss, right on the mouth, and real wet and everything, and that it lasted a long, long, long, long time, and then that it led to some other really hot and heavy stuff happening and everything, but then I kind of decided you wouldn't believe it.) And as I said before, I didn't want to stir up trouble with her new husband. Well, I won't try to tell you any more about fourth grade. It was all one wonderful blur. Sort of anyway. And also, I was the best student, meaning the best in the whole class, at learning my multiplication tables. Whatever. Just know that fourth grade (featuring MISS MYRA DIMONS) was by far my best year yet. (Except maybe for the wet pants episode and the lumpy vomit.)

Fifth grade? Not so good. I st-st-st-started to st-st-st-stutter again, g-g-g-goddamn it, and it was the t-t-t-teacher's fault. She, Miss G-G-G-Gidlap, made me (and everyone else I think) really nervous. That was because *she* was so nervous. At least I thought so. Kind of like what people call a "nervous wreck" or something. I don't know. Maybe she just needed to get laid. I have no way of really knowing. Anyway, it sure wasn't like fourth grade, I'll tell you that. There were lists and lists of things to memorize, and then lists of other stuff. And all these lists were written (and revised daily) all over the goddamn blackboard. The "other stuff" lists were mostly the names of everyone who hadn't yet memorized the lists about the first stuff. Believe me, fifth grade was not fun, and I was more than glad when it was over. In truth, however, Miss Gidlap took herself and her job (and her students) very seriously; and I have to say that we did learn a lot. I mean she wasn't a bad person or anything. Just maybe a little bit "wacked" by putting too much of an emphasis on details. I guess she never heard the expression "don't sweat the small stuff."

In fifth grade (to comment just briefly about classes and teachers other than my homeroom one), I really liked science class. Since nervous Miss Gidlap was the morning homeroom teacher (in the afternoon we got to go to other classes—a system which actually had started in third grade), science class was a welcome change. We learned about snakes and spiders and stuff like that. And, I started my very own butterfly collection, although the fact that the teacher had to first gas them to death seemed kind of cruel. The gas chamber itself, however, was in a closet at the far corner of the science room (there was no viewing area); and therefore, and fortunately, I (and the other kids in the class) never really saw it happen. Kind of sad, I thought (meaning not sad because we couldn't witness it, but sad because the executions had to happen in the first place). However, it probably would have been even crueler (and sadder) to have "mounted" them (i.e. the butterflies) alive. I mean what you eventually did, one way or the other, was to press them (after they were dead, if gassed) sort of spread-eagle-like, on four-by-four inch cotton squares (with cardboard bottoms), on which you then placed four-by-four inch cardboard-framed glass. It ended up being kind of like a little tomb that you could see into . . . maybe like some of the tombs for famous people.

Whatever. One way or the other the butterflies were going to end up dead, that was for sure, so I guess it didn't really matter how all this took place. And to tell you the truth, if they hadn't first been gassed they would probably have busted their wings and everything (antennas for sure), as they desperately, indeed frantically (and probably with a look of absolute terror in their eyes) fought to break away from the four-by-four inch windowpanes that were being lowered down on them—ever so slowly, but inevitably, nevertheless—ending their lives by suffocation, and thereby entombing them forever. Well, I guess that was pretty heavy. Anyway, as I said, it was the teacher who gassed them, not me. I don't think the school wanted us little kids to be going around gassing anything (including letting farts). I learned later that there were varieties of farts, by the way, from "sliders" to "bench rattlers," but I think that's so crude I won't tell you how you decided which was which (although you can kind of probably figure it out on your own). The most prized specimens of my little collection (butterflies, not farts), just in case you're interested, were a giant

Monarch butterfly and an especially pale (from its struggle to survive the gassing?), green Luna moth. The science teacher's name, by the way, was Miss Ballsover, and she was not only really nice, but smart too. Real smart. And now that I think about it, kind of pretty.

While I'm sort of digressing a little bit, you may also like to know that Miss Charlotte's art class was also a favorite of mine (I guess I had never really gotten over my second grade "moon coming over the mountains" episode). And, since I was now taking piano lessons (having pretty much given up on my career as an accordionist), it was becoming increasingly evident, although I think I attempted to pretend otherwise, that my interests were not developing along the lines usually (normally?) expected for a ten or eleven-year-old Midwestern boy who had only one more grade to get through before "going up" to junior high, where he was then expected to "go out" for football. And then basketball. And then a track. (It all followed the seasons and the high school sports schedule.) Whatever, I wasn't supposed to be playing the piano and doing art. That stuff, when I was little, was considered kind of sissy-like. In track, by the way (seventh grade, so I'm sort of jumping ahead for a minute), and on the very first afternoon, everyone had to run a "440," which meant you had to run around the track *once*, a distance of 440 yards (but you probably already knew that). You were supposed to go as fast as you could, which actually wasn't very fast for me (although I really did try). In fact, I tried so much and pushed myself so hard (I mean who wants to cross the finish line last?) that I threw up (again) at the four hundred and forty-first yard marker. And still finished last. Holy shit! And this was what I had to look forward to? Whatever. I don't mean to jump ahead; I need to get through sixth grade first.

Sixth grade? A big year, but another bad one too. Had the meanest teacher in the whole goddamn school. I mean she was really awful. Her name was Miss Kirter (should have been "Hurter"), and she was *not* a pleasant person. In fact, she was exactly the type that made it easy to understand why, when you talked about teachers in the 1940s, it was almost always "Miss." But maybe not. Maybe teachers just didn't get married very often because (as I told you before) they so often lived in rooms in other people's houses. I don't know. Or maybe it *was* because some of them were just so mean. What I *do* know, however, is that I really don't enjoy saying unkind things about people; and as I got older (as I also told you before) I began to realize that everyone has problems and some serious shit to deal with and everything. So don't think I get some kind of pleasure out of saying what I just did. In a way (and this is pretty hard to admit), more than not liking Miss Kirter, I think I actually felt sorry for her. And as I also told you before (there are a lot of "I told you befores" here), I was always, *always* feeling sorry for someone. What I also know, however, is that this Kirter bitch slapped me right across the mouth once, and in front of the whole goddamn sixth grade class! Painful as the experience was (in more ways than one), when I was little teachers were allowed to hit you, yank you right out of your chair if they wanted to, and even drag you around the room. For all I know it was probably even OK for them to go home and stick pins in some Voodoo doll with your name on it. I have to say though that I honestly didn't deserve to be slapped (really). It was just a misunderstanding (hers, of course, not mine). I mean, couldn't that woman see how exceptional I was? Sort of nervous and still self-conscious maybe, but nevertheless extremely sensitive, extraordinarily talented, and in fact absolutely wonderful in every way (and handsome and everything)? And becoming more handsome with each passing day? I mean Jesus! Couldn't she see it? I guess not. Whatever. In spite of the pressure, at least the stuttering, which as I said had gotten really bad again in fifth grade, hadn't come back. As a matter of fact, it was pretty much all gone. Well . . . p-p-p-pretty much anyway.

And then there were some other "novel" things I had to cope with in sixth grade too. For example (although I couldn't believe it . . . really, I absolutely could *not* believe it), I noticed that a buddy of mine (I learned this one day just sort of by accident in the gym class shower room) had pubic hair (I didn't even know the word *pubic* then, but I knew what I saw). I mean he looked like a father, not a sixth grader, for God's sake. Anyway, he sure didn't look like the rest of my buddies and me. At first I figured his parents must have lied about his age or something. *I* looked the way you were supposed to look in sixth grade, and I didn't have a single hair anywhere, except on my head of course. He probably had no idea how he made the rest of us feel. Sort of like "pubic envy" I guess, as in "penis envy" (which was one of the weird things that that crazy Dr. Freud guy talked about, although I of course didn't know anything about it at the time). Oh well. My buddy's name, by the way (wouldn't you know), was Dick; so of course everyone in the locker room started to call him "Big Dick," since that part of him was changing too. His parents, at least his mother anyway, still called him "Dickie," and sometimes even "Dickie Ray" (which probably made him gag), but she of course hadn't been in the boy's shower room recently. Actually, I guess, probably never. By the way, the only thing that was worse than Dick for a gradeschooler to be named was Peter. Prick of course would have been even worse, but no one ever named his son Prick. I mean that would have been really stupid. Cruel even. I mean think about it. Someone comes up to you and says, "What's your name?" And you have to say, "Prick." And every time a teacher called on you she would have to say, "What do you think, Prick?" Whoa! I mean that would have been really awkward. Anyway, "Dickie Ray" had miraculously morphed into "Big Dick." And he was only in sixth grade!

Two other things about sixth grade. And both of them sort of embarrassing, so I'll keep it short and to the point. First, during the spring All School Track Meet (which meant all four elementary schools were competing) at the big high school track, *and* with absolutely everybody who was anybody in the whole goddamn town watching, I dropped the fucking baton (sorry, but it was really that bad) during the 440-yard relay. (I guess '440" wasn't a good number for me.) And to make it even worse, for all I know maybe even the President of the United States and his wife were there too. (I know for sure the school superintendent was.) Anyway, and to make the whole thing even worse than worse, I was the "anchor man," which is to say that although I might not have been football material I was at the time pretty fast. Skinny kids often are. Of course the fact that I dropped it (the baton) was actually my friend's fault, since it must have been obvious to everyone that he passed it to me too late. And of course he said it was my fault. But (and again, of course) he didn't know what the hell he was talking about. So after that we weren't the best of friends for a while. (It *was* his fault, by the way . . . lots of people told me that.) And, wouldn't you know, that very friend (no kidding) was my (sometimes anyway) buddy, Dick, the one I just told you about ("Big Dick" . . . although his baton pass was more like a

"Dickie Ray" thing). Whatever. He was acting like a real dick. Both in name, and for having screwed me with the bad pass.

And then (and you really won't believe this one), late that same spring some absolute asshole of a physical education (gym) teacher, and a woman of course, came up with the idea of having an all school May Day Festival. It was supposed to be real "historical" and everything. Like in colonial days, I guess. In reality, it was just plain stupid. Stupid and shitty. *Really* stupid. And *really* shitty. Like TURD shitty (which is as bad as it gets). So anyway, guess who ends up prancing around this great big goddamn "Maypole" in the middle of the great big goddamn high school gymnasium (it rained that day or it would have been outdoors) wearing a homemade pink, that's right, *pink, pussy* pink (the other choices were like bumblebee yellow or a sort of puke purple), eighteenth century-like, phony silk costume? You guessed it. The forever nervous, self-conscious (but don't forget handsome), for-the-most-part recovering stutterer. Only now he's wearing this fucking pink silk suit (that's right, *fucking*), and weaving a "gauzy"-looking cloth streamer in and out of the "gauzy"-looking streamers that the other stupid-looking, silk-suited sixth graders are stupidly weaving (in and out). I mean just picture it: knicker-type pants (pussy pink), white knee socks (to accent my skinny legs), "swallow tail" coat (again, pussy pink), and a goddamn dirty white cotton wig that F.W. Woolworth's probably had left over from Halloween. I mean Jesus! Talk about a dog and pony show . . .

And as if the Maypole deal wasn't enough, the "festivities" terminated with, or one might say "climaxed" with (except that this was still only sixth grade, and climaxes were not yet being experienced, except perhaps by "Big Dick") . . . *anyway,* the whole goddamn thing ended with a truly piss-poor, and again really stupid (and *TURD*-shitty), eighteenth century Minuet (played by the Junior High School Orchestra . . . so you can imagine how goddamn swell *that* sounded). So now, in the same pussy-pink party suit, there I am skipping around in front of the whole town again, including this time for sure (it felt like it anyway) not only the President of the United States and his wife, but also his entire goddamn Cabinet. (And of course the school superintendent.) So I'm dancing around, bowing all over the place, and holding some dumb girl's hand (I can't even remember her name . . . and don't want to). I know it wasn't Marcia

Stringfinger though, since she moved away (maybe even eloped with Mike) when we were in third grade But shit! That's all I can say. Just shit! Solid, sixth grade, unflushed shit. I mean what a *fucking* mess that was (and no apology either). But at least I knew that in just a few more weeks grade school would be behind me, although I had absolutely no idea of the perils that lay ahead in seventh grade. So anyway, eventually it was "Good-bye" to Washington Elementary, where I actually did have pretty much fun and stuff (as well as all this trauma), and "Hello" (with an early pimple or two on my handsome face) to Washertown Junior High. So, "Step right up folks." The show's about to begin."

Except that before it does, i.e. before the show begins (because now that I think about it I should tell you this), there was another one of my grade school friends (using the term loosely . . . *very* loosely) that I haven't mentioned yet that you probably should know about. His name was Harold, and although he never really "fit" very well with my other friends (in fact he didn't fit at all), he did have an impact on how I got to be this way. Maybe even a pretty big one. So anyway, to begin with, Harold lived across the street from my grandma (my dad's mother . . . his father had died when he was just one) when I was little, and then up the street from my house when I got bigger. And here's how things got started with him. When I was little, like maybe four or five, I was over at his house playing in the back yard one Sunday (Sunday afternoon was when we always went to my grandma's house for "coffee time"), when for some reason that I can't even remember now he got really mad at me. Anyway, Harold told me to "eat shit." Well, I didn't even know what shit was then, and it was for sure I wasn't about to eat some if I didn't know what it was. I did know, however, that I wasn't having much fun anymore, so I decided to just go back to my grandma's house.

Well, when I got there and went inside everyone (meaning my grandma and my mom and my dad, and maybe my aunt Nell and some other people even), were sitting around the kitchen table drinking coffee and eating cookies and stuff. (My brother was probably in the backyard climbing one of grandma's plum or cherry trees.) So I just kind of sat there for a little while (remember, I was pretty shy and everything . . . and also polite). But then when no one else was talking or anything I spoke up and said, "What's shit?"

Well, that didn't seem to go over real well. I mean it was kind like someone had farted or something. Anyway, everyone just sort of sat there and stared at me. I don't think anyone even answered my question; but I do remember, (after the second time I said, "What's shit?") that my grandma suggested I not think about that anymore, and just go to the kitchen and get myself some butter cookies. She always kept butter cookies in her kitchen in a green-colored tin can. (Remember those little Nabisco cookies . . . round, with a hole in the middle and scalloped edges all around?) So anyway, I guess she (my grandma) thought it would be better for me to have a handful of butter cookies than a mouthful of shit. All of which just proves that people really do get wiser as they get older. So that was the *first* thing about Harold.

The second thing about Harold happened when I was in about fourth grade. At least I think it was fourth grade. Anyway, I know it was before I went to YMCA camp and was told all that sex stuff about "doing it," and not playing with myself and everything, so it was probably almost for sure in the spring of my fourth (or maybe fifth) grade year. I would have been about ten or eleven. Anyway, what happened was that this time when I was somewhere with Harold he started talking about how babies were made and everything (I don't know where he had learned all that stuff). But anyway, good little boy that I was, I probably looked real confused and everything, and then said something really dumb about the subject (since I didn't know much about it anyway). Maybe something like "I thought God made us." (I mean I wasn't totally stupid, meaning that I knew it wasn't a big bird or anything.)

Well, Harold had different ideas, I can tell you that, and he started using the *fuck* word all the time (if he had lived at my house, his mouth would have been totally burned out). And then after that he said (and this time I kind of knew at least part of what he was talking about because of what my friend Mike had taught me about sliding down poles) . . . *anyway,* he said that if my mom hadn't been home the night my dad "wanted it" (I figured out what that meant by myself), that I might have ended up just a white glob on the floor of a shower stall or something, or maybe been wiped away in a wet handkerchief even. And he used really bad words for this part too. I mean Harold could be pretty gross! And he always seemed angry, which I understood more when I got older. (His dad I found out, although it's really sad and I hate to have to say it even, had shot himself to death when we were in about third grade maybe, so that kind of tells you why Harold might have been kind of messed up himself.) But anyway, I just mostly tried to stay away from him after he said all that stuff about my maybe being a glob in a shower stall. And I also decided (for sure) not to bring the subject up and say the word *fuck* and other stuff that Harold had said when I was having coffee time (and eating butter cookies) at my grandma's house. Trust me, if I had said everything that Harold said in front of my grandma and everyone, my mom and dad would probably have put me up for adoption or something. Or maybe even had me circumcised some more. Especially because on Sundays you weren't supposed to work, or do much, or even say bad things. Not *fuck* anyway; that's for sure. And not at your grandma's house. (Man, it's really hard to keep away from that word sometimes.)

And then, and finally, one more thing Harold did was to grab my red and white striped, genuine wool stocking hat out of my school locker one winter day, take it into the boy's bathroom, and pee in it. Can you believe that? I mean Harold was a real asshole. A butthole even (which as I told you a long time ago was considered to be worse than an asshole). And it was pretty cold and snowy too, like maybe in the middle of January. Well, again, the good little "prince of peace" that I was, I picked my pee-soaked, wool stocking hat up off the floor where Harold had tossed it, and carried it home between my thumb and index finger. *Very* carefully, so as not to let it touch anything else. I mean I wasn't stupid enough to wear it or anything. That would have been really dumb. And it could have even started steaming or something when I got outside. (I mean can you picture a fifth grader walking down the street wearing a steaming stocking hat?) Well, I couldn't. So anyway, I carried it home, and when I got there I held it out to give to my mother (like some kind of goddamn present or something) and told her what had happened. I think it even had some ice crystals on it by then. And I remember she just sort of looked at me in disbelief and said, "Harold did *what*"? And so I said (again), "Harold peed in my stocking hat." And then she didn't say anything more, but just held out a brown grocery bag and had me drop it in (i.e. drop the pee-wet hat into the bag), which she then rolled up real tight and threw in the trash. I don't know; I figured she would want to just wash it. But somehow I guess the vision of Harold peeing in it sort of grossed her out. (As you can probably tell by now, Harold was really good at grossing people out.) Whatever. I guess taking it home was the wrong thing to do. So anyway, because of the things Harold said and did, I had to kind of do some rethinking about some stuff. I mean he sort of messed me up, if you know what I mean, and that's why I said up above that he probably had more than just a little bit to do with how I got to be the way I am. But anyway, now you know Harold, and we can move on to junior high. But watch out for that guy. Troubled as he undoubtedly was (and I did feel sorry for him), he could be really mean.

School Daze Part II
(As I got bigger.)

Washertown Junior High. I absolutely hated it! Well, not all of it, of course. But a lot of it. However, now that I think about it, I do have to admit that there were some really good times. It's the other stuff that makes for a better story though (sort of like on the evening news), so I'll just tell you about some of the hard parts. Anyway, the situation now is that all four elementary schools are in one building, so I wasn't going to know everyone anymore. And that was kind of scary. Maybe *no one* even, but that of course was an exaggeration, since for that to be true the whole Washington Elementary sixth grade class (except for me of course) would have had to have been wiped out by a plague or something. Or maybe been poisoned during hot lunch. Whatever. It was definitely true that not everyone would know me either. (So much for getting a shit load of Valentines.) And that was a little scary too. And all this just after I was doing better with some adjustment issues in grade school. I mean it may have taken six years, but I had gotten rid of at least some of the nervousness (or so I thought), and my self-consciousness was pretty much gone. And it helped, of course, that I knew I was continuing to become pretty handsome. Still skinny maybe (actually for sure), but good-looking nevertheless. The stuttering was gone too (at least it had been all summer).

However (remember how I told you a long time ago that there always seems to be a *however* to most things in life?), well . . .

after being at Washertown Junior High for just one week, and being sent to the nurse's office one day because I felt sick, I was told that she (the school nurse) thought that I had a "nervous stomach." Fine. Just fucking fine! (Guess I might as well keep on skipping the apologies . . . they don't seem to help much anyway.) That was *exactly* what I had been told by the Washington Elementary school nurse six years earlier. "Nervous stomach." Shit, I wasn't getting better after all! Maybe even worse, for the truth was I wasn't just nervous in the stomach; I was beginning to feel sort of nervous all over (again). So, poor problem solver that I apparently was, I started to hate the place. I knew what people were probably saying about me of course, if they were saying anything at all (and more than likely they weren't). One day I even imagined that the editor of the school paper might be preparing an article entitled "Thirteen-year-old Neurotic Male Student from Washington Elementary Enters Washington Junior High a Loser!" That's what I thought. Really. And then I was afraid they were going to follow it up in later editions with articles like "Could This Loser Hurt Someone?" or "Is This Kid Nuts or What?" Anyway, much as my imagination got kind of carried away (I may have exaggerated just a little bit), for a guy with my rather mild-mannered ways, there were just too many people going in too many directions in too many crowded hallways.

I, nevertheless (and of course), was becoming preoccupied with trying to come up with the right answers to all the important questions. Like "Will the teacher like me?" "Am I really the skinniest kid in class?" "Does the teacher even know who I am?" "When does football practice start?" (And later, "When the hell will it be over"?) "Will I get "cut" right away?" (To get cut meant that you weren't any good and didn't need to come back, which, in fact, I pretty much had hoped would be the case.) "Will I have to stick it out anyway?" And then there were the *really* big, "deep inside" questions to think about too, Like "Am I jerking off too much?" (I don't mean to sound crude or anything, but the only other term I knew at the time was "jacking off," and for some reason I thought "jerking off" seemed to describe the behavior better.) But then sometimes I would think that maybe I wasn't doing it enough, i.e. jacking off (which was doubtful, although I would have been happy to have someone tell me that). Shit! I didn't know what to think. And of course I also worried about girls, and what I wanted to do to them (I mean *with* them . . . I keep meaning to say *with* . . . no, goddamnit, I do mean to say *to* them). I wanted to screw 'em; that's what I wanted to do! Screw 'em. Every last one of them (at least the pretty ones). Shit! (Obviously my big word for the year.) I would probably have been too nervous to "do" anything anyway.

The truth is, regarding these "girl issues" and stuff, that I was mostly pretty sure that whatever I was thinking about doing to them was wrong, since everything I had been taught (which actually wasn't much) made me feel that way . . . whether I had been taught it in Sunday School at Washertown's First Methodist Church (the place with the diaphragm on top and the pigeon shit all over the sidewalk), or at YMCA camp (where, as I told you before, we were told not to play with ourselves *or* do it to girls). The YMCA bullshit (and the primary source of my "education") was from that talk we had to go to called "From Boy to Man" (remember?) that was supposed to let us know what was and wasn't OK. And if it *was* OK, then just *when* it was OK, and to *whom* it was OK (I mean *with* whom it was OK). And shit like that. One of the "whoms" of course was yourself, the subject during the half hour of the sex talk that had to do with what you did when you were alone in your own little bed (or maybe in the shower or somewhere). But then I pretty much told you about all that stuff before too. One other thing though, so as to be sure I haven't confused you. "Jerking off," and "jacking off," and "beating off," and "pounding your pud," as one pathetic little camp kid said (what a loser he was . . . I think maybe he was from a small town or had grown up on a farm or something) . . . *anyway,* those terms all mean the same thing. You can choose whichever one you want (but for God's sake don't be a "pud-pounder"). Anyway, according to the camp instructor at least, who claimed to know all this stuff (or was lying, or hadn't had much fun in life, or maybe was a closeted child molester . . . or "all the above"), I concluded that I was probably a somewhat normal and reasonably good little twelve-year-old, which (the being good part) eventually sort of turned into another problem. As I said a long time ago, being too good is sometimes *not* good. And in reality of course (and to be really, really honest), the sex talk guy (or anyone else) didn't have a clue as to what I was thinking about doing to some people anyway. If he had (i.e. had had a clue), he would probably have recommended that I be put in an institution somewhere.

So anyway, I let myself become pretty much convinced that all the rest of the guys at Washertown Junior High were probably "doing it" to (with) someone, or if not, were jerking, jacking, or beating their crazy heads off. That (i.e. jacking, jerking, or beating your head off) also meant, according to both the Methodist church crap (meaning some of their ideas about sex, not the pigeon shit on the sidewalks), and the YMCA camp guy (asshole idiot that he was), that you could get warts on your hands (or was it grow hair on your hands?), become sterile, and maybe even lose your mind. No kidding! That's the kind of absolute bullshit you heard back then. But that wasn't going to happen to me! No sir. I was more likely to end up losing my mind for *not* doing it enough. Man! Why was I the one who always, *always* took things so seriously? And I'd like to bet, if you really want to know what I think, that the YMCA camp instructor, as well as a few of the Washertown Methodists I knew, were probably real "jack-off freaks" themselves. *And* that maybe one or two of them even became wacked-out, Bible thumping, porn-prone evangelicals or something (I started to think that when I got older). The camp guy, by the way, could have even been peeking into our tents at night for all I know. Or even sneaking in sometimes. Maybe anyway. But in all fairness, I can't say for sure. What I can say though is that this whole subject is beginning to create my sort of wandering mind, kind of "out of it" and "off the track" feeling again. I haven't veered off center for a long time now; so let's just move on. Yeah . . . move on. And besides, it's almost like I've become obsessed with this shit. (I know; you've probably been thinking that for a long time now.) So anyway, how's that (i.e. to just move on) for a good idea? I mean it's at least one way of "handling" the situation (no pun intended).

At Washertown Junior High, by the way, although this may not be the best transition sentence right now, the boy's bathroom always smelled sort of like urine. The warm kind. Either the urinals were old, or the water pressure (when you flushed them) was too low. I don't know. But I decided it wasn't my responsibility to find out either. And actually, as I think about it more, the whole school smelled kind of funny. (I'm not sure about the girl's bathroom though, since I never took the chance of going in there.) Anyway, the whole school smelled, and mostly, I think, like "sweeping compound," if you can remember what that was. (If you can't, it was sort of granular-like stuff that they put on the floors when they swept them.) Probably, I guess, the problem was that they just needed to air the whole place out. Although with all the big windows the building had (which were in fact often open), that might not have been it. But let's get back to what was going on with me. Besides, I don't suppose it really mattered what Washertown Junior High smelled like anyway (except sometimes if you were a boy, and the radiators were running at full tilt, and you had to go pee in one of those stinky urinals).

I "went out" for football during the first month of my seventh grade year. As I said before, that's what *real* guys did. Anyone who had hopes of being *anyone* at Washertown Junior High went out for football. Unless of course you were a girl. Then you "went out" for cheerleader. And that could be a real killer too. So I of course, in my usual way, although burdened enough with football, felt sorry for them. I mean the whole junior high operated with just four cheerleaders, and the only girls who even had a chance were the ones with pretty faces. Cute butts (and was the word *cute* ever over used in those days) didn't matter so much in the 1940s (in fact we wouldn't even have said things like *butt,* at least not out loud), although a nice one (butt) could nevertheless be a real asset (again, no pun intended), since they (the cheerleaders) did wear sort of short skirts (with shiny, satin-like panties underneath them). At least I think they were satin. I never got to touch them or anything, so I can't say for sure. When I was in junior high, by the way, cheerleaders didn't have to do much other than to just jump up and down at the right time, yell a lot, appear to be not very smart, and, as I already said, be pretty. *Cute,* I should probably tell you (I mentioned the word up above), was what you always asked about first, if someone wanted to "fix you up" with a girl. "Is she cute?" Actually I guess girls used the same word for boys. "Is he cute"? Whatever. It was a really over used word. But anyway, I was just trying to kind of tell you that the cheerleaders (and the three hundred other girls who didn't get to be cheerleaders) had their own sets of issues to deal with. And I had mine. No big deal or anything. Just a little information.

But anyway, there's more to say about football. In seventh grade, you could go out for football and, as I said before, have a chance of being *someone;* or, you could not go out and probably end up a *no one* (or a "brain," or worse even, a queer or something). Well, as I also told you before, Washertown already had a queer, and since not very many of us were real smart (which as I just sort of hinted at was not something a *guy* was supposed to aspire to be anyway), most of us just bit the bullet, took the only reasonable way out, and opted for football. And? For me? Football? I hated the whole goddamn program! Not only did I not like to get pushed around and knocked down myself (the tackling part), I also didn't like to push anyone else around either (the offensive part, which was "offensive" to my entire nature, only in the other sense of the term). I'll probably regret having admitted all this shit, but the whole thing about football just seemed to me to be fucking (the only appropriate word) stupid.

So, right from the start even, I pretty much didn't think (or care) that my football days were going to be particularly spectacular. But at least I knew better than to say that to the coach. In fact, with my shitty attitude about the whole thing, and my reluctance to get roughed up (or maybe hurt anyone else), it was probably more pretty much for sure that I wouldn't even be worth the shoulder pads, hip pads, helmet, and other shit that they gave everyone for protection. You had to buy your own dumb-looking, high-top shoes (black), i.e. "cleats," as they were called (I even thought the word *cleats* itself sounded stupid . . . CLEATS?), *and* a "jock strap," i.e. an athletic supporter . . . you know, so your balls and stuff wouldn't get crushed if someone else's knee or other body part got too much between your legs. Of course being in just seventh grade you hardly needed a jock strap. (Mostly you were simply embarrassed as shit to have to go buy it.) You did though, meaning you bought the required jock strap, and you did it at the Washertown Sport Shop (where of course you also bought your *cleats),* and where the older guys that always seemed to hang out there would give you that "You've got to be kidding" look. Anyway, "Big Dick" that I already told you about (and maybe a few other guys) might have needed them (i.e. the jock straps), but not the rest of us. Oh . . . and all the pads, and the helmet for my handsome head, and the other stuff that I got thrown at me (for my so-called "protection") were either too big or too small, or had literally had the shit beat out of them. That was because the "not real aggressive" and kind of skinny guys like me always ended up with the leftovers.

Would you believe that the sides of the goddamn helmet I got had even been bashed in? I mean that thing looked like a limp, leather dome or something. (Washertown Junior High didn't have the new molded plastic helmets yet, so they were still handing out the kind that looked just like the "helmet," or whatever they called it, that executioners put on prisoners to electrocute them . . . or as they said, "fry them.") Whatever. The *real* guys, meaning the "first string" as they were worshipfully called (and the "second string," and maybe the third even), all got their stuff early. A "string" by the way, just in case you're not "into" football (and good for you if you're not) was another word for a team. And that seemed pretty stupid to me too. Anyway, I thought the whole thing was really depressing.

Speaking of depression (although I promise not to get all carried away about it), I remember a couple years later, when I was a ninth grader, our English teacher had us read a poem about a man named Richard Cory who was real good looking and rich and popular and everything, but then "went home one night and put a bullet through his head" (I remember that those were exactly the words too, which is why I put them in quotation marks . . . I mean I don't want to get cited for copying or anything). Anyway, something pretty bad must have been part of Richard Cory's life too. And so he got really discouraged and unhappy I guess (and I'll bet felt pretty lonely), and then got really depressed (probably because he didn't think things would ever get better . . . like nothing was going to change and so people wouldn't like him anymore maybe), and so he shot himself. Right in the head. I don't know who found him or anything. But man, that's really scary. And too bad too. *Really* too bad. I mean it kind of just made me sick, to tell you the truth. Well, I wasn't depressed in a way that I would do anything like that. I mean I would never go shoot myself just because of some lousy misshapen shoulder pads and a goddamn crushed helmet. But anyway, what I really liked about this poem that I'm telling you about was that the person who wrote it, Mr. Edward Arlington Robinson, described Richard Cory as being "imperially slim." And I really, *really* liked that. I mean being imperially slim sounded a whole lot better than being skinny. No one ever told me I was imperially slim, I'll tell you that. They just said skinny. And sometimes even made fun of me because of it. But anyway, I'll bet Richard Cory wouldn't have liked football either. He had too much other stuff going for him. I mean (among other things) he dressed real smartly and even "glittered" when he walked (that's what Mr Robinson said). Football players don't do that. And you know, and I think about this a lot, even today, I often have the feeling (to this very day) that Richard Cory and I could have been really good friends. And I mean *really* good. I sometimes even think I might know what it was that he thought was so bad. I don't know for sure of course; but I think I do.

But what I *do* know for sure (back to football and reality) is that I absolutely hated it! I said it before, and I just said it again. But now you get (or have) to hear the specifics (if you're going to hate something you should know why). So here's why: I hated the smelly dressing room (especially the musty, sour-smelling sweat socks and the unflushed urinals); I thought that the stuff that smelled like Wintergreen Lifesavers (only a lot stronger) was really bad too; I hated the slick, often sort of slimy (what was making it like that anyway?) shower room floor; I hated the ten-year-old pads I had to put on (which were discolored by ten seasons of some other asshole's sweat); I hated memorizing "plays" that I would never be a part of; I hated the coach (well, at least what he stood for); and, as I already told you, I hated getting blocked or tackled (i.e. having the shit kicked out of me), and hated having to do it (i.e. having to kick the shit out of other guys) too. In truth, however, I'm sure I never actually kicked the shit out of anyone . . . bumped them a little bit maybe, but that would have been about it. And they probably could have outrun me anyway. I guess what I'm trying to say is that I hated the whole goddamn system. What do you think?

By the way (and before I hang up my pads), you might like to know (regarding a situation that had to do with *real* courage and stuff, and as a further comment about what I thought of *fucking* football) . . . anyway, you might like to know that the same English teacher who taught us about Richard Cory was the second teacher to sneak up and slap me right across the mouth. (I can't remember why though, so it must not have been too serious.) But I'm just telling you this so you won't think that the reason I didn't like football was because I was some sort of a "pansy," or a "pussy," or a "goody-goody" who couldn't take punishment and was weak and everything. I mean she (the Richard Cory teacher) didn't tackle me or anything; but she sure as hell knew how to throw a face punch! And I just took it too. Just stood right there and took it! Like a man. A *real* man. No pads, no cleats, no jock strap, and no fucking goddamn helmet either! And, I didn't even cry.

Then (still seventh grade, but moving on), there was the school choir. It was called "Mixed Chorus" at Washertown Junior High, and it was directed by Roxie Hoage, *Miss* Roxie Hoage, of course. Miss Hoague was the aging daughter (and given what I know now, doing it pretty well) of the owner of a variety store (sort of like a stripped-down Woolworth's), who was a really nice man. His brother, Roxie's uncle, owned the adjacent grocery store, and wasn't so nice. He, as a matter of fact, Roxie's uncle, was rumored to be "doing it" with his bookkeeper (I think), whose name was Eileen, about whom (both of them) I shall have more to say later. Anyway, some people in town said that she (Roxie, the Mixed Chorus teacher, not Eileen) had at one time been involved with (meaning had "done it with," I guess) a rather well-known man named Fred Waring, or so she, or the townspeople (or maybe both), imagined anyway. He, Mr. Waring, was this older guy who was the conductor of "The Pennsylvanians," a nationally known singing group (remember them?). Sort of like the Washertown Junior High mixed chorus, only of course bigger and more famous and better and everything. A *lot* bigger. And more famous. And better. They were even on TV every week, meaning "The Pennsylvanians," not Roxie and Fred. (This is beginning to get complicated.)

Whatever. As I grew older and learned about some recently written (i.e. recent in the 1950s) and really strange plays and stuff, like some of the ones on Broadway (Broadway is that street in New York City where they have a lot of plays, but you probably already know that) . . . anyway, when I read plays like that I sometimes thought about Miss Roxie Hoague, and decided that Tennessee Williams would probably have really liked her. (It was Mr. Williams who wrote some of the weird plays.) At least I thought he would have (liked her), since she (Roxie) had some of the same characteristics as that pretty much wacked-out woman in *The Eccentricities of a Nightingale* had. If you ever saw it, or read it, and knew Roxie, or maybe just imagined things about her, you'd know what I mean. Whatever. Roxie also could probably have played Blanche, and rather nicely I think, in another of Mr. William's plays, which he called *A Streetcar Named Desire*.

Anyway, whether or not our own Miss Hoague had something going with Mr. Waring (or as far as that goes, with the whole goddamn bass section of "The Pennsylvanians"), there was obviously *something* distracting her. But I guess that was her problem. *My* problem was that in music class, which you had to take by the way, and you had to take it for sure if you wanted to be in the Washertown mixed chorus . . . anyway, in music you had to go up to the piano on the first day, *all by yourself,* and sing (i.e. "try out") in front of the whole goddamn class. That way Roxie, I mean Miss Hoague (I don't mean to be disrespectful here) knew whether to call you a tenor or a baritone. Or, in rare instances (this was seventh grade remember), a bass. I think maybe my friend who had the pubic hair in sixth grade, "Big Dick," (the one I saw in the sixth grade locker room), might have made it as a bass. The rest of us just hoped we would be baritones. Well, it probably won't surprise you, but my brief little audition led to my being "diagnosed' a tenor. Shit! A *tenor.* Is there no God? I mean tenors are just a notch or two away from being eunuchs or something (I learned about eunuchs when I went to college). Couldn't I at least have been a baritone? I mean Jesus! Here I was a "Dickie Ray," wanting desperately to be a "Big Dick." But oh no; I had to be a "Timmy the Tenor." Shit!

Oh well. I'll bet what really happened to Roxie and Mr. Waring (if the whole thing was even true), was pretty hard for her to take. I don't know of course. But I just sort of felt that it would be. Anyway, if it was true, I'm pretty sure (at least mostly sure) that being a tenor in the Washertown Junior High mixed chorus probably wasn't nearly as difficult as what she maybe was "mixed up" in. I don't know, but I just had this feeling that Roxie wasn't real happy. In fact, much as I resented her diagnosis (labeling me a tenor), I guess I sort of felt sorry for her. I wish I could have asked Tennessee Williams what he thought. And now that I think more about it, maybe it was *Streetcar* and not *Eccentricities* that made me really wonder about her. Or maybe both. But I guess I should get back to some other and maybe more important stuff that happened in junior high. I don't even know why I brought this Roxie and Fred thing up.

So, moving right along, once again we meet Miss Kirter (remember her?). The meanest teacher at Washington Elementary? The bitch who slapped me? Well, as fate would have it, she followed me right up to junior high (just my luck). And now I was in her seventh grade math class. There was another math teacher, but I of course got Kirter. Shit again. (There was a lot of shit in junior high.) She, as I just reminded you, was the very woman who had hit me in the mouth for nothing, absolutely *nothing,* and now I thought (this was just my theory, but maybe there was actually something to it), she was plotting to make my pimples worse or even something more awful happen to me. My hair seemed to be getting a little greasy too, and I decided that that might have been her fault too. Then, as though things weren't already bad enough, there was still the "not any (or enough anyway) hair in some places yet" problem. Again, it was probably Kirter's fault. To be fair though, I have to say that for some reason Miss Kirter seemed to get nicer as the year went on. And I do have to admit that she was a pretty good math teacher. Got me ready for algebra in ninth grade, and other hard stuff, so I have to admit that she wasn't *all* bad. (But mostly.)

Winter came (still seventh grade), and football practice became basketball practice. The only thing that really seemed to change, however, at least for me, was the shape of the ball. But at least I could use the same jock strap, and I was done with the "bashed in" helmet. I did get into one basketball game though (although it was two years later when I was a freshman), for about a minute, and blindly scored two points with a wild "set shot" from the far right corner of the court. To tell you the truth, I probably just wanted to get rid of the goddamn ball before I screwed something up. Anyway, it was pure luck, believe me; but so what . . . it was a basket! You know, something to be proud of. The next day, however (and I'm not shittin' you), the very next day the local newspaper, *The Washertown Daily News* (which, believe it or not, actually reported these kinds of things in its sports section), recorded the shot as having been made by a kid named Lyle Trier. No kidding! And you wonder why I have problems? My only score in *any* ball game *ever,* and the goddamn newspaper gives the credit to some other asshole. Holy shit! And he didn't even look like me or anything. I mean, what does that tell you? But let's keep going. I may have been a "loser" as an athlete, but I'm not a whiner. So anyway, I (once again) "bucked up" and took it like a champ. But Jesus! I mean I could have used a little credit now and then. Just putting up with the smells of the goddamn dressing room for three seasons should have been worth something. But oh no! The credit went to Lyle Trier. I'll tell you this though: I'll bet *The Des Moines Register and Tribune* (a *real* newspaper) would have gotten it right!

Spring came next of course, and now it was track instead of basketball. No ball now (same jock strap), but what seemed like a lot of unnecessary running. Always had to "go out" for some sport though. As I told you before, this was when I ran my first solo "440" (not that I wanted to, of course, but because we had to). As I probably also said before, it was the first chance you had to show the coach what you could do. Well, I certainly showed him (remember?). I came in next to last, and promptly proceeded to throw up all over the side of the track. Pretty impressive, I guess. I can't remember what the deal was with the guy who came in dead last. He probably had one leg in a cast or something. Anyway, I should have remembered the fiasco that was the sixth grade 440 relay, and somehow just avoided the whole thing. I mean I may have dropped the baton in sixth grade, but as I hope you will recall, it was in fact my buddy's fault ("Big Dick's" error, not mine). Anyway, a twelve-year-old dropping a baton in the sixth grade seemed now to be a whole lot less embarrasing than being a seventh grader and throwing up in front of everyone just because I ran too hard. Whatever. I pretty much began to get the idea (I guess I was a slow learner in some respects) that I wasn't terribly athletic. But at least when June came all this shit was over for the year. And believe me, there are not words enough to tell you how glad I was. I mean to throw up in front of all those other guys? I don't think the guy in the body cast (or whatever the hell it was) even did that!

Eighth and ninth grade were a lot like seventh grade, although by the time I made it to ninth grade it got to be kind of fun. In ninth grade, for "one brief shining moment" (to kind of borrow a phrase from another Broadway show, although it hadn't been produced yet), you were referred to as an "upper classman." That's *man,* by the way: upper class *man.* Still did sports (you didn't think I was a quitter did you?), although I hadn't gotten any better, and didn't like it any better either (especially after getting screwed out of my basketball points). As a matter of fact, I still fucking hated all the sports shit! (I guess you'll just have to keep allowing me an occasional fuck now and then . . . but I'm trying.) Whatever. I somehow just felt that I had to stick with it. The good news was, however, that in the fall (before the basketball disaster), and on the very first night of freshman football practice, I injured my knee pretty bad (at least I acted like it was pretty bad, maybe *really* bad even), and managed to sort of limp around and nurse that injury all through the rest of the season, while still somehow remaining on the team. What I did was to sit in a hot shower during practice time, and then wrap my whole leg up in "ace" bandages. That way I made it look as though I was still really suffering. The coach never said anything, which I kind of didn't understand at first; but then it hit me that he probably didn't give a rat's ass what I did anyway. In fact, I suspect he was probably as glad to have me out of the way as I was. He might even have needed my "super-duper" shoulder pads for some other guy. I don't know (nor do I care). Maybe even my crushed helmet. As I said before, none of that stuff ever fit me very well anyway. Whatever. It was becoming pretty clear by now (actually totally clear) that, as I said up above, an athlete was not what I was intended (or could be trained) to be. Somehow I just had this sort of gnawing kind of feeling (you know, like real deep inside you and always there) that not only had I not been destined to be a performer of distinction on the water glasses (remember the broken goddamn "g" glass?), or a great accordionist (more on that later), or a recognized impressionistic painter (because of Mrs. Doofus), I was also not going to be an all-star athlete (not even a flickering one). Hard lessons to learn.

But anyway, in addition to too many sports, junior high was also a time of too many pimples, an unsuccessful effort to gain weight (but I sure as hell tried), having some fun in the band, a couple of pretty heavy love affairs (a girlfriend or two anyway . . . both "cute" of course), and a curious and creeping sense of anxiety about going on to high school. I was pretty much ready, though. Had hair in all the right places now, and had actually been having more good times in school than I just made it sound like. And, *and,* in the southern part of Washertown, set among rolling green hills (actually on a pretty bare-looking "rise" that had had the top sheered off of it by what must have been the world's biggest bulldozer), there had risen a magnificent (well, sort of anyway), brand new, buff-colored, brick and glass block high school. (Actually, because of a painful error in the projected cost of the building, what had "risen" on the "rise" was only about half of what it was hoped could have risen.) Whatever. There was a building there, just waiting to receive Washertown's sophomore, junior, and senior students. And I, a mighty sophomore to be (or "not to be," to borrow another expression that doesn't much fit but just happened to come to mind), was determined to make the place my own.

But you're probably a little tired of all this school stuff, so let me just sort of speed along through high school. First, high school was *somewhat* to *considerably* better than junior high had been (actually probably more considerably than just somewhat). I knew lots of people, in fact practically everyone it seemed, and I was pretty good looking. Actually, *very* good looking (at least that's what most people said, so I believed it). In fact, all modesty aside, I *was* quite a handsome young man. Maybe even like Richard Corey. Still skinny though (i.e. "imperially slim"), again like Richard Corey, who I had decided by now could for sure have been a good friend of mine, which means I would probably have called him Rick rather than Richard (or maybe even just Corey, as in "Hey Corey, how ya doin?"). Anyway, I was still fighting occasional pimples, and always of course, as all pimple-prone adolescents know, the really big ones (i.e. "monster zits") popped out just before a big date, the prom, or class pictures or something.

Nevertheless, I was generally feeling pretty OK about myself. Secure enough, even my sophomore year, to say to hell with football, basketball, and track, and get involved in speech class stuff ("radio speaking" was what I did in contests), and in the high school plays. Not to brag or anything, but I graduated Washertown High School's "star" thespian. I suspect no one really gave a shit, of course. But I did. And so did my speech and theatre "coaches," both of whom had become very important people in my life. One, Mr. Grout, because he taught me a lot and really helped me feel good about acting *and* myself; and the other because she didn't mind if I smoked and stuff on trips we took to play "contests" in some other towns. (I actually "made out" with her my freshman year in college . . . well, not "clear out," but pretty far.) In fact, to back up to high school again, she might even have bought or given me cigarettes sometimes. So anyway, she also was making me feel really good about myself. And there was something about her that has always remained curiously erotic to me. Whatever, she was a real favorite, and a true friend. Unfortunately, her name (which I'm not going to say because I don't want to get her in trouble for buying me cigarettes or anything) was one of those names that people could kind of make fun of. But I didn't. Whatever. Anyway, because of all my success on the Washertown High School stage (although again I don't mean to brag), I actually secretly thought of myself as the Cary Grant of Washertown High. Well, maybe not quite. Maybe Alan Ladd though. I mean I didn't have any really big delusions of grandeur or anything like that (I never even knew what delusions of grandeur were about until I went to college). And then I still didn't have any (i.e. delusions). Unless maybe sometimes when I drank myself into a state of oblivion (but what happened then were mostly just hallucinations . . . at least I think anyway). But I guess that's a story best left untold. As a matter of fact, I'm sure it is.

The spring of my senior year at Washertown High was marked (stained forever . . . screwed up . . . whatever) by my being judged by a "select committee" of faculty members to be totally unfit to lead my class in "The Pledge of Allegiance" at our upcoming graduation ceremonies. Leading the class in the Pledge was something you got to do (I think) if you finished second or third (or maybe it was fourth or fifth, or fifteenth or fiftieth or something) among the male students in your class academically, which I apparently I did (although I don't remember being particularly excited about it). Unfortunately, however, during the previous winter, two of my buddies and I had been expelled (as in what happens to feces when bowels move), for getting caught smoking at play practice. That's right, *expelled,* and for a whole week, for smoking one goddamn cigarette (and actually just sharing it). And because of that horrendous sin, *and* more than three months later, the "select committee" of faculty shitheads (as I noted above) judged me unworthy to lead "The Pledge of Allegiance." I mean can you believe it? An honor student, inordinately successful socially (mostly anyway), musically talented, theatrically accomplished, *and* good looking, "feced" out of school for a week for smoking one-third of a goddamn cigarette? A *tobacco* cigarette? Shit! And then punished further five months later? Jesus! I might as well have raped one of the teachers or something. And by the way, and at about that same time, it was well known all over school that the son of one of our school administrators, the very same administrator who had taken part in "feceing" my buddies and me out of school (thereby ending any career I eventually might have had leading pledges to flags) had "knocked up" (one of the more eloquent expressions of our time) his girl friend. (At least it wasn't one of the teachers.)

Anyway, it was for sure *he* wouldn't be leading any "Pledge of Allegiance." But it was also for sure that he didn't get feced out of school by anyone either. Talk about corruption in the corridors! Whatever. It seemed to my buddies and me that getting some chick knocked up in the back seat of your father's car (which was usually where such "calamities" occurred in the early 1950s . . . there or on the seventh green of the Washertown Country Club golf course perhaps) . . . anyway, it seemed to my buddies and me that knocking someone up was a hell of a lot worse than taking a few drags off a goddamn cigarette. According to the members of the faculty committee ("select") on student conduct, however, smoking a cigarette (one-third of a cigarette) outside a stage door (at 10 p.m.) was apparently deemed to be a greater crime than "ruining" someone's sixteen-year-old daughter by getting her pregnant. So anyway, "fuck your ears off, Johnny!" (Sorry.) My buddies and I will just keep puffing away. And, by the way (there are *so* many "by the ways" in life), if you can believe it, this punishment of being feced ("shitted"?) out of school was imposed on us (we considered it a blessing) during the very week of the State Basketball Tournament in Des Moines. Therefore, thanks to another of Washertown High School's enlightened committees (an "association of assholes," we called them), and our skill at arranging transportation, my friends and I got to see almost all of the games. But (and this is pretty significant) you need to know one more thing about that whole incident. If I *had* led "The Pledge of Allegiance" at graduation time, I would have done it without even one single stutter! Mrs. Doofus (remember my second grade teacher, who had everyone take a turn leading the Pledge?) would have been *sooo* proud of me she probably would have wet her pants!

Actually, Washertown Senior High was a pretty good experience. And, since I told you I would sort of speed right through these years, I'll just tell you about two or three other things. First, as I already pointed out, Washertown High was a brand new building, so the boy's bathrooms didn't have that junior high school urine smell yet. So that was nice. And, it was mostly during my senior year that I had this string of pretty passionate love affairs, although actually I think I was only really and truly "in" love with Mary Lou. And that was nice too. (Having said that, however, Carol, and Gloria, and Janey, and another Carol weren't too bad either.) And now that I think about it even more, I might as well tell you that I had some pretty weird fantasies about one or two of those girls. Whatever, Mary Lou was for sure the love of my high school life. But I'll tell you more about us in just a little while.

There is just one other thing though that I should tell you about. It was kind of embarrassing for the whole school, I thought, but I should tell you anyway. You know how every school has its big "fight song" or whatever? Like when the "pep" band plays real loud and everyone sings at football games and all that shit. Well, I don't remember the words too totally well, since I was in the drum section (you didn't need to know a hell of a lot of words if your whole job was to bang out four-four time on a bass drum). But I want to at least *try* to tell you about the words, since they were just so goddamn stupid. I mean really, *really* goddamn stupid. So anyway, here goes.

Mostly the words all had to do with being "loyal and true" (but that meant just to Washertown High . . . I mean it wasn't like you had to have some big set of morals or anything). Part of the words (after the first part, which was "We're loyal to you Washer High") went something like this: "We'll back you to stand 'gainst the best in the land" (I think); and then there were a few more words that I can't remember. But then, *then,* and this was the really stupid part, there was some real loony tunes stuff (kind of like a chant, I guess) that went like this: "Che" (soft "e," as in "Chuh") "He" (long "e," as in "looney"), and then "Che Haw" (as in hawk), "Che Haw, Haw!" I mean when you look back, it was really embarrassing. And then on the drums, we all were supposed to go boom-boom (pause) boom-boom. I mean this whole thing was really, *really* stupid. And then everyone repeated the "Che He, Che Haw, Che Haw Haw Haw" stuff (and of course the drums came in with the boom-boom shit again). And *finally,* as if we hadn't sounded stupid enough already, everyone shouted (and really loud): "Washer High! Washer High! Washer High"! I mean it was as though we were proud of that goddamn chant, or cheer, or whatever. And then (no shit), "Washer High" having been yelled out at the top of our lungs, there came this totally goofy *scream* from everyone (swear to God) that went: "Osky Wah Wah!" At least I think that was it. Yeah. "Osky Wah Wah!" That was it. We sounded like some goddamn kids asking for a drink of water or something. I mean it was really bad. And then the song went on with some other words I can't even remember. (But maybe that's a good thing.) Anyway, I guess I need to calm down here. And maybe (probably) you didn't need to know about our "fight song" anyway. I'll bet your high school had some stupid stuff like that too though. But I mean it was just plain awful! Goddamn awful!

And so it was at Washertown High. Just one more thing though (really this time . . . I know I said that before). I went to the senior prom with Mary Lou, who (of course) wore the most beautiful dress of all. Her dad had actually bought it for her during a business trip to New York City (not where most Washertown girls did their prom shopping); and it was from a place called Saks Fifth Avenue, he said. Well, wherever it was from, I can tell you it was really beautiful, and soft-feeling (actually so was Mary Lou herself), and real "flowy." Most of the girls that year wore dresses that were made of stiff, scratchy stuff (called "net," I think). But Mary Lou's dress was made of limp, shrimp-colored, silky stuff, and had little tiny white pearls all over the top part of it. It was "strapless" too (which was nice for dancing, since I was just the right amount taller than she was to have a fantastic "view"). And it was even nicer for later on. So anyway, because the dress was so special, and since I was so much in love with her and everything, I bought her a white, that's right, *white* orchid to wear on her wrist (a wrist corsage was pretty much the "in" thing then). The purple ones (and not very many guys even bought those) cost four dollars. The white one (they had to get it special from Des Moines) was seven. But it was worth it.

But now hear this (I get turned on again just thinking about it)! Mary Lou's dad pretty much liked me, and trusted me most of the time (which once in awhile kind of made me feel a little bit, and sometimes a lot, like an asshole . . . but not so much of an asshole as to change my behavior). Anyway, he knew how crazy I was about cars. And therefore (and I could hardly believe it), he offered to let me take his Buick Roadmaster, two-door hardtop (with white-wall tires and wire wheels and real leather inside) to the prom. It was sort of like sea-foam green on the bottom, and dark green on top. And if you know anything about the cars of the early fifties, you might recall that the Roadmaster was what was affectionately called a "four-holer." That meant that it had four ornamental, chrome-plated wholes punched out of the front fenders, kind of like "port holes" on a ship. The less expensive ones (Buicks) only had three holes. Well, I told you all this stuff about holes because my buddies and I would once in a while stick our dicks in the holes (not in Mary Lou's dad's holes, of course, but in other people's holes) and pee. You know; just for the hell of it. It was kind of the thing to do late at night if you saw a parked Buick; and I just sort of thought you might think that was funny or something. Well, maybe not.

Anyway, and to get back to the prom, I felt like "king shit" (meaning so important I almost couldn't stand it) pulling up to the dance at the Washertown Country Club in that Roadmaster. A lot of the other guys probably thought I was some kind of a "stuck-up" ass-hole/butthole. But you know what? That only made the whole experience even better! (Some of those guys thought I was generally "stuck-up" anyway.) Whatever. I was "sitting on top of the world," to borrow yet another expression. I mean look at it this way. I had a white "dinner jacket," black pants (with a stripe down the side), two-tone powder blue silk cummerbund and bow tie *on* me. I had the most beautiful girl in the whole world, in a shrimp-colored, pearl encrusted, New York City, Saks Fifth Avenue gown (and white, "strappy," really high healed shoes) *next* to me. A two-tone Buick Roadmaster (four-holer), with wide whitewalls and real wire wheels *under* me. And Washertown Country Club straight *ahead* of me. Holy shit! I mean holy, *holy* shit! And the night had only just begun.

Then, just a few weeks later, came graduation (along with the absolutely devastating news I received concerning "The Pledge of Allegiance" issue), and then our first all-school alumni banquet, and then some other shit. And with that, it was over. Finished. My friends and I were out of there. Washertown High, by the way, and as I am sure you can imagine, was therefore (and of course) greatly, perhaps even tragically diminished by our passing (not that we had actually died or anything, but you know what I mean). Whatever. It was "Hail and farewell!" And so, for now anyway, it's love and kisses from a handsome, tall blonde asshole who not only drove his "could and maybe should have been" (I sometimes think) father-in-law's Roadmaster to the prom (and felt like "King Shit" doing it), but who also, in the Homecoming parade in the fall *before* graduation (I can't believe I forgot to tell you), had driven Washertown's only 1954, powder-blue Cadillac *convertible* (feeling also of course like "King Shit"), in which rode the Homecoming Queen . . . who should have been Mary Lou, but wasn't. (You just read through one of those long, hard-to-follow sentences that I cautioned you about, I know; but it was a good exercise for you, nevertheless, and certainly worthy of reading again if you didn't get it all.) By the way, I still don't know what the hell my classmates were thinking when they chose someone else as queen. I mean talk about assholes. Mary Lou was, however, an "attendant." *And,* hands down, the most beautiful woman in Washertown's entire Homecoming Parade. Ever. So, once more, dear reader, "Osky Wah Wah!" High School is over, and there's a lot of other stuff about Washertown that I want to go back and tell you all about anyway. And by the way, if you want that bashed in football helmet that I wore, it's probably still being recycled in some goddamn smelly dressing room at one of the current junior highs.

CHAPTER THREE

FIRST LOVE
OR
WOW, DOES THAT FEEL GOOD!

W ell, I hope all that school stuff wasn't too boring for you. But keep in mind that since this is mostly a book (indeed a masterpiece, as I reminded you before) about where I grew up and how I got to be this way, I had to tell you about school. I mean school has a lot to do with growing up. I guess anyway. That's what most people say. And besides, I'm pretty sure what you're going to hear about next won't bore you. At least I don't think it will. So here it is: my very first really hot and torrid (actually I just said the "really hot and torrid" part to get you excited) love affair.

To begin with, probably the most generally acceptable part of this first affair, I think anyway (if I choose to actually think about it at all), and the most ordinary or maybe even "normal" part, is that she and I were the same age. *Seven.* (Actually I guess that might not be so normal after all.) Maybe it was though. I don't however consider myself to be an expert on this kind of stuff, so I can't say for sure. And maybe I shouldn't even be writing about it, since some of my friends once told me they thought the whole thing was kind of strange. Meaning they couldn't recall having had an affair when they were seven. Whatever. I have to tell you about it regardless of what other people might think, since it was truly one of my more memorable experiences of growing up in Washertown. And as I've said before, I'm not going to leave stuff out or lie to you or anything.

Well, maybe *some* stuff I might leave out. But not much. *Anyway,* and to stay on track (I don't want my mind to go nuts on me again, and its beginning to feel a little bit that way), her (i.e. my lover's) name was Janey (as I actually told you a lot earlier in my book), and she made me feel things all over my little seven-year-old body that I think maybe I wasn't supposed to feel until several years later. You may not even believe that, but it's true. But anyway, this is how it happened.

I don't remember for sure just how or the very day we met or anything, since it was a pretty long time ago. It might have been at her grandmother's house (Grandma McCorsky), since she (Grandma McCorsky) lived just one street over from me and then down (north one block, and then just a little bit west, if that kind of detail matters to you). Or perhaps we met at school, since because we were both seven and lived in the same part of town (west side) we went to the same school, which of course was Washington Elementary. I learned, by the way (about five years ago when I went back to Washertown and drove by my old school and saw this new building with its big sign and everything) that it (Washington Elementary) had been torn down and replaced with a place called The Center for Unwanted Pregnancies (like a clinic, I guess). Well, it really made me sick to see that. Mostly because even though I hadn't lived in Washertown for a long, long time, no one had even asked me what I thought about the idea (which wouldn't have been much). I guess they just didn't know how important that school had been to me. I mean it's not that Washertown girls don't get "knocked up" and everything (I'm sure they do), or that they shouldn't have somewhere to go get fixed or something (I'm sure they should); but did they have to tear down *my* school? I mean Jesus! Is nothing sacred anymore? And besides that, if they had to do it (i.e. build a place like that on the site of my grade school) they at least could have spared us the euphemistic "Center for Unwanted Pregnancies" crap and called it what it really was, i.e. a "Knock-up Clinic." But anyway, and to get back on track (it's so easy to get carried away), maybe Janey and I didn't meet at her Grandmother's house, or at school, but somewhere else. Maybe even in another life even. I don't know. And it really doesn't matter. What *does* matter is that we met and had this torrid love affair (although "torrid" of course is another word I didn't actually know then).

It all began rather simply, I think, and innocently (maybe), when we went to the movies together. Saturday matinees at the Capitol Theatre (Washertown's finest) were what we went for. A lot of kids our age did that in the Washertown of the 1940s, since the whole town was such a safe and seemingly innocent place. I mean nothing ever happened to anyone. Hardly anyway. So anyhow, we went to the movies, and although I don't think I actually "took" her (she would be dropped off by her mother or grandmother maybe, and always had her own dime for her ticket), I did buy the popcorn at least once (five cents for a white paper bagful). The bags at Washertown's other two theatres weren't as nice as those at the Capitol. They were brown. Shit brown. Kind of like little grocery bags. Anyway, Janey and I would sometimes sit in the balcony, *if* we could sneak up there (and it wasn't easy). The balcony was supposed to be closed for the matinees, and the manager considered it "off limits" for minors, which of course at age seven we were. So most of the time we had to find a corner toward the back on the main floor.

Sometimes we would sort of slouch down in our seats, eat popcorn, and hold hands and stuff (if I could get up the nerve). It was almost like "necking," which was what the older kids did. But that (necking) seemed like a pretty strange word to me. I mean when I thought of "neck" I always conjured up this image of Sunday dinner at my grandfather's, my mother's father's house. (My grandmother had died when I was just four, so she wasn't part of those dinners . . . at least I don't think she was . . . unless maybe in some sort of scary-like spiritual way maybe.) And although I didn't know much about spiritual stuff then, I do remember that there was this thing called a "Ojai Board" (or something like that) at my grandpa's house. That was pretty spooky.

Anyway, there would usually be this big plate of fried chicken for Sunday dinner, with a really gross-looking chicken neck stacked up by the other, nicer pieces. (The "neck stack" also had the gizzard and the heart and everything in it.) It almost made me sick sometimes. Anyway, the point is (I guess) that what Janey and I did didn't have anything to do with chicken necks (or, as far as that goes, gizzards or hearts either). Well, hearts maybe, but in a totally different way. And I still don't know why people called it necking. But one more thing about those chickens; I also remember sometimes feeling sort of icky even when I would bite into a drumstick (considered a "good" part), and the veins would kind of be there, and maybe even sort of get pulled out and stuck between my teeth when I started to chew it and everything. Really bad. But I need to get back to Janey and our affair. I don't know why I can get so far off track with stuff that isn't important. I mean fried chicken necks and leg veins, when I'm just trying to tell you about my girlfriend? What the hell is it with me?

So anyway, one time at the movies we (at least I) got really lucky. It was a rainy afternoon, so we ended up kind of crawling (almost sliding) under her raincoat, sort of like it was a tent or something, and then ate our popcorn and stuff. I think I even put my whole arm around her that time. And you can bet that took courage. (I learned to love rainy Saturdays.) Anyway, I just now thought (going back to the fried chicken for a minute) that it always seemed to me that the heart on that plate was too little for the rest of the chicken. Did you ever think that? And if you can believe it (and it's true), my brother and I used to actually fight over who got the gizzard, so I guess looking at that thing didn't *always* make me sick. And now that I'm thinking about all this stuff again, I also remember (you may want to skip over this part) watching my grandfather chop the head off the chicken on Saturday, and then seeing the goddamn thing flop all over the backyard (my grandfather kept his own chickens in a pen behind the garage). It was really awful. I mean *really* awful. Blood spurting all over the place and everything. But I guess someone had to do it. And it was better than when he would sometimes put a broomstick across the chicken's neck, step on the stick, and then just pull the little fucker's head off. (Here I go again.) But Jesus! That was really gruesome.

Anyway, after murdering the thing, he would put it (i.e. the headless chicken) in a big tin tub full of really hot water (which was in the basement and usually used for rinsing laundry). And man did that stink! I mean *really* stink. But I guess that was the only way you could get the feathers to fall off. At least I think it was. And then the next day we would be eating that very chicken. Can you believe it? But again, none of this had anything to do with Janey and me, and I've *got* to stop getting off the track all the time. Really. And I'm sorry. But I mean it was *gross. Really* gross. However (as I said before, life has lots of "howevers"), and to go back (yet again) to where I seemed to have lost the "thread" of what I'm really trying to tell you about (I don't know why I can't get those goddamn chickens out of my mind), when Janey and I sat real close at the movies and held hands and everything (and I maybe even hugged her), it was called necking. That's the point I've been trying to make all along; it had nothing to do with headless chickens flopping around and bleeding, and maybe even gurgling too, or the actual Sunday dinner at my grandpa's house. In fact, I'm pretty sure Janey never even went to one of my grandpa's chicken dinner parties. They were just for family. (Like for my mom and my dad and my brother, and maybe my aunt Velma and uncle Lloyd and my cousins, and my grandfather's housekeeper of course, since she cooked the dinners, and my grandfather himself.) Anyway, that's who was usually there.

So at about the same time Janey and I were at the movies necking and stuff (my friends still tell me it was probably kind of early for us to be doing that), I became familiar with the term "pet," which seemed to mean that you messed around in a few more places than you messed around in when you just necked. Well, that seemed like a pretty good deal to me. Somehow though I had already gotten the idea that necking wasn't a particularly nice thing to do (I mean *I* thought it was, but I guess some people didn't), and that petting was *really* not nice, and maybe even "dirty" and everything. Those "some people," I suspect, were probably a few of the folks from the Methodist Church (I told you about part of what they thought before), although this necking with Janey stuff was happening before they (the church people) really got to me. Needless to say, sexual intercourse, i.e. *totally* "doing it" (which by the way I only knew by the word "screwing," or *fucking*, which I'm trying not to say anymore) was not really on my mind. In fact, until I went to that YMCA camp that I told you about and got straightened out about all this shit, "screwing" was something that only married people were supposed to do (again the Methodist factor, I'm sure). And then later I learned (from a little book I read) that the guy was supposed to actually "put it in" only when it was dark, and only when he and his wife (only) were in a double bed and in just the right position. The "right" position by the way meant that the man was on top (I learned that in the same book). Always on top. I think the Methodists even said that it was somehow better if he was also a missionary or something. Whatever.

That kind of talk pretty much confused me when I was little; and I always thought missionaries were kind of strange people anyway.

And then there was this one other thing (and then back to Janey and me). First, the man was also supposed to be sure that she (again his wife only) was breathing real hard and stuff (maybe because he was real heavy or something, I'm not sure), before he put it in. And then there was something about her also being lubricated (which of course was something I thought you did to your car or a door hinge, not to your wife). Whatever. And then finally he (the man whose wife was breathing real hard and was all greased up) was supposed to grit his teeth really hard and hold his breath and everything so that his wife would get to enjoy it (being screwed) too. If he didn't do that, i.e. grit his teeth and stiff (I mean stuff), he might enjoy it first, and then not be able to do it anymore. Something like that anyway. It was all pretty mixed up sounding, I thought anyway. Sometimes I can't even believe I remember all this stuff. But life can be so goddamn confusing when you're little. By the way, talking about getting your wife greased up and everything reminded me of one time when I was a lot older (like in college) and my date ("blind" date) spent two hours up in the air on a grease rack at this little gas station. That was because we didn't know it was going to take that long to fix the car (which had broken down on the way to this beer and dance place), and she said she would just stay in it. I probably shouldn't say this, but I was pretty much OK with that. She was one of those blind dates that wasn't working out so well.

Anyway (I'm so goddamn off track again), Janey and I were only seven, and of course didn't even pretend to be married or anything. So again, a lot of what I just said didn't have anything to do with us. Especially the screwing part (and the lube job and all the rest I guess). I mean I don't think *anyone*, not even a hard-breathing married lady, would let some guy "put it in" under a raincoat at the Capitol Theatre during the Saturday matinee. *After* the movie, maybe. But not during it. Whatever. I just remember that I liked the "pet rules" better than just the "neck stuff," so that's kind of what we did. So, as I was saying (I hope my mind isn't beginning to drift again), there we would be, slouched down, kind of nervous-like (at least I was . . . but what else was new), eating (popcorn), and petting. I loved it! And so did Janey. At least I think she did. However, as you might expect, and as all good Washertown Methodists (*First* Methodists) could have told us, our clandestine behavior (another big word I didn't know then of course) would lead to more. And eventually to damnation, ruination (actually I think ruination comes first), and a whole lot of other shitty stuff. The damnation and ruination stuff was of course also Methodist talk (and again, words I didn't even know). However, and as a matter of fact, that's sort of just what happened. I guess anyway. At least our necking and petting (God forgive me, but was it ever special) led, as we were warned it might, right to Janey's very own bedroom. But before I go on with this (there are lots of "buts" in the world too), I think I should first tell you more about the popcorn at the movie theatres and, as a matter of fact, the movie theatres themselves. I'm not exactly sure why, but it might not be as irrelevant to our love story as it sounds (or maybe it is . . . you can decide). Whatever. It's also probably a good idea to kind of cool things down a little bit anyway. Don't worry though. I'll get back to the good stuff in just a little while.

You see, if you happened to be more than just a little bit sensitive to some of the sights, sounds, and especially *smells* in Washertown, (and given some of the stuff I've already told you about, you know I was), and if you were especially sensitive not only to your surroundings in general, but to things like the popcorn at movie theatres in particular (and I was), *and* if the Casper County Courthouse, First Methodist Church, and Washertown Junior High School boy's bathroom (remember that place?) sort of lingered in your mind (and they did in mine), you would understand that all these places and things (especially the popcorn, the boy's bathroom, and the courthouse) did in fact have something very much in common. Which is to say they all *smelled* funny (meaning bad). Actually, the Capitol Theatre (Washertown's finest), the one where Janey and I did most of our "neck and pet thing," didn't smell funny. At least I don't think it did. But the other places I just recalled for you, and Washertown's two other theatres, the Rialto, where all the "westerns" were shown, and the Iowa, the home of Tarzan (which made not going there an impossibility, if you were any kind of a normal person and a boy), did (i.e. they did smell funny). I'll bet, by the way, that you don't even know what the word *rialto* means. (I do, but I'm going to make you look it up.) Anyway, it was the Iowa that *really* smelled, so

I can pretty much tell you this part of my story by just talking about this one theatre.

You could go there (i.e. to the Iowa theatre) anytime you wanted to, of course, but as I said up above, you *had* to if you wanted to see the Tarzan movies. However, you probably would have had a problem with the popcorn. And here's why, and how it all ties in with those other places I just reminded you about. (Man, I hope my little mind gets me through this part.) Anyway, it was the urine smell. Everything at the Iowa Theatre smelled sort of "uriney." Not all the time. But mostly. And the problem at the Iowa, compared to the other places I mentioned, was that the lobby was really, really small. In fact, it almost didn't have a lobby at all. You just bought your ticket outside and kind of walked right in. Therefore, the popcorn machine, unfortunately but by necessity, sat right by the entrance to the theatre auditorium itself, and next to the stairs that led down to the men's bathroom in the basement, which itself, as a matter of fact (i.e. the men's room), was a rather strange, cave-like place (but that's another story). Actually, men's rooms in those days were almost always in the basement, as you may or may not recall from my earlier comment about the bathroom at the Methodist, i.e. *First* Methodist, church.

Anyway, to get on with the story, popcorn (in all the theatre's actually, not just the Iowa) was available in paper bags, and for just five cents (brown bags, except at the Capitol, where they were white, although I think I already told you that), or in a usually red and white cardboard box, for just "one thin dime" (as the expression used to go). Unfortunately, what was also "available," in fact what "came with" the popcorn in the five-cent brown paper bags at the Iowa ("sacks," as we said in Washertown), was the faint aroma of "old urinal" urine, which seemed to have wafted its way up the stairs from the men's bathroom and kind of soaked right into both the bag *and* the popcorn itself. You could almost taste it. Which meant that you were better off, if you *had* to have popcorn at the Iowa, to "go the extra mile" (another common expression) and buy the ten-cent box (it wasn't good either, but it was better). Now, the "connection" between the Iowa Theatre and the other places in Washertown was, therefore (and I've been trying my hardest to establish it for you), that the same uriney smell wafted around the Court House, the Methodist Church basement (especially on hot, "muggy" Sundays), the boy's bathroom at the junior high school (especially on cold days, with the radiators going full tilt), and the Rialto Theatre. As I already told you, the "wafting" at the court house actually spilled out like some gaseous and menacing green cloud swirling across the floor, seeping under the doors, and flowing over the pigeon shit that covered the sidewalk, right up to the drinking fountain with the little steps by it. Really bad. It's a wonder it didn't kill the pigeons.

So I ask you, "Who wants to eat popcorn when it makes you think of (and almost tastes like) a smelly, musty basement, an old, unflushed urinal, or a cloud of deadly green gas?" Well not me! That's for sure. And I wasn't about to buy that stuff for Janey or anyone else either. As I said, however, this was really only a problem at the Iowa. Never at the Capitol, and only sometimes at the Rialto. At the Rialto, by the way, the men's room was also pretty close to the popcorn machine, but since it was also shared by a barber shop next door (The Rialto Barber Shop, of course), any urine smell there was covered up by the "fragrance" (and I use the term loosely) of the 1940s, hair oil and talcum powder and stuff. That hair oil, by the way (and you always got really slathered with it, especially if you were little and your hair wouldn't lay down), smelled (believe it or not) like roses. It was even kind of a rose-pink color (real sissy-looking), and was dispensed from a tall, "shake-top" bottle. Kind of like the tops of salad dressing bottles in restaurants, or booze bottles in fancy bars, as I found out later. However, if the barber liked you, or you were maybe just older, you got something from a bottle that had a label that said Pinaud. And that stuff (at least that's what they said) had been shipped to the Rialto all the way from France or somewhere. But I'm sorry. I suspect you'd like me to get back to my love affair with Janey. And that's probably a good idea. I didn't mean to get this carried away with the popcorn issue. And besides that, it's *not* a particularly good idea to hang around men's rooms anyway (I figured that out pretty early). So anyway, just remember that the popcorn at the Iowa Theatre is *not* good. Use your nickel to buy a box of "Juijy Fruits" (that's what we called them), or if you really like chocolate stuff, a big fat Tootsie Roll instead. Goddamnit! I'm so off track I can't believe it.

So anyway, it's springtime, 1943 (maybe 44), I think anyway . . . a warm (for April in Iowa) Saturday afternoon, and my "fancy" (as in "In the spring a young man's fancy turns to thoughts of love," or something like that) had indeed "turned" (although I was never sure what that expression meant). I knew a lot of names for some of the "feel good" parts of my body, but I had never heard any part called a "fancy." Oh well. Some people in those days might even have said that my "sap" was flowing (like a maple tree, I guess), but then if they said that they would have forgotten that I was only seven when this whole love affair took place. Sap (or whatever you want to call it) may have flowed in seven-year-old maple trees, but it sure as hell didn't flow in seven-year-old boys! And when it started to (flow) we didn't call it sap. I'm not sure by the way whether girls were supposed to have "fancies" (which also turned to thoughts of love), but if they did, I'm sure Janey had a really nice one. And I never even thought about the idea that a girl could have sap. I mean I didn't learn about that until I was a lot older. Like in seventh grade maybe.

So as I was saying, it's Saturday afternoon, and springtime in Iowa. You know, when it's still just a little bit chilly, but everything smells kind of fresh and clean, and the daffodils are sticking up out of the ground in pretty little clumps and everything. Anyway, I'm at Janey's house. I don't remember why, but nevertheless I was there. And, by invitation. I mean it's not as though I just went there or broke in or anything. What I *do* remember is that Janey's mother had a big plate of fudge on the table that she had just made (meaning the fudge of course, not the table . . . at least I don't think she made tables), and then eating a big piece of it (the fudge), and then eventually going to bed with her (i.e. with Janey, not, for God's sake, her mother). I may have been somewhat sexually precocious (although "precocious" of course was another of those words I didn't know then), or maybe "wired wrong" or something, but I wasn't crazy or anything like that. Well, maybe sort of, but not that much. I struggle with that (as you know). *Anyway,* Janey's mother had gone out somewhere, maybe to a friend's house to talk or something, since I learned later that she was going through a pretty hard time. Well, maybe it was the fudge that made me do it, meaning go into her bedroom and get on the bed with her, *not* (again, for God's sake), actually "do it" to her or anything like that. You have to remember here that we were only seven and in second grade. And actually (I hope this doesn't spoil anything for you), as I just said, we were only *on* the bed, not really *in* it. Anyway, let me tell you more about just how it all happened. I mean I don't mind sharing this stuff, since it was so nice.

We're in the bedroom, see, and as I said before when I was talking about just going to her house, I don't really remember (for *sure* anyway) just how we got there (in the bedroom) either. Anyway, we were (in the bedroom), and then Janey went into the closet, and then there was kind of a rustling sound, and then she came out of the closet, absolutely resplendent (another word I didn't know then, but that's what she was) in her mother's bathrobe. It was a pink, chenille bathrobe (although I didn't know the word "chenille" then either). I just knew that it was real soft and sort of fuzzy, and that it had little rows of really furry stuff, with "lower" rows of other stuff between them. (I figured out that it was her mother's, because it dragged across the floor behind her, i.e. behind Janey, just like she was a queen or a movie star or something.) In fact maybe that's what she was trying to look like. I don't know. However, unknown to Janey, but maybe not (she may have been trying to seduce me), but *probably* not, it (the pink chenille bathrobe) was separated in front just a little *little* bit, just enough for me to see that all she had on under it was her underpants. White, I think. And oh my God! Remember that goofy song with the words "I see London/I see France"? Well, I saw Janey's, and they looked pretty good too.

Not to get off the track again, but I had only seen one other little girl in her underpants, and that was in first grade. What happened that time was that after school one day another one of my little friends, this one named Joycie, not only showed them to me (her underpants), but actually pulled them down. We were hiding behind an old upright piano in her parent's living room, playing some kind of game I guess, and she did it so that I could "see hers." And then of course I was supposed to pull mine down too (underpants), so she could "see mine," which we both suspected was pretty much different from hers. (I think maybe she already knew that, since she had a little brother.) So anyway, I don't know if it was fear, or modesty, or shyness, or what the hell it was, but I reneged (another big word) on the deal, and Joycie got really mad. And I mean *really* mad. She must have been some kind of incipient (yet another word I didn't know then) sex nut or something. I mean she was chasing me around the room and everything! Now that I look back, I think that I maybe didn't do it, meaning "hold up" my share of the bargain, because I had already seen that there was a lot more to "mine" than there was to "hers," and therefore thought it was a bad deal. But man was she mad. And to tell you the truth (although I wasn't dumb enough to tell Joycie), I actually hadn't seen anything of much interest anyway (an opinion that would of course change considerably over time).

Whatever, I obviously had decided (as I just said) that showing Joycie my "thing" wasn't a fair deal. Speaking of deals (only now the "New Deal," not the one Joycie and I made and I broke), only a few weeks after this sex-crazed behavior on Joycie's part, President Franklin Delano Roosevelt died in Warm Springs, Georgia. I doubt of course that there was any connection between Joycie's goddamn sex problems and President Roosevelt's death. At least, I sure hope not. He, President Roosevelt, probably had his own problems to take care of. Whatever. It just happens that I remember the day he died, and that lots of people in my neighborhood were crying when they heard about it. But I also remember reading a lot later (a lot, lot later, like maybe when I was in college) that President Roosevelt had been messing around a little bit too. Not with Joycie, of course, but with someone (I think her name might have been Lucille, or Lucy, or something like that). And maybe he had an upright (piano) in his living room too. I really don't know. And I don't mean to be disrespectful. But you know it could be that he (President Roosevelt) even liked fudge and chenille bathrobes that dragged on the floor and opened up in the front just a little. I don't know. But maybe. When I think of his wife though, Mrs. Roosevelt, I somehow have a hard time thinking of fuzzy chenille bathrobes and stuff. But I saw her and heard her speak when I was in college. She was good too, and a really fine person. Whatever. To tell you the truth, I don't know much about the other lady that he, President Roosevelt, was maybe doing it to (although I think maybe her name was LuLu, rather than Lucille or Lucy, as I said before). But I guess I should probably just mind my own business and (no pun intended) "tend to my own affairs." By the way, another strange thing about Joycie was that she liked to eat soft butter by the spoonful. Makes me sick to even think about it. Big spoonfuls of greasy, yellowy shit. I mean that's disgusting.

Anyway, back to Janey, the bedroom, the bed, the chenille robe, her panties, and what we actually did. Read slowly now, and with feeling, since this is the good part. "Chenille Janey" and I, without speaking a word, got into bed. Sorry (exciting as it might have been), but as I already told you, that's actually not quite true. As I said before, we didn't really get *in* the bed, but just *on* it. There's a difference (although probably not much). Once more, however, you have to remember that we were only seven. So anyway, we got on the bed. I can't remember what I hard on (sorry, I mean *had* on) or off, but I suspect not much (off), because of my modesty and not too distant memories of Joycie the sex nut and everything. The modesty part, by the way, had started when I was real little, meaning real little all over (not like just age-appropriate real little in "certain" places). I mean it seemed I had always been pretty modest. Maybe it was the Methodists again, who knows. But anyway, I can say for sure that I would have hard on (damn . . . I don't know why I keep saying "hard on") . . . anyway, I would have *had* on something. And, by the way (just to make sure you don't make too much of this), if I had "gotten off," it would only have meant that once in a while I might have gotten off the *bed*. There was absolutely no way I would have "gotten off" getting off, if you know what I mean. And I suspect you do. Holy shit! Now I'm beginning to think *I'm* the sex nut or something.

Anyway, I remember (do I ever) how fantastic it felt just holding Janey real close, being on top of her, then kind of under her (I was an equal opportunity guy before anyone was even talking about it, I guess), and then just rolling all over on the top of the bed and stuff. The chenille felt really good too. But not as good as Janey herself. I mean I just wanted to hug and hug her. And then I don't remember some things (just time passing maybe), and then I *really* remember! (I'll bet you're beginning to get kind of excited.) Unfortunately, however, and this is an "unfortunately" and a "however" that I'll never forget, *ever,* the "bubble of love" (and the dam full of excitement you were maybe beginning to experience) suddenly burst. What happened was that I remember looking up from the bed (I was on my back, with Janey on top) and seeing Janey's mother standing at the bedroom door, absolutely aghast (I didn't know that word then either, but it probably describes pretty close the way she looked). Anyway, the woman was upset. *Really* upset. Like she was going to throw up or maybe even go crazy or something. (Had she thrown-up, Janey and I would probably have drowned in the stuff; that's how much of it there would have been.) I mean this lady was close to being certifiably nuts . . . to maybe qualifying for electro-convulsive shock therapy even. Like for twenty-four hours a day and ten years maybe. Or even more. In fact, it looked to me as though she might have to be locked up somewhere real fast. I mean it was just goddamn awful, the whole thing. So, as you might suspect, it had suddenly become pretty clear (to put it mildly) that I wasn't going to be eating any more fudge at Janey's house. No doubt about that! My challenge was simply to get out of there alive.

Of course, and as you might suspect, I was told, pretty strong-like, to go home. And right away too. And there wasn't any "Come back again soon" shit, or "I hope you had a good time," either. And for sure there wasn't any "Did you and Janey have fun playing with each other?" So anyway, painful as it is to say it, Janey and I were never to have such an encounter again. Never. *Ever.* It was over. *We* had "crossed the line." "Fallen overboard." And *I,* it was clear (like *really* clear), had "fallen off the wall." And believe me, neither Ann Landers, nor "all the king's horses and all the king's men" (as that treasured little poem tells it), were going to put me (or us) together again. I mean it wasn't that we didn't ever see each other, but something that was truly beautiful (well, fun anyway) had pretty obviously ended.

In one sense, however, Janey's mom proved to be a real trooper (meaning she didn't call my mom and rat on me). And actually, my mother would never have believed her anyway. Her fair-haired, seven-year-old "Wonder Boy" in bed with some conniving, chenille-clad, underpants-showing, seductive little blonde-haired bitch? Her very own "God from God, Light from Light," second born child? (My mother had by this time forgiven me for having had such a big head, as well as for the breast infection she developed following my birth.) So anyway, her "Very good" from "Very good" second grader was in no way to be accused of being a *bad* child. (By the way, did you ever see the movie *The Bad Seed?* Man, *that* was scary.) Anyway, for me to have "fallen short of the mark" (another one of those expressions I wasn't sure of) was simply something my mother would not have felt possible. The reason I knew Janey's mother hadn't told my mother was because when I got home (and believe me, I had walked *very* slowly), although my mother was upset, it was because I came in bare footed, carrying my shoes. (You don't think I was stupid enough to leave them under Janey's bed, do you?) Whatever. She (my mom) thought it was way too early in the year for me to be bare footed, and she worried that the sidewalks had been too cold on my dear, sensitive, and innocent little feet. I mean, what if I got sick? (Actually that would have meant ginger ale, chicken noodle soup, and ice cream . . . not a bad deal.) Anyway, little did she know that it was Janey's mother who was sick, probably "puking sick," and that I, "pure as the driven snow" (and what a nice expression that is), had been making love for the last two hours (well, kind of), and probably with more bare (but not much, as I already told you) than just my feet. All my mom knew, however, was what she could see; and what she saw were two precious (and, thank God, not frostbitten) little feet, belonging of course to her very own blue-eyed, blonde-haired "barefoot boy with cheeks of tan." Actually that last part wouldn't have been true; you can't get tan cheeks in Iowa until much later in the year.

But I suppose my rather feeble poetic references, and as a matter of fact this entire "sentimental journey" (and we probably should underscore "mental"), might be making *you* sick. I know it's becoming sort of really stretched out. I shall therefore "cease and desist" (I think that's what I mean to say anyway). And besides, as I said just a little while ago, I somehow knew that there was to be no more chenille for me for many, many years. And, as for fudge, it would only be my mother's. Oh well. "Sex at seven" (OK . . . "messing around a little bit at seven") was more than worth the consequences. And it also provided me an early example of what my father would remind me of when I was a little bit older, i.e. that "he who dances must pay the fiddler" (or something like that). Not that Janey and I were dancing; but you know what I mean. Finally, and to tell you the very, very truth, I do have to say that there really *was* something extraordinarily special about that time with Janey. Really. It was warm, and beautiful—an innocent, lovely, caring, and indeed *loving* moment in our lives. Really and truly it was. And obviously a time that "old sentimental me" hasn't forgotten.

CHAPTER FOUR

OF SWIMMING POOLS AND POPSICLES

Y ou might think that writing a whole chapter about swimming pools and Popsicles is sort of a strange thing to do. And you also probably think that swimming pools and Popsicles don't even go together, except perhaps as a sort of weak attempt at alliteration or something (which of course I didn't know anything about when I was a little). But trust me; they (i.e. swimming pools and Popsicles) do (i.e. go together). In fact, there still remains a very special place in my heart for at least four swimming pools and several flavors (one especially) of Popsicles. Orange. I can actually even say that it (the special place in my heart) occupies a sizeable amount of space; and also that that space is in the very most sacred realm of my entire being (well . . . that's maybe a bit of an overstatement). Whatever. I'm going to take a chance and tell you about why swimming pools and Popsicles are so special and go together, and then maybe you'll even agree with me. So anyway, what follows is about one *really* special swimming pool, two others that were pretty special, or at least maybe kind of special, and then one that was in fact goddamn *awful,* as in hideous and totally shitty and everything (it should have been drained and filled in, it was so bad). And then what follows is also about eating more Popsicles than a person could possibly count (there's that alliteration thing again, i.e. the *P* sound in Popsicles, possibly, and person . . . and also even the "could count" part is a little bit alliterative too, only now it's the *C* sound). I guess it's pretty obvious to you by now that writing was going to be a real strength of mine (and nothing like playing the water glasses or being a world famous accordionist or artist or athlete or anything). So anyway, here's the story.

Swimming pools were not common in Washertown when I was a little boy. And they probably still aren't. To be exact, there were only *four* swimming pools in the whole town. But you have to remember, this was Iowa in the 1940s, and so even just four made it a sort of special place. At least I thought so. I mean it wasn't like Hollywood or anything, with lots of swimming pools and movie stars and everything, but it was still a pretty nice place to live. So anyway, to talk about all this, and to make this part of my book more exciting for you than just kind of interesting, I've devised a special and sort of secret code system (alliteration again, only now S sounds) for the pools (sort of like the "code key" that came with my Captain Midnight ring). I'm willing to share it with you though (i.e. the code, not my Captain Midnight ring itself . . . which I can't find anyway). Captain Midnight, maybe you remember, was a pretty exciting radio personality when I was little, although I'll try not to get carried away with telling you about him, since you know I have this sort of peculiar mental tendency to digress and stuff (the point being that this is supposed to be about swimming pools and Popsicles, not Captain Midnight). And he (Captain Midnight) is dead anyway. At least I think he is. Maybe not though, since he wasn't like the rest of us. At least I know he's not on the radio anymore though (and he never did make TV . . . I don't so anyway). Just remember that he helped kids with life. But back to the code. (I kind of started doing it, i.e. digressing again, didn't I? So the code . . . the code . . .

OK, the sort of secret but not entirely secret code names of the swimming pools are (in order of how good they were) as follows: *MPP, EH, FL,* and *YMCA.* The last one you probably had in your hometown too, so I don't want you to think that I'm claiming to have made that code name up or anything. As I told you before, I'll always be honest with you. And besides, the person who made that name up was a Christian. I guess he was anyway, and it is not my practice to take away from or crap on Christians (well . . . at least not on most of them anyway), even though the *YMCA* pool was the one I thought should been drained. Bombed maybe. Whatever. It (the name) stands for what the words mean: *Young Men's Christian Association.* But you probably already knew that. Anyway, it was supposed to be a place where just wholesome Christian stuff happened (although I could tell you about a few "activities" I observed there in the boys/men's locker room that didn't seem so wholesome to me). Oh well, no one's perfect (as I've also said before). I just hope the Y pool you maybe had in your hometown holds better memories for you than the one we had in Washertown does for me. My memories, as I just sort of implied (at least for the most part), were in fact *awful.* As I said up above, but to kind of add to it and sum it all up, I thought our Y pool was *goddam*ed hideous, shitty, and "should be drained," awful. (I almost said *fucking* awful, but I kind of promised you that I would try not to use that word anymore . . . and also I don't want to use it along with something Christian that could therefore maybe cause me to eventually go to hell.) Anyway, I'll tell you more about that pool later. The first part of this chapter is supposed to be more about good stuff and special places, and that place, i.e. the *fucking YMCA* pool (there, I said it) was, for me, neither. Neither good, nor special. And it certainly didn't have anything to do with Popsicles, I can tell you that. I guess I just kind of put it in (i.e. in my story) since it was one of the swimming pools I went to, and because I thought that telling you about it would somehow sort of justify (maybe a little bit anyway) my bad language sometimes, and maybe make the other pools seem even better.

But as I just said, details about the Y pool are for later, and besides I'm sort of getting off the track again I think. Man, I don't know. Maybe there *is* something wrong with my mind. But no one's perfect. (Although I think I already told you that.) *Anyway,* to get on with it, *MPP* was the most wonderful place (swimming pool) in the whole world, and it's also where I bought most of my Popsicles (except for one summer when I bought most of them at Stub O'Brien's Grocery Store, which was near the cottage we went to at Clear Lake for our family vacation when I was eight-years-old). The *EH* and *FL* pools, to just sort of introduce them, were sort of like fantasy places for a boy in Iowa (at least they were for me), like Hollywood and movie stars and everything (as I kind of mentioned before). And they didn't have anything to do with Popsicles. But they were still really special just the same. Rita Hayworth (I used to like to think about Rita Hayworth with no clothes on, meaning that *she* didn't have any clothes on, not me . . . I mean I would probably have been in bed with my "jammys" on when I was thinking this) . . . *anyway*, I think that Rita Hayworth would probably have liked Code Pool *EH* a lot. But all this will become clearer as I keep going. Remember the codes though, since they make the stories about all these pool places more exotic. At least I think so. Kind of like Maureen O'Hara was exotic (I also liked to think about her with no clothes on . . . and Betty Grable . . . and Dorothy Lamour . . . and probably even June Allyson). Well, maybe not June Allyson. You know, sometimes I think that maybe I *am* a sicko. I don't know. I guess I could dial in to Captain Midnight and see what he thinks; except that, as I told you before, I lost the ring a long time ago and therefore can't dial. (Those Captain Midnight rings, by the way, now that I think about them more, were actually just for really stupid, naive kids who believed anything you told them, and drank something called Ovaltine all the time.) I think it was Ovaltine anyway. But I guess it doesn't matter. It might have been Nestle's Quick or something. No. It was Ovaltine. Hell, I don't know. Maybe The Shadow knows (he was another radio guy who helped kids). Man, this is going nowhere! Kind of like Burma Shave signs and Ipana toothpaste maybe. Shit! I've got to get back in control here. I mean I'm only just trying to tell you about Washertown's swimming holes . . . I mean pools . . . well, actually the *YMCA* pool was a hole of sorts (but I already kind of said that).

So anyway, *anyway,* I'm going to begin with Code Pool *EH*, thereby saving the best, *MPP*, for last. (All the stuff I want to tell you about Popsicles will come at the end.) OK? So, as I kind of already told you, *EH* was the most mysterious, romantic, and Hollywood-like of all the pools in Washertown. Just like a movie set. The pool, and the house in front of it (actually two houses), and all the other stuff around the place belonged to a member of Washertown's leading family (no surprise there). It was kind of strange though, because you almost never saw anyone living in those houses. As a matter of fact, I don't remember seeing anyone even *go* there. But anyway, the entire property, which included the pool, the two houses, the lawns, a bathhouse, and other stuff sat back from the street, quite elegantly, down a long, curving, U-shaped red brick driveway (with a lot of always-trimmed green grass growing between the bricks). When I was little I was afraid to take even one step onto that property;

that's how much the place made you feel as though you weren't even good enough to go there. My best friend's dog went there once, and he got shot just for being in the yard (way down by the pool). The groundskeeper did it. I mean that poor little son-of-a-bitch got gunned down for just running by the bathhouse. One hole, right through his hip; in one side and out the other! So that's how much you didn't want to go too near the place. Pretty exclusive, I guess, and with a really nasty groundskeeper to see that it stayed that way. And yet, as I already told you, I don't think I ever saw anyone there (at least not for long), and I never remember seeing anyone at the pool. Not even "E.H." himself (as everyone called the owner), or any other members of his family. My friend's dog died by the way. That's right; two days after the shooting, the little fucker just rolled over and died.

Nevertheless, the *EH* pool and the surrounding grounds still remained a real fantasyland for me, strange little romantic that I was. It just all seemed so wonderful and "not Washertown" (and even "not Des Moines" either). As I said before, it was Hollywood. I can remember walking by there often, just to look at the beauty of it all. I mean no place I had ever seen, in fact not even in the movies, struck me as being quite so grand and important. There was this magnificent, 1940's two-story red brick (the real smooth kind), Georgian-style house. And it had a real slate roof on it (gray, or perhaps I should say "grey"), not anything like the asphalt shingles on most of Washertown's other houses (or tar paper even). The whole place just sat there (kind of like a symbol for something, I guess)—majestically yet gracefully—down this beautiful, green sloping lawn, with all kinds of really nice trees in front. There were maples for shade, and several tall, stately elms. And in the springtime lilacs and magnolia trees and everything blossomed all over the place. I mean the whole thing was just plain gorgeous. That's the best word for it: gorgeous. The lawn, interrupted only by the gentle curve of the driveway, had a sprinkler system in it too, which was absolutely unheard of in Washertown in the 1940s (except for here and at the *FL* pool, which I'll tell you about later). The little sprinkler things, meaning the "heads" (I didn't even know what to call them when I was little) just sort of "popped up" and sprayed this mist-like, magical water all over the lawn. And I can remember times when I was real little (and big too actually) that I would have given anything to play in it. To just walk through it even. Especially on days when it was really, really hot out. I never did though, since I didn't much like the idea of getting shot and then dying two days later.

The backyard flowed on down from the house and right into really dense, "trimmed real square," and "so green that they almost looked unreal" hedges, that lined the *EH* pool's edge (we are finally at the swimming pool itself). There were squares of real tile all around the pool, and benches to sit on and everything, and a design carved right into the bottom of it (the pool). Again, just like Hollywood or somewhere, only better. And then, *then* there was this big bathhouse (which was bigger even than my mom and dad's real house) built of red brick, with colonial paned windows, and all in the same Georgian style as the big empty house up the hill. And always the "presence" of the pool . . . almost magical . . . smooth as glass, and filled with blue-green water. (At least it looked blue-green.) And then there's something else. I mentioned it just briefly up above, and although you'll probably have a hard time believing it, it really is true. Swear to God it is. So what it was is that not only was the main house that I've been telling you about big and storybook beautiful and like a mansion in Hollywood and everything, but there also was a *twin* house just east of it. Honest. Just like it! Bricks, slate, Georgian style and everything. (No one seemed to live there either.)

But then, to make this whole *EH* thing even more special (as if it wasn't special enough already), both of these houses, *both* of them (no lie), had these big, beautiful, really swanky-looking, green and white striped awnings hanging over every window. *Every* window! First floor *and* second floor. Again, real Hollywood-like. But then (to say just one other thing about no one living there) I do have to tell you that one night (but only one . . . as far as I remember anyway) there was a single light fixture burning in one room of the east house . . . real mysterious-like, and almost creepy even. (I didn't stay and look very long because I actually got kind of scared for some reason.) I still didn't see a person (not even a ghost), only just the light. But anyway, other than that, as I said, no one seemed to live in the east house either. Except for in my own mind. In just my own mind I thought that like maybe Lana Turner lived there. Or Hedy Lamar. Or Ingrid Bergman even (and maybe the other Hollywood ladies I already mentioned up above). Ingrid Bergman, by the way, was really something else. She was from Sweden or somewhere (no kidding), and had a love affair with a guy (an Italian I think) who directed her in a movie called *Stromboli,* or something like that. I think anyway. And I remember for sure that lots of people thought she was a really bad person for what she did. But actually, as far as that goes (and to get back to Washertown), maybe the person in the house was a man. Like Clark Gable or someone (I don't mean to leave the guys out). He would have had a convertible though, and I don't remember seeing a car in the driveway that night. Or maybe it was Joseph Cotton. Or Charlie Chaplin even, although I think he might have been dead. But, swear to God, other than all these people in just my mind, no one seemed to live there. Ever.

You know, now that I think about it more, it may be that the way I felt about these two houses, and the pool, the bathhouse, and the sprinklers and everything, was like what Robert Frost felt when he wrote "Stopping By Woods on a Snowy Evening" (which of course I had never even heard of when I was first experiencing all this stuff). Probably not though. I guess I was just trying to sound grown up. Frost's experience was probably different, although when I finally did read his poem it seemed to me that he might have gotten a little bit carried away (a tendency that he and I, as great writers I guess, share). But anyway, when I was a little boy in Washertown, frost was just frost, as in "Jack," not Robert. It didn't have anything to do with poets. "Jack Frost" was just a "nose nipper," I was told, or something like that (and don't, however, whatever you do, confuse him with "Jack the Ripper" though, who was some really wacked out dead foreigner who didn't like women very much).

Thinking about poems and stuff, I do remember a prayer that was kind of like a poem; I mean it rhymed and everything, and went like this: "Now I lay me down to sleep/I pray the lord my soul to keep/If I should die before I wake/I pray the lord my soul to take." Remember that one? It didn't have anything to do with the *EH* pool or the houses or anything (or Robert Frost). But I just wanted you to know that it wasn't as though I didn't know anything about poems and prayers and stuff when I was little. And I'll tell you something else, if you promise not to spread it around. OK? That little bedtime prayer used to scare the very shit out of me! Really. "If I should die"? *Die?* So what the hell kind of prayer is *that?* I'm supposed to go to bed and think about dying? I mean Jesus! That's really scary. The whole prayer was probably some Methodist plot or something (it's hard for me not to blame some stuff on the Methodists). Well, anyway, that's just something I happened to think about right now. Sorry. And as I just said, it doesn't have anything to do with code *EH*. At least I don't think so. But maybe it does. Goddamnit! It's that "mind thing" beginning to happen again. Let's just keep going.

So anyway, whatever it is that's going on here, just remember that as wonderful as the place seemed to be, and, as I already said, as close to Hollywood as anything in Washertown could get (and probably, as I also already kind of said, as close even as Des Moines could get too), you don't want to set foot on the *EH* property. Any of it. And whatever you do, do not, do *not* go down to the swimming pool. Ever. Unless of course for some reason you want to get shot in the butt doggy style. "If you go into the woods today/You're in for a big surprise." Remember the little song with those words in it? Well then, don't go there. But thinking about Teddy Bears (because of the poem, or song, or whatever it is that I just called to your attention) reminds me that I slept with my Teddy Bear longer than my dad thought I should. Like maybe until I was ten or even eleven maybe. Whatever. It's for sure it was making him (my dad, not my bear) a little bit uncomfortable. But that's another story too. And anyway, my mom finally sent him, i.e. my Teddy Bear, not my dad, to Europe in a World War II care package. To tell you the truth though, I still sometimes miss that little guy. I mean he was always, *always* there for me (even the night my chameleon committed suicide and when the first three of my dogs died). I guess all I can do is hope that he found a good home with some bombed out kid in England or somewhere. And I still can't forget the day my buddy's dog died. It was really sad. He cried. And so did I (but only after I got home and was all by myself). Anyway, I'm kind of getting "loose" in the head again, and I've probably told you enough about code name *EH* (and movie stars, and my buddy's dead dog, and Robert Frost, and Teddy Bears and everything). I didn't mean to get so carried away with talking about all this stuff. I mean this part of my book is supposed to be mostly about swimming pools. Just remember though (one more time), that beautiful as the place designated EH is, you can never really go there (regardless of how much you might want to). Maybe that's kind of like the moral of the story. But by the way (and before we go on), did you know that Teddy Bears were actually named for President Roosevelt (only Theodore this time, not Franklin)? Really.

Code name *FL* was almost as nice as *EH*, but not quite. As I came to find out, however, it had a considerably happier history. The house that went with this pool was also really nice too, but not as grand as the *EH* house(s), even though it also was built of brick, had fancy awnings and sprinklers and everything, and sat on large, well-groomed grounds. Not so Hollywood as *EH*, but again, much friendlier. The *FL* house and pool were also owned (again no surprise) by members of Washertown's first family. I later learned, by the way (which I thought was really neat), after I had grown up and everything, that my very own mother went swimming there, and had even (when she was in high school) posed for a kind of "cheesecake-like" picture on the diving board. She got to do that because her father was the caretaker for the *FL* property (and also for one of the dairy farms that they owned). He of course, my grandfather (and be sure to remember this), wasn't anything like the caretaker for the *EH* property. And it's for sure that he would never shoot anybody . . . especially my best friend's dog. (He might have chopped or pulled off the heads of chickens for Sunday dinner, but he never shot anyone.) So anyway, pool *FL* was a good place, a *very* good place, and I even got to go there once (a story I'll save for later).

There was a high, brick wall that enclosed the *FL* pool, but curiously, the wall was constructed so as to have an occasional brick placed "the long way out" from the rest of the wall. Those bricks, as you might suspect, were all it took to make the wall an irresistible climbing challenge to every little boy in (or out) of the neighborhood. It was almost as though it had been intentionally constructed as a "tease" of some kind. You had to be careful though, since just as it was pretty easy to step on and pull yourself up by these bricks, it was also easy to skin the hell out of your knees if you slipped and fell *down*. Anyway, it didn't seem to me that it was a very smart way to build a wall. By the way, in case you have forgotten (and you probably have), Robert Frost (the "Stopping By Woods on a Snowy Evening" man) also wrote a poem about walls. I won't tell you about it now though, since I already talked some about him. You might already remember his "wall" poem anyway, since it's somewhat better known than the "woods' one is. Or maybe you don't. But that's your problem. Whatever, the last time I started to talk about Mr. Frost was when I got off track and had to sort of "fix" my mind again. So anyway, when I was little I would sneak over to the *FL* pool wall all by myself, climb up *very* carefully (remember I didn't like getting hurt much), and then just hang there, staring over the top, and having kind of an imaginary movie star experience (sort of the same as at the *EH* pool). Like maybe I was even the star who lived there. Then I would climb down, hope no one had seen me, start to feel pretty ordinary, and go home.

Years later, although I maybe shouldn't be telling you this, I got to go to a party at the *FL* pool. It was when the owner's son, who was a pretty nice guy and who (of course) went away to private school in the east (of course), had come home for the summer, although (of course) not for long, and had a pool party. Well, it seemed that everyone who was anyone was invited, and I was too. It was all very nice, except that I was still in my skinny time of life, with yet a few pimples here and there, and exposing myself (if you know what I mean) was not one of my greater pleasures. *And,* the girl who was supposed to be my date for the evening (can't remember her name), with whom I was in love (at least for the night), spent most of the whole goddamn time looking at the biceps, and I suspect everything else that rippled or bulged, on this other guy (who, by the way, was once so *small* that no one thought he would ever grow). Shit! I finally get to experience the Hollywood lifestyle, and this guy is the center of attraction. So there *she* (my girlfriend) is, there *he* (Washertown's Marlon Brando) is, and there I (the handsome guy . . . as long as I had my clothes on) is (i.e. am . . . just trying to be funny). She had some pretty mind-boggling curves herself, by the way (meaning, quite frankly, pretty big tits). He had his big bulging biceps (and as I sort of suggested before, probably a rather decent bulge between his legs). And I (at least it seemed to me) had a protruding Adam's apple (to go with the rest of my physique), a somewhat lesser (but maybe not) bulge, and most likely a pimple or two (with probably at least one really bad one). Some party. But anyway, that's more than I care to recall about code name *FL*, and I really don't want to get wacked out or depressed again. I guess I should have tried harder to stay in love with Janey, and just mess around with her in her mother's (if I could ever get the woman to forgive me) separated-in-the-front (but only slightly), pale pink chenille bathrobe.

Well, I suppose I should go on to the *YMCA* pool (hell-hole that it was), and then I can finish my stories having to do with swimming pools by telling you about a really good place, "the best," and some of the also really good times I had there. And I haven't forgotten the Popsicles. Remember? The title of this whole chapter is "Of Swimming Pools and Popsicles." But I'm saving that part until the end too. Dessert is always better if you clean your plate first, i.e. eat your vegetables and shit. That's what I was told anyway. So . . . about the sinkhole, cesspool, absolute sewer that was called the *Y* pool. It was old, indoors, cracked around the edges, over-chlorinated (I mean it was like some kind of a liquefied gas chamber), and musty smelling, all at the same time. And cold. *Really* cold. *And,* to make it feel even worse, it was downstairs, kind of like in a basement (unless you went in from the alley entrance). Nevertheless, if you went in the usual front way, it was *very* downstairs—long, narrow, precariously steep, concrete stairs. Like there were a hundred of them, it seemed, and all steel edged; so you sure as hell didn't want to *fall* down, unless you preferred to die rather than have to go swimming there (a thought which at times probably ran through my mind).

So anyway, the pool that lay below, as I mentioned before, was so heavily chlorinated that as soon as you began your descent you were hit right in the face (eyes, nose, and mouth . . . maybe even ears) with this really obnoxious, wet-like and probably poisonous, "burny" stench. And in the dead of winter, the only time that even a swim freak would think of going to this pool (except for junior high gym class, when you *had* to), it was really, *really* bad. That was because the radiators that kept frost from forming on the locker room walls and everything made it even more obnoxiously wet and toxic, and way *way* too hot as well. It all made you feel as though you were being soaked clear through in a kind of heated, gaseous brine. Really, it was goddamn awful, and a grim reminder that the greenish-looking water that awaited you was going to burn the eyeballs right out of your fucking head, *and* the hair (wherever you might have it . . . and for me that meant not yet in some of the places where I wanted it) right off your whole fucking body. During gym class, by the way, this whole area was "presided over" by a gym teacher/coach that most of us thought was a real butthole (being a butthole, you may recall, my buddies and I thought anyway, was even worse than being an asshole). Whatever. "Coach" Mydol's attitude toward non-athletic kids only made the entire gym class ordeal at the *Y* pool worse.

So anyway, once you got down the stairs, the next thing you had to contend with in this hellhole was the locker room. This so-called "dressing area," including the floor, walls, ceilings, toilets, and benches was always, *always* wet and slimy. *Everything.* And of course when you took your clothes off, you ended up having to sit on one of the goddamn wet benches (God only knew whose pimply butt had been there just before yours). Then there were the toilet seats. The "shitters," as we called them. They were even wetter than the benches (probably from having been peed all over, as well as from the pervasive "room sweat"), so you didn't even *think* about sitting on one of those babies. I mean you'd be inclined to fill your pants or choke on it before you sat there. The ceiling, by the way (no kidding), was so wet that it literally dripped huge, hot drops of water on you (bacteria-saturated nodules of some shit-like substance, I'm sure) that had been hanging on the ceiling for hours, just waiting for you to walk under it. The one *good* thing about this pool, however (as if it was going to really make a difference), was that it could be used by everyone, just like all the other stuff at the *Y* (once you had a membership). Therefore, if you had aspirations to be a "real" man, you could make use of everything there as part of your daily training program or whatever. I guess anyway. And especially, as I said, during the winter. So, being somewhat eager to make the transition from boy to man, I did actually go there (i.e. to the *Y* itself, not the pool) a few times when I didn't have to, although I usually just stayed upstairs and played ping pong or something. But mostly, believe me, I would go there (at least to the pool itself) only when I absolutely had to, which meant during junior high school, when you didn't have any choice (it was part of gym class, as I said a little while ago). Junior high of course was when you would do just about anything to start becoming like one of the big guys (in more ways than one), although I didn't think going to that goddamn pool should have had to be part of the program. Whatever.

The *very* worst thing about code *YMCA* however (and you probably thought you had heard it all), was that you had to swim naked.

That's right. Naked. Stark naked! The ancient Greeks and Romans (especially the athletes, so I had read) did a lot of stuff naked (although some of the "stuff," again as I also read, was probably not exactly what the YMCA people might have had in mind); so anyway I guess the Board of Directors (or whatever they were called) of the Young Men's Christian Association thought that we should too (i.e. do stuff naked). Well, swim anyway. Maybe they thought it would kind of balance things out between pagans and Christians or something. I don't know. Maybe though. Anyway, it was no swimsuits. None. Spring, summer, fall, or winter even (although I guess swimming naked in cold water feels about the same, regardless of the season).

The only thing that I can figure out, now that I look back on it, is that this naked business was actually some kind of a plot, a heartless, devious plot—like a sinister plan that most likely had been designed by some strange person or persons (Jehovah's Witness's perhaps, or maybe a group of deranged and institutionalized Methodists who were also somehow involved with a few flesh-eating, blood-drinking, and also deranged Roman Catholics or something). Whatever. The "plot" or plan (at least as I have tried to understand it) had to have been the work of some really sick and evil people who were determined to actually shatter a lot of fragile young male egos (while enlarging a few others), and most of all see to it in general that kids who were pretty much unsure of themselves, and perhaps somewhat (to a lot maybe) undersized (generally and in particular), or maybe uncircumcised (which meant they looked pretty different from most kids in Washertown in the 1940s) feel like shit! Total shit! Like horse shit. And cow shit. And dog shit. (And diarrhea shit even.) All mixed together. That's the kind of shit and plot it was. (That was also another one of those sort of convoluted sentences that I told you about before.) Or maybe there wasn't really a plot after all. Perhaps I just got a little bit carried away there. I don't know. But maybe I did. I'm not paranoid or anything though . . . I mean I'm not paranoid or anything though (I just thought I should say that twice). And as far as that goes, i.e. the idea of a plot (and maybe being a tiny bit paranoid too), it could have even been the Jews who devised the plan (if there was one of course), since they didn't go there, meaning to the YMCA (because of the "C" part), although I think they could have . . . at least as guests. And they of course wouldn't have had to worry about the uncircumcised thing (issue) if they did go. But I'm kind of feeling a little bit confused here, and to tell you the truth maybe even sort of worried again about the way my mind works sometimes. So I think I'll just go on. As I said a long time ago, there are times when that's all you can do (meaning just "go on"). You probably already know that from some of the shit in your own life. So anyway, you'll just have to trust me. It was not real pleasant (at least not for most of us) to get naked and swim at the *YMCA* pool. I guess maybe for the few "early developers" it might have been. But not for the rest of us it wasn't.

To totally finish up here though, so I can completely get on with other stuff, the "everyone naked policy" at the *YMCA* pool, at least as I saw it (plot or not), at the very least served to increase the risk of your having certain body parts burned out by the over-chlorinated water, or frozen off by its coldness. The *burning* of body parts actually got underway, as I already pretty much told you, as soon as you began your descent down the stairs. But it got worse of course when you actually got in the water. That's when the "deep" burn started. Especially if you forgot and opened your eyes under water. The *freezing* problem was what you encountered after having been in the icy water for just a few minutes longer. Because now, as if it weren't enough to have had your eyeballs *burned out* from the chlorine, your other ones, meaning your other balls (i.e. your "nuts," if that's OK) would seemingly have been *frozen off* (i.e. they would have "retreated" and sometimes seemingly *vanished* even). That's how cold the goddamn water was! So how about that? Vanishing testicles!

But even *more* scary (and humiliating as well), you had to watch, actually *watch*, as the very most prized of *all* your body parts (like all two inches) shrank away to almost nothing! And right before your eyes (if of course you could still see). I mean it was totally fucking frightening! (*Fucking* is the only word that works here.) But then finally, as if all this other stuff wasn't bad enough, there was yet one more humiliation to be endured. The high school lifeguards (also naked, of course), and always better built and endowed (especially when you were only in seventh or eighth grade), mostly just walked around the edge of the pool and yelled at you for one thing or another. They, probably more than somewhat concerned about their own "manhood" (meaning in fact of course the size of their goddamn dicks), never

ever went into that eyeball-burning, ball-vanishing, dick-shrinking sea of arctic water. Oh no; they just paraded around. So I mean Jesus! Who needed that shit? I know I didn't. But anyway, so much for the *Young* (most of them) *Men's* (some of them) *Christian* (at least a few of them) *Association* and its goddamn swimming pool. And, by the way, regardless of what *they* called the organization, or thought about it, I have to tell you, there were times when the place seemed a lot more pagan to me than Christian. At least down in that chlorinated hellhole of a swimming pool it did. And you know what? I'll bet most of us could have become pretty good men without even going there. And for sure, for some of us anyway, with a lot less grief.

So, on we go to one of the very best and happiest places in all of Washertown. (And I still haven't forgotten the Popsicles.) This *best* place, this *very* best place (if "bestest" were a word I'd say it right here) was code name *MPP*. And believe me, there just aren't enough really good words to describe it and all the fun I had there. In fact, although I can't actually prove it, *MPP* was probably one of the most best places in the whole world. (I would say universe even, but I don't want to sound like I'm exaggerating or bragging too much or anything.) But I'm telling you, this pool had to have been the world's "eighth wonder." So anyway, *MPP* was named for one of the very finest and most generous members of Washertown's first family, and it was located in the very best part of the very best public park anywhere. Ever. (I know I'm saying "very" a lot, and "best" and everything, but that's because I have to, since all this stuff is really true.) So anyway, *MPP* was Washertown's only public pool, meaning that anyone could go there (although you probably already knew that that's what *public* means). However, it was actually kind of private too, since the first family had given it to Washertown and had endowed its maintenance and everything. Forever. That's how generous they were. So, for just four dollars you could get a "season pass" to go there anytime you wanted to (i.e. all summer long). And trust me, it was worth it. I mean it was like having a pass to paradise (although again I don't mean to brag or anything). Your very own ticket to warm summer sun (sometimes pretty hot though), clear, cold water, and really, really good times. The annual opening of *MPP*, a lot of us thought anyway, and especially when we were real little, was next in importance only to Christmas morning. And maybe not even next, but actually the same. That's how fantastic it was. I mean, Christmas morning, even if you kind of tried to stretch it out, only lasted about three hours; *MPP* lasted a full three months!

Opening day at *MPP* was always on Memorial Day, unless there was a tornado predicted, or maybe it could be proven somehow (and it never was . . . and I'm just kidding of course) that the Jehovah's Witness's bullshit about the end of the world was about to come true. Once open, the season went through all of June, all of July, and most of August (until just a few days before school started). And believe me, it was a sad day in Washertown when that piece of paradise closed for the season (sort of like the kids in "Mudville" felt . . . I think anyway, if you remember that story). I mean the place was just that wonderful! And since it was public and everything (as I already told you), no one had to be rich or be a movie star or anything to have something to do all summer. All you needed was twenty cents a day (or your four dollar pass) and a swimsuit! Which is to say there was none of that *YMCA* "let's get naked" shit going on at this place. (Although since girls went there too, it might have been kind of a nice opportunity to see some things.) Whatever.

But speaking of girls, if you were one (although my buddies and I were totally glad we weren't), you also had to wear a rubber "bathing" cap" with a chin strap on it, which (both the hat and strap) kind of took something away from the look most of Washertown's local "bathing beauties" had in mind. The caps made their heads look sort of like bullets, and if they were too tight they also made their cheeks sort of puffy-looking around the edges (like a gold fish looks when it seems to kind of "blow itself up" and then stick its face right against the bowl). I think the reason they had to wear those caps was to keep them from getting sucked into the drain by their hair. Something like that anyway. Also, if you were a girl (although I maybe don't need to say this), there were some days you couldn't go swimming at all. That was because of something people called "the curse," or something like that (I learned about what it really was later, and I might add, kind of the hard way). Whatever. I guess girls had it pretty bad in some ways. But let's just get back to the pool itself.

The setting of *MPP* was the greatest you can imagine. It was right in the very center of the whole park, nestled down in a green "hollow," in front of a two-level, red brick (the smooth kind) bathhouse, with a genuine slate roof (just like at the *EH* bathhouse). The building sort of bent around the west end of the pool, and rose up from the concrete deck that bordered the shallow end (which had a really neat "kiddies" wading area with a tubular iron fence around it). The "fence" was sort of like a corral fence, now that I think about it. Anyway, the whole place, both the pool and the bathhouse, was surrounded by these big beautiful oak trees, along with some maples and elms, and maybe other kinds of trees that I didn't even know the names of. There were also lots of bushes that I didn't know the names of either. And green, green grass.

Tickets, ice cream, popcorn, candy, and Popsicles (ahah! . . . be patient . . . we're going to get to the Popsicles pretty soon now) were all for sale on the upper level, which you walked right into from the circular drive that marked the front entrance. And right over that arching entrance, in great big, kind of chrome-like (but not real shiny) letters was the name of the Washertown first family man who had provided all this. His first name (at least as the sign read) was Fred. Just plain Fred, which said a lot about the kind of person he was. And I think probably the letters weren't shiny because the first family didn't like to be too flashy. Always present, but not flashy. And then also on this upper level (this place had absolutely everything) there was a screened-in area where you could sit and talk with your friends, and avoid the flies. There were lots of flies in Washertown, so that part of the place was a really good thing. And, when you got a little older, you could sit there and just look at the girls without flies. I don't mean that some of the girls themselves had flies, but just that once again the screened in area didn't have any (I mean what kind of a person would accuse girls of having flies?). Anyway, downstairs were the dressing rooms, showers and that kind of stuff. So, as I said, *MPP* simply had it all. And as I already kind of said before (when I was maybe bragging just a little bit), I'll bet there wasn't another place like it anywhere else in the world. Not even in Des Moines (although there was a place there called Birdland in Des Moines that had a pool with a really high diving board). But, back to Washertown's own paradise.

The pool itself was emerald green, just like in the "technicolor" movies (or so it seemed anyway, especially when you looked real far down into the "deep end"); and the pool was "emerald cut" too (no kidding . . . that was the shape it was . . . just like a really fancy ring or something). And then, right in the center of it, was this huge, plastered, concrete pedestal, over the top of which poured icy cold water on the hottest July and August afternoons. *And,* and this was one of the most special things you could ever imagine, up from the center of that same oasis of a pedestal rose a massive, majestic even, really tall (like a hundred feet, or maybe even a thousand, when I was really little), shiny steel pole, topped off by four big round "flood lights" that lighted up that whole entire pool at night. (I'll bet you could probably even see those lights all the way to Des Moines; that's how tall the pole was and how bright the lights were.) There were also lights in the deep end of the pool, recessed into the walls. And I'm telling you it was really something to see all those lights on, although I didn't go swimming very often at night. (It never quite seemed right to me to be there without the sun.)

And now (drum roll and trumpets please), let me tell you this. I mean this was truly the real "topper." So anyway, even though all the other stuff about *MPP* was really wonderful and everything, this was even "wonderfuller," like grand and glorious and everything all stuck together! (I knew even when I was little that *wonderfuller* wasn't a word, by the way, but it's OK to say it because of what I'm telling you about.) Anyway, right in front of the beautiful, red (smooth) brick *MPP* bathhouse building, and in the very center of a really nice and real green grassy area, with a big circular driveway all around it, stood another tall, shiny steel pole, only this one also had a big, polished gold ball on the top of it. *Really* big, and right on the very top! And flying from this pole, and I do mean *flying,* like with all the pride in the whole world and everything, was this great big (and I mean really, *really* great big), like gigantic almost, American flag. A bigger than big, and beautifuller (kind of like "wonderfuller") than beautiful, "flappy" American flag. I mean each one of that flag's thirteen stripes was a foot wide (at least I thought so anyway, and maybe even wider when I was really, *really* little). And every one of its forty-eight stars was bigger than a baseball (maybe a softball even). And sometimes when the wind blew real hard, like really, really hard, you could hear that flag flap all over the whole park. Well, almost anyway. At least I heard it. I mean the stars and stripes of that all-American banner were just what they were supposed to be: bigger and better and more beautiful than life itself. And there they were, smack dab in the heart of 1940s Washertown. Actually, in the heart of the whole United States even.

And that flag of ours was made of the reddest red, and the whitest white, and the bluest blue you can ever imagine. Like bluer than the sky even, like it's coming right out of heaven or something. And that flag was never worn. Never frayed. Always clean. And always *there!* *Always* there (except of course for when it rained). You could just count on it. I mean it was really something. The whole United States of America, *right there in front of you!* Sometimes even it almost seemed like those thirteen stripes were there (at least I thought) to just wrap you up and hold you tight. And the forty-eight stars to light your way to anywhere you wanted to go! And you should have seen that beauty at night, when a great big spotlight and some extra floodlights were blazing all up from and around it! Man was that ever beautiful! Better than fireworks at the State Fair even. And believe me, no one had to tell people in Washertown why Francis Scott Key had written "The Star Spangled Banner," Or Katherine Lee Bates a song called "America the Beautiful," Or Irving Berlin "God Bless America" (for Kate Smith to sing). That's for sure! You just knew. In your own heart, and sometimes even with a tear in your eye, you just knew!

And then on Thursday nights . . . wow, you just can't believe how really grand and exciting and everything this was . . . on Thursday night, *every* Thursday night, *all* through the whole summer, you could look at that big flappy flag seemingly floating over the whole park (maybe the whole world even), as you sat and listened to the Washertown Community Band playing patriotic songs, like John Philip Sousa's "Stars and Stripes Forever" and stuff. The summer concerts were played from the stage of what was called "The Band Shell," which was just a short distance from the pool; and, like the bathhouse over at the pool, had the name of that same Washertown first family man arching over the front of it (just "Fred" again, and then his last name). And I'm telling you, when that fantastically boomy and brassy band (with lots and lots of snare drum and cymbal sounds) opened the evening with "The Star Spangled Banner," you were up and on your feet and with your hand over your heart in less than an instant! *Everyone* stood. *Everyone* sang. Some people even cried, which made me feel kind of sad. I think a lot of them were crying because someone they knew or loved was fighting or had died in World War II or something. But anyway, you just can't believe how wonderful and "just right" patriotic it all was. And then, maybe for real, or maybe because you just thought it was real, you could once in awhile (even over the sound of the band) hear the reassuring flapping of that great big beautiful flag. I mean I'd give anything if you could have been there. It was one of those experiences when you learned "flat out" what it meant to get "goose-bumps" all over your body, I'll tell you that!

And then to just kind of top things off (although of course this was just sort of an "extra," meaning that it wasn't nearly as important or anything as the flag, or the band, or "The Star Spangled Banner"), there was a popcorn wagon on wheels sitting right there in the parking lot by the Band Shell. It sold peanuts and candy and ice cream bars too. And absolutely everything on that wagon, *everything* (but especially the fresh, hot pop popcorn of course), smelled really good. Just like it was supposed to. I mean, if you kind of stuck you face down right over the place where they had the candy and stuff, you could even smell the black in the "Black Jack," and the fruit in the Wrigley's "Juicy Fruit" gum. They even had "Teaberry"! And of course Popsicles, soon to be our subject. Whatever. It just doesn't get much better than that!

But back to the pool itself. In the shallow end (as I told you before), was a wading area for real little kids and babies and stuff. I remember my mother sitting with me there when I was little (like four or five maybe). It had metal guardrails around it, kind of like a two-rail corral fence (which I also said), so that some dumb little kid wouldn't go out too far and get lost or drown himself or something (which would probably have meant that they would have had to shut the whole pool down for a while, or maybe for a whole day even). Anyway, after that (the corral) there was this stretch of sort of but not very deeper water, and then you got to the pedestal and light pole where it was pretty much deeper, and then you got to the completely "deep end." And I mean *really* deep, deep end! It said right on the edge of the pool that it was ten feet deep! But I thought (at least when I was little I did) that it was probably more like *fifty* feet deep. And maybe it was too. (And maybe there was even an octopus living on the bottom.) You had to cross "the ropes," which were suspended by big, bullet-shaped wooden "floats," to get to the deep end; and you couldn't even go there unless you first proved to the lifeguard that you could swim across the whole pool. That's right, the whole pool; and that was pretty tough. Trust me. And there were always at least two lifeguards, one on each side, sitting in chairs up on poles so they could see everything. If they caught you trying to go into the deep end without permission they would kick you out (at least that's what they said they would do). Whatever. That was enough to make me stay out (but then, along with the rest of my "good little boy" crap, I was always one to play by the rules).

Then, at the very, very far end of *MPP* there were three diving boards. Two "low" boards, and one really scary high one, that the big kids always dared the little kids to go off of, so they could maybe watch them get hurt and stuff. The high one was ten feet, they said, but again, I'll bet it was more like fifty. I jumped off once without holding my nose shut, and thought it (the inside of my nose) would never stop stinging. I mean I thought my head was going to blow off or something. Like for ten minutes I thought that. I cried even. And man, I never did that again, I'll tell you that! But anyway (to get back to the pool itself), all around the pool people sat or lay on their towels, forming little "friendship groups" on the usually burny-hot, concrete deck. Sometimes, if you walked by a really pretty girl spread out on her towel (or one with big tits, even if she wasn't real pretty), you sort of hesitated as though you were thinking about turning around or something. That way she didn't know (you thought anyway) that you were really just stopping to stare at her. So anyway, as you can see, even just walking around the deck at *MPP* was pretty special. Actually getting there, however (i.e. getting into the pool itself), was another story. Listen to this . . .

First of all I should say, as eventually we all find out, that even the very best and most funnest (another word that should be OK) places often have something that isn't real good about them. I mean "that's life," as all my teachers and my mom and my dad and other smart people would say. I just thought I should tell you that before I tell you this next part. OK? (*MPP* was still the best of all places though.) So anyway, this is the part that wasn't so fun. Everyday, just before one o'clock, the area around the ticket window of *MPP* (but just on the boy's side) would get super crowded and pushy and everything. That's because some guys always wanted to be the very first ones in the pool. So tempers would sometimes get pretty much out of control (meaning some guys got pissed off pretty easily), which is to say you could once in a while get the shit kicked out of you by the bigger guys, if you weren't careful. Anyway, as it got closer to the time to open (that's one o'clock, as I said up above), everyone got more and more excited, and the older guys would start to sort of bend their knees just a little, as if they were getting "set" at a track meet, or ready for "take off" or something. Some of them (mostly only the older guy probably) maybe even started to sweat, for all I know. Whatever. I hated that part of getting into the pool (not just the sweat part, but the whole thing), because everyone just got more and more pushy and everything. And then, with the mob at its turbulent worst, you'd hear this little clicking sound from the other side (a lifeguard was unlocking the place), the oak-stained double doors would swing open, and the "run" would begin. (There weren't any bulls behind us, but there might as well have been.) Whatever. *MPP* was open for the day!

So, through the doors you went, and as fast as you could possibly go (you didn't have any choice unless you wanted to get trampled to death), down some really smooth, waxed, concrete stairs. (If you were lucky, you managed to hold on to the life-saving, shiny chrome handrail.) Miraculously though, in all these runs, I can't remember one serious fall by anyone. But anyway, it was down several stairs, onto the "landing," then a ninety-degree left turn, and on down more really smooth and waxed concrete stairs to "the window." The window was actually a large opening in the wall, with a cold (regardless of how hot the day was) and sort of damp-feeling chrome countertop, on which you tapped your season ticket (or your "single," if that's all you had), and groped and fought to grab a wire mesh basket, which was literally thrown at you or bounced across the countertop by some asshole of a lifeguard who was on "inside duty." It always seemed to me that they could have been nicer about it. I mean I didn't see any reason for all the yelling and throwing things around and everything. And I absolutely hated all the pushing and shoving and grabbing and stuff. Jesus wouldn't have liked it either (at least not according to what I had been taught at the First Methodist Church Sunday School he wouldn't have), but of course he never went swimming there. And if he had, he probably would have just walked across everything (including of course the pool itself).

But anyway, whether Jesus had ever been there or not, it wasn't very Christian behavior that was going on down there, I'll tell you that! And now that I think about it more (although I don't mean to digress too much), it would have been really neat though if Jesus *had* shown up there (maybe even with a season pass and everything), since he could have taught *everyone* how to walk across the pool, deep end and all; and that way we wouldn't have had to prove to the lifeguards that we could swim. But I guess it's pretty dumb of me to even think about stuff like that. (And it could make my mind get sort of "off" again too, so we better just move right along.) Keep in mind though (you know, sort of "just for the hell of it," as went another expression that we used a lot and for everything when I was little), that if Jesus had not only *gone* there, but had actually *worked* there ("inside duty"), he would never have thrown a metal basket at you. But again, it's pretty dumb of me to keep talking about these things. I mean none of this Jesus stuff would have even been possible. He died in 0033 (that's what I was taught anyway, although I don't think I've ever seen it written like that), and *MPP* wasn't even built until 1935.

Anyway, next, after having it (your basket) thrown at you, you jammed your fingers through the wire mesh, so no one else could grab it from you, and then, telling the bigger guys to leave you alone, you fought your way into the dressing room (actually "un" dressing room when you first got there, and then dressing room when you got out of the pool and had to go home . . . but you know what I mean). Anyway, a few words about the dressing room. It had a slick, concrete floor (smooth and waxy again), only it was now wet (everything down there was always wet), and the whole place was just a little bit smelly . . . but not enough to matter of course. The "wet factor" meant that when you got in there you had to sit down on a wooden bench that was always wet too (and felt especially funny on your bare butt). But that was OK. The excitement about getting into the pool itself made it worth it, and besides, this was only the beginning of the daily ritual (the *traumatic* daily ritual, when you were little) that you had to go through to actually get into the pool itself.

So, clothes off and into the basket. "Will the big guys make fun of me?" "Why am I still skinnier than any of my friends (than *everyone*, as a matter of fact)?" Oh well. I just reminded myself that all people are pretty much the same (basically anyway), if you really think about it. You know one head, two arms, etc. And I shouldn't have been so self-conscious anyway. So, as I said, clothes off, wad them up, stuff them into the basket, and now its time to head for the next stop. But don't forget to put the plastic band with the number tag on it around your wrist (or ankle, if you want to be like the big guys). It has to match up with the little tin number on the basket or you'll never get your clothes back when you get out. OK? Now run, naked, swimming suit in hand, back to the basket window. Slide your basket across the counter top, and head on into the shower room. The floors are really *really* wet (and waxy) in the shower room of course (and they slope toward the middle), so be careful! I mean who the hell wants to slip and fall on his skinny little ass right in front of everyone else (especially in front of the older kids, like the junior high guys and everything)? Can't you just see it? Some sissy-shit kid, flat on his back in the trough under the showerheads, hurting so much that he can't stand it, but determined to never, *ever* cry. Even if his fucking head (whoops) had actually broken open from the fall, or had blown up from all the pressure and everything . . . and therefore there were brains and blood and shit everywhere. Anyway, shower on (when you were little you had to jump up to pull the chain that turned it on, and therefore you once more had to be extremely careful, or you could slip and fall on your ass).

OK. Now squirt some soap out of the chrome, wall dispenser, and try to make some suds. Of course the "inside" asshole lifeguard guy who is peering over the wet counter top starts to yell at you some more: "Shower with those suits *off*, you guys! Yeah, you, or you're out of here before you even get in!" Again, I just don't know *why* they had to yell all the time. As I said before, I hated that. It made me feel bad, and maybe sort of nervous-like, even though *I* (the good little boy) hadn't done anything wrong. And of course no one else even gave a shit whether the fucking lifeguard yelled or not. But really, shouldn't that basket boy (that was a good name for him I thought) know that I'm an unusually nice little boy who always does the right thing? I guess he had never had a conversation with my mom, or my Sunday School teachers, or my real teachers, or all the other people who knew me and thought I was nice. Anyway, all the yelling and shit really made me upset. But this, however, was still not the worst "not-fun" part of getting into the pool.

So here we go. Showers off. Swim suits on. And the "lineup" begins. The next and (thank God) last thing you had to do to finally get into the pool itself was to go through this unbelievably complex and scary looking (to a little kid anyway) "needle shower" sort of contraption. The needle shower contained really freezing, high-pressure water that shot out of ten zillion little bitty holes that had been drilled into four or five strategically placed shiny chrome pipes. It must have been the coldest goddamn water in the world (except maybe for the *YMCA* pool). I mean it was like water that was going to be ice in the next ten seconds (or maybe just five even). Whatever. The chrome (steel?) shower pipes themselves had been installed in a really narrow, high-walled, yellowy brick, hall-like passageway that was about ten feet long (or maybe a hundred, when you were little). And the scariest thing was that when you went through this alley of agony (like torture chamber) you had to straddle a center pipe that was about two feet high. That meant, at least if you knew yet what it felt like to have your foot slip off a pedal and therefore crash full force onto the center bar of your bicycle—thus smashing your goddamn balls—that you straddled the pipe carefully. *Very* carefully. I mentioned once before about getting your balls crushed. And man, it was just *not* something you wanted to have happen. Ever.

So anyway, as you would try to walk (or maybe run), with that center pipe between your legs (actually you would just sort of waddle, since when you were maybe only five or six your little legs were too short to run and the pipe would be kind of brushing against your also little dick), sharp needles of ice water would shoot out from the goddamn thing right up between your legs and everywhere. And I mean *everywhere.* It was torture. Sheer torture. And at the same time your were waddling, other needles were shooting at you (piercing your very body) from two other pipes that were mounted on the sides of the walls. These "needle weapons" were, by design I guess, about armpit high (for a big person), so that meant that they shot you right in the face when you were little. You think *that* didn't hurt? I mean Jesus! And there were at least ten (it seemed like fifty, as I said before) feet of these pipes and shit! So, let me put this needle shower experience all together for you. There's a smooth, waxy, concrete floor under you (already all wet of course), dangerously slanted toward the middle (forming a trough under the center, "between-your-legs" pipe) . . . shiny, yellowish brick walls on both sides of you with two more pipes (almost like in a prison) . . . and, an ominous-looking (although I didn't know that word yet), gray, concrete ceiling, dripping ice water on you from someone else's earlier run. Goddamn scary; that's what it was. Goddamn scary! I mean why the hell anyone thought all this shit was necessary is a mystery to me.

But anyway, your turn in the shower line finally comes. And here's how it goes. The inside, basket-hurling, asshole (maybe even butthole . . . yeah, probably butthole) lifeguard guy yells at you (they *always* yelled), "GO!" And you do, to the clank of the lever he activates to start this fucking (sorry again), icy-needle torture tunnel. "DON'T RUN!" Goddamnit, he's yelling again! Jesus Christ! I mean this is total chaos. Anyway, blinded by all the goddamn water in your face, already half frozen, and being stung to shit, you nevertheless try to move as *slowly* as you can (so as not to fall or be yelled at even more), straddling the dick-rubbing, potentially ball crushing, center needle shower pipe. But then at least, *then,* you are almost there! Only one more obstacle to go (but this one doesn't even matter). So catch your breath from the shower run, and then take a quick left, jump out the door and into the square rubber box with the white, cloudy, "milk-in-water-looking" stuff (intended to disinfect your feet), and you're "home free." There it is. I mean *there* it is! *MPP* in all its glory! Emerald green. Emerald cut. And cool, clear, and sparkling under the noonday sun. Wow! Absolutely beautiful, and yours for the rest of the afternoon. And tomorrow? You guessed it. Tomorrow the whole routine starts all over again!

Before leaving ("all good things must come to an end," as they say), although I don't want to spoil the mood here, there's one thing more I should tell you. I want you to keep in mind that if you have to pee in an hour or two or three (and you probably will), I suggest that you pee in the pool, since if you go back inside you have to go through this whole goddamn shower thing all over again. OK? So just remember that. And don't feel guilty; we all did it. But anyway, you've survived being yelled at by an asshole, probably being picked on by some other asshole (or holes), and being "baptized by injection" in

that stupid, *stupid* goddamn needle shower. So enjoy the
while you do, it's also kind of fun to think that your own re
decontaminated feet, just like the feet of the big guys who jum
into and out of the rubber box fungus trap before you, are no long
subject to "athlete's foot." Indeed, they are now the feet, the clean
feet, of an athlete. Just like the feet of the high school "jocks" and
lifeguards. Maybe the feet even of a future Olympic swimmer (well . . .
maybe). But I mean how does *that* make you feel? And anyway, as I
said up above, the day has begun. *MPP*, which is to say "the world
in all its glory," is spread out before you. So have fun. And by the
way, I dare you to jump off the high board! If you do though, be sure
to hold your nose. As I told you, it can really sting if you don't.

And now, *now* (another drum roll please), about the Popsicles.
As you may recall (or perhaps not), this chapter in my little story
about Washertown is entitled "Of Swimming Pools and Popsicles."
And that's because there really was, for me anyway, a very real and
important connection between swimming pools, especially *MPP* of
course, and two thin flat "sticks" with pretty hard but sort of mushy,
flavored ice on them. My "kind of like an obsession," I guess, all
began, I think anyway, in the summer of 1944, at the chrome-
topped refreshment counter at *MPP*, where I bought my very first
one (Popsicle). It was orange flavored (the traditional best seller).
Popsicles had been hard to get during the war, i.e. World War II, along
with a lot of other really good stuff, like Hershey bars and Fleer's
"Double Bubble" bubble gum, so getting one (a Popsicle) seemed
pretty special. Not that anyone should actually have felt deprived
or anything. I mean our soldiers were dying all over the world, and
we should complain because we couldn't get Popsicles? That would
have been pretty shitty. That's for sure. But anyway, from the very
first Popsicle I bought, I absolutely loved the things. Perhaps even
unnaturally so. But maybe not. I don't know. I do know that for my
age (six or seven), I had a fairly long history of liking ice. It began
with what I could beg from the neighborhood iceman (neighborhoods
still had guys who delivered ice when I was little, like a toddler
maybe . . . and we also had a milkman). But that's another story.
Anyway, from my first piece of ice (read that carefully, i.e. piece of
ice), to the Kool-Aid pops my mom would make in a green rubber
ice cube tray (each little cube had a toothpick frozen in it so you

. grape ones were the best), to real Popsicles,
~~~g on frozen stuff. I used to even "saw" strips
off the whole chunk (Birdseye Foods, a pretty
~ then, sold frozen applesauce in square, flat
s of frozen foods).

~~~ the real thing. The first one I ever had (i.e. my first
~~~sicle), as I told you up above, was an orange one; but then other flavors too, like cherry, grape, banana, and root beer began to appear, and, as a matter of fact, in just that order. One summer they even made chocolate ones, but they weren't very good. At least I didn't think so. Too watery or something. And besides, if you had wanted something cold and chocolaty you bought a Fudgesicle. Anyway, as any real Popsicle lover would tell you, the original orange was always the best. And to tell you the truth (as I always almost do), I think I was actually addicted to those things (especially to the orange ones of course), maybe even until I was about twelve or so and started thinking about cigarettes. Cigarettes are yet another story, however, and at this point I only want to make sure you understand more about how good the Popsicles were when I was little, *and* why they were so important to me.

See, Popsicles, when I was a boy, sort of stood for everything that was right about America. In their own way they did, anyway. And not just Washertown and Iowa, but everywhere. I mean they were exceptionally well made, priced right, and even good for you (maybe). At least you could tell yourself they were. The way they were made is a lot of why I want to tell you about them, I guess. I mean it was almost as though each one was inspected before it went into the little bag it came in. Talk about pride of workmanship! I mean Popsicle makers were like craftsmen. So anyway, each one had *two* sticks (kind of like little flat "paddles," or, although not as wide, sort of like the sticks the doctor used to hold your tongue down when he wanted you to say, "aah"). Trust me, I'm talking about "quality control" here, as in the kind of quality everyone expected in American products.

As far as I can remember, all the Popsicles were made, at least the ones you bought in Washertown, by the Beatrice Foods Company in Des Moines. And believe me, they weren't at all like the sloppy, malformed things you get now. Each half, *each half,* with its own paddle stick planted firmly and squarely in the middle, had no less than eight sides. Really. *Eight* sides. (I've been just a little obsessive-compulsive all my life—although I didn't know that when I was little—so that's how I can remember about the eight sides and everything.) I suppose the obsessive-compulsive stuff was probably an outgrowth of some of the other mind problems that I've already told you about (maybe more times than I should have). But so what. Anyway, get this. Four sides of the eight sides of each half of these things (the Popsicles from Beatrice Foods) were slightly wider, with the other four not so wide and formed to be kind of like slanted "corners." Altogether then, when you bought just one Popsicle (whatever flavor it was . . . it didn't matter), you got the paper bag it came in (which was white and had red and blue colored dots on it that you could save up for prizes, meaning the whole bag, not just the dots . . . although I didn't because they were always sticky and stuff and I didn't like sticky). And as I already told you, you got *two* sticks to hold onto, and then the *two* identical *eight*-sided halves. That made for a grand total, by the way, of *sixteen* sides you got to suck (you always sucked some of the "juice" out before biting it, unless you got really carried away and couldn't wait any longer or something). I mean can you believe it? Sixteen sides? I was always pretty good at arithmetic, so I'm pretty sure that sixteen was the right number. When you first bought the Popsicle, by the way, you blew into the bag, one really big breath all at once, and the bag popped right away from it (i.e. from the Popsicle itself), although how hard to blow took a little practice. And sometimes the bag got stuck or ripped or something. But that didn't matter. At least not very much. The Popsicle itself was still good.

So anyway (is this really neat or what?), the two halves of the Popsicle were held together by what (you're going to love this part) could have been called, maybe by adult Popsicle aficionados, or cult groups, or clubs at least (of which actually and of course there were none), the "popsicle collosum," as in "corpus collosum," which as you may or may not know (and probably you don't) is what holds together the two sides of your brain . . . and cat and dog brains, and I guess maybe other brains too. (That was another of my probably I guess kind of too long sentences.) Whatever. Of course when I was little I didn't even know what a corpus collosum or anything like that was. I only learned about brains and stuff when I got older and went to college, and then went to graduate school, and then became a psychologist. A clinical psychologist is what I was actually, although my friends for some reason liked to say "clinical psychopath" instead of clinical psychologist. But I think they were just kidding. (Why am I telling you this?) And now it kind of feels as though I told you that already. Like maybe way back in another chapter. Did I? Well, anyway . . .

Anyway, a good clean whack on the fragile connecting band of the Popsicle (the "popsicle collosum," if you think that's kind of neat to say) and you ended up with two separate, self-contained halves, just as surely as you would end up with two separate, self-contained halves of a brain if you whacked through the corpus collosum in someone's head . . . or if you whacked a cat's head, or a dog's head, or some other head . . . which you probably wouldn't be inclined to do though, so just forget it. Of course I would never want to do that either (meaning be a "brain whacker"). By the way, if you didn't do it right (i.e. whack the Popsicle with just the right amount of pressure), it would break off funny, and you couldn't eat the broken part very well. That's because sometimes the broken part would slip out of your fingers or something and you would lose it (meaning lose the Popsicle, not like "lose it" yourself). I think that's right anyway. I don't know what would have happened if you didn't do it right (i.e. whack right) with a brain. Or drop part of it, for God's sake. Wow. That's sick! Anyway, if you did it right (again, whacked the Popsicle right), you could enjoy sucking on each half separately, all by yourself; or, although I didn't do this very often (although I wasn't particularly selfish about most things, just this), you could share half of it with a friend. Man, can you imagine sucking on half of a brain though? Like with blood coming out of it, and sticky, maybe even slimy-like parts and everything? Makes me almost want to throw up just thinking about it! I mean Jesus! What a disgusting thing to do! I mean *really* disgusting. Like something some kind of a serial-sicko-freak maybe would do. But I'm sort of getting off track again, and maybe even a little bit strange in the head too. I'll try to finish up real fast. But suck a brain? Goddamn! What a nightmare that would be.

So just one more thing about those "vintage" Popsicles (I trust you are still at least a little bit interested). If you sucked on the thing real, real *slowly,* and real, real carefully (so as not to bite the top off), you could watch it turn from its original orange color (unless it was some other flavor, and then it would turn from that flavor's color) to pale orange, and then to frost white, which it would be just before the one final suck crumbled the whole thing apart. Remember? And as I said, it was the same thing with all the other colors too. And, since no one in Washertown knew anything about Freud (remember him?) and stuff like that (except maybe one or two of the town's doctors, or some really weird person who spent too much time at the library), you could suck on as many popsicles, and for as long as you wanted to (at least when you were little), and no one would think anything about it. It probably wouldn't be that way today; but that's the way it was then. You could just suck it to your heart's content! Well, I could maybe say even more about all this, but you probably think I'm on the brink of losing it again (my mind, or at least my concentration), and as I just said a few lines up above, I'm kind of feeling like it too, so I'll completely stop telling you this stuff.

But just remember, however (sometimes it's so hard to stop), that for me, *MPP* and Popsicles (especially orange ones) were kind of like a hot dog stand and weenies. They just always went together. (Or is the expression "a hot dog and a bun . . . or a beer"?) Whatever. I guess it really doesn't matter. But such connections, at least I think anyway, are not to be taken lightly. And so what if I may be just a little bit strange? So what? I mean whose problem is it, anyway? And remember, as I said when I started all this, Popsicles used to be almost like a symbol of what was good about America, and everything that we used to make. So then finally (and again), since I know you probably already forgot that I mentioned this before (and I guess I couldn't blame you if you did), I want to say (only kind of like really totally this time) that I lived up to my reputation for having an obsession with Popsicles partly because I ate so many of them when my mom and my dad and my brother and I went on our first family vacation to Clear Lake (I was seven or eight, if being reminded of that matters to you), where "Stub" O'Brien sold them at his little grocery store, which was located real close to the cottage where we stayed and where (at the cottage and in the morning) my dad gave my brother and me each a quarter to spend anyway we wanted to. Well, I spent all my quarters at Mr. O'Brien's Grocery Store buying Popsicles. One quarter (which bought five Popsicles in those days) times six days (that's how long we were there) equals *thirty* Popsicles that I ate in one week (all orange, except maybe once in a while a cherry one). Although now that I think about it I may have spent one or two of those quarters for tickets to ride the roller coaster at Bayside (an amusement park), which unfortunately, regretfully, and tragically (I found this out when I went back years later to ride the roller coaster again) isn't there anymore. I used to really love roller coasters. Anyway (and this ends it), so maybe (because of the roller coaster tickets) I actually only ate twenty-five Popsicles that week. Whatever. Twenty-five or thirty, that's how good they were! Also, would you believe that until I was about ten or twelve I always called a roller coaster a "rolly" coaster? Really. That's the way I thought you were supposed to say it. (I guess that's just one of those kind of peculiar but dumb things that you remember all your life . . . like saying *Warsher*town when it's really Washertown). Oh well.

CHAPTER FIVE

(A Rather Short One)
TOP SECRET

My aunt Velma had one in her utility room before anyone else in town. Not the "top secret" one that was going to revolutionize the industry, but one that was made by Washertown's serious competition (actually its one-time nemesis . . . although I didn't know that word then). And the competition, having experienced instant success, was really putting the pressure on the local folks to get their butts in gear, the show on the road, and their model on the market (as the loosely put expressions go). So anyway, what my aunt Velma had (having behaved in an almost traitorous manner) was a Bendix automatic washing machine. A Bendix, for God's sake! I mean Bendix was a dirty word in Washertown (maybe almost as bad as "fuck"). Well, probably not *that* bad, and again I'm sorry I had to use that word. But anyway, the Bendix Corporation had its "automatic" in an increasing number of American homes months before the Washertown product went on sale. Of course everyone knew (at least the executives at the Washertown facility knew) that its product was to be infinitely superior to the Bendix, or anything else that might come on the market. Therefore, although both design and production were a little bit slow getting out of the gate (as goes yet another loosely put expression), the company was convinced that it was poised to crush the competition and thus control the world (once again). Whatever. To have a Bendix in Washertown was an act of apostasy (although of course I didn't know what that word meant either), which therefore also meant, unfortunately and however (I guess anyway), that my aunt Velma was an apostate. But a nice one.

A few words about the Bendix automatic washing machine (like it or not, it *did* exist). First of all, the thing had to be screwed (bolted) down, or else when it went into its "spin" cycle it would vibrate so much that it could jump clear the hell off the floor, and probably (although to the best of my knowledge it was an event never documented) right out of the laundry room as well. And, as future automatic washing machine buyers of America would soon be told (by the Washertown marketing people of course), it, the Bendix, was by its very nature (probably in fact from the very moment of its conception in the post World War II industrial womb) not only likely to self-destruct and spin out of control, but was simply a totally inferior product in numerous other ways as well.

For starters, the Bendix "tumbled" instead of "agitated" during the wash cycle itself. And as any clear-thinking American woman should know (men could have known too, only men didn't use these kinds of machines in those days . . . they *built* them), you can't get the family wash clean, at least not *really* clean, if all that happens is that your clothes gets turned upside down a few hundred times, as happened in the Bendix. Clothes, if they were to be truly clean, had to be beaten and sloshed to death by an "agitator," and furthermore, by an agitator of a certain shape and churning power found only in the Washertown products. It was simply assumed that people knew that. And as I also kind of said before, you either screwed *it* (the Bendix) to the floor, or it could screw *you,* "the laundry ladies of America," to the wall. And now that I said that, and think about it more (in my sometimes sort of sick and sordid way of course), maybe the Bendix people *did* have the better product. I mean if you were a housewife who was bored out of her mind by the daily and incessant drudgery of housework (and most American women were in the 1940s), it just might have been fun to think about being screwed to the wall. Even by your washing machine. Like by "Big Ben the Bendix" maybe. But I don't know. You'd have to ask the women doing the laundry. (Monday mornings would have been the best time to check this out.) As you know, I tend to be a little twisted though, so I probably shouldn't even be thinking about, much less talking about this kind of stuff. I do recall, however, when I was in junior high, that screwing someone to the wall (or at least wanting to) was a frequent topic of conversation. At least it was in the boy's gym class dressing room. Jesus! Here I go again.

Whatever. I guess I started to get pretty much off the track again. (But at least I think I'm getting better at recognizing when it begins to happen.) So *anyway*, "Top Secret," *the* top secret, the *real* top secret, could be found (and at about the same time my Aunt Velma was enjoying her Bendix) in the basement of my best friend's house (the same best friend who wet his pants with me at the Frankenstein movie, and next to the dry cleaning "blowpipe," and in fourth grade . . . and also whose dog got shot). Anyway, several of these top secret machines had already been placed in "select" homes, and by now were aggressively beating and sloshing the shit out of clothes in basements and utility rooms all over Washertown. Sometimes even they were *literally* sloshing the shit out of things, especially if the person whose basement it was in had a little baby, since disposable diapers hadn't become part of the American way yet. (Otherwise, I just kind of used the expression, i.e. "sloshing the shit out of things," as sort of a just ordinary way of saying something.)

Whatever. The point is that Washertown's "automatics," which by the way did not have be screwed to the floor (and therefore would not be screwing any users to the wall), were being thoroughly home tested, since before being placed on the market they had to be absolutely perfect. And, *dependable*. Especially dependable, since that's the way they were to be advertised. After all, Washertown products had achieved their present success by being dependable (from the time the very first models were produced). I mean that's what they were all about: dependability. So that's what the new automatic would be about too. And, if you'll pardon my pride, their reputation was well deserved. So anyway, "Top Secret" was there in the basement, and my friend told me he would let me see it (kind of like Joycie pulling her underpants down, I guess), but only, *only* if I would promise to never, *ever* say anything—*anything*—to *anyone* (again like Joycie did). I mean that's just how top secret this whole project was supposed to be. So, I did (promise), and so he did (show me his mother's automatic washer), and therefore, although my dad didn't even work at the washing machine company (at "Plant One" *or* the now secretive "Plant Two"), I, an outsider, had nevertheless become part of top secret. Pretty exciting for a ten-year-old boy in Washertown! I kind of lied though, since I told my mother about it. I mean I just had to tell someone. You know how that goes. But she probably already knew anyway, although she acted like she didn't, and she promised she wouldn't tell anyone either.

So here's what that early, top secret automatic looked like. It was a white, *really* white, porcelain enameled, really plain-looking "box," about four feet high, and maybe about two and a half feet deep and wide. It had a square lid on the top that was hinged and opened to the back, and two control knobs positioned on top and kind of toward the back two corners. A Spartan—looking machine, but that was part of the Washertown "salt of the industry" idea of quality (once again, the strategy of the marketing people). The most exciting thing about top secret (at least I thought) was that you were almost led to believe that it had some kind of a "mind" inside of it. I mean it actually knew when and how high to fill up with water, then wash, then rinse, then rinse again, and then spin the stuff dry (pretty dry anyway), with no one doing anything to it. In fact, all you had to do was put your clothes in, add some detergent, and turn the knobs to what you wanted it to do. Amazing. Absolutely amazing! Probably some of the people who designed and built it even said, "fucking amazing," but as you know I'm trying pretty much not to use that word. So anyway, it's no wonder that with the introduction of this plain-looking but futuristic top-secret machine the modern age had dawned in Washertown. I mean it was like today the town, tomorrow the world!

In fact, to kind of summarize it all, it was like I'm going to say now. I mean this could be sort of like an advertisement on the radio or something. So here's how it would go . . . sort of anyway. "No longer will the American housewife face the drudgery and the blues of Monday morning wash day"! (And then maybe there would be some music or something.) "No longer will rinse tubs and hoses and shit like that be all over the basement"! (Actually if it was really an advertisement they probably wouldn't say the "and shit like that" part.) Whatever. (More music.) "No longer will some unhappy first-grader destroy his gold, wire-rimmed glasses (or anything else he might wish to destroy) in the wringer of a pre-automatic-age washing machine"! (This part would maybe be to make the advertisement "personal" or something.) Maybe, anyway. (Again, more music.) Then finally, "No longer will you or a loved one risk running your goddamn arm through an old-fashioned wringer"! (Again, if it was really an advertisement or a commercial they would probably leave out the *goddamn* word.) Meaning probably for sure. (And then even more music, like maybe sort of a great big "Tah Dah" sound!) And then they could say more stuff about the automatic being so modern and everything. So as you can see, the world had changed. Gone were the "Furies," the "Eumenides," and all that shit (bet you don't even know what that means . . . and I didn't either, until my freshman year in college). Whatever. I was kind of getting carried away there, and I probably didn't even remember the Furies and Eumenides shit right anyway. Nevertheless, the age of automated bliss had indeed arrived. *Dependable* automated bliss. OK?

But to get back to reality, and my best friend's basement, I actually got to lift that lid, twist those knobs ("you 'git' a little drunk and you 'lands' in jail") all by myself. And that was about as exciting (although not quite) as when I (without my dad having to tell me what to do) got to turn on (and "adjust") our family's new TV set for the very first time. So (back to the automatic washer) . . . lid up, clothes (and detergent) in, lid down, turn those knobs (one for the water level and temperature, the other for the "cycle"), pull up on the right knob (really hard), and "off" (actually of course meaning "on") it goes ("into the wild blue yonder," if you happen to remember World War II songs and have a kind of strange imagination). So anyway, that was "Top Secret." And *I* was part of it!

Weeks later the Washertown automatic washing machine, with a burst of publicity (although I don't think they used my advertisement), hit the appliance show rooms of America. The nation's laundry needs would therefore be met at last (and, as I keep reminding you, dependably). Families would be happy (and clean). And the wives and mothers of those families would be fulfilled (unless of course they rather liked the idea of what the Bendix might do to them). Whatever. Washertown, wonderful Washertown, would forever be the undisputed "Washing Machine Capitol of the World." Speaking of which (i.e. the world), it may even have been thought that it might now (and at last) be truly "safe for democracy." I mean "God was in His heaven, and all was right with the world" (or something like that). And now, *now*, after centuries of dreams, wishful thinking, and prayer, "cleanliness" could *in fact* be "next to Godliness." *The* "automatic," the *Washertown* automatic, was here! "Deus ex machina" (again, or something like that). I didn't learn this stuff until college either, and then (obviously I guess) not very well. *Anyway*, slosh and agitate. Rinse and spin. And (and these will be my absolute closing statements): as if post-war America were not already beautiful and overwhelmingly satisfying enough, the much sought after security of knowing that neither your wife, nor your mother, nor your grandmother or daughter or any other loved one even, was in danger of getting screwed to the wall in the laundry room of your new, probably too small, and more than likely ranch-style home (assuming of course, as I suggested above, that they didn't *want* to be screwed . . . to the wall) . . . *anyway*, such security was yours. (That, by the way, was another pretty kind of hard sentence, so you might wish to read it again . . . I mean I had to reread it a time or two myself.) Whatever. At least there would be no "taking a tumble" with *this* new beauty. No sir. You can depend on that!

CHAPTER SIX

(A Really Big One)
AROUND THE SQUARE

So much for short stories and even shorter chapters. It occurs to me that if you're *really* going to know what it was like growing up in Washertown (where it all began, and how I got to be this way and everything), I need to take you on a real, live, person-to-person walk around the Washertown "Square." I know it sounds like something of a contradiction to walk around a square, but you know what I mean, and that's precisely what a lot of people did when I was a little boy. They just "walked around the square." That was their entertainment when nothing else was going on (which meant fairly often). They especially walked, when I was really little, on Saturday night, because that was when the stores were open late. Some people, if they got downtown early enough (on Saturday night), just parked their cars and *sat* there and watched other people walk around the square. But you had to get there pretty early to do that, since all the good places, meaning the "head-in" places, would otherwise be taken. Curiously, by the way, in Washertown you always said "downtown," not "uptown." I'm not sure why. Maybe "uptown" sounded too snooty or something. Whatever. You always said "downtown" when you referred to the Washertown Square (even when it wasn't Saturday night). Maybe uptown was hidden somewhere that I didn't even know about. Like maybe it was a secret place just for adults or something. But my mind could probably start to get goofy again if I think about stuff like secret parts of town, and since

I'm pretty sure there weren't any anyway, it's probably best that I don't ramble or scramble my thoughts too much. I'll just take you there (downtown). Rambling or scrambling actually makes me think of eggs anyway. And besides that, the idea of a secret part of town (which as I just said probably didn't exist anyway) simply shouldn't matter. Should it? Well, maybe I guess. I mean if it was really *really* secret it maybe should (matter). Stop (it's happening again). What *does* matter is that you to get to know Washertown better. So let's walk.

First of all, one thing (and a really nice one) is that you will notice that almost all the buildings around the Square are two-story, "turn-of-the-century" (i.e. nineteenth to twentieth), Victorian-looking structures. All attached, of course. One exception though, in terms of height, is the three-story building with the Masonic Temple on the top (meaning on the top floor, of course, not on the top of the whole building itself). It wasn't really a "temple," by the way, but you probably understand that. I mean it wasn't like some Egyptian place, like where Cleopatra let a snake bite her boobs or anything (she died, by the way). Or the temple in Jerusalem, where the Jews go to rock back and forth and wail and everything (I always thought that was pretty dumb . . . I mean wouldn't you think they could find something better to do?). Anyway, it, the Masonic Temple, was just kind of a club (which is to say it was kind of like a secret cult place or something). At least I think that's what it was. Whatever. As I already told you, there were only three Jewish families in Washertown, and no Egyptians (at least there were none that I knew of), so they didn't need to have any temples there anyway. Just the Masonics did (and I think they had a lot of Methodists who were Masonic). I'm not sure though.

But to get back on track, there was one other exception to the height rule (i.e. the height of the buildings around the Square), and that was a hotel (a pretty fancy place that I'll tell you more about when we get to it). And then of course there was The Casper County Courthouse in the middle of all this, with its kind of "dick-like" dome (phallus) on the top, and the funny smells, and the drinking fountain with the little stairs for kids. Remember? It was pretty high too. Especially when you included the penis part (I'm trying to decide which word is the best sounding) and the flagpole. But anyway, to get back to the Square itself, another thing that you just can't not notice when you look at the Washertown Square is that almost all the store fronts have these really pretty, genuine canvas awnings hanging out over the sidewalk (at night, or if it was real windy maybe, they rolled them up). I mean they were really, *really* pretty, especially when I was just little. They were all different colors too: like there were blue ones, green (both light and dark) ones, and a few brown or yellow or red ones, and some that had stripes even. A few of them would once in awhile be sort of tattered in places (another example of the "nothing's perfect" idea I guess), but even with the tatters they still looked pretty good.

So anyway, what you're looking at is the Washertown Square in the 1940s, the decade when I was pretty much doing most of my growing up, and getting to be the way I turned out, which (not to brag or anything), I think is actually pretty good. At least I don't think anyone would have called me a loser, or thought that I was a total asshole or anything. Or even a shithead or a butthole either. A pain in the ass? Well . . . maybe, but not real often. Anyway, downtown Washertown, *my* Washertown, with its Square and everything, was truly a very special place. An "American Masterpiece," as I first said in the title of this whole book (if you look at it again, meaning the title on the cover, you'll see that it really stands out). So, come with me and you'll soon agree. (I'm not trying to sound like a poet or anything; those last words for some reason just sort of came out that way.) It kind of reminds me though, because of the way it rhymes maybe, of the words of a 1950s' song (when I was still getting to be the way I turned out) that went: "See the USA in your Chevrolet!" Remember that one? Dinah Shore (but maybe you've forgotten her) sang it on television to help Chevrolet sell more cars than Ford. She was pretty good too (but not as good as Kate Smith of course), and I think it worked. But I suspect we both know what's beginning to happen with my mind again, so as I said we should a few lines ago, let's just take a walk, and talk. (There's that rhyme thing again.) Whatever. I've learned (although it really took me a long time, as I may have said before) that *doing* something can sometimes help me stop *thinking* something. Not all the time. But a lot of times anyway. So let's go. (And I'm sorry I keep drifting so much . . . but man, sometimes it's really hard to control.)

OK. We'll walk the west side of the Square first (starting at the southwest corner). Actually, I guess we could have started at the northwest corner, but then we would kind of have been walking backwards (at least it would feel that way to me). We're beginning though (please God, keep me on track!). And that's what's important. Right? Right. First stop: "Gurdy's Drugs," a "Rexall" store of course, since almost all the drug stores in those days were (Rexall). Had there been no sign telling you, you would have known anyway, because of the smell, that it was a Rexall. I mean these stores were always filled with that difficult to describe, sort of "hanging over you" and always there, "mediciney" smell. However (and fortunately), the air in a Rexall store was made just a little more pleasing by the faint fragrance of cosmetics and talcum powder and stuff, and also by just a hint of the contents of the boxed, cellophane-wrapped (usually) chocolates. Most often, at least when I was little, they were "Whitman's" chocolates. Or maybe "Russell Stover." But it was almost as though, try as it might, the cellophane just couldn't quite contain the deliciousness of what was inside.

Whitman's, when I was little anyway (I guess to help people who were afraid to take risks), was the candy company that put little labeled squares on the inside of the lid so that you knew what was inside each piece before you bit into it. Looked pretty confusing to me, but maybe I was just stupid or something. Anyway, with Whitman's you didn't have to take any chances, unless you wanted to, and the labeling system also helped you avoid having to spit gooey little pieces of bad shit in your hand to hide your poor choices (and there were some). The Whitman box, just so you'll know, was always sort of a straw-yellow color, and looked like it was quilted or something, with delicate little designs all over it. I guess Whitman's was mostly for little girls and old ladies. But I don't mean to be impolite or disrespectful or anything by saying "old ladies." As I've already told you, I was a pretty nice little boy. I just must mean to say that ladies who are old enjoy boxes like that; not "*old* ladies," like some guys who were married would say about their wives. Especially if they thought they were real bitches, or were maybe real fat or ugly or something. You know, like "My old lady says I can't come," and stuff like that.

But candy and old ladies were not the only things that Gurdy's Drug Store was all about. Not by a long shot. You see, "hanging" in that same fragrant (somewhat) Rexall air, only now near a metal rack at the very back of the store, was the smell of printer's ink. It was really heavy too (meaning the ink smell). And that area of the store, my friends (the nearly sacred space that it was), was where the so-called "dirty" magazines and "pocket books" ("paperbacks" in today's jargon) were displayed. They weren't really very dirty in the 1940s though, which of course was kind of a disappointment. But anyway, (and this is a fact . . . swear to God), the inky smell back there was so strong that it sometimes seemed to just pull a young man (and more than a few little boys too) right to it. And therefore to the dirty book rack itself. Whether they wanted to be there or not, it just pulled them. And I'm telling you, a few of those pocket books had some pretty good parts in them (but as I sort of said up above, for Iowa in the 1940s anyway). And if you were lucky, some other kid had already "dog-eared" the best pages for you, so you didn't have to waste a lot of your valuable time flipping through them to find the good stuff. The full-sized magazines, like *Esquire* and *Stag* (especially *Stag*), were pretty good too (mainly the pictures, of course), but you had to be especially careful when you were looking at those, since Mr. Gurdy, or even worse, *Mrs.* Gurdy, might see that you were getting excited or something.

And a *really* neat thing about being back by the magazine rack (although actually not as neat as the good parts of the dirty books themselves) was that you could stare at the wall behind the counter right across from the rack, where the "rubber" drawer was. (Not a rubber *drawer,* but a drawer with *rubbers* in it . . . you know . . . like your dad used on your mom, or a high school football player used when he was banging his cheer leader-type girlfriend in the back seat of his old man's car . . . that kind.) Pretty exciting for a little kid not even in junior high yet. I mean it was sort of like "playing with the big boys," if you know what I'm getting at (I don't mean actually "playing with" them of course, like you were some kind of a queer or anything, but playing *like* them . . . OK?). Anyway, I sometimes wondered if there was something wrong with me for liking to stare at that drawer. And there might have been, for all I know. Once in a while you would even see Mr. Gurdy go there and get some (i.e. rubbers) for a guy, and then you could try to figure out who it was, and if you knew him, and who it was he was "doing" and everything. Never Mrs. Gurdy though (meaning never did Mrs. Gurdy open that drawer). Her job was to get the gigantic blue boxes of Kotex off the shelf and wrap them in brown paper so no one would know what the lady who got some had just bought. Of course the "big blues," as we called them, were about twenty times bigger than anything else in the store, so it seemed kind of stupid to spend the time with the camouflage paper. Anyway, when you saw Mr. Gurdy get some rubbers, you always watched to see who he was selling them to (and then maybe wished you were that guy . . . but sometimes not). And as I sort of already said, I guess I must have been kind of weird of something for watching the way I did.

Actually, and to keep telling you the truth (well . . . mostly anyway), I wouldn't be surprised if some guys didn't even get their first "hard-on" at Gurdy's. I mean reading some of the really good parts in those dog-eared pocket books, and then maybe following it up by looking at a picture of a woman with really big tits in *Stag*, could do it to you. And then add to this that you were standing right by the rubber drawer and everything. Actually, now that I think about it more, if you were a Boy Scout, which I wasn't (I think I already told you a Bear Cub was as far as I got), the placement of that magazine rack, the possibility of getting a good solid hard-on, and the fact that you were right next to the rubber, would have made it pretty easy to "be prepared," or whatever it was that scouts were supposed to be. Maybe it could even have helped him (the Boy Scout with the hard-on) on his way toward becoming an Eagle Scout or something. I know it took a lot of different activities to become one of those. (By the way, I don't mean to be crude or anything, so if you want to you can substitute the word "woody" or "boner" for "hard-on." It doesn't matter to me.) But whatever you want to call it, it's what could happen at the dirty magazine rack sometimes. That's not where I got my first one (i.e. "hard-on"), but as I said up above, it might have been for some guys.

I'm not telling you where I got mine (and its not because I'm afraid to either, or that I'm trying to withhold important information from you or anything). Its only because when it happened I was in kind of an unusual place, and also because the whole thing was pretty exceptional, and therefore I don't want you to think I'm bragging or have no class or anything. And since I was only about five or six (or *maybe* seven), it might even seem kind of strange to you. But I will tell you that I saw my first real rubber when I was staying all night at my best friend's house and he showed me one in his dad's sock drawer. We were in fifth grade. I also remember thinking about a certain girl when I saw it. Her name was Carolyn something. OK . . . I might as well get straight with you (no pun intended), and tell you the other stuff. I got my first hard-on at Washertown's First Methodist Church during Sunday School when I was looking at this little girl who was sitting across from me, and whose chair was real low, and whose dress was kind of too short (or maybe just bunched up or something), and whose legs were sort of spread apart (although I'm sure quite innocently). I think anyway. I mean it wasn't like she was some kind of a whore or something, like from the bad part of Bethlehem or somewhere (or that *really* bad town in *The Bible* with the name I could never pronounce and can't remember). Anyway, I knew I was getting it (i.e. the hard-on/woody/boner) when my pants started to get kind of curiously tight, and I couldn't seem to get them straightened out and stiff. I mean *stuff*. But I'm really getting off track again. Jesus! What a place for a hard-on. I guess some of my "mental issues" have just always been really hard to contain. If it helps any, I also remember that little Carolyn was wearing "Mary Jane" shoes, and "anklets" with little ruffles around the top. I mean it was all something that just sort of innocently happened.

Gurdy's was also where I bought my favorite grade school teacher that small (very small) bottle of "Evening in Paris" perfume that I already kind of talked about. She's the one I told you I was in love with (remember when I told you about fourth grade?), and I thought the perfume in the little blue bottle with the silver cap and the little silver label was probably *the* most important thing a guy could give a girl. I mean it was obviously French and everything (like who ever heard of Paris, Iowa?), and I knew what French stuff was all about, even though I was just in fourth grade. Everything that came from France was supposed to be special when it came to buying something for your girlfriend. (So were "dirty" pictures French and special, but that's another story that I sort of already told you about when I introduced you to the Washer City Café.) Anyway, it was kind of embarrassing when (as I also told you) I found out that this teacher I loved so much wore "White Shoulders." Oh well, I probably couldn't have afforded "White Shoulders." I only had thirty-two customers on my entire paper route, and that didn't provide me a lot of "disposable income" for romance ("disposable income" is something I of course didn't know anything about then; I just threw it in there to sound more grown up). Whatever. We'd better get out of Gurdy's, since I don't want to get all excited again thinking about the magazines, and the rubber drawer, and the memory of my innocent little Sunday School friend Carolyn sitting in that low chair with her legs spread apart.

Next door to Gurdy's Drugs was Hoage's Grocery Store, and next to that, connected on the inside by a double archway, was Hoage's Variety. It was kind of like a dynasty, I guess. At least for Washertown in the 1940s. My mother hated to go to Hoage's Grocery, but she had to "trade" there (a rather quaint, 1940s midwestern term for "shop"), because Mr. Hoage "did business" (another sort of quaint expression) with my dad. In Washertown, you did business with those who did business with you. It was sort a commercial "Golden Rule," I guess. So my dad told her to, and my mom did (i.e. trade at Hoage's), even though she didn't want to; and my dad, being the good guy he was, wished she didn't have to. Whatever. Hoage's Grocery smelled sort of old, although if you stood right over the produce counter just after they had wet it down, and then sucked in real hard (*really* hard, kind of like you were trying to make your lungs explode or something), it smelled nice and fresh, almost like a real garden after a June or July thunder storm. Sometimes it seemed as though you could even smell the black Iowa dirt. Especially if you sucked in right where the potatoes, or beets, or maybe even the carrots were piled up.

Towards the back of the store was the meat counter, and believe me, it smelled too. Really, *really* bad. Like fresh cow blood, and chicken insides, and old, icky fish parts, all kind of mixed together. And there was always this sort of mushy-looking, kind of wet sawdust all over the floor, with little scraps of meat parts in it that had been trimmed off of some horse or something, and were getting stepped on all the time by the butcher. That stuff made it smell even worse of course. Real dead-like sometimes. Not as bad as a dead frog, or a run over skunk or beaver, or maybe a smashed bird that had been in the sun way too long, but bad, nevertheless. I mean some days that meat counter smell could actually make you feel sick, especially if you smelled it at the same time you were looking at the yellowy, blood-smeared, supposed-to-be white apron of the greasy-looking butcher (who was always wiping his nose on his sleeve). Even his hair was greasy (I guess to go with his apron), and slathered down on his head too much. I don't think it was from the meat grease though; it was probably from using too much hair oil from Gurdy's Rexall or the barbershop he went to or something. Maybe even from the Rialto Barber Shop (where the hair oil was in the shake-top salad oil bottles . . . remember?). Anyway, this part of the store could smell puking awful. I mean the whole back end of the place just smelled raw. *Really* raw. "*Stenchy*" *raw.* And on Fridays, when Mr. Hoage got his fresh (at least sometimes) fish in (so that the Catholics could be sure to go to heaven and still have something to eat), the entire store was absolutely gross. Like you wanted to gag or actually throw up or something. Mississippi Catfish (man are the heads of those things ugly!), and who knows what else. It even affected the way the potatoes up in the front smelled. That's how bad it was! I mean it smelled as *bad* as the A&P Grocery (especially near the coffee grinder machine) smelled *good*. But we won't be going there (to the A&P), since it wasn't actually on the Washertown Square. (The A&P was around the corner from Gurdy's and on west about a half a block, in case you want to go there later.)

Across from the meat and the blood-soaked sawdust at Hoage's grisly Grocery, and up about five steps, was the "office alcove." This little overlook was almost continually occupied by Eileen, the office lady (at least when the store was open), who seemed to have some kind of a contest going with Mr. Hoage to see who could be more rude to the customers. Eileen was curiously attractive, I guess, but plain. But she had that non-orgasmic look too (although that's another word I didn't know then), sort of like the ladies you expected to see standing in front of a Washertown grade school class, or, if they were *really* (like totally) non-orgasmic, sitting behind a principal's desk. All of the teachers didn't look that way of course (never forget the one I was so much in love with). But I could get off track here, and I don't want to do that. I mean this part of my story isn't about teachers (I already did that part). It's about Hoage's Grocery Store, and we aren't finished there yet. So anyway, this Eileen person seemed to stare at you all the time, peering down from her alcove with that kind of pinchy look that made you wonder about her underwear being too tight or something.

You know, now that I think about it more (and maybe stretch my imagination just a little), those two, meaning Mr. Hoage and Eileen, may, just *may* have been "doing it" or something. Maybe even right there on the alcove floor, as far as I know. (Certainly not in the sawdust behind the meat counter though, or probably anywhere else in the store, as far as that goes.) The alcove was the only sort of like private area. But *maybe* they did do it in the sawdust. I don't know. Anyway, how I can even think this stuff sometimes surprises me. Some people, however, as I learned later in life (and probably in the wrong places and from the wrong people), sort of liked to do weird stuff and mess around in strange places. But I don't know why I'm even saying this. I never had any hard evidence, and therefore it's probably totally unfair to these more than likely basically moral, maybe even unusually moral, people. So I do apologize. It must have been that I got off on this (meaning "got off" just in general, not, you know, sexually or anything) because I mentioned Eileen's underwear or something. Anyway, there was one other kind of strange thing though (and this will help get me back on track). It was what the floor in Hoage's Grocery was made of. Not just the bloody, meat market floor, but the entire place. It was all made up of large, black, somewhat soft when you walked on them sheets of asbestos board or something, all butted up to each other. Real tight-like. Strange, I thought, but maybe not for the 1940s. Anyway the floor came to mind (when something really needed to), so I just thought I would mention it.

But then, believe it or not, in the very back of Hoage's Grocery Store, I mean way, *way* back, even past the meat counter and Eileen's alcove, were bags of "feed" and blocks of salt for cows to lick. So it smelled kind of funny back there too. Almost like a farm, which can be (but actually isn't always) bad. Whatever. This should pretty much do it for Hoage's. *Except* that, and in all fairness, I need to tell you two really good things about the place, which probably as a matter of fact were part of what helped them stay in business. First, you could phone in your grocery order, which would then be put together by a store clerk (of which there were few), or maybe even Eileen, during an "out of alcove" moment (but never Mr. Hoage himself, I'm sure). And then everything would be promptly (most of the time anyway) delivered to your house in a wooden cart-like thing that was wedged between the two back wheels of a strange looking, three-wheeled motorcycle. Obviously it wasn't a "Harley," or anything like that, but it did what it was designed to do. And second (i.e. the second good thing about Hoague's), you could "charge" your groceries. Everything would be written up on a little "order pad," just like in a restaurant.

There was however (there's that "however" again), and to be totally honest, a bit of a downside to all this. When you called in to order your groceries, you didn't necessarily get the brands or the special items you asked for, and you soon learned (very soon) not to count on those folks to choose the best produce for you either. It was sort of as though Mr. Hoage and Eileen enjoyed conspiring against the customers who, as was the case for my mother, were "locked in" to shop there by unspoken trade agreements. (I told you before that in Washertown you "did business" with those who "did business" with you.) So, as it worked out, Mr. Hoage's and Eileen's call-in and delivery service, convenient as it was, was also doing a pretty good job of clearing their shelves of slow-moving canned goods, and emptying their produce counter of days-old, wilted vegetables. Nevertheless, in Washertown in the 1940s, with most families having only one car (if any), and sometimes not enough money at the end of the month (especially when the washing machine workers were out on strike), phone-in deliveries and charge privileges were pretty good things to have available. But it really is time to be moving on.

Hoage's Variety, next door to Hoage's Grocery, was mostly just that—next door. (Actually, as I mentioned above, you could simply walk through an inside archway from one Hoague store to the other.) Anyway, the place was no match for J.J. Newberry on the north side of the Square or F.W. Woolworth on the east side. And Hoage's Variety didn't sell goldfish. But more about that later. Anyway, the Mr. Hoage who owned the variety store was an exceptionally nice person; it's just that his store wasn't so nice. Actually, in its own way, I guess it was. Maybe because they made you feel like they really appreciated your business. So perhaps it was just in the wrong location or something. Or maybe its association with the not-so-friendly Hoage's Grocery worked against it. But then it had a smell to it too; it wasn't really bad, but it wasn't really good either. (It seems as though everyplace in Washertown smelled kind of funny.) Oh well. I guess you could just say that at Hoague's Variety the smell was simply "so-so," and came mostly from the oiled wood floor and the ever-present sweeping compound that was the preferred treatment for the narrow, age and wear darkened hardwood slats that the floor was made of. (Less toxic than the asbestos stuff on the floor of the grocery store, but smelly, nevertheless.)

Hoage's Variety had lots of stuff, for a small store, but no lunch counter; and, as I said before, no goldfish (which both J.J. Newberry and F.W. Woolworth had). I guess what I'm trying to say is that the place just sort of lacked excitement. This Mr. Hoage, by the way, was the father of Roxie the "mixed chorus" teacher (remember her?) who was rumored to have been in love with Fred Waring and his boys (not all of them, as I'm sure I said before, but just Fred). Anyway (and then we'll just go on), the one thing I remember most about Hoage's Variety was that sometimes when my brother (who didn't like me much) and I were there, our mother would ask if we could use their bathroom. (Take two little boys *anywhere* for very long, and one of them is going to have to go.) They always said yes, but I don't think they liked it very much. Sometimes it was even hard to start "going," since you somehow knew they really didn't want you in there. And so (most of the time anyway) we tried to be pretty careful not to pee on their toilet seat or anything. This didn't mean that we necessarily put it up (the toilet seat), only that we usually took turns and tried to aim well. (In case you're a girl or someting and don't know this, it can be kind of a challenge to leave the seat down and try not to hit it.)

Next to Hoague's Variety was this place called the Mode O Day (which later became a hobby store). I don't think I ever even went in there, since it was a store just for women. I remember though that it always seemed to have mostly underwear and stuff in the window (at least I think that's what it was). Whatever. I may have been hanging out around the dirty magazines and rubber drawer at Gurdy's Rexall, but I wasn't so weird (yet anyway) as to hang out around the Mode O Day. So if it's OK with you, let's just move on. I don't even like the way the name of the place sounds . . . Mode O Day, like it thinks it's some kind of "hot shit" sort of place or something. I mean as far as I could tell it was just a women's underwear store.

Next door to Mode O Day was Beyer's Bakery. Good stuff in that place, I'll tell you. I mean *really* good stuff. Fresh baked everyday. In the morning, especially on really hot summer days, you could smell the place from a hundred feet away (maybe a hundred miles even). You know . . . that really neat "doughy" smell, as the stuff was baking. And they had perfect Danish pastry (although I was actually more into donuts and cookies), with just the right amount of white icing on it. And Byer's Bakery had the very best maple "long johns" you can ever imagine. Ever. The long johns had just the right amount of icing on them too . . . sweet, but not too, and real "mapley," but not too much. Beyer's made really good little one-person cherry pies too, but they cost a dime, and that was usually more than I could afford. Most of the other stuff, except of course for the big cakes and things like that, was just a nickel. And although I already told you, I have to say it just one more time; Byers Bakery smelled better than anyplace else in the whole town. Even better than perfume, like "Evening in Paris" or "White Shoulders." I'm not totally absolutely sure, but I think it did anyway. Yeah . . . Byer's smelled better. Even better in fact than the smell from the Wonder Bread Baking Company in Des Moines. And speaking of smells again, other really good Washertown smells came from the "A&P" fresh ground coffee (which I mentioned before) and gas pumps (the gas pump smell was *really* good I thought, although once in a while, if I sucked in too much of it, I kind of got a headache). The A&P coffee, especially if I stuck my face right into the grinder (well, not completely "right in," but you know what I mean), was really good too though, and that didn't give me headaches either. Or anything else, as far as that goes. Anyway, Beyer's Bakery was a super good place. A hometown, Washertown, treasure. Sometimes I think I would even give my left nut (not really of course . . . that was only a "guy expression" we had then) to have just one more of their maple long johns. Man were they good!

Next door to Byer's came Powell's Drug Store. Rexall again (of course). Same funny smells, like at Gurdy's, i.e. medicine, talcum powder, and chocolates wrapped in cellophane. Powell's actually outdid Gurdy's in at least two ways though. First, it had a better soda fountain, where you could get a cherry-vanilla phosphate just as "icky-thicky," syrupy sweet as you wanted it to be (which was pretty sweet). Of course that meant that the person who worked behind the fountain (who of course was never Mr. Powell) was willing to cheerfully forego any profit from the drink. But I'm telling you, those phosphates were really, *really* good. Their chocolate cokes weren't bad either, but neither were the ones they made at Gurdy's (or at Rollens, which I'll be telling you about when we get over to the center of the south side of the Square . . . which will be a little while, but that's OK). Anyway, for just a nickel you could get some pretty fantastic drinks.

The second way that Powell's was better than Gurdy's was that they had better school supplies. Every fall, on one long table right in the middle of the store, Powell's had these really neat (at least I thought so) zipper notebooks (the "in" thing to have in the 1940s). I remember they (the notebooks) smelled kind of funny too. Probably because although they looked like leather, it was really only make-believe stuff. (You found that out later when they got sort of scuffed up and everything.) One year, I think maybe when I was in eighth grade, I bought this incredibly beautiful two-tone zipper notebook ("three ring") that was dark brown for the most part (with a kind of woven leather look to it), and had "piping" around the edges that was light tan. It sort of matched the brown and tan loafers that I had that year (although I had to talk real hard to get my mom and dad to let me buy those beauties). So anyway, I thought that was pretty neat (meaning the way my shoes and notebook kind of went together). To tell you the truth though, I don't think anyone else even noticed; which, as a matter of fact, was probably a good thing. An eighth grader (at least a guy anyway) wasn't supposed to look that good.

Powell's was also where you went to buy your Duncan yo-yo. And trust me, in Washertown in the late 40s and early 50s, if you didn't own a Duncan, you didn't own a yo-yo. The Duncan was the only one that would "free wheel" the way yo-yo's were supposed to, and let you do "'round the worlds" and other really hard things like that ("baby in the cradle" was probably the hardest one to do). And later, Powell's carried those really neat, square plastic "number puzzles" which, if you wanted to be anyone at all at Washertown Junior High, you had to have. They came in their own little snap-cover cloth case, so you could kind of hide them from the teachers when you had to. In fairness to Gurdy's however, Powell's didn't have any dog-eared pocket books or *Stag* magazines, and I never could figure out where Mr. Powell kept his rubbers. Not his own, of course, but the ones he sold to other guys (he probably kept his own in his sock drawer, just like my friend's dad did). Furthermore, I didn't have a big "crush" on Mr. Powell's daughter, although I think he had one (meaning that he had a daughter, not that he had a crush on someone . . . I mean he was married for God's sake), the way I did on Mr. Gurdy's daughter. I think Mr. Powell's daughter (if for sure he had one) would have been too young for me anyway.

Now that I think about it, by the way, I don't know why I forgot to tell you about Mr. Gurdy's daughter and my big grade school crush on her (and later again in high school). Maybe it was because I got so excited talking about the rubber drawer and stuff. Anyway, had Mr. Gurdy known about my fascination regarding that particular drawer, and my interest in, if not obsession with his dirty books and magazines, he probably wouldn't have wanted to think that I also had this kind of romantic-like interest in his daughter. In fact, he probably would have thrown me out of his store even, which, had he actually done so (i.e. thrown me out) would have probably pissed me off enough that I would have "accidentally" knocked over the whole goddamn stack of Mrs. Gurdy's camouflaged Kotex boxes on my way out. I would have done something anyway. Whatever. My crush on Mr. Gurdy's daughter didn't lead to an unwanted pregnancy or wedding or anything. And since I've finished up with what was and wasn't so good about Powell's, we should probably get out of the drug business for a while and just move on.

Oh. I forgot something else. I really should tell you about what happened a few doors back. You should enjoy it too, and it was major enough (in terms of how I got to be this way) that we really should go back to it. OK? OK. So anyway, next to Hoage's Variety Store (and before the dopey Mode O Day place), and up some really long, and I mean really long, and really steep (and really narrow too) stairs, was that Masonic Temple place. As I told you before, it wasn't really a temple, like in Egypt or anything like that; it was simply where the Washertown men who said they were Masonic went. Well, my dad was Masonic, as not only the temple itself was called, but also the activities that went on there (although I always thought Masonic sort of sounded like someplace you could maybe contact with a Captain Midnight ring) . . . anyway, my dad was Masonic, and that meant that my brother and I got to go there with our mom and dad for the dances they had on certain Saturday nights during the winter. Almost all the

Masonics took their kids with them, since they sort of considered the temple to be a place for families too. Or, I don't know, maybe they just didn't want to have to pay a babysitter. Whatever.

The other temples in Washertown, by the way, (only they called them lodges), like the "Elks" and the "Moose" and the other animal clubs (all of which I actually already mentioned), weren't so family friendly. People drank beer and stuff at those places (which I also told you before). In fact, I think the animal lodges were kind of maybe more like the Washer City Café (remember that place?), only not as bad (and I may have already said that too). At least I don't think they were as bad. But anyway, as I was saying, my dad was Masonic. (I think my grandfather was too, now that I think about it, since his wife, and therefore of course my grandmother, was called a "worthy matron," or something like that (only not like in a prison or anything), in their sort of "sister" club that I think was called the "Eastern Stars," or maybe the "Satellites," or something.) I think that was it anyway. But to keep (or get back) on track (which again we probably need to do), I started to tell you that my mom and my dad and my brother and I went to the Masonic Temple for dances. Actually though, now that I think about it (and if you will allow another really *really* brief digression), I should probably tell you that my dad was actually more athletic than he was Masonic. (I just thought you might like to know that.) But then I guess he was a pretty good Masonic Temple dancer too (my mom said so anyway). And he was also good at a lot of other things. Like softball. And volleyball. (Remember, I just said he was athletic.) And he was good in his business. And at teaching a Sunday School class at The First Methodist Church. And that's only just *some* of the stuff he was good at. But this isn't supposed to be about what my dad was good at, so I'll just sort of stop here. It's time to get on with the dance.

So anyway (and we're back on track for sure now I think), I'm going to tell you about what happened once at a temple dance, and then we'll go back downstairs to finish our walk around the square, since I think you'll really like it (meaning you'll like the temple dance story). Maybe not. But I think so. Probably anyway, although the whole thing is pretty painful to hear. Meaning emotionally painful. Anyway, I know at least some of you will like this story ("The Future Sadists of America" perhaps), although I'm only kidding. And as I learned over the years (and the hard way, I might add), "you can't please all of the people all the time." (In spite of my best efforts, however, this is once more beginning to feel kind of like I'm sliding toward another one of those times when my mind seems not to be real OK, so I'm going to just sort of keep going, and it probably will pass.) I've learned, as I said at least once before, that to keep going helps. Not always. But mostly. Well, sometimes anyway. I mean you don't want to let yourself get stuck in some kind of "mind pit" or anything. Or like in a "dark" place, where God only knows what evil may lurk. Or other places like that.

Anyway, when I was still pretty little and went to the temple of the Masonics with my mom and my dad and my brother, they (not just my mom and dad, but everyone) would let us gradeschoolers try to dance too. I suspect they thought it was "cute" or something. And probably wholesome. However, to dance was something you could only do of course if you weren't afraid of girls, or maybe too shy to ask them. Some guys (the brave and fearless ones) would just sort of shuffle around the edge of the dance floor, kind of mindlessly rocking back and forth. But not me. I was really good. I could trot like a fox (I figured out later though that the correct expression was "foxtrot," so I hope I never asked any girl if she wanted to trot), and "fast" dance too. Also, when I danced I would sort of imagine that the two of us (the little girl I was dancing with and me) were in Hollywood or somewhere (and if not Hollywood, at least Des Moines, where they had this place called The Tromar Ballroom . . . I think that was the name of the place anyway). But even dancing right there in Washertown kind of felt like Hollywood (at least maybe a little bit), since the Masonics always had a pretty big band for their temple dances. I mean they actually had two or three trumpets (sometimes with mutes in them), a couple of slide trombones (also with mutes in them), lots of clarinets ("licorice sticks"), a saxophone (maybe two even), and a piano player, a drummer, and a pretty good, but I thought sort of fruity-acting, bandleader. He (the bandleader) bounced up and down a lot (sort of like he had an apple in his underwear or something), and also (at least I thought) smiled too much when there wasn't anything to smile about. That, by the way, is something that has always bothered me, i.e. people who smile all the time, when there really isn't anything funny going on. I'd rather they'd just be honest. I mean I'll bet that bandleader was just counting the minutes until he could get out of that goddamn place and go home. Anyway, he was strange. Very strange.

Mostly however, my brother and I and the other kids didn't dance. Instead, we would hang around the room where the billiard tables were (each of which had a shiny brass pot next to it, into which the old guys would spit). Really. I think it was "the age of the spittoon" or something. (That's what they were called: spittoons.) What they spit could be really gross too. So gross in fact that I hardly want to think about it, much less write about it. I mean it was so bad it would probably even make most normal people sick, if they looked at it very long anyway. Some of the stuff would sometimes actually be hanging around the edge of the pot even, or maybe be all dried up on it. And some of it (the spit) was kind of like real thick and greenish-yellow, and way too fresh looking, like one of the "spit guys" had recently gotten sick or something. As I said, it was pretty disgusting, and especially when you could even see the wet globs of the stuff all mixed in with the water in the bottom of the thing (i.e. the spittoon). So anyway I won't even talk about it anymore. Nice people don't talk about spit and shit like that. I don't think, by the way, just to wrap things up here, that women ever spit there (and for sure not the "Eastern Satellites" or "Stars" . . . I sill can't remember for sure what they were called). They probably weren't even allowed in the billiard table room (and wouldn't have wanted to go there if they had been). In fact, I don't think I ever saw a woman spit anywhere. Not even to this very day. Only the men spit (spat?). Unless maybe the women spit/spat in the ladies room or somewhere. I just can't say for sure. I doubt it though.

But anyway, as I started to tell you, most kids would just hang around in the room with the billiard tables, and also run up and down the steep stairs, and sometimes even sneak out to go have one of those famous cherry-vanilla phosphates at Powell's. We weren't supposed to though, so that of course made them taste even better. But I've got to tell you about this one really bad that happened to me at the temple (that's mainly why I took you back here in the first place). I mean I wasn't sacrificed on a pile of burning sticks or anything like that, but it was still pretty bad. In fact, now that I think about it, maybe being sacrificed on a pile of burning sticks would have been less painful. Anyway, you can decide. And this is one of those stories that should remind you that I'm willing to trust you with some pretty embarrassing information; and furthermore, that I always try to be honest with you (although just once in awhile I may leave something out). The point is, how are you supposed to understand me (and how I got to be this way and everything) if, as I've said before, I don't tell you some of these hard-to-say things? I mean someday someone is going to write my biography, probably fairly soon even (literary people always write biographies about famous authors . . . eventually anyway), and they'll need to know this stuff. OK?

So one Saturday night when I went to the temple of the Masonics, with my mom and my dad and my brother, I wore a brand new, brown and tan and sort of white sport coat (I had the sport coat because I was growing up . . . or at least older . . . meaning I think I was maybe in about sixth grade). It (my sport coat) had a sort of "checkered' pattern all over it, with the checks sort of lined up in a "V" formation, like the way ducks fly (kind of). At first I thought that the material it was made of was called "chicken bones" or "herring bones" or something like that; but eventually I learned that it didn't have anything to do with chickens or fish, but was called "hound's tooth." After someone's dog, I guess. Anyway, I looked really good in it. At least I thought so. I was also wearing a real wide, plain yellow necktie (which probably *didn't* look so good . . . even though it seemed to at the time) and a grown-up, starched white shirt that itched me around the neck. My dad had tied the necktie for me (I kept trying, but just couldn't get it right), and he explained to me (he was always teaching me stuff) that the knot was called a "double Windsor," so I felt pretty important about that. I had pants on too of course, tan ones, and also I was wearing brown shoes and argyle socks (which again, like my necktie, may not sound too hot now, but were OK then). *And,* to top it all off (literally), I think I had on (and probably too much) some of that rose-smelling hair oil they used at the Rialto Barber Shop. Remember that stuff? The shit they used when you asked them to "slick it down" (and again maybe too much . . . meaning to "slick it" too much)? Anyway, since the dance was most likely on one of those Saturdays when I got my hair cut, chances are I was pretty slick.

And, to tell you the truth (although not to brag or anything), I wouldn't be surprised if I wasn't looking pretty much like Washertown's own Richard Corey (I hope you haven't forgotten him). In case you did though, he was that guy I learned about in junior high English class. Rick (remember I told you that I thought he would have been a good friend of mine and therefore I would probably have just called him Rick?) . . . *anyway,* Rick Corey was the really handsome guy in the poem written by Edward Arlington Robinson, who everyone thought was pretty much with it and everything, and who had lots of money, and who (according to Mr. Robinson anyway) even "glittered when he walked;" but who (meaning Rick) nevertheless "went home one night and put a bullet in his head." That gets pretty scary again, at least when you really think about it. I mean ending up with a bullet in your head isn't a very good thing to have happen to you, even if you did it yourself. And I still don't know why our teacher had us read stuff like that. Especially when we were only in ninth grade. I mean I can remember (I know I already told you this too, but it's worth saying again) how that poem (not a bullet, thank God) just sort of sank into my own head, and then sank in some more. It gave me a pretty weird feeling, almost sick-like, and one that I never forgot. But I don't mean to make you sad or anything. This part of my book is supposed to be about dancing, and running around, and the one not-so-good time that I had at the Masonic Temple

So remember Janey from second grade? The one whose mother made fudge and then went away for a while, and who (Janey, not her mother) wore that chenille bathrobe for me that I liked so much (that kind of "opened up"), and who therefore sort of got me turned on and everything? Remember her? Good. Well, she was always at the dances too, since her grandparents were also Masonic. Actually of course just her grandfather was . . . grandmothers and other women, as I said before when I mentioned my own grandmother, were called "Ladies of the Night," or "Satellites and Stars," or whatever . . . I still can't remember for sure. I think "Stars of the East" maybe. And now that I think about it more, it was for sure not "Ladies of the Night." Whatever. These local "stars" though weren't like movie stars or anything (like Lana Turner, or Hedy Lamar, or Betty Grable, or any of the other ladies that I've already told you about . . . some of whom may have died in my hotel fire, if you remember that story). Trust me. They weren't like that. They (the temple ladies) pretty much had a style all their own. And it wasn't Hollywood.

Anyway, Janey was there at the Temple, and we danced together. "Slow." Sometimes *real* slow (and close). Slow dancing, at least when I was little and then in high school even, was when a lot of you touched a lot of the other person, and you moved against each other real slow; whereas "fast" dancing, which I mentioned before, was just the opposite, meaning not much of you touched and it almost seemed as though you were moving away from each other . . . and real fast. Well anyway, I was probably thinking about the fudge and the bathrobe and maybe seeing Janey's underpants and everything (not at the dance of course, but just at her house when we were in second grade). And besides, we couldn't "do" anything at the Masonic Temple, unless we maybe sneaked off into a far corner of the billiard room. And I wasn't about to do that. Not with all that green shit and other runny-like stuff in those brass spittoons. So anyway, Janey and I danced . . . and sort of drifted all over the place . . . and played around in the hallways . . . and eventually went ("snuck") down the long stairs to Powell's and drank cherry-vanilla phosphates . . . and then went back where it all started . . . and then danced some more. I remember that it was about then that I started to get this real hot and kind of sweaty feeling (because of all the running around, I guess). And of course my new wool sport coat with the hound's teeth all over it was probably making me feel extra hot too. And maybe this time it was again part Janey that made me hot. But "hot," in that sense (meaning the Janey sense), would probably have been somewhat of an age-inappropriate exaggeration. Although maybe not. Whatever.

So after we got back up the stairs and had danced and everything, and I got hot, we went to a room where there were tables (not billiard tables this time, but just the kind you sat at and played cards and stuff), and I began to feel not only hot, but then cold, and then "sweatyer" and "sweatyer," and then just kind of "funny," like *real* funny (as in sick funny). I think some of the people in the room might even have gone to tell my mom that I didn't look so good. And then it happened. I threw up all over the whole goddamn table! Just missed Janey, but my chicken bone (I mean hound's tooth) sport coat and tan pants (and my shoes), and everything else within about ten feet of me, took a pretty big hit. Trust me. And then it happened right away again. I mean it was bad. *Really* bad! At first I guess I was too sick and goofy feeling to be embarrassed, or really even sure where I was or what had happened to me (and the table and walls and everything else). So I just kept sitting there. But I remember I threw up a lot. A *whole* lot! It was really, *really* disgusting too. So bad that I wouldn't even be telling you about it (except for my pledge of honesty). Like there were these little brown chunks of kind of half-digested food. And some other real icky and "runnyer" stuff (which I think was green maybe). And there was also even some "fizz" (at least I think that's what it was) from the cherry-vanilla phosphate. And smell? Man did it smell! I mean it was bad all right. *God-awful* bad.

And then I remember being rushed to the bathroom where something else started happening. So now I've got the shits (pardon me . . . diarrhea), and I'm just sitting there (on the toilet now, not at the table) suffering (but not like I'd been hit by a car or anything), and just kind of spinning around in my own head, looking at the throw-up stuff all over my chicken bone/hound's tooth sport coat, my now not-so-tan pants, and spattered shoes. All I could think was "Holy shit!" (no pun intended). And then more diarrhea. It was not, you might say, turning out to be one of my better evenings. I'm just glad that if I had to throw up and everything, and right in front of Janey, that it was then, and not four or five years earlier when we were at her house in her (i.e. *on* her) bed. *That* would undoubtedly have messed up my entire sex life (in more ways than one), more even than being caught by her mother. Well (if you can believe this), I learned a lot later, when I took some really off-the-wall psychology course in college, that the night I got so sick at the temple was maybe like I had had both some kind of "oral expressive" and then "anal-explosive episode," all kind of rolled into one or something. That never really made much sense to me though (as I said before, I never really "got into" Freud very much). I just figured I had downed one too many of those icky-sweet cherry vanilla phosphates, barfed, and then had the shits. (Real bad.) Whatever. It was one experience I wouldn't want to repeat. Like its bad enough to get sick and throw-up and have diarrhea at home. But at a temple? And with your girlfriend (sort of)? I mean *holy shit!* Again, bad choice of words I guess (given the circumstances). But I'm telling you, it was BAD!

One other sort of interesting story about the temple (at least I thought it was, and since we're still here I might as well tell you) was when the governor of the whole state of Iowa came there one night. His name was Governor Blue (really). That was his name. Blue. Like in red, white, and blue. And I remember he had real silvery hair and looked really important (maybe like Richard Corey would have looked, had he lived longer). Anyway, he (Governor Blue) came to the Masonic Temple for its fiftieth anniversary celebration (I think that's what it was). And they had ice cream (real white-looking vanilla) that was cut into sort of diamond-shaped pieces. And then each piece (you won't believe this) *each* piece actually had the Masonic Temple emblem in the middle of it, made out of candy or some other kind of real hard stuff you couldn't eat very well. You either just kind of spit I out or put it aside (without calling attention to what you were doing), or you had to suck on it a while before you swallowed. Well, I can tell you that *that* was the fanciest piece of ice cream Washertown had ever seen. I mean they must have had that stuff sent down from Des Moines or somewhere. Maybe even from the Beatrice factory that made the Popsicles I already told you about. Or I guess the governor's people might even have brought it all with them. (Probably not though . . . I mean you don't expect governors to arrive in ice cream trucks.) I don't know though; they may have. Whatever, those things were no "Dixie Cups" with little, paddle-shaped wooden spoons attached to the lids. I'll tell you that! I mean this was pure "class." As in *high* class!

So anyway, I remember I ate two of them (had to sneak the second one). I don't know how many Governor Blue ate, or how many pieces of the "candy" he sucked on, but it was probably just about as many as he wanted. Then he gave some big boring speech abut how good he was, and how good Iowa was, and how good Washertown was, and then topped it all off of course by saying how good it was to be Masonic. Trust me, it was enough to drive a kid right back down the stairs to Powell's for another cherry-vanilla phosphate (whatever the risks). And no (I know what you're thinking), I did *not* get sick and throw-up and have diarrhea this time. I mean, when the governor comes to Washertown and they put colored candy emblems on diamond-shaped pieces of really white vanilla ice cream and have speeches and everything, you don't throw up and you don't get the shits. You might think you're going to; you might even wish you could; but you don't. As they say (another expression that I learned later), "it just isn't done." And besides, it hadn't been that long since I had gotten my sport coat, pants, and shoes cleaned up from the other time. Anyway, so much for trauma and treats at the temple. But I just thought you should know how both good *and* bad things could be for me sometimes. And try to forget about Richard Corey. That was a long time ago. But man, it was a shocker.

So . . . back down the stairs, out the door, past Powell's, cross the alley, and we arrive at Stooley's Music Store. Stooley's display window usually featured a variety of "mouth harps," i.e. Hohner harmonicas (if it wasn't a Hohner, it wasn't a harmonica . . . at least not a good one), two or three pieces of brass, which always included at least one cornet, and, believe it or not, an accordion or two (and if they, i.e. the accordions, weren't from Italy, they weren't very good either). There were usually a few pieces of "sheet" music scattered about as well. Inside, Stooley's was about as dingy as any place could be, although in fairness, the rather dark and dingy look was rather prevalent in 1940s Washertown. Stooley's had one wall covered with patches of old, weird wallpaper (chartreuse, with "Chiquita Banana" women printed on it) that showed through whatever else had been glued or plastered to it over the years. And of course the place smelled. This time the smell was mostly from the musty, unsold paper music books that had accumulated over the years, and the ubiquitous smell (how's that for another of my big words?) of oil and sweeping compound (like at Hoage's Variety) from the worn, dirty-brown wooden floor.

The Stooleys were nice people. Perhaps not terribly sophisticated regarding their tastes in music (or décor), but then neither were most of customers who patronized the place. I mean Washertown wasn't exactly New York City (although I guess I didn't need to say that), and most of the Stooley crowd was more at home in Study Hall (where you went in high school when you didn't have a class) than it would have been in Carnegie Hall. But anyway, the place was good enough, and I have to say that when I was little it was thanks to Stooley's that Washertown had a place to buy up-to-date "45s," and whatever "78s" still remained in stock. And, believe it or not, before you bought any of these recordings, you could actually go play them in a "listening booth" (which of course meant that almost every new record sold at Stooley's was in reality used). Everyone knew that, so you always tried to get there early whenever you thought the latest "hits" had come in. (That way you not only got to be the first to play them, but the first to scratch them up, as you hurriedly jammed them back into their sharp-edged, cardboard "jackets" and returned them to the shelf.) But that was Mr. and Mrs. Stooley's problem, not mine.

By the way, since we're at Stooleys's and talking about music and everything, let me tell you something really fascinating. Well, at least perhaps somewhat interesting. I think anyway. Maybe kind of like famous even, in a strange sort of way. Whatever. It happens that Dick Contino (his name was probably really Richard, but everyone on the radio just called him "Dick") was one of my childhood heroes. You may not remember him, but he played the accordion, I guess better than anyone, and won the "Horace Heitt Original Amateur Hour" radio contest. He was a lot better on the accordion than I was, of course, actually a lot, *lot* better (I sometimes have a hard time even saying that I played one of those things). Anyway, I think that may have been (meaning the reason Mr. Contino was better on the accordion than I was) because he was an Italian, and I was just an Iowan. Maybe. Or it might have been that he was better because he was older and practiced more than I did. Whatever. But although I might not have been as good as he was, I nevertheless played a lot of pretty challenging songs on the accordion myself, like "Red River Valley" (which I mentioned when I told you a long time ago about my musical experiences in second grade) and polkas and stuff like that. And I even had some of them memorized. Really. When I got older though, and didn't get much better (which is probably an understatement), I decided to quit. So I never even came close to being on the "Amateur Hour." But, as they say (I think this is how it goes anyway), "it isn't whether you win or lose, but how you play the thing." Something like that. Anyway, let me tell you two things about my years as an accordionist. You might find them instructional even. Well, at least entertaining. I find them mostly just sort of embarrassing. Nevertheless, if I had ever been chosen to be on "This is Your Life" (another early TV show), I suppose they would have included this stuff.

First, and this was *really* special (then anyway)—and therefore it's OK for you to get excited about it too—I did in fact have my "one big moment" on the stage. When I was only about ten years old (although I don't mean to brag or anything), I was asked to play my accordion at the Casper County Fair in the neighboring city of Fairfax. Actually Fairfax was just a town, and smaller even than Washertown. But this is show business, so I think I should be able to exaggerate just a little bit if I want to. So anyway, I may not have been "Amateur Hour" quality (actually the "amateur" part is probably pretty accurate), but there I was one hot August night, with a veritable sea (that means in truth a whole lot) of people sitting on this grassy knoll and everything (I mean like there must have been 10,000 of them at least . . . maybe more even), all just watching me up on the stage. (Some of them perhaps weren't paying much attention, and were just there to maybe eat popcorn and stuff, and talk and everything, but that was OK.) And I can tell you I was pretty scared, *really* scared as a matter of fact; the kind of scared that makes you think you have to go to the bathroom and everything when you really don't.

But anyway, there I was up on that stage and all alone (except for the accordion that I had strapped to me), and there were all these little lights shining on me, and one great big spotlight that I remember, and probably about 50,000 people (the crowd had grown) were screaming my name and everything. (Actually, there were maybe only two or three hundred people . . . and maybe not quite as many lights as I made it sound like . . . and no screaming.) But two or three hundred is a lot of people, and even one kind of small spotlight is pretty special. Especially when it's shining just on you. Also, as long as I'm whittling this whole thing down a little, I guess there really wasn't much of anything going on with that crowd. In fact, one could pretty easily get the idea that no one gave a shit if I was up there or not. But I *was* there, and doing my best to play "The Twelfth Street Rag," even though as I already told you I was really nervous and stuff. Whatever. Just understand that I was truly "playing my little heart out," as the expression goes. (My cousin had taught me how to play that song, by the way; only she was better than I was too.) But not better as much as Dick Contino the Italian guy was better. Maybe together (meaning my cousin and me) we were about as good as he was though. I don't know. My cousin of course wasn't Italian either.

But I really should stop this (you guessed it . . . that mind wandering thing is starting up again). So anyway, *anyway,* the people clapped a lot after I played, and that made me feel pretty good. (I would have felt a lot better though if I hadn't heard them clap just as much for a skinny little five-year-old, grotesquely made-up and dumb-looking little blonde girl from Fairfax, who twirled her fucking baton just after I had played "The Twelfth Street Rag.") I mean every time she tried to do anything special she dropped the goddamn thing! Why clap for that? But I guess I shouldn't judge ("judge not" . . . more Methodist crap). So anyway, after my "limelight moment" (and the baton bitch's stupid "drop the stick" finale) everyone left the absolutely enormous outdoor theatre where I (we) had just performed (in fact a somewhat grassy knoll with a makeshift stage of saw horses and planks), and went to see some of the fair's other main attractions. Like the pigs, and the cow stalls, and the quilts and homemade jelly and shit like that. I just unstrapped myself, packed up my accordion, went home with my mom and dad, played with my dog for a while ("Snippy"), and went to bed.

The other thing about my accordion had to do with a worm. Really. No kidding. An *Italian* worm I guess, since that's where my accordion had come from (just like Dick Contino's). Mr. and Mrs. Stooley, who had sold the accordion to me (actually to my parents of course), tried to make us believe it wasn't just any old worm, but some exotic kind of very special imported insect or something. I guess they would have said just about anything to try to make things not look so bad. Anyway, what happened was that on one of the most very special days of my entire life (up until when I first had sex maybe), my parents bought me this brand new *red,* sort of marble-looking but plastic accordion (almost all accordions in those days had some kind of marbleized plastic stuff on them). *And,* it was "the big one" too, meaning that it had one hundred and twenty base buttons (accordion aficionados would say, "120 bass" . . . aficionados being another word I of course didn't know then). Whatever. So that meant that mine was just as big as Dick Contino's (meaning that my *accordion* was just as big . . . I was only about nine or ten when I got the thing). Anyway, this big red accordion sometimes had sort of a "squeaky" sound in it, or maybe more like a slight "crunch." Not real loud, and not all the time, but there, nevertheless. It was sort of spooky I thought.

Well, what happened was that one day, about a year after I got it, and just a few weeks after my big performance at the Casper County Fair, I took it out (meaning I took the accordion out of its case) to play it, and there was this hole in the top of it. Right where you could look straight down at it. I mean holy shit, I thought; what the hell is this all about? So anyway, it (the hole) was about the size of a fat pencil, or maybe a regular size Crayola (crayon). But then, *then*, out of this hole (I swear to God this is the truth) came the sort of greenish head of a worm, and the little sucker was looking right back at me. Right at me! Sort of like he thought he owned the thing or something. Then it went back in (meaning the worm went back in its hole). It didn't turn around or anything; it just kind of "backed up." So I told my mom, who called my dad, who came home from work, who picked us up, "who lived in the house that Jack built" (forget that last part . . . I was just trying to be funny), and he drove us down to Stooley's to see what the deal was with this goddamn worm that was living in my hundred and twenty base Italian accordion. I mean holy shit (again)! This was serious.

Well, believe me, Mr. and Mrs. Stooley didn't want to believe that my accordion had worms, but just after I opened the case and got it out (my accordion), it (the worm) came crawling right up from its hole again, and now sort of seemed to be staring at *all* of us! You can be sure Mr. and Mrs. Stooley were just a little bit upset. So anyway, Mr. Stooley pulled it out (the worm), right in front of everyone (I guess he was more of a "take charge" sort of guy than I had thought). He just grabbed that little sucker right around the head, pulled it out of its hole, and put it in a glass of water. I don't know what he planned to do with it. Drown it, I guess. And then, a day or two later, Mr. Stooley (or maybe Mrs. Stooley . . . I don't really know, since I wasn't there) filled in the hole with some kind of plastic wood or something, told us some story about exotic worms, and declared the situation to be taken care of. Well, maybe *they* thought so, but I didn't. The hole with the plastic wood in it (that wasn't even the right color), I thought anyway, looked pretty shitty. I mean I'll bet Dick Contino wouldn't have been expected to play an accordion with a plugged up and not even the right color wormhole. That's for sure! However, it seems the Stooleys were two more of the people that my dad "did business with" (remember that arrangement?), and he (my dad) didn't seem to think we could do anything more about it.

Later on, by the way, I found out that Mr. Stooley had kept the worm (to have it investigated, I guess). He said, and I kind of liked this part (not that I believed very much of it), that he had found out that the worm was *definitely* Italian, and that it was very rare for this to happen (no shit), and that it had probably hatched in the wood, and had therefore been there ever since my accordion was put together in Italy. (He probably thought the fucking worm was Catholic too.) But anyway, as I said, I did kind of like some of what Mr. Stooley was saying, at least when I put it all together, since it made me think that I might therefore someday get to be as good as Dick Contino. I mean he, Dick, as I already told you, was Italian. The accordion was Italian (as I also already said). And the *worm* (according to Mr. Stooley's "story") was even Italian. Therefore, although I was just Iowan, and not Catholic, but Methodist, all the Italian talk somehow made me kind of wonder if part of it would maybe rub off on me. But I didn't wonder much. I mean I'm not stupid. In fact, what I just said is total bullshit. I don't even know why I said it. And I still didn't like having an accordion with a goddamn wormhole in it. Patched or not. Whatever. Several years later I traded my accordion back to Mr. Stooley for my first "Hi-Fi" set. I was pretty sure that it (my newly acquired "Voice of Music") didn't have worms, and I had decided that playing the accordion was not a very sophisticated way to become famous. Maybe in Italy. Maybe in Poland. And maybe at the Casper County Fair even. But not at The State University of Iowa, where I was soon to be a freshman. But we need to get back to our walk around the Square, and I'm going to try real hard from now on not to digress so much. You might miss out on some good stories and a little bit of other important stuff, but you can't have everything. And anyway, my book isn't supposed to be some kind of *Encyclopedia Britannica*.

Next stop, believe it or not, is a place called The Washertown Seed and Feed Store. Really. The forerunner of the suburban plant nursery, I guess. I never spent much time at this place though, since it made me think too much of hot summer days, sweat, the neighborhood yards that I had to mow, and being really thirsty. The Seed and Feed Store smelled good though (with one exception). Both inside and out. It had a real fresh and "earthy" smell, if you know what I mean . . . and you probably do. And although it looked like they had piles of just sandbags or something stacked out on the sidewalk, the bags actually contained totally pure and natural stuff, like black Iowa dirt, and mulch. The bags of fertilizer were another story (the one exception to the smell-good areas). They were pure in one sense (since it was mostly lamb shit), but really smelly. Bad smelly, as in stinky smelly, especially when the stuff got wet. I also remember that the grass seed you could buy at the Seed and Feed Store (to get away from the shit) came in great big gunnysacks. If you wanted less, it was weighed out for you on a large, old "balance" that had a big tin scoop hanging next to it. They would pour the seeds from the gunnysacks into the scoop, weigh it, and then put it into brown paper bags. (Actually, in Iowa and Washertown things were always put in "sacks," not bags.) Even at the grocery store they "sacked" your groceries, which of course had nothing to do with anyone trying to destroy them or anything.

Once in a while there was also a rather unpleasant chemical smell at the Seed and Feed Store (kind of like the pharmaceutical smells at Gurdy's and Powell's, only stronger). I think it (the chemical smell) was from stuff that was supposed to kill insects, even though it was still just the 1940s, when people pretty much thought that God and the heat should take care of most bad bugs. Whatever, the Washertown Seed and Feed Store was a decent, proper, almost moral-feeling even, necessary place. After all, it provided us the basics for life on our part of God's earth: packets of seeds, trays ("flats") of plants, some shrubs and stuff, bags of dirt (black, Iowa dirt of course), and real sheep shit for fertilizer, as I already told you. Sorry about the shit word (although I guess I've used it lots of times before), but I never heard that stuff called anything else. I mean shit is shit. And man, as I sort of hinted at before, if it rained real heavy right after you spread the stuff, you wanted to leave town. I don't know who owned this place (The Seed and Feed Store), by the way. It might have been the Burpee family, but I doubt it; although you saw that name (Burpee) on just about everything in there. The Burpees didn't live in Washertown though. At least as far as I know they didn't. But anyway, just one more thing. At Christmas time they stacked lots and lots of Christmas trees in front of the Washertown Seed and Feed Store. They were sort of "tied up" with twine, and then leaned against the wall of the building, right out on the sidewalk. And trust me, the scent of fresh cut pine from those trees, especially when the air was already heavy with that sort of friendly, moist, December air smell, was absolutely wonderful. You just wanted to stand there and suck it in. And it more than made up for any chemicals or sheep shit that may have been left over from summer. But let's keep going here.

Walking towards the north end of the west side of the Square (don't fall behind), we come to Keefe and McNaughton's Jewelry Store. *The* jewelry store of Washertown. It had real, mahogany-framed, beveled glass cases, in which they displayed what (at least when I was little) seemed to be thousands and thousands of dollars (maybe millions even) worth of real jewels. Mostly diamonds, but they had some pearls and rubies and emeralds too (and also those purple stones that were hard to spell). I even kind of didn't feel real comfortable in there by myself, since it was so nice and everything. And they sold genuine Longine watches there too (not just Bulova's and Elgin's, like some other places). Longine watches were only for the really rich people. Bulova and Elgin ones were for the more ordinary people. And Timexes and Westclocks were for everyone else. Some people in Washertown probably didn't even have a watch at all. At least when I was little they maybe didn't. Unless perhaps it was a "hand-me-down" from their grandfather or something. I still have my dad's Bulova, by the way. It was one of the better ones that Bulova made: fourteeen carat gold and everything. And it has engraving on the back, since it had been a gift from the people in the Sunday School class he taught. In Washertown, by the way, and maybe other places too, but I don't know for sure since I obviously didn't live in other places, they talked about "Bulova Watch Time" on the radio. I think that was supposed to mean that that was what time it *really* was, in case you just had an old Timex or something. At least I think that was it. Whatever. Keefe and McNaughton's also sold "fine" china and silverware and everything, and you could see real "loose" diamonds there, if you were a grown-up and maybe wanted to get married or something. As you can tell, it was a pretty fancy place. Especially to a soon-to-be older guy (like high school) who not only appreciated nice things, but was becoming an increasingly, and eventually incurably, romantic young man.

Next to Keefe and McNaughton's was Wormley's Men's and Boy's Store. Remember the worm in my accordion? Well, Wormley's didn't have anything to do with that of course; the name just kind of made me think about it again. Anyway, the boy's department at Wormley's was where I got most of my good stuff when I was little (the other, less good stuff came from Montgomery Ward's, or maybe J.C. Penney's), although most years I actually got a lot of my good school clothes at Younker's Department Store in Des Moines. Anyway, the boy's department at Wormley's was at the back of the store, up a sloping, ramp-like section of floor that was covered with ribbed, rubber stuff; I suppose so you wouldn't fall or roll down or anything. I don't know why the floor went up that way. Perhaps it was because of some furnace pipes in the basement, or maybe because they just liked it that way or something. But as I just said, I really don't know (and also really don't care), and probably you don't either. At least I doubt if you do. You might though. Anyway, you don't even need to know the details about the floor. Just remember that there was a sort of strange-like "bump" in it. But it's always things like this (as you know) that are what can sometimes get my mind messed up and stuff, and I *hate* when that happens. So let's just forget it and go on. I mean a funny bump in the floor of a men's and boy's store isn't exactly the kind of thing a person should obcess about. And besides, all that this makes me think about right now (i.e. the word *obsess,* which comes of course from the word *obsession*) is a movie that was pretty big when I was little called *Magnificent Obsession,* or something like that. I think it was a book first though. Or maybe not. Whatever. (I can't even remember now what it was about.)

It was at Wormley's that I got to buy my first mid-1940s, shiny, "stretchy-type" swim suit, although it took a lot of talking on my part to get it. I think that was because it cost so much . . . like maybe two dollars even. Anyway, it was made of some kind of real new and fancy material. I also remember that I had a hard time deciding between the emerald green one and the one that was real "maroony" red. I finally chose the green one; I think because it seemed shinier. And not only did I think it looked really neat, but it also meant that I no longer had to wear the hairy, scratchy, belted and baggy, *wool* swimming suit that I had had for the last two years. It was sort of faded yellow, if you're interested (meaning the old hairy one), although that's probably not real important to remember. Anyway, another thing that made the shiny green one special was that when the yellow wool one got wet it always kind of gaped open around your legs, especially if you had skinny ones (I *hated* the word "skinny"), which of course I did (i.e. have skinny legs). They sort of went with the rest of my body.

So anyway, when that happened (meaning. when the wool swimming suit gaped) you could kind of see up it, or maybe (if you didn't watch how you sat) you cold even see clear in it. Actually of course, when you were in fourth grade there wasn't a whole lot to see (as if anyone cared or was even looking). And if by chance the gaping actually allowed your "thing" to accidentally hang right out, there still wasn't much to see. But even when you were just a little kid, and especially if the pool water was so cold that it had shrunk you up to nothing, you still had your pride. What your parents called your "wee-wee," or maybe your "pee-pee" (and you called your DICK, which is what it was), seemed just a little too personal to be displayed like that. Big or little. Frozen or thawed. Anyway, my emerald green swimming suit didn't gape. It *did* however make me stick out a little more in front; but there wasn't a guy in Washertown who didn't feel pretty good about sticking out in front. Especially when you got older, and your "wee-wee/pee-pee" DICK and "stuff" started to get bigger, if you know what I mean (and I'm sure you do).

I also bought some of my school clothes at Wormley's, although as I already told you, I got a lot of that stuff at Younker's in Des Moines. In early August, however, when it was pretty close to time to get ready for school to start and everything, Wormley's would often have three or four (or maybe even five or six) plaid shirts to choose from. Sometimes though they wouldn't have the ones I liked best in my size. In fact, it seemed like that was usually the case. So, since there were more shirts at Younker's, most years (and especially when I got older) my mom would take us (my brother who didn't like me very much, and me) there to get our school clothes. Actually, I think some of the reason we went to Younker's was because she liked to go there herself. I learned that for a mom in the 1940s, getting out of town for a whole day, with lunch at "a lot nicer than Washertown had" restaurant (or maybe even at Bishop's Cafeteria, which was *really* special) was pretty much fun. However, my mom always spent most of the money she had on my brother and me, since she was a really good mom and loved us a lot. And so was my dad good, since he of course was the one who made the money to give to my mom to buy the stuff. She still got an occasional nice lunch in Des Moines though.

Also, by the way, for most of our school clothes trips to Des Moines, my grandfather's housekeeper, who later became his wife (after my grandmother died kind of early), and who then even more later became pregnant (which of course surprised the hell out of everyone, and among lots of other things resulted in my having an uncle who was eight years younger than me) . . . anyway, she (the housekeeper/wife/eventually mother of my uncle) went with us. And that made it even more fun. She always drove the car, my grandfather's gray (of course), 1936 Chevy two-door sedan. The official Washertown pronunciation of Chevy was *Chivy*, by the way). Later on, although I hate to have to tell you this, my grandfather and his wife had some really sad and pretty awful things happen. That was because their little boy (that no one thought they could have, since they were older), and the one who was my "little" uncle, died after being hit by a car when he was only nine-years-old. He was a very special little boy, and I thought it was really neat to have an uncle younger than I was, so when that car hit him, for those reasons and lots of others, it was really, really sad. For everyone. I hid out in my room and cried. And on more days than just when it happened too. But I don't want to make you sad, and I don't want to be either, so let's just go on.

Next, and before we go on to the place on the corner, I want to tell you about one of our Des Moines trips that I thought was really special. I know you'll like it, so that's mostly why I want to tell you. Anyway, it was on a cold, gray (like the Chevy), rainy day in November, and we all (my mom, and my brother who *still* didn't like me very much, and my grandfather's housekeeper, and me) went to Des Moines to get more school clothes (winter stuff this time). It was when I was in kindygarden, and since I hated school so much I really, *really* liked getting to skip school to go. My grandfather's housekeeper, by the way, and our driver, and later on his wife (as I just told you) was a really special lady. Her name was Jessie (at least that's what we called her), and she was always doing nice things for us. She liked my brother and me a whole lot . . . kind of as though we were her own kids. I sometimes even used to stay all night with her when I was little, like maybe when I was just four or five, and the next day she would get up and bake sugar cookies for me, and let me help. As I said though, what eventually happened to her and my grandfather and their little boy was really sad, and since this story isn't supposed to be about sad things, I'm going to try real hard not to say anything more about all that. Besides, I already said I wouldn't (up above). And also, if I'm not careful, I might get that kind of crazy in the head thing going again, only in a different way than usual, by just thinking about them. But anyway, we need to get back on our way to Des Moines.

So here's how it worked that day. I got to choose three new shirts (flannel, for warmth) and two pairs of pants (corduroys, again for warmth), and all at the same time! Talk about fun. Pants usually meant "Levi's," of course, the kind you put on and then got wet in (either by hosing yourself down or by getting in the bathtub with them on). That supposedly made them shrink to your body (or so we were led to believe by the older guys, like the third and fourth graders maybe). But now of course, as I just said, given the approaching winter, it was corduroys (brown or gray). Shirts, by the way, as I mentioned a while ago, still meant plaid, but that was OK. Shoes were another and not so fun story, so I'll wait and tell you about shoes when we get to the north side of the square where the goddamn Buster Brown shoe store that I had to go to was. (I hated that place.) Not as bad as I hated school, but almost.

Anyway, getting to skip school and ride to Des Moines on a cold, rainy, November day was cozy and fun and real safe feeling and everything. And we not only went to Younker's that day, but also to another department store called The Utica (a name that sounded pretty strange to me). And then we had lunch at a place called Skondra's (or something like that). Supposedly (at least this is what my mom said), Skondra's made your complexion look good, since it had soft, kind of "glowy" lights on the ceiling. Anyway, women liked the place, so that's where we ate. And then on the way home, we stopped to get ice cream at a store called Reed's, where they sold their ice cream in real long "tubes" that were wrapped in paper (really), which they whacked off at various lengths. Mostly five cent or ten cent lengths. I liked vanilla best, or orange sherbet. My brother liked chocolate. But that gets into yet another story that I think I should leave alone. Anyway, going to Des Moines was really fun, and if I hadn't had to grow up and everything, I'd probably still be going. But also, every time I think about all these good times and stuff, I remember my mom and my dad and my brother and Jessie and my grandfather and their little boy and all my other family people who aren't here anymore. And sometimes it can make me feel pretty bad. (I guess I'm having a hard time here getting away from sad feelings.) I'm OK though, so don't worry about it.

So let's keep going and finish up this side of the Square. On the corner, west side, north end (Gurdy's, where we started, was the west side, south end . . . just so you won't get confused or lost or anything) . . . anyway on the corner was what I thought was a pretty strange, Washertown "institution" called The Scoreboard. That's right, The Scoreboard (its real name). It was a really dingy place (kind of like Stooley's Music Store, only worse), and it was filled with lots of sort of peculiar and pretty icky smells, including the odor of old and really awful cigarette, pipe, and probably even cigar smoke, along with a lot of other musty stuff. All mixed together. And there was also just a trace of that "unflushed urinal coming from the bathroom" smell, suggesting that the place might not be too clean. In a sense then, The Scoreboard could sometimes kind of make you think of the Courthouse in summer, the Methodist Church basement all the time, and that Iowa theatre, with the popcorn machine that was just a little too close to the men's room.

Anyway, guys went to The Score Board to get all the "ball" scores (mostly baseball), which were written by hand on a long chalkboard that was placed above and behind a bar (sort of a bar anyway, although you couldn't buy beer there or anything) that stretched the entire length of the place. Anything you could smoke, however, and candy and gum and gigantic, red "Delicious" apples were sold over that bar. Had those over-sized apples been available anywhere else, by the way, they would have been really good. The rumor was, however, that the owner of The Scoreboard "spit-polished" them. Not a pleasant thought. Whatever, I wasn't sure why anyone would want to go there anyway, except for the ball scores; unless maybe some clandestine (a word I of course didn't know then) activities were going on that I hadn't figured out yet. What I know for sure is that *I* wasn't supposed to go there. It wasn't thought of as a good place for gradeschoolers (or even junior or senior high guys) to go.

I guess they probably sold black market rubbers or something. I don't know. Or maybe "pocket" books that were even better than (meaning of course "dirtier" than) the ones at Gurdy's. I just don't know. I *do* remember however, now that I think about it more, that The Scoreboard had what were called "punch boards." I can't remember for sure how they worked, but I know that they were just about the best you could do (at least in public) with a gambling habit in Washertown. But enough of this place. It stinks.

Across the street from The Scoreboard was a place I absolutely *must* tell you about, even though to do so represents sort of a "side trip," since this particular establishment was not really on the Square, but was instead the cornerstone of an adjacent block. But that doesn't matter. You simply cannot not hear about this place. I mean it was a genuine, "one-in-a-million," Washertown-only phenomenon. And, one of my very most favorite and often frequented stops. The place was called The Orange Bar (again its real name). The emphasis was on "orange" (as in *orange* bar, not orange *bar*). And that's just what it was. A bar that sold orange juice, *fresh squeezed* orange juice, pineapple juice (again fresh), and sandwiches, candy, and other good stuff. All year long, *all year long,* there was fresh orange juice, right there in Washertown, Iowa. Even in the winter there was fresh orange juice. And believe me, for the 1940s that was pretty unusual. So anyway, let me tell you what it looked like, since that was part of its charm.

The outside of The Orange Bar had great big plate glass windows and really nice, bleachy-clean white awnings that protruded over the sidewalk. The windows were sort of framed with orange and white siding, and the door was on the corner, at an angle, just behind one round, iron post that sort of held the area up. And, if you looked down at the ground, just before you went in, there were these really little, eight-sided pieces of tile (white, with black lines around them). And inside (with all this detail, you can tell I really liked the place) there was a classic, black and white tile floor (big squares this time). Then there were "chin-high" (when you were little anyway), glass-front display cases on one wall, just loaded, and I do mean loaded, with candy and gum and stuff. And the bar itself, the ORANGE bar, was a long, white, really clean-looking, smooth-topped, shiny counter that ran down the whole length of the place, right opposite the candy cases. The bar was quite a bit more than "chin-high," so when you were little you had to kind of reach up when you were getting something. But that just made it seem all the more special! It got lower of course when you got older. Just like the candy cases.

Large, arching, polished chrome spigots, with sort of round and flat ceramic levers attached to them, allowed the juice to be pumped up from big vats that were hidden under the bar, and into medium-tall, kind of like "fluted" and "footed" glasses. And when that juice, that super-fresh, really foamy, bright orange orange juice came up through that pump, out of the spigot, and into your glass, it did so with this really neat and wonderful kind of "whooshing" sound, that made it so you could hardly wait to start drinking the stuff. And you could have all orange, all pineapple, or half and half. All you had to do was to tell the owners (who were always there running the place). And, (ready for this?) that juice was only five cents a glass! That's right. For five cents, all the sunshine in Florida and vitamin C in the whole United States (maybe the world even) were yours. And *then,* as if this place wasn't already paradise enough, they also sold tuna and ham salad sandwiches, for just ten cents each (and I'm not kidding about the price either). On really special days my mom would give me a quarter to go there from school to have my lunch. Two sandwiches (I usually had tuna) and a glass of fresh juice (all orange), all for only one quarter! Not bad. And you got to enjoy your lunch even more because you could sit in one of the two white, steel, outdoor-type, sort of "springy" chairs (the kind rich people had on their porches) that sat at the front of the store right next to the window. They had steel mesh seats and backs, with pretty big holes in the seat bottom part. Just big enough to get your finger stuck if you were messing around and weren't careful.

Actually, one time I did that (got my finger stuck in a seat hole), but it wasn't at The Orange Bar. It was on a two-decker boat with my mom and my dad and my brother (who didn't like me very much, then either) when we were on vacation at Clear Lake (remember the twenty-five Popsicles?). Clear Lake, I forgot to tell you before, actually wasn't very clear; in fact it wasn't very clear at all, but it was an exciting place to go for vacations to swim and go boating and everything. Especially if you remembered not to open your mouth when you were under water. Anyway, it (i.e. my finger that was in the seat hole on the boat) swelled up and hurt pretty bad and everything, and seemed to me to be becoming like sort of a big emergency or something. I mean I couldn't even get off the boat after the ride was supposed to be over. I suppose some people probably would have just left me there, since I shouldn't have been sticking my finger in the seat holes anyway, but not my mom and dad. They (actually, it was probably just my dad, since my mom was getting pretty emotionally upset herself) got a man who worked on the boat who had a screwdriver and some pliers and stuff, and he pried open the seat hole just a little bit so my finger could come out. Well, it did; and even though it hurt really bad, I didn't even cry. I think I was just glad that I wasn't going to have to live the rest of my life on a boat with my finger in a hole. But I've kind of gotten off the track again, so lets get back to Washertown and that little piece of paradise called The Orange Bar.

I never threw up at the Orange Bar, like I did after eating "hot lunch" at school and drinking too many cherry phosphates the night of the Masonic Temple dance. In fact I don't know why I even said that. I mean The Orange Bar was just too nice a place to throw up in, and besides, there wasn't anything about it that would have made you have to (like rotten tuna or something). Anyway (I'm trying to get back on track here), since my mom and dad had enough money, but not a lot, I ate lunch mostly at school or at home, so orange juice and two tuna sandwiches at the Orange Bar was actually only an occasional thing. I'll always remember it though, since it was a real treat. And healthy too. The people who owned this incredible place, by the way, (an older couple, or so it seemed at the time) were just as nice as the place itself. And they even looked as clean too. Also, as I told you already, they seemed to be the only people who ever worked there. So I guess what I'm trying to say is that the owners looked as though they not only owned the place, but also actually "belonged" to it. "Just right," 1940's Americans: that's what they were!

Oh, and one more thing. It was at The Orange Bar that they got the very first box of Fleer's "Double Bubble" bubble gum near the end of World War II. You couldn't get "Double "Bubble anywhere during the war because (at least this might have been the reason anyway) it probably had some of the same stuff in it that the army used to make tires out of or something. I think so anyway. And they

(Mr. and Mrs. Foster, the owners) let me buy *five* pieces all at one time (at a penny a piece). Five pieces! I told you they were really nice. They sort of "rationed out" the rest of it so lots of other kids could get some too. However, as the saying goes, "all good things must come to an end," so I guess we have to leave this place. At least for now. But believe me, it's one place I'll never forget; and you wouldn't either if you had ever gone there. (You can probably tell that it was really special, since I only said good things and used all nice words the whole time we have been here.) Well, that's it. The Orange Bar: a Washertown, an *American*, treasure.

OK. North side. West end. Sander's Grocery Store. A good place. My mother would have liked to have shopped at Sander's, but I guess my Dad and Mr. Sander didn't "do business" with each other. A friendly place too. I know, because I went there at least once with my grandfather's housekeeper who, as I told you before, would later become his wife. She always shopped Sander's. In fact, she just might have been their best and most loyal customer, at least for Folger's coffee and CocaCola. She liked her cokes so much that she always bought them "by the case," which meant that she got a total of twenty-four of those classic-shaped green bottles for (believe it or not) just one dollar! And in a wooden "case." You have to remember though, that this was the 1940s. Anyway, now that I look back, I think the dear lady may have had some kind of an out of control need for the stuff or something. Sort of like she was a coke addict maybe, only when that mostly just meant someone who liked CocaCola a whole lot. And I remember she would really argue with you if you even suggested that any other coffee, even Maxwell House (the "good to the last drop" stuff), could compare to Folgers (which of course was "mountain grown"). And trust me, she would have had no time for anyone who tried to suggest that PepsiCola was in the same league with Coke. Pepsi might have had a few more ounces in each bottle, but it sure didn't have the flavor. But anyway, I guess there isn't much more I can say about Sander's, except that it was one place that smelled really *good*. They, like the A&P, ground their own coffee beans sometimes. (I guess that meant that not everyone wanted Folger's in a can.) I also remember (can't seem to get out of this place) that Sander's had a really classy-looking awning, perhaps even the best of all the stores on Washertown's

Square. I think it was kind of chocolate brown, with maybe a real skinny yellow or ivory stripe. And just one more thing. To the best of my knowledge, Mr. Sanders had neither an alcove in which, nor an Eileen with whom he "did" anything. Sander's Grocery was simply your basic, friendly, all-American, family owned and operated place to buy groceries.

Next door to Sander's was McBond's Men's Store. No boy's stuff though, so I was not to know much about the place until I got older (high school), and had a part-time after school job there. My dad bought most of his clothes at McBond's (not only did he and Mr. McBond "do business;" they were good friends and neighbors). The neighbor part gave me a real edge when looking for the part-time job. McBond's, by the way, was considered a pretty first-class place to work, for those of us who chose after school jobs over football, basketball, and track. It won't surprise you to know, I'm sure, that I chose early. As I already said, I didn't like sports much, didn't do well when I tried, and therefore felt really good about having this job instead. My "career" as a clothes salesman was sort of an interim period for me though, since it was pretty much wedged in between my early and abortive junior high athletic career (disaster that it was) and my eventual debut on the Washertown High School stage (which, but only momentarily, was also somewhat abortive also.) The latter "abortion," as you may recall, was because I smoked *one*-third of *one* goddamn cigarette at *one* play practice (at night and in the parking lot), which activity (and I still can't believe it) led to my assumably total moral collapse, which therefore resulted in the bullshit of my being "feced" out of school for a week, and subsequently rejected (three months later) by a dumb-ass faculty committee of "select" shitheads, as the person to lead "The Pledge of Allegiance" at our fucking graduation exercises. Whew . . . what a sentence! And I'm sorry about so many bad words, but just thinking about that crap still pisses me off. (You do have to say though, that I've been doing a lot better with my list of adjectives.) At least *some* better anyway.

Whatever. Next to McBond's was Gottlieb's Ladies Apparel. The Gottliebs were one of Washertown's three or four Jewish families (I can't remember for sure just how many there were). Max, you may recall (earlier story), another Washertown Jew, was the guy who wanted to hit a few golf balls at the Country Club but couldn't, because of the Board's fear that he may have connections with the Jewish Mafia in Des Moines (or maybe something even worse). Mr. Gottlieb was undoubtedly a friend of Max's (the "birds of a feather" phenomenon perhaps), but he (Mr. Gottlieb) didn't play golf, and therefore the town leaders at the Country Club didn't have to tell him where he could go (or play). Anyway, Gottlieb's was a women's apparel store, and the finest one in Washertown, although in the minds of Washertown's most fashion conscious ladies it was not, of course, as fine (i.e. as sophisticated, or elegant, or fashionable, etc. etc. etc.) as "The French Room" at (you guessed it) Younker's Department Store in Des Moines. When I was little, that "room," i.e. the "The *French* Room," was considered to be someplace *really* special, so special in fact that when you went in there you sort of felt you shouldn't talk very loud (like in a library or a bank maybe). I know, because I went there once with my mother. She just kind of wanted to see the place.

So therefore (brief digression), because that French place was at Younker's, I sort of felt extra important sometimes about buying my school stuff there (at Younker's in general, not of course at "The French Room"). I mean French stuff at Younker's? The very same store where I bought my Levi's and plaid shirts? For all I know (although no one ever told me this), the area where I got my Levi's may have been called "The Jewish Room" or something. But I don't think so. I mean I never saw any signs saying it. Anyway, I just kind of thought of that "on the spur of the moment" (another expression I never really understood), since Levi is a Jewish name. At least I think it is. Whatever. As you might suspect, of course, my dad didn't "do business" with the French, but he did with Mr. Gottlieb. He (meaning my dad) not only did business with Mr. Gottlieb, he even quoted a lot of sayings and stuff from the *Old Testament* for the adult Sunday School class that he taught at The First Methodist Church (the place, as you might remember, with the sort of smelly toilets, too many pigeons, and diaphragm for a dome). So how's that for having an open mind? Anyway, my dad and Mr. Gottlieb were friends, and, as I said, "did business" with each other. So Gottlieb's was where my mother bought some of her clothes (actually, not very many though, since as I said up above, the place was pretty expensive). But every once in a while, on special occasions, she would buy something really nice there.

In fact one time I remember, just after the War (WW II), when everyone wanted to buy nice things again, she bought a black, "Swanson's" suit there (a pretty fancy label at the time . . . at least Mr. Gottlieb said so), that had a big "swirly" skirt. It was just like (well almost just like) some of the suits you saw in the movies that were created by this really famous designer named Christian Dior (who, although French, probably never even heard of "The French Room" at Younker's). At least I think that's who it was. But I remember for sure that it was important that my mom's new suit was a "Swanson," since (as I already sort of said) that was supposed to make it special. And then (as if this "Swanson" and "Dior" stuff wasn't enough), for one really special Christmas (two or three years later), my dad bought my mom a full length, "mink-dyed" muskrat fur coat at Gottlieb's. I remember she cried and everything, since she was so surprised and excited. My dad giving her that coat was so special that my brother and I even had to hold off opening our own presents and stuff until she got herself under control. And then, a few more years later, after the plastic "piping" on our car's seat covers, and other experiences of wear and tear, had worn some of the hair (I guess I mean fur) off the bottom part of the her coat, it got sent to a tailor shop where it was changed into my mother's "mink-dyed" muskrat fur *jacket*. I know this is a little off track again, but I always thought it was strange that people in those days almost always bought seat covers for their cars, even when they were brand new. I guess you were supposed to save the good seat for the next owner or something.

But back to Gottlieb's and the fine things for the ladies of Washertown. Gottlieb's was a kind of narrow, deep, and very plain looking store, and it was carpeted from your very first step inside the door (which made for some really slushy and dirt-stained areas in the winter). The center of the store was all open space, with absolutely nothing there at all, and the clothes racks were recessed into the walls on both sides, going all the way to the back of the place. Way, way back. Gottlieb's didn't smell, by the way (a Washertown rarity), except maybe for a really, really faint smell of some perfume they may have sold (but not French, of course). So "score one for the Jews." Or maybe the place didn't smell simply because it was a ladies' store, and ladies aren't supposed to smell. At least not bad anyway. But let's not get into that. I mean I really don't consider myself to be an expert on every kind of smell, and I guess it really doesn't matter how ladies (or Gottlieb's itself) smelled anyway. Or maybe it does. I don't know. Whatever. All this was a long time ago, and I really don't want to let it get me too off center here and then end up wacky in the head again. God knows (and of course so do you) how hard that is for me to control sometimes. I mean who gives a rat's ass about these kinds of things anyway? And we all know that what smells good to one person might not smell so good to another. (And "vice versa," or something like that.)

So to just keep going here, I also remember that whenever I was in Gottlieb's (which admittedly wasn't real often . . . and probably shouldn't have been), the place was always real quiet (a little bit like the French place at Younker's, only not nearly as much). Kind of like the Washertown Library though, or maybe like something was wrong, or something bad was about to happen. And the only person I remember seeing there (other than customers) was Mr. Gottlieb himself. He was a gracious man (I wouldn't have used that word then, but I would now). Maybe even too gracious at times, but then he knew it was an uphill climb for a Jew in Washertown, so he probably once in a while tried just a little too hard. You have to remember, as I pointed out a long time ago, that more than a few Christians in Washertown still thought of the Jews as "Christ killers." In fact, that kind of thinking was so prevalent that some of the wealthier Washertown Catholics (although there weren't many) would probably have preferred that their wives shop at a store named for the Virgin Mary or something . . . as if Velma Coyle's Ladies Shop (on the east side of the square, which we'll get to later) could perhaps have been renamed "Virgin Velma's" or something.

Actually though, she (the Virgin Mary, not Velma Coyle) wasn't much of a "dresser" (at least not in most of the pictures I saw of her), so a fancy ladies shop named after her probably wouldn't have done very well. Casual stuff, maybe. Or maternity wear. Yeah . . . that's it! A maternity shop! "Virgin Mary's Maternity Shop." But still nothing fancy. Whatever. (Why do I get off on these things?) Anyway, I think most Washertown ladies thought Mr. Gottlieb's dresses and things were quite lovely. And I didn't mean to say anything bad about Mary the Virgin. I mean although her clothes were pretty plain, I thought she herself was kind of pretty. At least in one of the pictures that hung in the "Ladies Parlor" at The First Methodist Church she was. And give her a break; she was only about fifteen (someone told me that anyway) when she got pregnant. Man, now that I think about it, had she gotten pregnant in Washertown at fifteen, she would have had some real problems! *Real* problems. I mean she wouldn't have been able to go to school or anything (and no graduation "Pledge of Allegiance" for her either, that's for sure). In fact, her mom and dad would probably have had to take her to some farm for unwed mothers on the other side of Des Moines or somewhere. Maybe Chicago even. Whatever.

Given the cultural climate of Washertown in the 1940s (not that it was probably much different in this sense from most other towns), let me say just a little more about the Gottlieb's as a family. First of all, they were simply very nice people. I knew their two children from when I was real little, mostly because we lived close by and the neighborhood kids used to slide down the hill in their backyard when it snowed. Their daughter's name was Goldene, so of course I figured they were really rich. And actually, for Washertown anyway, I guess they were. They lived on Fifth Avenue. South Fifth Avenue West to be exact. I know . . . that was Washertown's strange way of stating addresses (i.e. not Fifth Avenue SW, but South Fifth Avenue West), as you may remember from my telling you before. Whatever. Living on South Fifth Avenue West was *almost* but not quite as good as living on South *Sixth* Avenue West. And of course Washertown's Fifth Avenue had absolutely nothing to do with Fifth Avenue in New York City. Except in the springtime, I guess, when just about anyone who lived on a fifth avenue *anywhere* couldn't help but think about a much-loved song and all the Easter stuff and everything. Remember that "Easter Parade" song? "On the Avenue/ Fifth Avenue." It was always on the radio, kind of like Christmas music, only at Easter when it was warmer. The composer, as you probably know (I talked about him before), was an extraordinarily talented young American song writer whose first name was Irving, although Washertown Christians wouldn't have wanted to think much about what *that* implied. Just think. A Christ killer wrote their favorite Easter song! Somewhat ironic, isn't it? And maybe, but in a different way, almost as bad as thinking about Cole Porter's "Love for Sale" or "Anything Goes," and stuff like that.

Anyway, "In your Easter bonnet/With all the frills upon it" (etc. etc.) was really big in Washertown. But I remember Easter mostly because of the Easter Bunny and all the candy and colored eggs. And I also remember the caged rabbits at the Seed and Feed Store that you could take home and put in a box in your own house, and the tinted and tortured little Easter chickens that you also let live in a box, and then threw away when they started to grow up, get ugly, and sprout wing feathers. Of course, people are *really* supposed to remember Easter because that was when Jesus (having been dead for three days) got up, walked out of his tomb, talked to his girlfriend, Mary, and a few of his other close friends, strolled around town for awhile, and then went up to heaven and everything (in a cloud). Fascinating! A little hard to believe maybe, but that was the story (actually the Mary part remains sort of controversial I think). And I'm not saying I didn't believe it (when I was in Sunday School anyway). And also, I don't mean to be disrespectful or sacrilegious or anything. Nevertheless, when you're little, the Easter Bunny is pretty much more exciting. However, I'm getting off track again. But do you remember those candy eggs though . . . the ones that were pretty big and a little bit too long, and all different colors, and shiny and hard on the outside, but "marshmallowy" and sugary on the inside, and that had kind of like pushed-in (but only slightly) sides? Man were they good!

But back to my story. The Gottlieb's, being Christ killers and everything, and given the local "rules" probably not very good at golf, obviously didn't believe this story about Jesus; and I'm pretty sure therefore that they would have had no interest in torturing tinted chickens in April, so I'll just try to jump back a little and finish this up. After all, this part of my story is supposed to be about the Gottlieb family and their store for the better dressed ladies of Washertown. So I won't talk about Easter anymore. Sometimes however I do wonder what the Gottliebs thought about the Easter Bunny (or at least the ones that were caged at the Seed and Feed Store or imprisoned at some kid's house). I suppose they would have thought that he (the "big guy") was OK though. I mean I don't see how anyone could not like the *real* Easter Bunny (or bunnies in general, as far as that goes). At least not when they were just little (meaning when both they, i.e. the Gottlieb children, *and* the caged bunnies were little), or when they were just stuffed maybe, and sitting on a shelf somewhere (meaning this time that just the bunnies were stuffed, *not* of course the Gottlieb's children). I think I said that right (although it kind of got to be another one of those sentences that I admit are sort of hard to get through.). Anyway, the only thing that he (the Easter Bunny) ever did was leave you candy and stuff. And Jews ate candy. At least I think they did. Maybe not Easter candy though. I'm not sure, since I never was one. I *am* sure, however, that my mind has still not yet totally stabilized from a little while ago, so enough of this "wandering." No more talk about rabbits. Or Jesus. Or faded and feathered "throw away" chickens. Or even Easter bonnets. Just remember that the Gottlieb family, and Gottlieb's Ladies Apparel, were both really OK. I just somehow wanted to be sure that you knew that.

Next to Gottlieb's was another of Washertown's many drug stores (there was at least one on every side of the Square). Piersall's. Its name was also (of course) followed by the word *Rexall*. Piersall's had no awning, but instead had installed a big neon sign that protruded rather rudely over the sidewalk. I didn't much like that they had done that, and given my attraction to Mr. Gurdy's daughter (and the dirty books and rubber drawer), and to Powell's cherry vanilla phosphates (and zipper notebooks and Duncan Yo Yo's, etc.), I actually didn't have much reason to go inside Piersall's, although I'm sure it was a perfectly nice Rexall. As fate would have it though, and for all the reasons I just reminded you about, I already felt pretty much at home at either Gurdy's or Powells, so there isn't much more that I can tell you about Piersall's Rexall. I hope though that I never find out that Mr. Piersall had a daughter who was prettier than Mr. Gurdy's, or that he had better dirty books, or maybe even gave out free rubbers or something. That would be pretty disheartening.

One door east of Piersall's was Marsh's Hardware Store. I didn't go in there much either. Marsh's and the Seed and Feed Store (the "for the most part" good-smelling place I already told you about) were both sort of there for a different kind of person. You know, the kind that's pretty much into hard work and "earthy" things. Like healthy people. And farmers and stuff. I was skinny and not real healthy looking, as I've also already told you (at least a couple of times by now), and sort of "soft" I guess, if you know what I mean. And of course I played the accordion and took piano lessons (remember?).

Not that work was unknown to me though. I mean there was no way anyone could accuse me of not working. In the first place, my dad believed in having his sons do real stuff, and work and everything, and we got disciplined pretty bad if we didn't. So I always had my home jobs (garbage, making my bed, carrying heavy stuff for my mom etc.), and also my outside jobs, like I was a lawn mower in the summer, walk "shoveler" in the winter, and had my own paper route (both summer and winter). And I can prove all this stuff too. I mean I wasn't some kind of a "pansy" or anything. Just not real rugged. Maybe more like a flowering bush or something.

When I was a lawn mower, by the way, I worked really hard, and ran the whole business all by myself. And in Washertown in the 1940s you *pushed* the mower, unless you were really, really rich, and then you had one with a smelly gasoline engine on top of it and a goddamn rope starter that you had to pull real hard and fast (and that usually didn't work right even then). Anyway, a "power" mower was something I never had; I wasn't rich, so I pushed. And the mower I had was the real heavy kind too, with an old wooden handle and some loose screws, and blades that turned over from top to bottom and then around again, making a real clear cutting sound (when it was oiled up and sharpened and working well anyway). And you had to adjust the mower just right so that the turning blade hit the bottom, "fixed" blade with just enough, but not too much, clearance. Which adjustments, by the way, I'm proud to say I also did by myself. But I don't guess you need to know all the details. I'll tell you though that going uphill with that mower was no easy push; especially it wasn't easy if you started early in the morning when it was cooler, but the grass was maybe still a little bit too wet. And it was even harder sometimes if you had put the job off one day too many and the grass got too tall or thick, like maybe if it had rained a lot of days straight, or you had been on vacation or something. So as you can see, I worked pretty hard at my mowing business. And I never "wimped out" either.

The really *good* part of my "mower-boy enterprise" though (just to dress things up a little), actually the *best* part, was the smell. I mean it (the smell) was sometimes so good that you almost hoped it would soak right into you. And sometimes it seemed like it almost did. On the very best days, usually in early July (about 10 a.m. or so), the smell came from the perfect combination of the grass being fresh (i.e. just cut), really, really "heavy" (like thick and everything), greener than green, kind of wet and warm (like almost hot and steamy), and just about ready to decay in the Iowa summer sun. And that's a lot of stuff for one smell (and a lot of sentence). But that's the way it was. You just kind of wanted to stick your face right in it, if you know what I mean. But I'll bet you most likely don't. You probably would have to have been a mower guy yourself to know.

Anyway, it made me want to do that (i.e. the smell of the grass made me want to stick my face in it). And although that might sound pretty weird to you (I already said that I knew it was kind of hard to understand), I really believe that you wouldn't think so if you had ever done it. Even just once. I mean there's something about Iowa grass (obviously . . . for me anyway) that can be just that special. And (as I also pretty much explained), it would be at its "smelly best" in July (early), and sometimes even all the way into August (but only if it got really, really, *really* hot). August hot, by the way, was the kind of hot that made it so that you couldn't even sleep at night, especially in a smaller than small, second story, under the dormer with only one window bedroom. I mean it got so goddamn hot sometimes that even though you only had your underpants on, and tried to flip over (back and forth) all the time, you still couldn't sleep. Anyway, to get back to what this part is about, the grass smell was just as special as the even heavier and sweeter August corn smell. And not to get off track and then kind or lose it again or anything, but I just might point out that I think maybe that that man named Walt Whitman, the perhaps just a little bit strange person who wrote some poetry that we had to read in junior high, and who had a really long white beard, and took care of Civil War soldiers and everything . . . you know, the one who wrote that really long poem called "Grass Leaves" (or something like that) . . . well, I think he might have had a lawn mowing business when he was little too. Among other things. I don't know that for sure of course; it was just a thought. But it kind of makes sense to me. At least in some ways.

To get that super good corn smell, by the way, you had to be up real early in the morning and be on a farm, or be on a farm about two hours after the sun went down. Anyway, you had to be on a farm (you didn't have to live on one, but you did have to *be* on one).

And, as I think I maybe told you a while back (but even if I did, it's worth saying again), when you drove out from Washertown into the countryside, especially to the river "bottom" (that meant almost right to it, i.e. the river), where the ground was flatter than anything, and the corn taller than *everything,* and when it was a really steamy hot July or August evening, you could almost take a bath in the scent of that sweet corn. That's just how totally thick and heavy it was. A lot of people did this in the 1940s (meaning they drove to the river bottom), just to let the wind blow on them and kind of get cooled off. (I need to tell you though that it wasn't as if you could *really* take a bath in the corn smell.) I just sort of made that up. And besides, in Washertown in the 1940s, a lot of people took a bath only on Saturday night. That way they were sure to be clean for Jesus on Sunday morning. At least I think that was why.

Anyway, at the peak of the season the corn smell at the river bottom was mostly kind of a yellowy-greenish one that was maybe even *icky* sweet (too much yellow perhaps), but still really good. Sometimes this "fragrance de la farm" (just to add a slight touch of class to corn smells even) seemed to rise from the rapidly ripening, haze-covered cornfields and form a huge, silent, vaporous sea. And on some nights it made you think you could maybe almost swim through it! Anyway, even though Iowa doesn't have any real seas (but you probably already knew that), it *does* have these oceans and oceans of cornfields. And in the heat of the summer, the misty, musky smell from every one of them would not only form the vaporous sea I just mentioned, but would sort of rise up even more, right into the silence (except for the constant, "droney," and kind of "buzzy" bug sounds) of the black and vacant (except for the stars and the moon sometimes) sky. (I guess I really get off on this corn smell shit, don't I?) Whatever.

But as I'm trying to tell you, it (the smell going up into the sky) was (almost anyway) sort of like some kind of religious experience you might have in church. Well, maybe . . . only better. I mean, I don't want to sound sacrilegious (a big word I used before and didn't know when I was little) or crazy or anything, but I'll bet Jesus Christ himself could have walked on the waters of those river-bottom, cornfield-fed oceans. Only of course Jesus never lived in Washertown, or at the river bottom, or actually anywhere in Iowa, as far as that goes (but that's another thing you probably already knew). At least if he did live there no one ever wrote about it or anything. Not even the crazy Mormons; and God knows, the Mormons wrote a lot of pretty weird stuff. Anyway, those evening rides out to the corn oceans were really special. *However* (I get off track *so* easily), this part of my book is supposed to be about our walk around the Washertown Square, not some drive out into the country. And to tell you the truth (I hope you don't get too pissed off at me), when I was writing about all that hazy, vaporous, misty, musky, "smells rising up into the sky" crap, and about Jesus walking around on cornfield oceans and everything, I knew I was just kind of bullshitting you, and repeating stuff a lot . . . and then even stretching it a little. I was having such a good time doing it though that I guess I just couldn't stop. (I had that problem when I got a little bit older too, i.e. the problem about having so much fun I couldn't stop . . . but in a sort of different and "we don't need to talk about it" way.) So anyway, back to our walk. Don't forget though; Iowa river bottom corn smells awful good. Really. No shit.

After Marsh's Hardware, you crossed another alley (the Washertown square had perfectly placed alleys that kind of radiated or went out from three of the four sides of The Casper County Courthouse). It was almost as though the whole town had been laid out by Lafayette or someone. Kind of like Washington, D.C., only there wasn't as much of it (meaning as much of Washertown), and the buildings (meaning in Washertown again) weren't as nice . . . or as big. Maybe the courthouse almost was. But actually that would be pretty much of an exaggeration. Whatever. To tell you the truth, Washertown of course wasn't anything like Washington, D.C. (I was just bullshitting you again). Anyway, next to this alley was one of Washertown's really big ones (stores). It was one of only five doublewide stores in the whole town. And emblazoned on a Chinese red sign, right across the front, and in big gold letters (not *really* gold of course, but gold paint though), was the announcement, J.J Newberry (real name, of course). It may have said "and Co." (for Company) too, or maybe "and Sons," but I can't remember for sure. I mean I don't know if the Newberry's even had any children . . . boys or girls. Anyway, the whole place (actually only on the outside, I guess) was real big and proud looking. J.J. Newberry! Really dark green and whiter than white striped awnings were stretched across the whole front of the place,

246 Ernest Arlington Twain

and it had two sets of doublewide, wood-framed glass doors (as I already said, the whole place was doublewide). *Swinging* doors too. All you had to do was just push on them and they opened. No knobs or latches or anything. One set of these doors was at each end of the front, with display windows between them. Pretty impressive; but then it was J.J. Newberry's, so it should have been. Those doors weren't as much fun as the revolving doors at Younker's Department Store of course (in Des Moines), but you could still pretty much just sort of swing your way right through and into the store.

Inside, Newberry's had oiled wood floors, just like the ones at Hoage's Variety, Stooley's, the Seed and Feed Store, and a lot other places in Washertown (which of course meant the smell of sweeping compound), and more other smells than all the Rexall drug stores combined (always, *always* it was the smells that seemed to define Washertown stores). Lots of oily smells were the first to greet you at Newberry's: floor oil, which had been applied to the wood to keep it new looking; hot and kind of stale smelling oil from the supposedly "Fresh Roasted Peanuts" counter; and buttery-smelling oil from the never silent popcorn machine. Then of course there were the usual cheap perfume and powder smells. And a faint smell of bird shit rising from the bottom of the birdcages (Newberry's always had a parakeet or two, a few canaries, and perhaps a sick and sometimes even almost dead-looking bird of some kind also). And of course there was the *really* stale, unclean, sometimes almost swamp-like smell that emanated from the fish and turtle tanks. Trust me; that could be pretty awful. And then as you walked around in Newberry's, you couldn't miss the "dry-goods" smells, especially the ones coming from the coarse, "burlappy-looking" cloth which was kind of wound around big cardboard "bolts" (that had their own smell).

But Newberry's had good smells too. Like the chocolate malted milk balls, which just happened to be my very most favorite candy in the whole world (except for when my dad would bring home some of those real runny "Brach's Chocolate Covered Cherries," or a box of really fancy-like "Peggy Ann Chocolates" from Des Moines). The "Peggy Ann" chocolates came in a soft-feeling, peachy-pink box that had a sort of raised brown cameo of some woman on it, and were always purchased (at least when my dad bought them) as a big surprise for my mom. Other than for the "Peggy Ann" stuff, my mom's favorite (candy) was the chocolate "Stars" at Newberry's. But I still liked the "malty balls" (that's what I called them when I was little), so when she (my mom) had some extra money to buy candy (like maybe a dime or fifteen cents even), she would get half stars and half malted milk balls. Anyway, that was about it for J.J. Newberry smells, except for the kind of funny smell coming from the pile of hairnets and combs and stuff by the cash register. "Funny," but not too good either. I can't remember just what the smell was, but it was sort of slightly yucky and unclean or something. Like old hair maybe. Oh . . . one more thing (smell). Do you remember Circus Peanuts? The candy that was pretty much faded orange and spongy, and trying to look like puffed up peanuts? Well, Newberry's had those too, and they gave off a pretty icky smell all their own. Sort of like old marshmallows, with some kind of cheap orange perfume sprayed on them.

J.J. Newberry was a great place to go, nevertheless, and it was well patronized by the people of Washertown. Personally, I preferred F.W. Woolworth's, on the east side of the square (more on that place later). That's because they (Woolworth's) had better fish tanks, less bird shit, and they sold hamburgers and stuff at a lunch counter. Actually though, I think the birds (with the exception of the ones that were trying to die), sad-looking creatures that they were, may have been a little bit better at Newberry's (in spite of the fact that the people there didn't clean the cages very well). Whatever. At least the birds didn't have to sit in their shit (maybe "droppings" is a nicer word . . . although it sort of loses something), like cats and dogs had to do at the county "pound." By the way, I remember how disappointed I was when I learned that the parakeets at J.J. Newberry's weren't baby parrots. And how even worse I felt when my black and really ugly (I probably felt sorry for it when I bought it) "gold" fish died. You might remember them . . . the kind with the gross looking, bulgy, almost "popped out" eyes. I mean those suckers were really ugly. But when mine died, it was pretty sad, nevertheless. Those little guys always seemed strange to me, by the way. Black goldfish. (I mean you'd never expect to see a brown blue jay, or a green flamingo or something.) I mean would you? But man was that thing ugly! Especially the morning right after it "passed away" (swam away?) and swelled up and floated to the top of the pretty little bowl that I had put it in (however briefly). I mean you just dropped to you knees and thanked God that it hadn't actually exploded or something. The thing was just fucking disgusting! (And I've been doing so much better with my words, so give me that one.) Since I said it though, I'll stick with it. It was *fucking* disgusting! I figured out later, by the way, that those black goldfish might have had thyroid problems. That's what can make eyes bulge out.

Well, we have to walk right by the next place or two. I'm sorry to have to admit it, but I have indeed forgotten just what was there. Maybe another hardware store. Garrett's? I'm just not sure (but as I already reminded you a long time ago, no one's perfect anyway). But that's OK, since the story that goes with the next stop should make up for Garrett's (if indeed that's what the place was called) and the other store I can't remember. So anyway, the next store that I *do* remember was (makes me sick to even think about it) Buster Brown's Shoes. I absolutely hated that place! All you could get there, at least all *I* ever got there, were these stupid-looking, hideously utilitarian (like from a concentration camp or someplace), plain brown, Boy Scout oxfords. Goddamn oxfords! Oh, I forgot. And sissy-looking, shit-brown sandals, with girl-like buckles and lots of little holes punched in the leather (those were my summer shoes). Everything at Buster Brown's was brown. Brown shoes. Brown socks. And even more brown stuff. It just occurred to me (but I'm probably too upset to be thinking clearly here) that that's why they called the place Buster Brown's. I don't know. But maybe.

Anyway, and to forget about the goddamn oxfords for a minute, I'd like to bet that those sissy sandals probably led, eventually anyway, to more than one or two of Washertown's otherwise pretty much OK guys becoming ministers or something. Maybe priests even. And it wouldn't surprise me if those same brown sandals didn't even lead one or two guys (again, eventually) into becoming homosexuals (or, to stick with Washertown language, homos or queers). I mean those shoes were toxic. Totally sissy-shit, as I said before. In fact, if I had worn those things (the sandals) to Janey's house for the big love affair I told you I had in second grade, it probably wouldn't have happened. But at least (and to try to keep on track here) I wasn't the only one who had them (the sandals), and I didn't have to wear them to school. And besides, I went barefoot a lot in the summer time, so I could avoid them even then. And most summers I eventually, sort of anyway, became a "barefoot boy with cheeks of tan" (to borrow from another poet), which, I guess anyway, maybe would have helped my feet and other parts blend in more with the brown sandals (when I absolutely *had* to wear them). Probably not though (again too much of a stretch). Whatever. Those sandals were really bad! Shitty, *shitty* bad. (Sort of like "Chitty Chitty Bang Bang," although that came later.)

But more about the standard, wear-to-school-everyday Boy Scout oxfords. They were fucking awful! (Sorry again about the *fuck* word, but as they say, "If the shoe fits wear it," . . . and being so logical about everything, I sort of decided that if "the *word* fits" I therefore have to say it.) That may or may not make sense. I'll let you decide. Anyway, if the children of Europe, or Asia, or wherever the hell else they were supposed to have been starving to death and to not have anything to wear (because of World War II) had been given shoes, I'll bet they would have been Buster Brown Boy Scout rejects. And I'd also bet they probably would have preferred to go barefoot. I know. I know. I didn't know what it was like not to have shoes, and I should have been counting my blessings and all that shit. After all, these were difficult years, and things were pretty terrible all over (shoes were even rationed, if you can believe that). But those goddamn Boy Scout shoes! Shit. "Give 'em to the Europeans." That's what I would have said. I would even have wrapped them and paid the postage. But anyway, there's still more I need to tell you. Mr. Buster Brown, patron saint of America's little boys that he was (although I'll bet he never wore a pair of those goddamn oxfords in his whole life), was determined not only to sell shoes, but also to teach American boys the virtues of capitalism as well. So Buster Brown's had its own stupid little "incentive plan." When you bought a pair of their totally shitty shoes, you got a coupon, several of which (enough to keep some kids buying those hideous goddamn things forever) could eventually be redeemed for prizes. Most guys traded them in for "jackknives" or army canteens or some other "out-doorsy," real guy thing. I traded mine for a globe (wouldn't you know). And you don't need to tell everyone. I was just sort of admitting it to you.

So anyway, out of Busters, past another store I can't remember, and on to the big concrete bunker (east end, north side) that was

Washertown National Bank. An almost ominous, but of course very important-looking place. "Neo" architecture, sort of like the Courthouse. Gray concrete (or maybe some other kind of faux stone), with six Greek (Doric style) columns, fully round and fluted (nothing half way about this place!), adorning the front. And they were really tall-looking too. They, the columns, didn't really come from Greece though (but you probably already were thinking that). Maybe from Des Moines. I'm not sure. Anyway, at the top, where the columns themselves became the square part, there was a lot of room for Washertown's pigeons to sit. And from which, therefore, to shit. Remember the columns on The Methodist Church? (If you don't that's OK, since I'll be telling you more about that place later.) Well anyway, these two buildings, the bank and the church, were pigeon heaven. I mean those birds may have done a lot of pecking and scratching and generally annoying people on the Courthouse lawn, but the tops of the columns on these two buildings, Washertown National and First Methodist, were without question their "toilets of choice." Real shithouses. So be careful as we go in here, and whatever you do, *don't* look up!

Inside, the whole bank felt almost like a vault, and it was probably the most serious-looking place in all of Washertown. I mean it meant business. But back in the 1940s that was the way banks were supposed to be. Very important, and very secure. And the bank didn't smell either. That's for sure. It wasn't allowed to. As a matter of fact, the place gave you the impression that the really starchy-looking people who worked behind the teller's windows and desks didn't smell either. Not even if something made them sweat, like maybe an attempted robbery or some other big major event. In fact although their sort of "pinchy" (but of course proper) appearance made it seem like they maybe had indigestion, or needed to have a bowel movement or something, they probably were expected to "hold it" until they got home. I mean I don't think they even would have allowed the bathroom itself to smell. And if you had to fart? Forget it! Anyway, going in there (i.e. in the bank, not the bathroom) was a lot like going into the library or a church. You somehow felt as though you shouldn't talk very loud. I know all this because I had my very first savings account at Washertown National. And every time I went in to make a deposit from the profits on my all-year paper route, or winter snow shoveling business, or summer lawn mower jobs, I felt kind of almost embarrassed. Self-conscious anyway. It seemed to me that giving them my little green savings book, with its one to three dollar (but maybe also sometimes plus some cents) entries, made it look as though I wasn't terribly successful or something (like maybe my deposit would be $2.67 for one week). I guess anyway that that's why I was so self-conscious. Oh well. I think I already told you that I was generally just kind of scared of some things and places when I was little, and one of those places was the teller's window at the bank. But enough of Washertown National. We have more exciting places to go.

I probably should tell you just one more thing though, since it was so important to the people of Washertown. When I was little, you almost *never* made a withdrawal from your savings account, even though you had earned the money and maybe wanted to buy something really, really bad (meaning that you wanted whatever it was a whole lot, not that what you wanted a whole lot was something bad . . . although I guess maybe it could have been). Anyway, I think you know what I mean, and I don't want to get too far off track again. Just remember that when you went to the bank you were supposed to leave a deposit. To "withdraw" was almost considered to be a weakness, or maybe even un-American (like as if you were the commander on some battlefield and lost and then left, or the captain of a ship and had to abandon it or something). Sort of like that, I guess. Anyway, you weren't supposed to withdraw. Unless of course (the one exception to the rule) you were Catholic and were having sex with your girlfriend (or perhaps your wife even). In that case you were *supposed* to withdraw, and *not* make any "deposits." (Just the opposite of what I said about savings accounts.) At least I think that was how it went. But I didn't claim to know a lot about that stuff when I was little, and I guess that situation (i.e. a Catholic having sex and not making any deposits) could get a little sticky (theologically speaking of course . . . and with no pun intended). And besides that, it (i.e. the Catholic sticky sex issue) doesn't really belong in this part of my story anyway. Probably not even in *any* part of my story, as far as that goes. Being a Methodist, I could maybe talk intelligently about sticky issues regarding Methodist sex, but I don't think that would be very useful either. And it's also just the kind of subject that makes my mind start to go in too many directions. Whatever. Just remember that you were only supposed to deposit stuff when you went to the bank. And look out for the pigeon shit as we leave.

Before going on to the east side of the Square (we are presently still on the north side, although at the east end of it, so we have to cross the street one way or the other), I just have to take you to another of Washertown's finer and indeed unique establishments. (For some reason, it seems as though the places that occupied the corners of the blocks that keyed into the Square itself were of considerable significance to the economy and social well-being of Washertown.) As you may recall, the last corner place I took you into was The Orange Bar, that wonderful institution that dispensed fresh-squeezed juice, and was the source of tuna (and ham) salad sandwiches and Fleer's "Double Bubble" bubble gum. Well, the corner we are now approaching is almost Orange Bar good. Not quite . . . but almost. Well, maybe as good. You can decide for yourself. Anyway, we're outside the bank now, so be careful (as I already suggested) that you don't step in any fresh pigeon shit (or get "bombed"). Also, watch out for turning cars as we cross the street (there is no traffic light; they're all a block south of here along Highway 6.) Remember?

Bigelow's! Like in "Billy Bigelow" in *Carousel* (although I'm not sure that show had been produced yet). Anyway, this fantastic place is where the east end of the north side of the Square intersected with the north end of the east side. I know this sounds a little bit confusing again, but if Lafayette could *lay* it out, you should at least be able to *figure* it out. So anyway, on that corner, in all its glory, stood Bigelow's (its real name, just like The Orange Bar, J.J. Newberry's, The Scoreboard, F.W. Woolworth's, Walgreen's, and a few other places where we haven't been yet are real names). Bigelow's, like The Orange Bar, was one spot that very simply "should never be forgot" (kind of like in another musical called *Camelot* which, however, I'm sure hadn't been written yet). Ice cream, candy, apples (with no spit polish, which as you may recall was a problem with the apples at the Scoreboard), and sometimes even *caramel* apples. There was also lots of other good stuff too, like ice cream sodas and sandwiches that were served from a solid marble, soda fountain counter. And Bigelow's had penny boxes of "SunMaid" raisins, which my dad sometimes brought home to my brother and me when we were little for a nightly "surprise." (He, our dad, sort of established a tradition of bringing us candy or raisins or something.) Bigelow's also sold cigars, cigarettes, and newspapers, which he didn't bring home (which isn't to say that my dad didn't smoke or read the newspaper, but just that he didn't buy his cigarettes at Bigelow's, and the newspaper was delivered to our house). So anyway, Bigelow's had just about all the necessities of life.

But since I just mentioned the newspaper, let me digress for just a moment to tell you about someone else I used to worry about (I'll keep it short). *The Des Moines Tribune* (an evening paper) carried a cartoon strip (although not a funny one) about a person named Scarlet O'Neil. The "strip" itself was actually called "Invisible Scarlet O'Neil." I've never found anyone who remembers her, but I certainly do (this was in 1942). Whatever. When she pressed her left wrist she became invisible, and could therefore help solve crimes and stuff (she was sort of like a detective, I guess). This was about the same time that I listened to "The Lone Ranger" on the radio, by the way (but that's another story). Anyway, when she (Scarlet) was walking in Central Park in New York City one time (I learned later that that was where it was) she fell through the ice on one of the ponds there, and for almost a whole week, she was under water trying to find the hole she fell through so she could climb back out. Well, I'm telling you, I couldn't wait for the evening paper to be delivered, since I was so worried about her and everything. I mean really worried. For a *whole week* (five nights of the newspaper) she was under water. And toward the end it looked as though she for sure was going to breath her last little "bubbles." Eventually, however, a rather odd looking man who was walking through the park had his hat blow off his head, and it landed on an ornamental concrete ball that decorated the bridge over the pond. Then, in his anger, he knocked the concrete ball off the bridge. And then the ball made a "just-the-right-size" hole in the ice, and Scarlet managed to pull herself up through it. Man, I was so relieved! I mean there was just something truly special about her (and she was also pretty), and I really *really* worried that she might drown. But she didn't. Anyway, I don't have any idea where she is now. She's probably dead even (but I hope from natural causes). I think the Lone Ranger's dead too. OK. We'll go back to Bigelow's now. Thanks for listening.

Bigelow's also had a bathroom for their lunch and soda fountain customers to use (although you only used it if you really *had* to) that was down some dark and extremely steep, worn-in-the-middle, wooden stairs that led to a bone-dry, dirt-floored, cobweb-strewn cellar. (In the 1940s in Iowa most people called cellars "basements," but I think cellar sounds scarier, and so that's the word I use.) I remember that bathroom, because if you were a little guy with an appropriately little bladder (I didn't know what a bladder was then, of course, only that I had to go to the bathroom a lot, and especially after having had a great big ten cent coke, root beer, or phosphate or something). Those "ten centers" seemed enormous to a five-year-old. So anyway, after you drank one, especially if your mom and a friend she might have brought with her just wanted to kind of sit around and talk and stuff the way women but not men usually do, you were happy to make the somewhat hazardous trek down those stairs to "relieve" yourself. Nightmares of dark, "down under" places were still occasional visitors to my little mind, however, like stories about the "fruit cellar" in the basement of our house, where I was told really scary things might live, so that I wouldn't go in it (the fruit cellar) and maybe knock some stuff off the shelves or something. Therefore, going downstairs to Bigelow's bathroom could be pretty frightening. And even though I didn't really think there were monsters down there, I couldn't help but wonder if some great big spider was going to drop on my head or something. Or maybe a huge, poisonous snake. Or a dragon even. Well, maybe not a dragon. Anyway, when I went (i.e. both when I went down the stairs and when I actually "went"), I went real fast, and was always glad to get back up those stairs. I mean that place was almost as scary as the storm sewer down the street from our house. "Trolls" lived down there in the tunnel (storm sewer) that went under the street to the next street over; that's what I was told when I was little anyway. Which was my parent's way of making sure I wouldn't go crawling around underground in the tunnel and drown in a flash flood or maybe get eaten up by roaches or something. I don't know. Maybe trolls did live there.

Bigelow's sold an ice cream bar that I absolutely loved, that came in a long, cardboard box. A red and white box, I think, with a perforated line around the center. You pushed on it real careful-like (the perforated line), and then when the box came apart, you pulled out this really good, chocolate covered ice cream bar. I never saw those things anywhere else (not even at the State Fair), and although I could never get enough of them, for some reason I can't remember what they were called. Something like "Whiss Lambs" keeps running through my mind (yeah . . . I think maybe that was it), but it could be I think that just because I was pretty little and didn't pronounce some words right. "Whiss Lambs" sounds kind of like baby talk or something. But that's what keeps coming to mind. Oh well. Bigelow's tuna sandwiches were really good too. Probably even better than the ones at The Orange Bar, since the ten cent ones at The Orange Bar were pretty much thinned out with a whole lot of mayonnaise ("Miracle Whip" probably). Anyway, the tuna sandwiches at Bigelow's were *fifteen* cents, so they were a little thicker (with less Miracle Whip), and came with a leaf or two of lettuce (if you were a big person and wanted it). I didn't; so when I was little they always left it off for me. That's sort of an example of how nice they could be there.

Anyway, I spent lots and lots of good times at Bigelow's with my mom and my brother (who still didn't like me), and my aunt (of "Top Secret" Bendix fame), and Jessie (my grandfather's housekeeper and then wife), and sometimes my dad even, if he happened to stop by. And always, *always* there were those delicious ice cream bars in the red and white box to look forward to, which I *still* can't remember the name of for sure. Oh, and I meant to tell you that when my dad would stop at Bigelow's on his way home from work some nights (to get the surprises I told you about for my brother and me), sometimes (when he didn't get raisins) he would get these really special pieces of penny candy that were supposed to be salt water taffy made from real ocean water (I think anyway). Iowa didn't have any oceans of course, but somehow my dad managed to get it (meaning the salt water taffy) for us. He was pretty smart. Anyway, Bigelow's was an all-around neat place! Good times. Good memories. And a curious sort of "safe and at home feeling" (except during the race down and back from that "cellar of horrors" bathroom that they had).

East side. North end. The Palace Hotel (with some storefronts on the street level). Actually, the hotel bore the name of Washertown's first family, and was indeed and of course (meaning absolutely and without question) *the* grandest hotel between the Mississippi River and Des Moines. We thought so anyway. Whatever. For Washertown, it was truly a palace. Much, much nicer than the other two hotels in town, neither of which was even on the Washertown Square. One of the other hotels tried to be important though. It was named after Prime Minister Winston Churchill, I guess anyway, since that was its name, i.e. The Churchill. It housed the Greyhound Bus Terminal (which kind of argued against it being too fancy or anything), and maybe also a few displaced English people (although I never heard anyone say that). The hotel itself was constructed of red brick that had then been *painted* red too (sort of strange, I thought), was Victorian in design (of course), and therefore had lots of tall, narrow windows, all of which were arched at the top. But to give the place its due, The Churchill was no less than *three* stories high, an uncommon height for Washertown buildings. So that kind of made it maybe a little (but not) a lot more important-looking. Unfortunately, the porch that went across the front of the place was pretty beat up looking though. The other of the lesser Washertown hotels (and I do mean lesser) was, I presume, built for commoners. It was called The Miller. Really. The Miller was only two stories high, was faced with stucco (which had then been painted sort of a dirty, gray-white color), and it had a wooden floored porch around it that sagged even more than the one at The Churchill. I mean you almost had to go uphill, or at least lean forward, to even get into the place, (if you wanted to get into at all, and most people didn't).

But back to the Square and The Palace. Ready for this? The Palace was *five* stories high! And I'm not kidding either. Five stories high. Swear to God. And although I might be but don't think I am mistaken, I'm pretty sure it was the highest point in all of Washertown, except perhaps for the water tower (or maybe the very tip of the flagpole on top of the Courthouse dome . . . which I won't describe this time). The Palace had a coffee shop, an almost separate, but nevertheless attached-to-the-coffee shop dining room, a barbershop (in the basement), a men's room (also in the basement and too often frequented by guys other than hotel guests), an upstairs ladies room (never went there), and a pretty large meeting room called The Wedgewood Room. And, *and,* a ballroom! That's right. A *ballroom.* Like in the big hotels in Des Moines. That (the Palace ballroom) was the place where some of Washertown's finest held their parties and wedding receptions and other fancy affairs. This was especially true, I think (meaning that the ballroom was where fancy affairs were held), for a person who might actually have preferred The Washertown Country Club, but wanted (or maybe needed) to invite a Jew (or maybe was one), or an Italian even, or something (or both, if you can imagine that . . . and probably you can't . . . not in the Washertown of the 1940s anyway).

Washertown's Rotary Club met at The Palace in the Wedgewood Room; Kiwanis met there (Wedgewood Room); Lions met there (Wedgewood Room); and ladies met there too sometimes (in the Wedgewood Room) for "benefits" and bridge parties and things like that. *And* (swear to God), the high school band (all fifty pieces of it) even jammed in there one noon (the Wedgewood Room) to play for the Kiwanis Club. Almost blew the entire membership right out of the place too, with a rousing, almost riotous rendition of John Phillip Sousa's "Stars and Stripes Forever." I know, because I was the base drummer (and cymbal "crasher"). A pretty stupid thing to do, I thought (I mean can you imagine a fifty member high school band playing "The Stars and Stripes Forever" in a room that maybe measured twenty-five by forty-five feet or so?). But I was only the base drummer, not the director (who of course was the Washertown High School band director). I think he (the band director) was a member of Kiwanis, and probably had volunteered to provide the entertainment. You do have to say it was one way to make an impression. What kind, however, is another story.

I can't be sure of course, but I think (to get back to other activities at the Wedgewood Room) that maybe some secret lovers might even have met there. Surreptitiously (a word I for sure didn't know then), of course. I mean I may be getting a little bit carried away, but it seems like everyone else met there, so why not? And then, as I sort of had it figured, they (the super-surreptitious cheaters) most likely got their own room upstairs, under some fictitious name like Mr. and Mrs. Smith, or maybe Dr. and Mrs. Jones, or some other name, and also wore sunglasses and stuff while they were doing it (i.e. checking in . . . "doing it" came later). They probably weren't from Washertown though, since in small towns like Washertown too many people knew too many other people. They (the secret, super-surreptitious, cheater lovers with the sunglasses) probably came from Des Moines, or maybe from a farm or someplace like that. Or maybe from a foreign country even. I don't know. I was too young to really understand it anyway. Well, maybe not, but sort of. I mean I pretty much would have known what they were going to do up there in their room though. Like really "do it" and everything.

Anyway, everyone who was anyone went to the Palace Hotel. And the Wedgewood Room was the sight of most of the meetings there (as I just said). And, you might like to know, you could get your shoes shined right off the Palace lobby (see next paragraph for more detail), which, by the way (meaning the lobby, not the shoe shine stand), had real potted plants placed everywhere (kind of tropical-looking, and probably not quite right for Washertown, but nevertheless kind of OK), great big sort of brownish and awkward-looking upholstered furniture (with wide, flat, dark-stained wooden arms and "loose" cushions), and a really big area rug, which served to kind of both cover up and warm up the gray, terrazzo tile floor. Get the picture? It wasn't exactly "The Ritz" (and frankly I always thought pretty disappointing), but a real cut above The Churchill lobby (trust me). And don't even think about The Miller.

The shoeshine man ("boy," as you may recall from some earlier comments regarding the local mentality) was the adult male member of one of the two Washertown Negro families. And not only did he do shoes (again as you may recall), he also operated the hotel elevator. And, I might add, in a most gracious and friendly manner. It was always "going up 'mam,'" or "missus," or "sir," when you were down, and "going down" (with the same respectful attitude) when you were up and heading back to the lobby. And of course there was the occasional and appropriate "you all watch your step now," when he didn't quite line up the elevator floor with the other floor height (which was a frequent occurrence in the days of "attended" elevators). Everything that man did was done with both style and a smile, which I hope (at least most of the time anyway) he felt really good about. He was supposed to smile, of course, since these were the 1940s, and as more than a few people (including too many in Washertown) thought (as yet again you may recall), Negro men (among other things) were supposed to smile for the white folks, eat watermelon, and father "pickaninnys." I just hope that most Washertown folks who spoke to him knew that he was indeed one fine human being. I mean this man was graciousness, and patience, and a whole lot of other things personified.

On the ground floor of The Palace, occupying a quite limited amount of space, was a jewelry store called Humperdincks, which you could enter from the street or from the hotel lobby itself (just like in the fancy hotels in Des Moines). A small, but smartly decorated store, as I recall, having been remodeled to reflect the style of post World War II modern (which at the time meant that a lot of junky-looking trim and crappy other stuff had been eliminated from the walls, counters, and window displays). I can't think of much more to say about Humperdincks though, except that a lady who looked and sometimes sounded a lot like Ethel Merman, and was actually named "Mermal" (no kidding), and her husband owned and operated the place. And one of my high school buddies worked there too (after school hours), so I sometimes went in and just talked to them and stuff. Nice people. The only other memory I have of Humperdincks is that I thought the name itself sounded sort of like a dirty word. But then I had already (eleventh grade) become somewhat "twisted" in some ways. Time to move on.

Next is Velma Coyle's, a pretty expensive dress shop that I already mentioned when I was talking to you about the Virgin Mary (and probably maybe, if not pretty much actually, inappropriately). Anyway, Velma Coyle's was kind of a "style house" (mess that it was) for a few of Washertown's female elitists (especially, as I also told you before, if they didn't like Jews and therefore avoided Gottlieb's, and didn't want to make the trip to The French Room at Younker's Department Store in Des Moines). "Velma's," as it was affectionately called, was a really small place, I mean *really* small, and it was absolutely packed with clothes (dresses mostly) on racks that bumped up against each other and made it hard to walk even. Nevertheless, Velma's was known as *the* place to find that "just right dress" (if you were going to find it in Washertown at all). I know this stuff (you may have been wondering) because once again my mom told me. I think I even went there once, when I was a lot, lot older, to buy a Christmas present (a dress of course) for the person I was engaged to and then married, and then had a lot of trouble with (some her fault, some mine), and then got divorced from. That wasn't Velma's fault though. And it's a story that doesn't belong here anyway.

Actually, and to get back to Velma Coyle's Dress Shop in the 1940s, I just have to tell you again that this place was so small (not that "size matters," as they say . . . although it does), and so packed with so many of those just right dresses (as I said up above, the place was a mess), that not only could you hardly move, you sometimes couldn't even breathe. I mean a person could have suffocated to death in there, or maybe just fainted, or even been trampled and then just sort of (but probably unintentionally) kicked or rolled under one of those over-crowded, "just-right" dress racks and forgotten about. Maybe anyway. And of course Velma's, like so many other Washertown places, had a distinct smell (and *not* because of a dead woman under the dress rack . . . I was just kidding). Velma's smell (meaning the store's smell, of course, not her own smell . . . I don't know what that would have been like) was that kind of funny, just a little bit musty but not really, "clothy" smell. (Part cloth, and part the boxes the stuff came in.) I think anyway. The smell at Velma's was thought of course to be one of *quality*. Certainly it was not like the dresses might have smelled at Montgomery Ward's. There was no Sears, Roebuck, and Company in Washertown (did I already tell you that?), but I'm sure the smell there would have been a lot like Montgomery Ward's. Pretty musty. And certainly not "Velma Coyleish."

But to get back to Velma Coyle's once more (I don't know why I'm having such a hard time getting us out of here), as I said before I only know all this stuff (i.e. about the crowding, and the "just-right" dresses, and the "clothy-boxy" smell, and the potential victims of fainting or trampling and everything), because I went in there once in awhile with my mom. I never went to Velma's alone or anything (not even to look for the Christmas dress I bought for my favorite divorcee whom I mentioned up above, but chose not to talk about since all that was so much later in my life and hard to think about and everything). So anyway, don't worry about me just because I know a lot about Velma Coyle's Dress Shop (for discriminating women), or be thinking anything weird. OK? And it's for sure that if anyone really did suffocate, faint, or get trampled to death, and then rolled or kicked (again unintentionally of course) under a dress rack there, I had nothing to do with it. But anyway, and to make you feel better about Velma's place, I don't honestly think any of those faint and get trampled things actually ever happened.

Maybe though. It wouldn't have been the only really sort of strange and maybe even grisly thing to go on in Washertown; I can tell you that. And there could have been some kind of a cover up or something. At least as far as I know there could have been. Shit. I mean like maybe a woman from Des Moines, or a farm or whatever, who was having an affair at the hotel (starting perhaps, as I said before, in the Wedgewood Room, and ending up in a bed in a suite on the third floor or somewhere) could maybe have killed her married lover (like stabbed him repeatedly with a hotel letter opener, and then cut some pieces of him *off*, and then the rest of him *up*), and then tried to dispose of his body (meaning the parts) under one of Velma Coyle's crowded but "just right" dress racks or something. After all, Velma's was right down stairs from the hotel, and she, meaning the probably "in more ways than one" fucking bitch who killed the probably asshole of a married guy could (maybe anyway) have done it at night, i.e. could have disposed of the body parts at night. I mean who knows *when* the hell she may have mercilessly killed, cut up, and then disposed of him? (Brutally, and without conscience.) I mean this bitch might even have been a full-blown sociopath or something, or "borderline," which means *really* fucked up. (Since I used the word once, I figured it wouldn't hurt to use it again).

Anyway, I know about this stuff. Remember? I became a clinical psychopath myself (just kidding . . . that's just what my friends used to say, although I already told you that). So anyway (and to get back to the facts), it could have been a day or two before when she actually killed the guy (meaning a day or two before she put "him" under the dress rack). At least as far as I know it could have been. Whatever. Maybe their whole goddamn affair had been going on for a really long time, and was getting more and more messy and everything, and then the guy came right out and said he was screwing someone else or something (hopefully some*one,* not some*thing*), and then she maybe got really pissed off. It's hard to tell though. And I don't remember reading anything about it in *The Washertown Daily News,* so it could be that I just sort of (perhaps anyway) got a little bit carried away here . . . or that my mind is hopelessly drifting again . . . or something. Whatever. I guess I don't know what the hell's happening, so it's probably a good time to just move on. You know, like "get out when you can."

But before we do (i.e. move on or get out), and speaking of drifting minds, I think this is a good place to point out that all in all I think I've been doing a pretty good job of keeping my mind (such as it is) on track. Mostly anyway. Don't you think? I mean not perfectly of course. I've never claimed to be perfect, and I never will. I mean everyone is a sinner (another piece of wisdom from my fantastic if not magnificent experiences at Washertown's First Methodist Church). So anyway, even in Velma Coyle's I didn't really "lose it" or anything. I was maybe getting close, but maybe also there was a reason for it. Or maybe not. Anyway, I would appreciate it if you would "give credit where credit is due," to borrow yet another expression. I mean it wasn't so long ago that I kind of *really* started to lose it (back when we were still on the north side of the Square, I think); so I'm actually pretty happy with myself right now. Whatever. That (the north side of the Square incident) was then, and this is now, and as you probably learned once (I know I did anyway), when you get older you often have to remember not to look back. At least not too far back. I mean if you do you can pretty much always find something to worry about (just to share a little of my accumulated wisdom with you).

That's what I think anyway. My dad told me some of these things (especially about the "worry" part). And also I read about the "not looking back" part in the *Bible*, when the writer (although I don't know who the writer really was, and if people who talk about the *Bible* all the time would be more honest, they probably don't know either) . . . anyway, I read about not looking back when this *Bible* writer was telling a story about some dumb-ass of a farmer whose plow would pop out of the row (or rut, or groove, or whatever it was he was trying to keep it, the plow, in) if he kept looking back. To see where he'd been, I guess. (The "plower" guy seemed to have been a slow learner too, since the way the story went, it, i.e. the plow jumping out of the row, had obviously happened to him a lot of times before it was explained to him what was causing it.) Well, maybe you don't agree with me (and my dad and the *Bible*), and of course that's OK, but I really think the idea about not looking back is a pretty good one. So you might want to be a little bit careful and not do it yourself. By the way, do you remember that Christmas song when we were little, the one that went: "You better watch out/You better not shout/You better not pout/I'm telling you why"? (It was because

Santa Claus was coming, in case you forgot.) Well, it's kind of like that, I think. Maybe anyway. Oh well. And just when I was going to tell you something important that now I can't even remember. But I guess it doesn't matter. We better (for sure this time) just get on our way. I hope you enjoyed the little "wisdom lesson" though. Does anyone know how to get back to the Square? (Just kidding.)

So *anyway,* next door to Velma Coyle's was the entrance to *the* office building of Washertown, which, like the hotel building it was part of, also carried the name of the town's first family. I went there a lot, since our family doctor (who was actually the only kind of doctor you had in the 1940s) had his office on the fourth floor. And every time you went there you couldn't help but notice that the entry area for the whole building always smelled the way an entry area to a place like that was supposed to smell. Clean and professional. Really clean, and really professional. The message was that the most important people in town worked there. Anyway, the office building was the site of Washertown's second elevator (The Palace Hotel of course had the only other one), and although when I was little I liked riding in it (and for the most part liked our doctor too), I didn't always like what he (our doctor) did to me. So let's just move on. I mean he didn't do anything bad; it's just that some of the stuff he did hurt.

One thing that wasn't too bad though (and I've known a few doctors might want to think about going back to this) was that when he wanted to get some of your blood to look at he used something that was sort of like a "punch" tool (kind of like what teachers and secretaries and people like that still use to punch holes in paper). And he "punched" you (meaning punched the hole to get the blood) in your ear lobe. Really. Right in your goddamn ear lobe. When he did it to me it was usually my right one, although I don't know which one it was for other people, or as far as that goes why I even remember this. And it didn't hurt very much at all (this is the point I'm trying to make), because you couldn't see him doing it. He always talked to you real fast about something else, and then just did it (i.e. "punched" you) before you knew what was happening. It was a lot better than having your finger stuck, or a needle put in your arm, I'll tell you that. *That* stuff hurts.

So anyway, our doctor was a pretty good one. And if you were too sick to ride the elevator and go see him, or if it was night maybe and you were real sick but not sick enough to go to the hospital, he would even come to see you at home. No kidding! As I said a little while ago though, it's probably best to just move on. But first take a look out the window from his office. You can get a pretty good view of The Casper County Courthouse across the street. And then, but only if you don't mind, let's walk down, rather than take the elevator. That way you can see this big, round, really polished up, mahogany handrail that curves all the way down to the first floor. Without ever ending even. When I was little I thought it looked sort of like a great big real long Tootsie Roll (the kind that cost a whole nickel). At least when I was real *real* little I thought that. Or maybe a big fat snake or something. And always when I was little (and this is the truth too), I couldn't even get my hand all the way around it (the handrail). I mean that's how big it was!

Next stop, The Capitol Theatre. Probably the best way to start to tell you about this place is to say that the Capitol was to Washertown's theatre district what The Palace was to its hotel industry. *Really* fancy-looking (well, for a small town in Iowa anyway). Furthermore (you may recall that I told you this a long time ago), The Capitol was the one movie theatre in Washertown where the popcorn was always good. And (as you also may recall . . . or maybe not . . . but it doesn't matter because I'm going remind you anyway), it was the theatre where Janey and I went in second grade to "neck/pet" (or whatever it was we did), and also the theatre where, along with my buddy, I peed on the floor during the Frankenstein movie. So anyway, it was a really important place, and I have lots of memories to prove it. The Capitol was also where (in the men's room) the town's one homosexual "hung out" (as I also told you a long time ago, and don't know why I even brought it up again). Since I did, however, I might mention that I still pretty much think there may have been more than one (homosexual) in Washertown. Maybe anyway. Even though no one ever claimed to actually have seen one. But that could be, at least partly it could be, because a "queer" (again the town's word, not mine) walking down the street is not as obvious as a Jew playing golf at the Country Club or a Negro shining shoes. But don't let any of this detract from the shine of the Capitol Theatre.

In fact, however (although I might be wrong but I don't think so . . . and I have evidence), I might as well just go ahead and tell you what

I eventually found out. Then we can for sure just go on. Anyway, I learned, but only after I got bigger of course, that one of Washertown's prominent ministers (Oh my God!) and one of Washertown's school administrators (Oh my God but more so!) just *may* have tilted a little bit that way. Meaning toward the queer end of things. Just like Mr. Lewis (only these guys of course would never have hung out in the men's room at the Capitol Theatre). Well, I guess they could have, but I don't think it would have been a very good idea. I mean they were married and everything, I suppose anyway, and I know that at least the minister guy had children. Whatever. I don't know where they hung out. Maybe Des Moines. Or in a rectory somewhere. And also (there seem to be almost as many as many "alsos" in good writing as there are "anywayses"), I found out that a friend of mine, who was the daughter of a Washertown schoolteacher, and another person, who was the daughter of a Washertown polititian, were *lesbians.* (Oh my God once more!) I mean Jesus Christ! It's beginning to sound like the whole goddamn town was a haven for homosexuals or something. Of course very few people in Washertown (including, at the time, myself) had a clue about what a lesbian was. And if you had even heard the word you probably would have thought that it referred to someone who had some sort of a skin rash or something. Or, if you didn't hear very well, maybe someone who was an actor.

Actually though, there was probably one Washertown resident who was an exception to all this ignorance and naiveté regarding the existence of homosexuals and lesbians and maybe even some other not exactly "in the mainstream" people. Enter Miss Phoebe Bilcox. Miss Bilcox, who was the Washertown Junior High School Latin teacher (and a very good one), just may have known the truth about all this because of her knowledge of the Greeks and Romans and a lot of the stuff they (i.e. the Greeks and the Romans) did to (for? . . . with?) each other. But then Miss Bilcox probably wouldn't have dared talk about it either. So anyway, there's no reason to get carried away here. Just remember that Washertown perhaps was not quite as "straight" and upstanding as its many flagpoles might have suggested. In fact for all I know, maybe some of those flagpoles kind of represented more than just a pole with a flag on the top.

As I'm sure you know though, I didn't even think about things like flagpoles being anything other than flagpoles until I went to college and learned some stuff about Freud (as I told you a long time ago), and then took a crappy "Modern" literature course that was taught by a totally weird-looking, wacked-out teacher who bit her fingernails, chain smoked cigarettes in a "made in France" cigarette holder, and talked about sex symbols and stuff like that all the time. She even once told us that Robert Frost was queer (pardon me . . . homosexual) because he wrote a poem about swinging in birch trees. And then that Ernest Hemingway was obsessed with breasts because he talked a lot about climbing mountains. Really. I mean that lady was really fucked up. But this whole thing is getting further and further off track. Just remember though that when I was a boy, as I told you before, you were supposed to believe that Mr. Lewis was the only sexually "disoriented" person in all of Washertown (if not Casper County). So let's leave it at that. What I started out to do was just to tell you some stuff about The Capitol Theatre. And besides that, as far as I could tell, the sex lives (and lies) of Washertown's more (or less) prominent citizens were, with the exception of Mr. Lewis of course, not played out in or around the Capitol Theatre anyway. The Wedgewood Room at the Palace Hotel? Maybe. But who the hell should care, anyway?

So, the fact is that the Capitol got all the big important movies, like *Gone With the Wind* and *From Here to Eternity* and everything (except for the occasional "big one" from *RKO,* which always played at The Iowa). Remember the Iowa? That was the movie theatre with the urine-scented popcorn. Anyway, to get to the really important stuff about the Capitol, every two or three months there would be a Saturday morning cartoon extravaganza (big word) there. And I'm telling you, it was wonderful. *Really* wonderful. I mean it was so wonderful that after it was over you almost felt the same way you felt when Christmas was over. You know, like it was the best thing in the whole world, but now you had to wait a really long time before it would happen again. I mean when these cartoon shows took place you sometimes had to stand in line for about two blocks (it seemed like two miles even . . . especially if it was raining) just to get in. That's how good they were. And you were always afraid there wouldn't be any good seats left when you finally got in, or that you wouldn't be able to sit with your buddies, or that you would have to sit way at the side, where it made everything on the screen look real "slanty" and stuff, and also made you get a stiff neck.

So the deal was that you tried to get in line really early, or, if your conscience let you do it (and if you were lucky it always did), you would find someone who was willing to give you "cuts." Some of the big guys (ass-holes that they were) "took cuts" anyway, but unless you were a whole lot braver than I was, you just let them. I hated it when that happened! Mostly because it made me feel like a chicken. "Chicken," by the way, when I was little, was about the worst thing you could ever be called. At least if you were a boy. I don't know what the worst thing was if you were a girl. Maybe "smelly" or something like that. And the *very* worst thing you could be called was a son-of-a-bitch. The term was taken more literally then; so if anyone ever called you that, no matter how big they were (or little you were), you were supposed to try to "beat them up," in defense of your mother's reputation. And if you didn't, of course, you once more turned into a chicken, only now even more of one, like a "big fat chicken." Which is a reminder that it wasn't always real fun and easy growing up in Washertown. But this chicken shit got better as you got older, since you eventually could be the ass-hole and "take cuts" just about anytime *you* wanted to; and also of course you could call the kid who was now littler than you a chicken, or son-of-a-bitch even, or anything else you wanted to. "Turd" even. Yeah. That was a good one. *Turd.* Being a turd was pretty much like being a butthole, which, as I told you a long time ago was considered to be even worse than being an asshole (although we probably have somewhat of a redundancy going here). Something like that anyway. *Redundant* of course, was another of those words I didn't know then.

"Beep-Beep!" "The Roadrunner" was my favorite cartoon, and "The Three Stooges" was the all-time best "short subject" (that meant like a little movie). At least that's what I thought. The Saturday morning shows at the Capitol always had at least two or three "Roadrunners" and "Three Stooges," and I absolutely loved them all. *Loved* them! I also liked "Tom and Jerry" of course (it would have been un-American not to like those guys), and "Daffy Duck." And then I also thought there was something really special (in a maybe sort of pathetic way) about "Goofy" and the way he could make me so happy. I'm not sure why. But anyway, Goofy was important to me. In general, however, given my tendency to feel sorry for everyone, and worry about everything, I sometimes had to be careful not to get too involved with or attached to all these cartoon characters, since if I did then I would feel bad myself. I mean they were always getting blown up, or beat to shit or something. But to tell you the truth, that didn't much get in the way of laughing your ass off, and the Saturday cartoon shows provided some of the very most best times in my whole Washertown childhood. In fact, it probably was the Capitol Theatre cartoon shows, *MPP* (the swimming pool with its big flappy flag), and feeling really safe at home and everything (and maybe even orange Popsicles), that were the very best parts about being little in Washertown. (It's for sure it wasn't throwing up at the Masonic Temple, or getting vaccinated in the nurse's office in elementary school, and shit like that!)

"They," by the way (probably some "big shot" designers that came down from Des Moines or somewhere), redecorated the esteemed Capitol Theatre after the end of World War II, and of course ruined it. Absolutely *ruined* it. It was the time when television was threatening the entire movie industry, and I guess they thought that if they remodeled and redecorated the place it would bring more people in. So as I said, they did ("redo" it), and as I also said, *ruined* it. Before all the changes, the Capitol was pretty much a 1930s, important-looking, "succeeding at being a little art deco" sort of place. It had an outside ticket booth, right in the center as you walked up, with two sets of double, dark-wood and glass-paned doors on each side. (Going through those doors made you feel really important and everything.) And I can still remember the little lady who sold tickets in the ticket booth, and also her husband, who sometimes took the tickets when you went through the double doors, because they were both always so nice (they did that after selling their own store and retiring, which I'll tell you about in just a little while). But anyway, in front of the ticket booth was a big brass rail to help keep people in line, and it was always polished up real, real shiny-like (even though there were usually also lots of finger smudges on it too). In front of this polished brass rail and the special doors and everything, and hanging *way* out onto the sidewalk, was the Capitol's big, square "marquee." It was always just sort of "there," like a symbol of the arts maybe, and always announced (in great big letters) the latest Hollywood love story or musical . . . like *Casablanca,* or *Song of the South,* as well as other "big" ones that I've already mentioned. And when you were downtown on the east side of the Square and it rained real hard, like during some of Washertown's really scary, but also kind of neat July thunderstorms (which also smelled really good), you ran up to stand under the Capitol marquee, even if you weren't even going to the movies. You just stood there, waited, smelled the "suddenly-getting-cooler," sort of sweet, clean, and "all around you" rainy summer scent, and felt real safe and cozy and everything. Like if you were riding in a convertible and listening to the rain splatter on the roof sort of cozy.

Inside the Capitol (before they ruined it) there were fancy lights on the ceiling of the lobby, and also all along the walls of the auditorium itself. Most of these lights had little pieces of colored glass in them, like stained glass windows in a church (only not so much of it), and they glowed a sort of mysterious and dreamy-like, orangey-yellow, Hollywood color (at least that's what color I thought it was). The first part of the lobby, just after you entered the theatre, was where you got your popcorn and candy and stuff. And then you walked through sort of another entryway to the next part, which had a really low ceiling and was where the pretty lights were that I just told you about. And the walls had great big "scrolly" plaster carvings on them. And then when you actually went through the next doors (into the auditorium itself) to find your seat and sit down, the ceiling was really, really *high*. Especially when you were really, really *little*. And then (and this part was unbelievably fancy and everything), at the very front of the theatre, on each side of the movie screen itself, hung these big, tall, heavy-looking, maroon velvet drapes that looked kind of like they should have been hanging in a palace or maybe a castle even. Perhaps they had been once. I don't know. Anyway, even the carpet in this place was fancy. It had big "splashes" of multi-colored (but not real bright) flowers woven into it, and it was thicker than thick, and spongy feeling, except where everyone had walked a lot, like right down the very center of the part of the lobby with the low ceiling and pretty lights. Even the stairs that went up to the balcony (one set at each end of the lobby) were carpeted. I mean this place was *fancy* fancy! Maybe like French fancy even.

And would you believe that when I was little (before the ruinous remake), and for some really special times, like maybe Friday or Saturday night, or even sometimes on a Sunday afternoon, the

Capitol had real live ushers to help you find your seat? I mean these guys wore uniforms and had flashlights and everything! They were there mostly because the place could get really crowded. At least I think that was why. So anyway, this was the Capitol at its very best! I also should probably tell you though, so you don't get in trouble or anything, that some of Washertown's kind of strange (I thought) religious people, like maybe the Baptists from the South (something like that anyway), and the Jehovah's Witnesses from the street corners, and some other people whose church was called "The "Four Squares" (I think that was its name) said you shouldn't go to the movies on Sunday (I guess because it might make you too happy). The word *square* by the way, in the 1940s anyway, was what you called someone who was pretty much "out of it" (you know . . . like a "dick-head," or a "wacko," or a "nut-case," or something), so I thought it was pretty strange that that church wanted to call itself "Four Squares." I mean Jesus! How goddamn stupid is that? (Sorry, but stuff like that really cracked me up.) Anyway, on special days (actually mostly nights), as I was kind of telling you up above, if something as wonderful as *Gone With the Wind,* or maybe a Fred Astaire and Ginger Rogers movie was playing, there would be ushers (the guys with the flashlights) to help you find where you were going. Some of the ushers were pretty old, but others were more like only in high school, and sometimes I thought I might want to be one of them (when I got older), mainly though just because their uniforms were really fancy and had brass buttons on them and everything. It was kind of like when I wanted to be the king in the grade school play or a wise man in the church Christmas pageant (because they were real special too, and got to wear robes and crowns and everything). But then I decided I didn't want to be (an usher), since I also thought they looked just a little bit sissy-like. And, as you may recall, I wasn't about to set myself up to be some kind of a sissy.

So anyway (to "bring the curtain down" on the Capitol), it was truly some place. But, as I said, and as fate would have it, "they," the design loonies from Des Moines (I really don't want to hang the blame on Washertown people) redecorated the place around 1948 or so, and *ruined* it. Within weeks it went from a 1930s, classy, sophisticated looking place (for Iowa and Washertown anyway) to cheap, 1950s, really tacky "modern." A truly sacred space, desecrated (big word). To be sure, it simply shouldn't have happened. But it did. A foolish decision, and a shitty job Trust me. Goofy, Daffy Duck, the Three Stooges, or even the goddamn Roadrunner could have done it better; but they probably would have had the good sense to just leave the place alone! Whatever. One final "beep beep," and we're out of there . . .

Next to The Capitol Theatre was another of Washertown's OK but rather non-descript jewelry stores. A very narrow little place, and not especially deep. In all fairness, however, I have to say that my brother and I chose this store in which to buy our mother a piece of jewelry for Christmas one year, so it must have been pretty special in some ways. I mean we wouldn't have gone just *anywhere* to get something for our mom. She was far too good for that. I can't remember the name of the place though, so I think we'll just pass by. And anyway, not everything (or place) in Washertown could be great big and special. (But most things were.)

But, *but,* just across the alley (another of Washertown's "Lanes de Layfaette" that reached out from The Casper County Courthouse) was another truly magnificent and special Washertown establishment: Roswell's (real name)! Roswell's was to Washertown what Sardi's or maybe The Rainbow Room (perhaps anyway . . . I of course had never heard of those places when I was little) was to New York City. It had a beautiful, wide awning, and plate glass windows that were almost sidewalk to ceiling high. Roswell's, trust me, was not just "one more" Washertown store. No way. Roswell's was candy, ice cream, more candy, more ice cream, surprises, and sandwiches. *And,* a soda fountain, booths, a big Wurlitzer jukebox, a great big dance floor (with a slowly spinning, silvery-mirrored big ball hanging over it), and even more really good stuff that I'll tell you about later. This veritable (again a word that came to me later) "palace of pleasures" was only one storefront wide; but it was long, *very* long, and deep (almost maybe, but probably not I guess, like Robert Frost's woods. Remember? "The woods are lovely, dark and deep . . ."). Anyway, Roswell's had a kind of strange, almost dark and scary feeling about it, especially if you looked from the very front all the way to the back. I mean when I was just little the place seemed cavernous (although then I would just have said "really big" or something). It smelled kind of musty too, although a good musty. Of course lots of stores that were long and went way back were kind of dark and just a little bit musty in the 1940s, so I guess that part didn't make Roswell's real different. Whatever. The point is, Roswell's wasn't real bright inside (especially, as I just said, at the back), partly because the interior lighting was provided mostly by only single, incandescent bulbs that were inside sort of milky-looking, "bulgy" glass fixtures that hung on skinny metal rods from the rather high ceiling.

For about two-thirds of the way back, the walls at Roswell's were lined with high, glass-front candy counters, some of which sometimes didn't even always have anything in them (that's how many there were). But that didn't matter. And in the center of the store there was always this big, long, makeshift table, covered with sort of faded-looking, white cloth (maybe even old table cloths) that hung all the way down to the floor. Kind of like a skirt or something. But makeshift or not, on this table was the finest assortment of penny candy and "novelties" that a little kid could ever imagine. I mean it had to be the world's (well, Washertown's anyway . . . no, actually the world's I think) biggest and best display of foil-wrapped candy kisses, "cigarettes" (both the ones that were like white sticks made out of chalky tasting stuff, with red on the end to look like fire, *and* the chocolate kind that actually had white paper wrapped around them, like real cigarettes), and also individual, cellophane-wrapped caramels and hard candies of every kind and color you could think of. Then, as I just said, there were novelties: little tin or lead medals that you could pin to your shirt (or just collect), and "clickers," which were little tin devices that when you pinched or pressed on them made a sound kind of like crickets chirping in wet grass somewhere, and stuff like that.

And (get ready for this), on that very same table was a Roswell's exclusive—a whole bunch of brown paper bags that they called "grab-bags," which were stapled closed at the top so you couldn't see what was inside until you bought them. These bags (like a box of chocolate cigarettes) cost five cents each (pretty pricey for a little boy in the 1940s), but they were worth it; that was because we knew that each and every one of those bags, I mean *each* one, contained Mr. and Mrs. Roswell's very own, handpicked assortment of penny candy and novelties. Actually it was the same stuff you could choose for yourself, only the bag, your "encounter with the unknown," made it a lot more exciting. So, if you had a nickel, which wasn't real often, and could resist spending it on an ice cream cone (which also wasn't real often), you bought a Roswell's grab-bag. I mean (if you had that nickel earmarked for other than ice cream) you never even thought about choosing your own stuff, since your curiosity about what was in the little brown bag was just too overpowering to resist. And if you didn't have a nickel, you sometimes went into Roswell's just to see which bag you would choose if you did have (a nickel). You never knew when you might be looking at (or feeling, if Mr. Roswell wasn't watching you) a special treasure that had been stuck into one of those mysterious bags. Like maybe even a real small, but solid, lead soldier or something (not just an ordinary, flat, tin one), or maybe some kind of really important medal (like maybe even as important as the Captain Midnight ring I told you about a long time ago). Only, as I think I also told you, you couldn't get Captain Midnight rings except by mail order (so that the Captain Midnight people could officially register the secret code you got with it). Anyway, once in a while a Roswell's hand-selected bag might even have an extra "clicker" in it (the kind that I already said sounded like a cricket in wet grass).

Almost in the middle of Roswell's, meaning just about but not quite halfway back, and on the right side, was the soda fountain. Roswell's fountain was really big and high (at least when you were little), and was all scratched-up-looking, since it was made out of real, but also pretty old, faded-looking solid marble (white, with some shadowy gray places in it). But I'm telling you, that fountain contained limitless amounts of ice cream and an infinite variety of syrups and other really good and thick and gooey stuff (by using words like *limitless* and *infinite,* I'm trying to talk about it in a sort of adult way). And on the very end of the fountain, toward the front, sat this inverted glass jug, with a kind of pebbly finish on it (so that you couldn't really see the stuff that was in it I guess, only that it was green), cradled in a shiny white ceramic base with a spigot on one side. And there was this big label glued to it that had a moon picture on it and said "Green River." Talk about something that made a really "wowy" lime phosphate! I mean that stuff was fantastic. Worth resisting an ice cream cone, a grab-bag, or maybe anything else even (if you could control your hunger and curiosity, or maybe were real, real thirsty). And you didn't even have to tell the soda jerk (a "soda jerk" was the "name" for the person who worked behind a soda fountain, by the way, not a "jerk" as in an asshole or anything like that) . . . anyway, you didn't even have to say that you wanted a lime phosphate or anything. He (the soda jerk) would say, "What'll you have?" And you would just put your nickel on top of the counter and say, "Green River." And next thing you knew, there it was right in front of you! Now that I think about it, dying and going to heaven would have been like being in Roswell's with not one, but *two* nickels, all at the same time; one would be for a grab-bag, and the other for a "Green River." And if you had a third one even (i.e. a third nickel), which would have been pretty unlikely, you could use it for an ice cream cone. By the way, I think Roswell's was the only place in the whole world that had "Green Rivers." Only I can't say for sure of course, since I hadn't been to a lot of places. (I was only five or six when I first started going to Roswell's.)

The back third of Roswell's, the kind of dark and almost scary part, seemed to exude a kind of palpable (although I of course didn't know the words *exude* and *palpable* then), but apparently innocuous (another word I didn't know), sense of evil. At least when I was little it did. I thought so anyway. I mean it just kind of felt sort of unhealthy or something; although I guess maybe those big words I used before describe it better. But it always seemed to me (although I can't say for sure why) that there was something wrong back there. Whatever. Anyway, the very back part of Roswell's was where the dance floor was, and it was surrounded on three sides by high-backed, wooden, "love-carved" booths. (I guess Mr. Roswell couldn't watch the dance floor, protect the booths, and guard the grab bags all at the same time.) The dance floor itself was made of that "seen-in-a-lot-of-places-in-the-1940s," gray, pebbly-looking terrazzo tile (I think that's what it was anyway), with a little fancy border around the edge. (It seems that most floors in Washertown stores, if they weren't oiled wood, were some variation of this shiny tile.) But of course you couldn't dance on oiled floors. Just this shiny tile stuff. Maybe on polished hardwood you could. I'm not sure.

Anyway, Roswell's tile dance floor was always highly polished and sometimes almost sticky in spots because of the "dance wax." Dance wax was the stuff Mr. Roswell shook out of a cardboard can (sort of like an "Old Dutch Cleanser," or "BaBo," or fish food can), when customers convinced him that the dance floor was too "slow." And then (to help the dancers not to miss anything, I guess), all around the dance floor there were mirrors lining the upper half of the walls, into which, and sadly I thought, one could too often observe a certain Washertown grade school teacher (from *my* school too) kind of looking at herself too much. Maybe anyway. Primping, when she thought no one was watching. Sort of in the manner of one of those pretty much, if not really strange ladies in a Tennessee Williams play, like *A Street Car Named Desire* or something (which I mentioned a long time ago). At the time of course (and as I said before) I didn't know anything about Tennessee Williams and the "eccentricities," or "nightingales," or "glass menageries," or any of the other southern shit that he seemed to want to write about. Mr. Williams, by the way, went to the same state university I went to . . . which would indicate that I am not the only great writer the place produced. (And I'm sorry about the *shit* word that I just used when talking about him. I continue to do better limiting the number of bad words though, don't you think? Except maybe for a while ago when I let loose with a couple of "fucks.") Whatever.

Even though, as I just told you, I didn't know very much about Tennessee Williams stuff, I did know something about streetcars, since when I was little they had them (streetcars) in Des Moines. But I didn't know about eccentric people. I mean I'm sure Des Moines had some (eccentric people); it's just that I didn't know any of them, and if I had I still wouldn't have used that word (eccentric) to describe them. But I guess that could just be because I didn't know it (the word) yet. I mean maybe the guy at the State Fair who sold me the ill-fated chameleon (my little lizard friend who committed suicide . . . remember?) was eccentric, but I don't think Mr. Williams would have been interested in him (meaning the salesman, not the lizard), since he (Mr. Williams) wrote about women, not men. Maybe though. But something is beginning to tell me that I might be getting a little to a really lot off track. You know, the mental thing again—my "cross to bear," if you want to get religious about it—(which I don't, but you can if you want to I guess). At times though (although I know I have to get focused again) I sometimes wonder what kind of medications I would have been on if I had been a little person just a few decades later? Like when they invented Thoraziine, and Librium, and Valium and everything. (Actually, although maybe I shouldn't tell you this, I think Valium feels pretty good sometimes.) But anyway, let's just keep going here. There's still more to say about Roswell's. By the way though (before we do keep going), I don't think any of the streetcars in Des Moines was named "Desire." (I just thought I should sort of clear that up, in case someone from Des Moines was reading this and wondered if I really knew what the hell I was talking about.)

Anyway, the behavior of this teacher that I mentioned a while ago (i.e. "the Roswell's primper") was strange. *Very* strange. Even to a fourth grader, which is about what I think I was when I would see her there. In the first place, she probably wasn't even supposed to be at Roswell's, since in the 1940s (as I told you before) women teachers weren't supposed to do much of anything except teach. I mean (as I also said before) I think they weren't even supposed to have a private life, and it's for sure that they hadn't been hired to have fun So it was a pretty good bet that this teacher wasn't supposed to be in the back of Roswell's looking at herself in the mirror. But here's what will *really* get you. Believe it or not, and this is no lie, this seemingly sorry and somewhat pathetic looking (at least I thought) person's name also spoke to her condition. Her name was Payne. Really. Payne, as in *pain. Miss* Payne, of course. Honest to God, that really was her name. A sad lady, I thought. And she was always, at least it seemed so to me, alone. *Always* alone. And she, Miss Payne, as you might suspect, was not only seen there (i.e. at Roswell's), but (of course) was also undoubtedly talked about a lot (again at least at Rosewll's). I remember my older cousin telling me that she was. And she (my cousin) knew stuff like this. (I'll tell you more about her after while.)

Anyway, the more I saw Miss Payne, the more I felt sorry for her (don't forget . . . I was the one who was *always* feeling sorry for someone). I might have been just little, but I guess some "little people" (even little boys) can understand loneliness. Their own, and that of others. So anyway, when I saw the eccentric Miss Payne at Roswell's, although in fact it was actually only occasionally, I think I really did feel her pain (kind of anyway); it was almost as though someone *needed* to. I know now that I wish I had been big when I saw her, so I could have told her that. Maybe it would have helped. And who knows? Maybe Miss Payne and I could even have had a dance together. Anyway, it was pretty sad. I guess she was just real unhappy. But mostly lonely, I think. *Lonely.* Miss Payne, by the way, not lacking for a sense of style (remember, this was the 1940s) had a big braid of hair which she kind of wound around her head. Sort of like a crown. Or maybe not. (I thought it looked like a crown anyway.) I do know however that I'm continuing to feel a little strange in the head, and that I can't chance letting my mind get funny over Miss Payne's hairstyle. Whatever. I was just trying to make an interesting and somewhat flattering comment about her appearance. She wound it (her hair) only once, by the way, meaning that when she wound it at Roswell's she did it only once. I imagine she probably wound it around lots of times at other places. I just hope, I really do, that Miss Payne eventually found someone else in the mirror at Roswell's, and then got happy. (Someday I would also hope to understand better why I felt so compelled to watch her.)

My cousin, who was named for a lady in the *Bible* (although it didn't seem to affect her much), and who was in high school and therefore really grown up and everything, went to Roswell's to "jitterbug." I wasn't sure what that meant at the time, but I figured it was probably pretty much OK, since she did it, and did it at Roswell's. Lots of high school kids went there and did it (jitterbugged). My cousin, we called her "Meme," wore "slacks," and black and white saddle shoes, and white socks, and one of her dad's old, long dress shirts that she tied in a big knot in the front. At least when she jitterbugged at Roswell's that's what she wore. The back of the shirt she just kind of let hang out. (I think that all this stuff she wore was kind of like what you were supposed to wear if you were "with it," like "in the groove" or something.) The problem was that just about everyone in the family thought she didn't look real nice that way. But I did. Maybe because I liked her so much. And she liked me too. Actually, I think she maybe kind of felt sorry for me (she was a person that I sometimes thought also felt sorry for some people, and I think perhaps she knew I was pretty self-conscious and everything). Anyway, I thought she looked just fine in her jitterbug clothes.

She, my cousin Meme, and I (if you'll pardon the digression . . . and I promise not to get mentally wacked or anything) would sometimes, and especially on rainy days, go down in the basement at her house and make "plaster of paris" frog people and other strange little characters in red rubber "molds." What you did was to fill the molds (they came in a "set," sort of like a kid's art or hobby materials) with the plaster, and then hang them upside down in fruit jars (with the lids off of course) until they got hard and you could (very carefully) try to take them out of the molds. You had to be really *really* careful taking them out though, or they would break. Then we would paint them (but only the good ones . . . not the ones that had broken or had been "deformed" because of air bubbles in the plaster stuff). Painting them was the most fun part. Anyway these "molding sets" were pretty popular when I was little, and molding on rainy days with my cousin was really fun. She was special all right. And I have never ever seen a frog painted as pretty as the one she painted once. It (the frog) was shaped to kind of be standing up, with its legs crossed (like a "dandy," I learned later), and leaning on a walking stick (sort of like a gentleman frog . . . maybe even like Richard Corey, if he had been a frog), and she had painted its face sort of ivory, and the top hat it was wearing red, and its coat ("tails") a really "purpley" purple. (She explained to me that the reason it was wearing a "swallow-tail" coat was that it may have been going to a wedding or something.) Otherwise, the rest of the frog was painted green, the way frogs are supposed to be. You would have liked my cousin. But we better get back to Roswell's, since (believe it or not), there is still more to tell you about.

On the very, very, *very* back wall of Roswell's (I told you the place was real deep and long . . . almost like a cave or something), and framed (most unfortunately) by the entrances to the restrooms, sat the very latest "jewel" of the jukebox era, an absolutely magnificent and magical-looking Wurlitzer. Roswell's always had the very latest Wurlitzer jukebox. This one, the model I remember most, was arch-shaped on the top, and for the most part was made (or so it seemed anyway) from sort of cloudy, milky-looking (*skim* milky-looking), "swollen" tubes of plastic, each of which was filled with some special kind of diaphanous (a word I *really* didn't know then), gassy-colored light. The color of the light varied from tube to tube, but I remember that they were all kind of cheap, carnival colors . . . sort of "lavendery," and light pink, and blue clouds "bluey" maybe. Whatever. These tubes were absolutely beautiful in their own make-believe, mysterious, sort of Hollywood (I guess anyway . . .

as I've said a few times before, I'd never been there) sort of way. Really big tubes flanked the outside of the thing (the whole jukebox itself), with smaller ones more towards the center. And then, in even smaller tubes, thin, translucent ones that arched right around the larger swollen ones, little bubbles of water seemed to be rising and somehow flowing into the jukebox itself. I mean this jukebox was really something.

Anyway, when you stood and looked at this Wurlitzer all together, and all at the same time, and if you imagined it to be a lot (like a really, really, *really* lot) bigger than it actually was, it could kind of make you think of a huge but hideous plastic cathedral (meaning a great big church . . . although of course we didn't have any churches big enough to be cathedrals in Washertown). But anyway, it was as though this sort of monstrous cathedral had somehow risen from (or had maybe even been pushed up out of) the earth itself, perhaps signaling the advent of some kind of a "to-be-dreaded" age of pestilence, and decadence, and suffering, and other really sick stuff. And I mean really sick, like *shitty* sick. Maybe even like what was going to happen to you if you were Catholic and had had sex before you got married or something. You know, and even made "deposits," when you should have been doing "withdrawals" (return to our time at Washertown National Bank, if you have forgotten about that particular "crime"). Or maybe "did it" in the wrong position. Or (Oh my God!) maybe also "jerked off" too much or something. I don't know. Or perhaps that bubbling, multi-colored and milky-looking stack of plastic tubes was just a goddamn jukebox after all; and the whole cathedral crap a dream. I don't know. I didn't mean to get so carried away either. And besides, when I was in fourth or fifth grade I didn't even know what pestilence and decadence and all that shit meant anyway. Whatever. I'll tell you this though: I'm not going to let my mind spin out of control again just because I had a maybe sort of strange vision regarding a goddamn jukebox that I thought looked like the Notre Dame Cathedral or something (wherever in the hell that was). Or maybe it *was* a cathedral. A cathedral trying to look like a fucking jukebox! Oh my God! Whoa . . . just slow down here. I mean Jesus, this is bad!

You know though, the honest-to-God truth is that the thing probably looked more like a little colored neighborhood church somewhere (meaning that the little church itself was colored as a result of the gases in the tubes and the lights, not that the people who went to the church were Negroes or anything). Yeah. Just a little, plastic, diaphanous church. Maybe even (if you could have turned the lights off) it might have looked like "The Little Brown Church in the Vale." (I know where that is, by the way, since it's in Iowa . . . really.) Or you know . . . maybe it, the magnificent Wurlitzer, just looked like a jukebox! But anyway, *anyway* (I'm trying to get focused again and transition away from that goddamn thing) you might recall that a few years later some company evidently borrowed the bubble feature from the big Wurlitzer jukebox at Roswell's (or big cathedral maybe . . . just *maybe*) and started to manufacture "bubble lights" for Christmas trees. We never had them on our Christmas tree though, since my mom thought they weren't traditional enough, and my dad said watching lights that moved kind of made him crazy. Well, no one should have to give up important traditions (or be driven nuts) for the sake of a few goddamn bubble lights, I guess. Maybe for some great big serious really God-awful calamity or something, but not for bubble lights. Holy shit! I mean Jesus! I think I'm losing it again! OK. OK. So let's just get back to where we need to be. I'll think about calm things. Like Christmas trees, and my mother, the remarkably sane, tradition-bound mom who didn't think bubbles were acceptable, but who nevertheless actually chose to buy a pink "flocked" Christmas tree about five years later. Anyway, I think I'm getting "leveled out" again, so lets get back to the remaining stuff about Roswell's. Sorry about the extended "slip-up." I guess it's too bad one of those grab-bags that I told you about didn't contain some Thorazine or something. But of course, and as I already kind of told you, they didn't even have stuff like that when I was little (not just in Roswell's grab-bags, but *anywhere*). And now that I'm getting totally level again, I've got to admit that my little "flight of fancy" regarding the jukebox was really unnecessary. I mean what Roswell's had was just a jukebox: a Wurlitzer jukebox. Nothing more. Nothing less. So do you want a Green River or something? I'll buy.

Well, as I already said (and we're almost done here), the dance floor at Roswell's was that mock terrazzo stuff; but always shiny, and sometimes, as I also said, sticky (because of the dance wax). Curiously though, now that I think more about it, I actually don't remember seeing anyone dance there, except my cousin and some of her friends jitterbugging once in awhile. But anyway, to sort of sum things up, my memories of Roswell's are primarily grab-bags, Green Rivers, and Miss Payne, all of which (or whom) I have already told you about enough. Just one more thing though, since I always have to be honest with you (even in a place like Roswell's), or you might think I'm just selecting the good stuff to make Washertown sound better than it really was.

So, the "one more thing" is that I can remember a strange squishing sound that my shoes made once when I went to the bathroom at Roswell's and walked (waded) across the several puddles of urine on Roswell's men's room floor, which of course (the whole men's room, not just the puddles) smelled really bad. And I do mean bad. Kind of made a person want to "tiptoe" and hold his nose, all at the same time (if you know I mean, and I'm sure you do). I guess the drain on the old, "all the way to the floor model" urinal was plugged up or something; probably with soggy cigarette butts. And now that I'm back to smells again, I just don't know why so many men's rooms in Washertown had to smell bad. Especially this one (since Roswell's was so special in every other way). I mean our bathroom at home didn't smell bad. (Well, maybe sometimes it did; like right after my brother or me or someone else maybe "went" big time.) But mostly it didn't. I guess Roswell's problem (in addition to the plugged up urinal) may have also been because the little crystalline deodorant discs that they bought (you almost always saw those things in urinals) might not have been strong enough. I don't know. But I don't mean to spoil Roswell's with bathroom talk (I was just trying to be honest). Just know that the men's room floor might be wet, and that the whole room could smell pretty bad. So therefore it wasn't always the best place to go unless you really had to.

However, never, *never* forget (as in the "Camelot manner" again) that Roswell's was a Washertown treasure. A genuine, "should be in *The National Register of Historic Places* even," treasure. ("Don't let it be forgot/That once there was a spot.") A *Washertown* phenomenon that was right up there with The Orange Bar and Bigelow's. And dark as it sometimes seemed in there, it was nevertheless, in its own very real and extraordinarily special way, "bright lights" (with most of them bubbling away in the Wurlitzer), "and Santa Claus," and everything else "coming up roses" (what a great show *Gypsy* would be some years later). *And,* some of the very best times any little kids (and big people too) could possibly have. I mean it had to be. After all, it was Roswell's of Washertown!

So, out of Roswell's, past the Singer Sewing Machine Store, a place in which (I'm sure you will understand) I had no interest, and on to the superstore of Washertown Square's east side. F.W. Woolworth! This place was even bigger than J.J. Newberry's (although the background red of its sign was not as deep-red rich, and its gold identifying letters were not quite as shiny). However, Woolworth's was almost three, that's right, *three* storefronts wide. It had two sets of swinging doors that made that distinct "swooshing" sound when you pushed them open (just like at J.J. Newberry's), a lunch counter (which J.J. Newberry's did *not* have), and just about everything anyone could possibly wish for or dream about. That's how big and good it was! Woolworth's, at least to a little boy in the 1940s, was like a living Sears and Roebuck or Montgomery Ward catalogue, only without the furniture and machinery and farmer's stuff. And Woolworth's had the absolute best goldfish tank in the whole world (however small my world may then have been).

Again of course, you walked on oiled wood floors. Years later, however, when I was getting big (bigger anyway), those "oiled to death," thin wooden slats were replaced by "genuine" squares of asphalt tile . . . but that's another story for another time. Woolworth's also had the usual mix of "dry goods," cheap cosmetics, and mixed, "bulk" candies, all of which contributed to its ever-present, kind of bad, but also often pretty good (and sweet) smell. The pale orange "circus peanuts" contributed big time (as they also did at J.J. Newberry's). In general, as a matter of fact (as you might expect), Woolworth's smells were mostly a lot like Newberry's, only at Woolworth's you could also suck in some greasy smells coming from the hamburgers frying at the lunch counter, and a sort of steamy, "hard-to-know-just-what-the-hell-it-was" smell that spilled over from the metal box in which they kept the steamed hotdogs and soggy buns that they served them in. Woolworth's hotdogs were usually pretty good though, except that the steam treatment (if they over did it) sometimes made the dog and bun combination just a little too spongy, if you know what I mean . . . and you probably do.

Woolworth's was where I spent a whole two weeks of my allowance (fifty cents total) on what I was sure would become one of my mother's most treasured pieces of art. It was a kind of big, all white vase in the shape of "Uncle Sam's" head, meaning the Uncle Sam who "lived" in Washington, D.C., not my own Uncle Sam. I didn't even have an Uncle Sam. Anyway, the vase was complete with Uncle Sam's "top" hat. What made it really special (although I thought it was pretty much special enough anyway) was that the hat part had a great big hole in it so you could put flowers in it. Just think; Uncle Sam with real flowers coming out of his head! I mean, the thing was goddamn beautiful, I thought (I'm trying to sound sort of tough now, since we're actually kind of talking about girly things). Anyway, the same Uncle Sam vase also came in blue or green (for some reason not red). I don't know why that was. You would think it would have come in red, white, and blue. I don't know. Maybe they were out of red. But I don't think so, since they had a lot of them in the other three colors. Oh well. Anyway, given my impeccable (one more big word I of course didn't know when I was little) taste, I of course chose the white one, and gave it to my mother for her birthday. Curiously, I don't remember that she used it very much. But that was probably because it was so special that she was afraid it would get broken or something. Maybe anyway. As a matter of fact though, I don't remember her ever using it. Oh well.

Woolworth's was also the place (although maybe I shouldn't be telling you this) where I stole a ten-cent ring during a minor, pre-pubertal (another big word) fall from grace. (I had a few . . . meaning "falls" not rings.) I just now thought of the Woolworth ring, because of telling you about her vase. Anyway, my mother would have been really upset had she known I stole something. (It might even have further affected her appreciation of the Uncle Sam vase I gave her.) But I guess I don't think she would have been *really* mad. Just a lot disappointed. Anyway, let's get out of here before the police come and arrest me. First, however, take a good look at that slow-moving, fat, black, pop-eyed goldfish that's kind of looking right at us from the fish tank across the aisle. See him? The really, *really* ugly one? And remember when we were at Newberry's and I told you that I felt kind of sorry for those guys? Well, I guess I sort of still do. I mean they are *so* ugly (like butt-ugly even), that it almost makes you want to puke. Or maybe just poison them or something, so they won't have to go through life looking that way. I mean they really look like shit!

So, out of F.W. Woolworth's (with one final swoosh of the doors) and on down the street. We just passed an auto parts store, which also didn't interest me much (although it was better than the sewing machine store), except one time when right after World War II ended they had a little motor scooter for sale that they called a "Doodlebug," and I thought maybe, just *maybe*, I could get my dad to buy one for me. Or even let me save up for it from my paper route. Well, it didn't happen. It was sort of one of those lessons about "you can't have everything," or "into every life a little rain must fall," or "it's always darkest before the dawn," so "look for the silver lining," and all that shit. I guess anyway. Whatever. I never got my scooter (and they weren't even big or expensive or dangerous or anything). But again, and to add to the stuff I just said, "life isn't always fair." (Which is another true but piece of shit expression.).

But anyway, right next door to that place, and on the corner, was the biggest and best drug store in all Washertown. At least in its way it was. My father didn't think so though, since it was a "chain" store, and people who owned their own businesses (as I said more than a couple of times before), and "did business" mostly with just each other, didn't appreciate people who "did business" with chain stores. And besides, everyone knew that these huge and sinister chain store places were owned and operated by "God only knew" what kind of people, who lived "God only knew" where (but probably in some evil big city or someplace . . . like bigger even than Des Moines). And furthermore (of course), these chain stores were known to be backed by millionaires who (of course) were probably Jews, who (of course) having already killed Christ were determined now to crucify the "little guys" in the world of independent businesses too. Nevertheless, regardless of how painful all this may have been for some local merchants to tolerate (including my dad), on the south end of the east side of the Square was Washertown's own and mighty Walgreen's Drug Store!

Walgreen's was another of Washertown's "double-wide" establishments. And what I remember most about it (and you would too if you had been there) was that on every Sunday noon they put white linen (actually cotton I suppose) table cloths on top of the booths and tables (the entire south side of the store was a fountain and eating area), adorned each one with a fresh flower, which was usually a red or pink carnation (talk about "high class"), and served this really fancy Sunday dinner for the after church crowd. The Sunday menu was always the same: Baked Ham (spongy, and never hot enough); Chicken (also baked, and usually too oily); and Roast Beef (cooked to death, and way too chewy). Gravy came on everything of course (white on the ham, yellow on the chicken, and brown on the dead roast beef). And, *and* everyone got one sometimes warm (most of the time not) "Parker House" roll, or maybe two if you had a nice waitress. All three segments of the roll (usually still attached) were served to each diner on a separate little plate (unless the table was real crowded, and then they served it right on the dinner plate, and next to your meat, I guess so it could get gravy all over it). You also got one "patty" of butter (on a little cardboard square), which you had to be kind of careful to keep from sticking to the side of, or sliding under the roll itself, and therefore melting. The rolls, by the way, regardless of where they were placed, were almost always soggy on the bottom and dry on the top, but pretty warm (usually), as I already said. I think they kept them in a hot dog steamer (or in the steam room of the "Parker House" . . . just kidding). Whatever. Therefore however, and unfortunately, they (the rolls) were also pretty much squashed, if not in fact smashed. Especially if the sermon at the church you went to ran too long and you got to Walgreen's *table d'hote* (words I *really* didn't know then) a little bit late.

Anyway, Sunday dinner at Walgreen's was *not* your ordinary Sunday dinner (more in a moment). However, there was one thing about this weekly spongy pig, oily chicken, and dead cow ritual that just didn't make sense to me. I never quite understood why, if it was wrong to work on Sunday, and the minister at the Methodist church where we went (the one with the pigeon shit all over the sidewalk, and diaphragm dome), and also lots of other ministers in Washertown, said that it was (i.e. that it was wrong to work), then how was it somehow OK to have Sunday dinner at Walgreen's (or anywhere else), which meant of course that other people had to work to fix it for you? Maybe they (the ministers) thought that Walgreen's and some other open-on-Sunday restaurants had special agreements with God or something. Or perhaps it was considered to be part of the overall (and overlooked) immorality of Walgreen's, since it was a chain store. I don't know. Or maybe it was a Catholic plot to see that the Methodists and other Protestants who ate spongy ham, oily chicken, and cooked-to-death, chewy beef were all going to hell or something. I just don't know. Whatever (and to get us back on track), if you had Sunday dinner at Walgreen's, you weren't going anywhere until you had had your cherry pie for dessert. The cherry pie, by the way, was the only part of the entire dinner that didn't have gravy on it. If, however, you could get your mom and dad to go the extra five cents, and knew what the expression "a la mode" meant, your cherry pie arrived with ice cream on it. Pretty special. Maybe even worth going to hell for. Anyway, I just thought I should tell you that part.

Walgreen's was also a good place to stop to call for a ride home from the movies ("picture show"), if you were too young to walk, too lazy when you got a little older, or it was maybe raining or snowing or something. It was also the place you called on the telephone (from somewhere else) and asked (convinced that this great joke was original with just you and your buddies), "Do you have Prince Albert in the can"? (For those of you too young to remember the hapless Prince Albert, it was a brand name for pipe tobacco that came in a flat tin container.) Then, whether the person at Walgreen's who had answered said "yes" or "no," or just tried to hang up on you, you yelled, "Well, you better let him out!" We thought we were so goddamn funny. Oh, and one more thing. Walgreen's was managed for a while by a man on whose daughter I had an unbelievable and like almost incurable "crush" when I was in fourth grade. Tragically however (well, unfortunately anyway), she, Virginia (her real, and I thought rather exotic name), liked my buddy (the one I wet my pants with) better than she liked me, so I had to remain content with my interest in someone else (I would not be so cruel of course as to name this "second" choice). Once even I held Virginia against the side of our grade school building so that my buddy could kiss her (he told me to). And then he was supposed to hold her so I could kiss her. But even though she liked him better, she got all mad at *me* for holding her there while *he* did it (kissed her). I mean what the hell was *that* about? He's the one who kissed her, and I'm the one she gets pissed off at. But I'm telling you she was so fucking upset that I thought she might even report me to the principal. And then tell her mom and everything. I mean that's how mad she was.

Of course had this big love thing involving Virginia happened today, my buddy and I would probably both be in jail for attempted rape or something. And then *we*, innocent boys that we were, probably would have been gang raped by a bunch of perverts and everything. Anyway, the whole thing just goes to show you how bad and how unfair life can be sometimes. I was just glad that I had my affair with Janey to look back on. Second grade wasn't that far behind me, and I talked myself into thinking that Virginia wasn't such a hot deal anyway. In fact, now that I think about it, I should have just told my buddy to hold her down himself. And it just so happens, by the way, that this "hold her down so I can kiss her incident" ended up sort of disrupting our "best friends" status for the whole goddamn summer! And then (check this out), Virginia's dad got transferred a few months later anyway, so she moves to some other state (Ohio). Wouldn't you know? Oh well. Just down the street from Walgreen's, by the way, was where my dad had his office, and where I got my hair cut when I was little (remember the Rialto Barber Shop?).

Anyway, out the door, and here we are on the curb, looking at a not insignificant piece of property that occupied another of those corners adjacent to Washertown's Square. Just a few comments will do though. I mean this wasn't any Orange Bar or Bigelow's. In fact this corner was just a hole in the ground when I was a boy, an enormous, weed-filled, fenced (with rotting wood) *hole*. (I would use a word other than *hole,* except there really aren't any.) Anyway, whatever had been there had burned down years before, and it had been just a big ugly hole ever since. But then, *then,* in the heat of one summer, there arose from that vast hole an absolutely magnificent (somewhat at least) new grocery store called The Thriftway Super Market, a food emporium (another word I had never heard of then) of such grandeur as to cause Mr. Hoage and his girlfriend Eileen to quake in their alcove. (Remember them? Hoage's Grocery . . . with the smelly meat department?) So anyway, there it was, in all its glory: The Washertown Thriftway! And in the basement of that new building, in what some people soon thought of as the very bowels of that new Thriftway (well, sort of anyway), was a twelve-lane bowling alley, a place that would soon spell the demise of the YMCA bowling lanes, and the beginning of stories of the occult. (I didn't know what that word meant either, and I'm probably maybe getting a little bit carried away . . . but only just maybe.) Whatever. We'll have to see. But strange things did begin to happen there.

The story is that it was rumored that at the bowling alley (in the very *bowels* of the mighty Thriftway) there lurked evil, devil-driven people who were attempting to sell marijuana, yes, *marijuana,* to the fine, upstanding, and unsuspecting young men (boys) of Washertown! And perhaps even to the fine, upstanding, unsuspecting, young but "nicely developing" (if you know what I mean . . . and you probably do) women (girls) of Washertown as well! But it was only a rumor. Rumor or not, however, it was of real and almost epic concern to many of Washertown's fine, upstanding, but *not* so unsuspecting, parents. Too bad that the bowling alley at the YMCA (and the age of innocence that it represented) had closed. Too bad indeed! "Reefer madness" was upon us. To tell you the truth though, *I* never saw any marijuana there. And for a while I even "set pins" (a pretty manly and somewhat dangerous job) in the "pits" of the Thriftway basement bowling alley (talk about being "in the bowels"). So I guess that pretty much tells you that I probably knew what I was talking about. I mean there might have been a lot of other shit going on there, but I don't think anyone was smoking it. "Setting pins," by the way, was what you did before the invention of automatic pin-setting machines robbed you of your thirty-five cents an hour job (but also eliminated the very real risk of your getting your head crushed in the pin-setting mechanism).

Before putting this stuff about the bowling alley aside though, I probably should remind you that I of course wasn't exactly the picture of a young man trying to get into trouble; and therefore (but just maybe), I might not have been the most reliable source of information about this reefer madness business after all. In fact, by now I had become a fine, upstanding, unsuspecting member of The First Methodist Church "Youth Fellowship" which, if you don't mind my bragging a little bit, was undoubtedly one of Washertown's premier youth groups (and how pathetic is that?). *And,* the Methodists were not shy about telling people either. So, although my job as a pin-setter put me in the company of some rather unsavory people, I for the most part was free from peril and safely engaged in learning about the Godly life (with several other young Washertown innocents), and all within (under anyway) the protective and magnificent First Methodist Church "Dome of the Diaphragm," the huge stone cap that topped off that entire and most noteworthy building. Furthermore, I was also learning to be especially careful not to step in the pigeon shit that covered, and seemingly in ever-increasing amounts, the church entrance. Simply put, I was earnestly seeking and enjoying friendship with other fine, upstanding, unsuspecting (although often-times boring as hell) Christian young people—*Methodist* Christian young people—popping our pimples, and practicing our prayers. Marijuana? No way! Not us! That kind of shit just wasn't what we were about. In fact, one could probably say, and with considerable accuracy, that we were (at the time anyway) "shit free" (well . . . at least in some ways).

OK. South side. East end. The Iowa Southern Utilities Building. Being just a boy, and therefore not a property owner, I had little to do with this place. The heat and light for our family were taken care of by my dad. What I do remember about the Iowa Southern, however, is that my uncle fell off the scaffolding while he and his associates were painting the exterior, and he got hurt real bad. Broke his leg in more than one place (like maybe three or four), and scared everyone a lot, since he fell so far. So anyway, because of his busted leg, he couldn't attend his daughter's wedding (the wedding of my cousin, Meme, who was named after a Bible person and jitterbugged at Roswell's (as I already told you), and so this made him, and my cousin, and the rest of their family, and lots of other people actually, pretty sad. I played the organ (a real pipe organ) for the wedding, since I had been taking lessons to learn how, and also because my cousin really liked me (as I also already told you) and asked me to do it. I'm not sure I did it very well, although the people who were at the wedding said I did, and my cousin and her husband at least pretended I did. So even though I was only in seventh grade and hadn't been taking lessons very long, I guess my organ debut was pretty good. (Not that it was going to lead to some kind of career or anything.) I remember that the wedding was at The Presbyterian Church, so I was really scared, since the Washertown Presbyterians were more upper class and stuff than Washertown Methodists, and

I thought kind of not as friendly. Maybe not though, and to tell you the truth I would have been scared even having to play the organ at the local roller rink.

The Presbyterians, by the way, had a big high tower on top of their church (instead of a diaphragm, like the Methodists had), and they didn't have any columns in front either. So I guess that was at least two *good* things about the Presbyterians. Especially the no columns part, since that meant that Washertown's pigeons seldom shit on their sidewalk. I know for sure that they didn't on the night of the wedding (although I suppose there was always the possibility that they could have staged a fly-over from the Methodist church, since it was just down the street). Probably though, had that happened (i.e. a shit attack by a squadron of flying Methodist pigeons), the Presbyterians would have hired someone to shovel it right back down the street. I think anyway. Maybe just to make the Methodists look bad or something. Whatever, I just know I was pretty scared to be playing that organ. So anyway, my uncle was in the hospital and in "traction," and really disappointed (about his accident, not the wedding); and my cousin the bride, although of course not in traction, was also pretty sad (again, about the accident, not the wedding). And me? The little seventh grade Methodist organ virtuoso? I was just glad when the goddamn thing was over.

Next stop, J.C. Penney Company (James *Cash* Penney, as I later learned). Another "double-fronter," maybe even a triple, I'm not sure. Let's say it was a "two-and-a-halfer," just to be safe. Again, it was another of Washertown's stores with the smell of oiled wood floors. And "dry goods." Lots and lots of dry goods. Really dry, dry goods. Anyway, Penney's was also really big, and there was more than just one floor to it. The street-level had just about anything you could ever want in a sort of "general" store (including the only refrigerated drinking fountain in Washertown). And at Christmas time (man, you should have seen it!) Penney's basement had the most wonderful, maybe glorious even, display of toys and stuff that you could ever imagine. And I mean ever. (Actually the Christmas toys in Montgomery Ward's basement were pretty good too.) But "Monkey Ward's," as it was affectionately called, wasn't on the Washertown Square It was about a block down from Bigelow's, and up just a little ways from the Methodist (First) Church. Not that it matters though.

Anyway, Penney's was topped off (not the whole building, but just the inside) by a real fancy area that they called the mezzanine (my mother told me that was what it was called), which provided space for frilly things (like old lady stuff, I think), the baby department, and the store offices. Then you went up another four or five steps to where there was even more stuff. Gifts, maybe, but I can't remember for sure. I just know that going up more steps probably made people feel real important.

The very most special thing about J.C. Penney's, however, and I do mean *special* (at least when you were little it was), was their unique but also pretty weird network of saggy, rubbery-looking "cables" that hung from the ceiling and carried little metal "pods" traveling from the main floor sales counters up to the office (on the mezzanine that I already told you about). It was all pretty strange. And complicated too. At least I thought so. I guess the reason they used it was because the J.C. Penney sales people didn't know how to make change or something. But I'm not sure. Anyway, all these overhead cables kind of made you think of a miniaturized version of the streetcar cables that ran down the middle of some of the streets in Des Moines. (You probably don't remember streetcars, but that's all right . . . and besides, I think we kind of talked about streetcars once before anyway.) Washertown, as I think I also said (I'm pretty sure anyway), wasn't big enough of course to have streetcars. We just had regular cars, and once in a while some big buses that drove around with no one in them. Whatever. The cables at Penny's were strung up over the whole store, and the pods, when a salesperson had made a sale, were attached to them (i.e. to the cables), and then sort of "fired off" towards the office. The pods themselves, by the way, looked a little bit like giant, hollowed-out metal corncobs, only with little hinged doors in them (the doors were so that the clerk could open the pod to put the sales slip in it). Well, they kind of were like corncobs anyway. But the corncob would have had to be really fat. And smoother.

Penney's cable and pod system could result in people getting bumped into, and kind of even getting pushed out of the way and stuff sometimes (especially during busy times like on Saturday nights and at Christmas time). That was because curious, wide-eyed, necks-bent-back little kids wandered around the place (away from their mothers) gazing upward . . . always upward . . . toward the mysterious "pod traffic" traveling from the sales areas, over their crooked little heads, to the cashier's station (on the mezzanine). Then of course, the pods eventually (and somewhat magically it seemed) were sent back to earth, also by way of the transporter cables (somehow not colliding with the ones going up though, which I never quite understood), landing with kind of a "shush" and "thunking" sound, as they fell out of a "missile receiving tube" (I just added the "missile" part to make it sound more exciting) and into a "pod return box." Now that I think about it more, those cables and "Penny pods" could have been part of a like maybe kind of goofy (but ahead of its time) miniaturized space odyssey or something. I guess that's what it might have been anyway, although in 1940s Washertown we didn't think much about space and that stuff (unless you went to the "picture show" which once in a while had a really fake looking and usually pretty shitty "short subject" about space ships. It was called something like "Space King," I think. I'm not sure though. Maybe it was "Captain World," or "Meteor Man." Whatever. It was pretty bad.

So . . . even with the refrigerated drinking fountain, space pods, transporter cables, and Christmas toys (all of which I thought made J.C. Penney's a pretty special place), it nevertheless wasn't one of the stores where my mother shopped very much. Again, that was probably (at least partly anyway) because of the all-prevailing "do business with those who do business with you" ethic, which I've already told you about (several times now). But since Penney's of course was a chain store, they didn't "do business" with my dad, so my mom didn't "do business" with them (but I'll try not to talk about that anymore since you probably already understand it by now). Except sometimes she went there though, like to get a baby present or something. But anyway, my mom and dad and brother and I were pretty much happy at other stores. So that was another reason not to shop at Penney's very much. And mostly I think the reason my mom didn't go there was because just about everything that could be found at Penney's could also be purchased at Montgomery ("Monkey") Ward's, only for less money. Montgomery Ward's (I told you a little bit about that place just a little while ago) wasn't as fancy as Penney's was though. I mean it didn't have a mezzanine or anything like that, and things there weren't quite as nice (although I remember that the farmers from around Washertown seemed to think it was nice enough). I also remember that the oil on the floor at Ward's was just as smelly as it was at Penny's. Maybe "smellyer" even. So I guess in some ways it was kind of a toss up. Maybe. But on the other hand, everyone knew, at least everyone in Washertown knew, that Montgomery Ward's "Airline" brand radios were as good as you could get *anywhere.* So if you put it all together I guess maybe Penney's wasn't that much better after all. Penney's didn't even sell radios. But they did have that refrigerated drinking fountain.

Next-door to Penney's was Larkwood Florals, the only downtown, i.e. "on the Square" flower shop in Washertown. And talk about smells! If anyplace had them, it was Larkwood's. And they were all *good* too (no sweeping compound, cheap perfume, or bird shit and fish tank smells in this place). I didn't know that damp things could smell so good, but trust me, those really deep green (or mottled or stiff and "striped" even) houseplants . . . and all the ivy . . . and especially the ferns, smelled totally delicious. Like the woods around where the Prince kissed Snow White smelled maybe (I trust you for sure saw that movie). And then there was the sweet and sort of heavy (in fact *really* heavy) smell (I mean *fragrance)* of the long-stemmed roses (at fifty cents a piece). *All* these smells and fragrances just kind of enveloped you as soon as you went into Larkwood's, kind of like (at least maybe anyway) you had walked into a jungle (although I had never actually been in a jungle) that had a lot of flowers in it. I think I like the comparison to the woods and Snow White better though. Whatever. The "just beginning to unfurl," velvety dark red ones (roses) smelled more than anything else. And some of those beauties were really, *really* dark too. Almost *black* red, like some of the peonies in our yard (or on the side of my grandmother's house) that we took to the cemetery on "Decoration Day."

Some years though the peonies wouldn't have bloomed yet, which, as you can imagine, created pretty much of a major crisis for a lot of Washertown grave diggers (I mean *decorators* . . . I suppose I could have just changed *diggers* to *decorators*, but I thought maybe you would think it was kind of funny to just sort of leave it the way it first came out). Anyway, that was because (i.e. the reason the peonies didn't bloom) the goddamn ants hadn't eaten enough of the sticky stuff off of the buds yet. And by the way (although this might seem kind of strange), when I mentioned the ivy plants up above it made me think of that really goofy song that you heard in the 1940s that went, "Mares eat oats/And Does eat oats/And Little Lambs eat ivy." Remember that one? When I was little though I didn't understand it because I thought it was saying, "Maresydoats and Doesydoats and Little Lambsydivey." (I guess for some reason it all just kind of "ran together" for me.) But to be honest I also guess it really doesn't matter. But maybe it does. I mean I remember reading somewhere that sometimes when you look back at your life, meaning your *entire* life (like maybe when you're almost dead or something), you can kind of see that everything sort of went together (although maybe in a rather strange sort of way). As I said though, I just thought about this because of the ivy at Larkwood's. But maybe you can take it as another lesson in life or something. If you want to anyway.

I also can remember thinking that I shouldn't go into Larkwood's too often, since it wasn't exactly a macho, tough-guy place to be. In fact, when I was in high school I thought about applying for a job as the Larkwood delivery boy. (That way I would get to drive their truck all over town.) But then I got sort of worried (*always* worried, remember?) that it might make me look a little too "soft" or something, so I didn't do it. My brother said I should take the job; but then he played the drums and did whatever the hell he wanted to do anyway; whereas I played the piano, and thought a lot about being good and doing the right thing all the time. Easy for him to say, I guess. But not so easy for me to do. Whatever. I decided to just rely on my summer soda-jerk job at an ice cream store (which, now that I think about it, wasn't exactly a "Charles Atlas" kind of position either). "Soft" ice cream, by the way, like the still present Dairy Queen places, had become the big treat in town in the 1940s.

Larkwood Florals was where you went if you were part of Washertown High School's "elite" (sort of anyway), upwardly mobile, and "got the whole world in your hands" group of guys (and my buddies and I thought we *were* that group), to buy your girlfriend a corsage for the "Rainbow Girls" dance. (The "Rainbow Girls" were the future "Ladies of the East," or whatever they were called, that I already told you about.) I think anyway. One thing for sure though is that there were too many of them (i.e. too many dances, not too many "Rainbows" or "Ladies of the East," although actually there may have been too many of them too). I don't mean to be disrespectful though. Some of these Rainbow dances were really kind of fun; but then others could be as goddamn awful as the fun ones were fun (if you know what I mean). And then of course you also went to Larkwood's to get a corsage for your date for the Junior-Senior Prom. And chances are your girlfriend had also gone there to get you a carnation for your lapel hole. A "lapel hole," buy the way, was of course a "nice" hole (a "slit" in your lapel actually) . . . and nothing like the other kinds of "holes" that I occasionally mention when referring to some shithead or something. (But you probably already knew that.) In fairness, however, and before continuing on, I should maybe point out that some guys went to a different flower shop (more like a greenhouse) run by a woman called "Pansy" (wouldn't you know); but Larkwood's was really *the* place to go. At least that's what my friends and I thought.

So anyway, Larkwood's got your bucks at least twice annually, if you had any social life at all, unless of course a last minute break-up with your "steady" resulted in absolute chaos and a whole lot of tears and shit like that (*her* tears, of course, not yours). And threats from her girlfriends, all of whom, of course, would have consulted with each other and concluded (in ten seconds or less) that you were a total asshole (some of them might even have said you were a "prick," but only if they were kind of crude about things and knew they wouldn't be overheard). And then there were some *real* losses involved too (meaning if you had a last minute breakup there were). The losses of course, as "the system" worked, were all at the expense of the so-called assholes (the losses being flowers that Larkwood's wouldn't take back, screwed up dinner reservations, and a very long night alone). Unless of course one of your buddies had become an instant asshole too, and then the two of you could just hang out somewhere. And maybe even find someone to buy you a six-pack (unless you were a Methodist).

Prom time, by the way (more than Rainbow dances), was often even further complicated by the usual "who has to drive" issue (which actually determined who got the back seat for some extra heavy, late night/early morning, post-party "messing around"). Speaking of which (i.e. messing around), if you were smart you always checked out, and *very carefully,* exactly what girl the guy who you would be "doubling" with (i.e. double dating and therefore riding with) was taking, since you constantly lived (at least most guys did) with that nagging fear of somehow being messing around in the back seat with your "new" girlfriend, only to discover that your "old" girlfriend (like from a week ago maybe) was sitting in the front seat with your buddy. I'm telling you, this prom shit could sometimes be stressful. *Really* stressful. Even dangerous. I mean everyone knows how really and totally wacked some girls can get about this kind of stuff. But on to a more pleasant aspect of the prom saga.

Tradition at the time (Washertown in the early 1950s), was that you bought your prom date an orchid, if you wanted to really impress people, and most of us did (i.e. want to impress people), even though she, your date, may have preferred something less awkward to wear, and a color perhaps more flattering for her dress. So, aware of all this flower shit, and being "Mr. Smooth," I decided (senior year) to stage a really big "impress absolutely everyone" kind of event and bought Mary Lou, the love of my life (at the time anyway), a *white* orchid. That thing cost me three dollars extra (meaning three bucks more than the purple ones), and it had to be shipped down to Larkwood's all the way from Des Moines. It probably was sent down with some other really important stuff, like special roses for a funeral or a wedding or something. Anyway, the white orchid (sounds like a movie title) proved to be a real success (meaning I scored really big), since Mary Lou's father, who was an executive with a local manufacturing company, had bought her a shrimp-colored prom gown (with little white pearls all over the top), during one of his occasional trips to New York City. That's right, *New York City!* Saks Fifth Avenue is where he got it, if you can believe that (and if you had even *heard* of Saks, which most people in Washertown of course hadn't). But no shit, that's where the goddamn thing came from: New York City and Sak's Fifth Avenue! (Yeah, I know; I'm getting all carried away again with stuff I've already told you . . . but sometimes a guy just has to relive the really good parts!)

So anyway this was the absolute greatest. I mean I could talk about this shit all day. So give me this one break, OK? I've just gotta tell it again (and I'll add some different details this time). Thanks (I said that because I'm assuming you'll keep reading). So here we go again. Mary Lou's dad, being aware of my obsession with cars (and I had a really big one, i.e. obsession with cars), offered to let me drive his brand new Buick Roadmaster "hardtop convertible" to the prom. That thing had the maximum of four, *four* chrome-ringed "port holes" in the front fenders (a big styling detail at the time), genuine wire wheels, whitewall tires (the really, really wide and extra white kind), a "wrap-around" windshield (which, when getting either in or out, you cracked your goddamn knees on . . . but didn't care), power brakes, power windows, and "Dynaflow" (Buick's patented, super-smooth and powerful . . . once it got going . . . automatic transmission). And the thing was "two tone" too: real, *real* light green (almost white) on the bottom, with a shiny, dark green (almost black) top. Talk about a set of wheels! I mean I couldn't have dreamed of anything more exciting (my dad drove a Ford "Mainliner"). I mean getting to drive Mary Lou's dad's car was even better than having a "wet" dream for God's sake! (Well, probably anyway.) I wouldn't even have cared if Mary Lou had stayed home (well, I guess I don't really mean that). But maybe I do.

Anyway, I went to that prom thinking that I was one handsome guy (at least that's what most people said), and knowing (for sure) that I was driving one really classy car. Furthermore, I had lucked out that weekend and had absolutely no "zits" (fantastic). *And,* I had the most beautiful girl in the whole world (well, Washertown anyway), wearing a really sexy, Sak's Fifth Avenue "cocktail" dress, and sitting right up against me, "thigh to thigh" (that's what your "steady" did in those days, which therefore left the outside third of the genuine leather front bench seat completely empty). The truth is, I felt like the goddamn "king of the road." Like "hot shit," as one of our expressions went, and I mean *really* hot shit. Like boiled shit even. (Or to be a little nicer about it, "King Shit," as I said when I told you about all this the first time.) I mean a Buick Roadmaster was just about as good as it got, especially since there were only three Cadillacs in all of Washertown. One of those big beauties, i.e. one of the Cadillacs (brief digression here), belonged to the president of the Washertown washing machine company. Another, and shorter one, belonged to the washing machine company's *vice*-president (which seemed only appropriate . . . meaning that his, i.e. his *car,* was shorter than the president's . . . I would have had no way of knowing how the two "stacked up" in other ways). And the third one (Cadillac) belonged to the owner of another manufacturing company. I don't remember how long (or short) his was. Whatever. The Roadmaster was a lot sportier than any of the Cadillacs, long or short. And even if Mary Lou and I had gotten into a big hairy fight or something, and even if a bunch of her therefore instantly and totally bitchy girlfriends had tried to crucify me, I would have taken it all, just to have that car under me. Not that MaryLou wasn't a real prize herself. She was that and then some. And to tell you the truth (although this might sound kind of tacky, and I guess maybe I even thought about not writing it . . . but obviously not for very long), I would have liked to have had her under me that night too. (Didn't happen.) But man, what a car! A four-hole Buick Roadmaster, and with more extra stuff on it than I can even remember.

By the way ("by the ways" seem to be occurring often), the only dumb, or careless, or maybe even bad thing we did that whole prom night (I just thought I should tell you this to let you know how generally good . . . or maybe stupid . . . we were) was to stand a half-drunk bottle of "Canadian Club" up against the hood ornament of the Roadmaster, kind of like a trophy or something, as we watched the sun come up over Red Rock Lake the next morning. I mean had some highway patrol or sheriff kind of guy seen us, we would have been in deep shit (and it probably would also have signaled the last time Mary Lou's dad would have let me drive the Roadmaster). Whatever. I just thought you might like to know that. "Canadian Club," by the way (one more time), was top shelf stuff. So it went really well with the Roadmaster. *Anyway*, right now you and I are still standing around in Larkwood's, and it's time to move on. We have a few more stores (and stories) yet to go.

You might like to know, however (and this will wrap things up for sure), that one balmy summer night, about three weeks (or less even) after this absolutely Hollywood-like, totally fantastic prom experience, the love of my life (and truly the most beautiful girl at the prom), and my so-called best buddy (the "wet our pants together" guy), decided to get together and "make out" (which didn't mean quite as much then as it does now . . . or so I prayed anyway) on the "No Jews Allowed," Washertown Country Club golf course (Seventh Hole). Well HOLY FUCKING SHIT! I mean *that* hurt! Mary Lou and I might have had a pretty big fight and have sort of "broken up" shortly after the prom (and I just might have been, and probably was messing around with someone else by then anyway), but that didn't mean that *she* had to start messing around right away. And that goddam orchid had cost me seven dollars. *Seven* fucking dollars! To tell you the absolute truth though, I would let it all happen again . . . whatever it was that actually happened . . . if it meant that I could drive that two-toned, four-holed, wire-wheeled, white-wall-tired Roadmaster just one more time! Man that was a nice car.

Next door to Larkwood's was Rollen's Drugs and Gifts, another Washertown landmark of sorts, and (you guessed it), another Rexall. The Rollens family had owned this place for years, and when I was little, the business was being managed by the original owner's daughter, Noreen. Rollen's was really nice, but it didn't offer some of the excitement of the other drug stores in Washertown. Gurdy's Drugs, you may recall, had the "dirty book" rack, the rubber drawer, and Kotex boxes all over the place (and their daughter was one of my girlfriends). Powell's had cherry-vanilla phosphates, zipper notebooks, yo-yos, and number puzzles. And Walgreen's (the manager's daughter being only an "I wish" girlfriend) had the big, super-fancy Sunday dinners, *and* Prince Albert in the can. So anyway, in some ways Rollen's wasn't real exciting. Washertown's "establishment" liked it though. Maybe because it just seemed so sort of "correct."

However, what *was* exciting about Rollen's, and I mean *really* exciting, was the over all quality of the soda fountain (better even than Powell's . . . although I still would vote for Powell's cherry-vanilla phosphates). But what made Rollen's soda fountain extra, *extra* special, "specialer" than all the rest of Washertown's soda fountains put together (including even Roswell's), was a really pretty, and I mean *really* pretty, high school girl named Nancy who worked there and made "Rainbow" cokes for my buddies and me. "Rainbow" was what we called them (Nancy helped us decide on the name), and it meant that she gave us one shot of every flavor, right down the line, and *then* a big shot of coke syrup, all in the same little five-cent-size glass (which therefore left almost no room for the carbonated water). As you might suspect, those cokes were just a little bit sweet, and actually got kind of syrupy-thick sometimes, but they were still really good. And Nancy would just smile at us as we sort of choked them down.

Of course when Noreen was watching Nancy couldn't make them for us; but otherwise she made them all the time. We didn't even have to ask her to. Fountain cokes, by the way, in the 1940s, were always served in glasses that flared slightly at the top, and actually had the words "Coca Cola" written right on the side of them. No kidding. And it was written out sort of in script. Anyway, somehow those glasses seemed to make the "Rainbow" cokes (and everyone else's cokes) even more special. As I kind of already said, a grown-up might have found our special cokes somewhat sweet (to say the least), and maybe even awful, but stuff like "Rainbow" cokes (and rainbows in general . . . and pretty girls like Nancy) are always more exciting to little kids than to grown-ups. Anyway, not even thinking about the cokes, Nancy was really special, and I always kind of thought that she maybe liked me best of all (how could she not have?), although some of my buddies might have thought she liked them best. I think it was me though. And Nancy was a high school cheerleader too, just to make her all the more special. She was almost like a movie star, I thought; only I could actually reach out and kind of touch her. Or at least I always thought about wanting to. Later on, when I was more grown up myself, I remember seeing Nancy in a cashmere sweater (in a different store), and *really* wanting to touch her. I think I kind of wanted to marry her even. But I was too young.

I also remember having really good "Dusty Road" ice cream sundaes at Rollen's when I really little, like maybe five or six (just a little bit bigger than kindygarden anyway), when I would go there with my mother and big brother, who already didn't like me very much (as I said a long time ago). Chocolate ice cream, marshmallow topping, and malted milk powder sprinkled all over the top: that's what made it a Dusty Road. And three things made it even better. First, it was served in a funnel-shaped metal dish with a paper liner in it. That way frost would form on the metal sometimes and make the ice cream taste even colder. Second, you got this neat little kind of rounded spoon to eat it with (smaller even than a regular teaspoon), which made it last a real long time, and again somehow taste better. And third, it was always followed by an icy-cold glass of water (in a coke glass), with "sweat drops" all over it. You got the water (you didn't even have to ask for it) to help put an end to your thirst, and also to get rid of that sometimes awful, too-full, icky-sweet, sick feeling that made you think you maybe might throw-up or something. Anyway, "Dusty Roads" were really good. If Rollen's hadn't taken their soda fountain out about the time I went to college, I would go all the way back there just to have another one. Really. That's how good they were (along with Nancy's "Romance is in the air 'Rainbow'" cokes of course).

Rollen's gift shop, which was on the mezzanine at the back of the store, was where my brother and I bought small, pocket-sized *Bibles* for each other for Christmas one year. The whole idea of course was thought up by our mother. I mean why else would two grade-schoolers buy each other *Bibles*? Yo-yos maybe, but not *Bibles*. Anyway, my brother's *Bible* was brown and had darker brown letters on the front that said *Holy Bible*, and it looked as though it should be for an army guy. Mine was white with gold letters and gold-edged, real thin paper, and looked like it should belong to the Pope or a nun or someone like that. Or maybe even to some other kind of holy person like someone I'm going to tell you about later. So anyway, Rollen's mezzanine also had a bathroom, clear at the very far back, that my brother and I used to use once in a while when we were real little and had to go real bad and weren't at Hoage's Variety or somewhere else. The nice lady clerk at Rollen's ("nice" meaning real proper acting and everything) didn't like it very much, however, since we (my brother and I, although he more than I) would sometimes pee on the toilet seat (like little boys are supposed to do, and like we also did, only not very often, at Hoage's Variety . . . which I already told you). Anyway, we always pretended it was an accident, but mostly it wasn't. Mostly it was just fun. Sometimes anyway. Other times we were afraid we would get caught, and so we lifted the lid.

One other time at Rollen's my brother and I bought a *Bible* for our father (Rollen's was a big *Bible* outlet, I guess). I think we bought it for his birthday, and I know for sure (as I suspect you do to) that it was our mom's idea again. We wouldn't have bought him a yo-yo, but we wouldn't have bought him a *Bible* either. It, the *Bible* that we bought for our dad, had covers made from genuine olive wood from the holy land (wherever that was). At least that's what the clerk told us (it may have been bullshit, but that's what she said). Anyway, as I said, I wasn't quite sure what she meant by holy land, since I was only about five, but I knew that she probably wasn't talking about

Iowa. By the way, I feel really bad about it now, but our mother never got a *Bible* from us (she always was the "doer," not the "getter"). I wish I could change that, but of course I can't. I mean, if anyone should have been given a special gift it was our mom. But I guess that's just the way it is when you're the mother.

Two other things about Rollen's, and then we'll move on. One is that Rollen's, like all the other drug stores in Washertown (and I guess even in other places), smelled really weird-like. Maybe sort of just "Rexally," as I've kind of said before. But for some reason Rollen's smelled just a little bit different from the others. It had all the same stuff in it, meaning cellophane wrapped candy, medicines, little piles of forgotten sweeping compound, and of course perfumes and powders and all that girly shit. But Rollen's seemed to smell just a little ickier than the rest, almost sort of milky sweet, and like they kept an open bottle of peach-flavored cough syrup or something somewhere. And the other thing I can tell you is that Rollen's was a good place to go at Christmas time, *every* Christmas time, to buy the two-bottle set of "Old Spice" cologne and talcum for your father and grandfather. One time even, I guess when our mother had some extra money to spend, we bought the "three-piece" set for our dad. It not only came with the cologne and talcum powder, but also included a sort of octagonal-like chunk of soap with a rope going through it, which (the rope itself) was made of real fancy-looking, twisted cotton cord.

So, out of Rollen's and continuing on west, we arrive at the Dependable Department Store. The Dependable was Jewish owned and operated (Washertown's third Jewish family), and one storefront wide. The store itself had two extremely narrow aisles, both of which were lined with tables displaying some pretty shitty-looking jewelry and just about anything else shitty that you could imagine. Some of tables were piled way too high with crushed, creased, messed-up looking, and kind of cheap and smelly clothes (almost like sweaty smells). And The Dependable sold stale "Brach's" chocolates (maybe to try to keep you from thinking about the old clothes' smells) from smudgy, glass-front candy "bins" near the front door. I don't know for sure what was sold from the back. I never went that far. Probably because I was afraid of getting lost in one of the of the piles of clothes, or maybe knocking over one of the tables with the shitty jewelry on it. I'm not sure. Once I kind of thought that they might be selling special Jewish things back there, like maybe "Old Testaments" and bulrushes and stuff. And maybe even Moses statues and those really little round hats that they sometimes wore. I just don't know. Actually (although I probably didn't think this until I got older), those little hats, or "beanies," or whatever they were supposed to be, were a lot like the little beanie the Pope wore (when he wasn't wearing his big cone-shaped hat). And he wasn't even Jewish, so that sort of made me think that maybe all really religious people were supposed to wear stuff like that. I don't know. But then that didn't seem quite right, since I also knew that the Pope didn't like the Jews. But I told you some stuff about the Pope already, and, to use another and kind of watered-down expression, "enough is probably enough." Whatever. I'm pretty sure the Pope wouldn't have had much interest in The Dependable Department Store, even if he for some reason had been visiting Washertown. Like if he had been in Des Moines or something and just decided to drive over.

Speaking of Jewish things though (a brief digression), it was made very clear to me and my buddies the summer when we went to the YMCA camp "sex talk" (you remember . . . when they told us about not thinking bad thoughts and not "doing it" and everything) that "they," meaning little Jewish boys, were circumcised (meaning, as my friends and I used to say, "had had the ends of their dicks chopped off") for religious reasons, whereas "we," meaning the little Christian campers, had had our dicks chopped off (just the end again . . . thank God) for hygienic reasons. ("Hygienic" is the word the camp guy used; it means clean . . . but I guess you probably already knew that.) Anyway, I think he thought it was important for us to know this shit (i.e. about what had happened to us and why, and the importance of having a clean dick and everything), although none of us had probably even thought about it (and it was pretty rare to see an unchopped dick at a YMCA camp in the 1940s anyway).

Whatever. I guess Christians were supposed to distinguish themselves by having clean dicks (the camp guy always used the word *penis* of course, but that word made my buddies and me squirm). I mean your dick is your dick. Not a *penis*. And by the way, this was the same sex talk guy who also told us not to "play" with ourselves (or, if we absolutely couldn't control ourselves, at least not very often). And that meant whether you'd had the end of it chopped off or not. I guess anyway. To tell you the truth though, my curiosity about my dick (and I'll bet almost every other kid's too) had more to do with all the things I could *do* with it, not just whether it had been whacked off. Actually though, to "whack off" was another expression for what the camp teacher meant by "playing with yourself," so I probably should just stay with the word "chopped" when I'm talking about being circumcised and stuff. I mean I don't want anyone to become unnecessarily confused here. Anyway, I didn't give a flaming shit (more camper talk) about what the guy was telling us. As I grew older though, I somehow envied those guys who were obviously neither Jewish nor hygienic. You know, the ones who had just been left alone. Like the way God made them. But then I also grew up wanting my tonsils back, so maybe I was just a little strange even then. Maybe.

Tonsils, by the way, when I was little anyway, were sort of like foreskins, in that you lost them at an early age. One or two snips at the back of your throat (unless you're still thinking foreskins), and you were a changed and supposedly healthier person. And if the good doctor wanted to make even more easy money in his "snip and clip" shop, he also cut your adenoids (whatever they were) off (out?). I don't know. I've never been sure about adenoids. At least the chop-job on your "wee-wee" happened early though, so you probably couldn't remember the pain and suffering (which I'll bet was extremely excruciating, and god-awful bloody, and gory, and incredibly cruel and everything). Someone even told me once that some of the little Jewish boys had it (the chop-job) done with rocks. Man, I'll bet *that* hurt! (I guess it's one good reason to be a Christian!) I mean at least Christian doctors probably used razor blades or scissors or something. Or at least a really sharp jack knife. But I'm getting the feeling that it's time to change the subject and leave the Dependable Department Store (with all its finery) for other and more exciting places. Safer anyway. I mean the more I think about it, that circumcision shit is really scary. Maybe that's even what went on in the back of the Dependable (chop-jobs). Probably not though.

But just one more thing (since I already sort of brought the topic up). Maybe I shouldn't make such a big deal out of it, but if you'll be kind enough to let me get this out of my system I'll really appreciate it. Anyway, it has always really pissed me off (big time) that so many doctors think they know better than God himself just what parts of our bodies we're supposed to keep. I mean if God made foreskins and tonsils and adenoids and everything, it seems to me it must have been for a reason. Don't you think? It's like doctors have to cut stuff off just to prove they went to medical school or something. I mean Jesus! (Sorry.) But what kind of logic is that? Do lawyers and judges and people like that have some poor guy electrocuted or hanged just because they don't like the way he looks or something? Or just for the money? Anyway, it's this kind of stuff that can really set my mind off. And you can be sure I would never tell a "head doctor" (like a psychiatrist or someone) about any of these thoughts (even if my friends told me I needed to), since the way I figure it he (the head doctor in the psychiatric sense of the term . . . not the "head" doctor, like the guy who is in charge of everything) . . . *anyway,* the doctor would probably have me lobotomized or something (a big word I learned later). Just to shut me up. I mean like run razor wires up between my eyeballs and forehead and then twist them back and forth. Or drill a hole into my fucking brain. And when they do that (i.e. "perform" a lobotomy on you), at least this is what I was told when I was little, you end up selling vegetables. I think that's what they said anyway. Or maybe they said you actually became one (a vegetable). I don't know. But that would be pretty awful too. Like especially if you turned into a turnip or something. I mean who the hell would want to be a turnip for the rest of his life? Or a brussel sprout? I mean Jesus! Or a "head" (get it?) of lettuce even? But I'm getting really off the track. Keep giving me credit though; I'm learning to check myself before I go too far. Usually anyway.

In fact though, I'm afraid I might actually be losing it again. Just by talking about this stuff. At least that's what I think. But you've been pretty good about overlooking my little mental episodes so far (at least I think you have been), so at least now (since I'm sort of doing it again, but still bringing it under control) I want to pause to thank you for that. So, "Thank you for that." And besides, as I said once before, no one likes a whiner. (Well maybe some people do, but not very many.) And no one likes a wacko, scalpel-wielding doctor either. I mean Holy Shit! I'm actually beginning to think there may have been some kind of black market for foreskins and tonsils

306 | Ernest Arlington Twain

and adenoids (and maybe even other body parts too, for all I know). Like maybe a "package deal" or something. Oh, and then I learned later about one other kind of chop—job that a lot of doctors seem to have fun doing. It was called a "hysto-wreck-your-tree" (or something like that). That's the way it sounded to me anyway (at least when I was little). But "hysto-wreck-your-trees" were just for girls, and as I understood it only when they got real old. Or at least pretty old. And cranky too, I suppose. So anyway I didn't have to worry about that. But you know, it's no wonder that doctors make so much money and have the fanciest houses in town. I mean I'll bet some of them would have cut your fucking balls off when they were doing your "wee-wee," except for the fact that they (meaning your balls, not the doctors) wouldn't have been hanging down far enough yet. (When you're little, in case you're reading this and you're a girl and don't know very much, a little boy's balls are stuck up in his body, sort of like they get when he's older and has been in a really cold swimming pool for too long . . . which is why there's the expression "freeze your nuts off.") But anyway, as far as this medical crap goes, I just don't get it. There are times though (I also was taught this when I was real little) when you just have to "let bygones be bygones." (Or "things" gone be "things' gone.) So I will. But I still don't get it. However, right now I'm going to rise above all this shit and *do* more and *think* less, since as I told you before, it helps me control my mind. Sometimes.

Across the alley from the Dependable (still going west) was the Coast to Coast store (another "chain"). Hardware, automotive stuff, and a bunch of other things (even some furniture in the basement). But as was true of a few of the other Washertown stores I already told you about, the Coast to Coast was not especially my kind of place, so I don't have a lot to say about it. I do remember, however, buying bicycle accessories there, like "struts" for my handlebars, and fancy handlebar "grips" (with streamers coming out of the ends of them and everything). B.F. Goodrich (not on the Square) was the best place for bike stuff though. But since I'm talking about my bike, you might like to know (maybe anyway) that I got it by getting lots of "starts" on my paper route. And I was only in fourth grade too! In my bike's brand new, shiny, glory days, it was maroon and white (actually sort of ivory), with chrome spokes and rims, and big "balloon" tires (all bikes had balloon tires in the 1940s, except for the English bikes that Mr. and Mrs. Smith rode). Mrs. Smith, by the way was really, *really* pretty, and one time made ice cream cones for all the kids in my neighborhood. But that's another story.

Anyway, over the years, and as the glory days faded, my bike acquired chrome fenders. And then one day (I must have been going through a sort of crazy adolescent surge or something), when I was in about seventh or eighth grade, I painted the frame yellow. I don't know why, except as I just said I may have been into an adolescent, i.e. testosterone-induced, crisis. Yellow wasn't a very good color for a bike, and I used a brush, so you can imagine it didn't turn out too good (well). In fact, my brother told me it looked like shit. And it probably did. But he was always telling me my stuff was shit. Anyway, so then I took the fenders (chrome) of my bike off, I guess so it would look like sort of a "hot rod" bike, and then a few days later, and after having done all this work, I kind of got run over and the bike got bent to shit (to use my brother's favorite expression).

Whatever. I probably shouldn't have been messing around the way I was; in fact, getting run over was probably mostly my own fault. I did manage to jump off before the actual crash though. Whatever. The guy who ran over my bike would probably have run over me too (I think anyway), if he could have. He said that my buddies and I were blocking his path as he circled the swimming pool (*MPP*) in his mother's new Chevy "Bel Aire." What he was really doing was just showing off for the high school girls and the guy he had with him. Anyway, he told us to get out of his way, and although my buddies did, I didn't, and so the prick just ran right over me (again actually just the bike). He wasn't really a bad guy though; in fact I kind of looked up to him; and if I had had a Bel Aire "hardtop convertible" I would probably have done the same thing. He helped me pick my bike up and everything (probably so I wouldn't tell and get him in trouble), but now that it was all scratched up (the yellow paint sort of just pealed right off) and had a bent frame, I couldn't ride it. In fact the thing was pretty much *all* smashed. I guess it didn't matter though, since it wasn't worth much anymore. I mean there wasn't exactly a big market for "fenderless" yellow bikes, even if they hadn't been run over. Oh well, let's just get on with the final stops on our "around the Square" tour. I just told you what happened to me that day, thinking you might like to know about it. Especially if you like bikes. But maybe you don't. I really have no way of knowing.

Next came Spurgeon's Department Store (again, a "chain," I think anyway). One more "double-wide," and filled mostly with non-descript, "you can get it anywhere," department store stuff (it was kind of half-way between F.W. Woolworth's and J.C. Penney's, classier than Montgomery Wards, and light years beyond The Dependable). We aren't going to go in though. Partly because the most important thing about Spurgeon's, at least I thought, was the way it looked from the street. The rest of the reason is that there just isn't much to see. So let me describe the outside. Spurgeon's had big, black, shiny, square glass tiles stuck to the front of it to make it look real "late 1940s modern" and everything. In fact it was, I think anyway, the first of Washertown's lovely "turn of the century," Victorian buildings to be totally desecrated by some obviously shortsighted, post World War II, "trying to make a statement" urban designer. I have to say though that it looked pretty fancy to a fourth grader. Real "uptown," if you know what I mean. Maybe even just a little bit like some kind of store in Hollywood or somewhere. But not New York. I'm pretty sure anyway. There were also two oversized, but again pretty stylish-looking big square columns (with the same shiny glass tile on them) that seemed to almost stand guard outside the entrance to the place. So at least take a look as we go by. You have to say it's pretty futuristic looking (in a black and white and maybe kind of moody sort of way). It almost makes you think (but probably not very much I guess) that Washertown was a city (i.e town) "on the move."

Dorn's Shoes is next. Quality shoes, which, for the men of Washertown in the 1940s, meant Florsheim and Nunn-Bush. (I don't remember what the women's brands were, which is probably at least one indication that I was still enjoying reasonably sound mental health.) Anyway, it was at Dorn's that the gentlemen of Washertown purchased their "dress" shoes, and the ladies could find the very latest styles (well, maybe not the *very* latest, but fairly latest anyway) for whatever occasion. (The very latest were probably being shown at "The French Room" or Chandler's in Des Moines.) Whatever. Dorn's also had a little shoe repair shop located in the back of the place, *and* Dorn's was the only shoe store in Washertown that had an X-Ray machine (to guarantee an excellent fit). Talk about futuristic! It (the

X-Ray machine) looked sort of like a stripped-down, walnut-colored juke box There were a couple of buttons to push on the top of it (one green . . . probably for "go," or "on," and one red, for "stop"), a "scope" to look down, and a big slot in the bottom where you were supposed to put your feet. If you did everything right, your feet would look kind of gray, and you could see your toes and everything (right through the shoes you were trying on!), with the rest of everything (in the slot) looking kind of gassy green. My brother and I used to put our hands in there when no one was looking, which just might not have been a very good idea.

In fact (and this is really true), sometimes I think, from what I've heard anyway, that playing around with the X-Ray machine at Dorn's may have contributed more to how I got to be this way (meaning sort of strange and off-center at times) than I might like to think. I really don't know. And as far as that goes I guess there's no way I ever *can* know. I'll just have to wait and see (meaning see if things get worse for me). But it's not just what I heard; I also read some articles in a newspaper once about "radiation poisoning" and other stuff like that. So maybe I have an X-Ray problem. I mean, who knows? And now that I think about it more, it could be that even if you had turned the thing on (green button) and off (red button) right, that the X-Ray machine itself was nevertheless *leaking* some kind of poisonous material. Maybe anyway. I mean as far as I know the whole goddamn store might have been filled with toxic shit. Like think about Hiroshima and then tell me there aren't some questions to be raised here. And also, you don't know if the shoe salesmen (they all were guys at Dorn's) had received adequate training to even run the thing. Or if they knew what to do in the event of a massive explosion or something.

Anyway, I was probably only about eight years old when we (my "didn't like me" brother and I) did that (i.e. played around with the X-Ray machine), so some early damage *is* a possibility I guess. Whatever. It's a good thing we weren't older though, and that they didn't have the X-Ray machine behind a curtain or something. I mean God only knows what we might have stuck in there (the foot slot) to look at. Whoa! Talk about radiation problems! I mean (again I read this) the stuff going on in that machine could make you instantly sterile and shit like that (although of course at the time I didn't really understand what that meant). Some people even said too much of that shit could make you glow green. But anyway, I think maybe playing around with the X-Ray machine was pretty serious, and I know Dorn's had the thing moved out after about a year or two. Or maybe it burned through the goddamn floor and fell into the basement. I don't know. But whatever happened (even if I have a greater price to pay in the future), I can tell you that I still liked Dorn's Shoe Store a lot better than Buster Brown's.

I mean, to start with, Dorn's didn't sell Boy Scout shoes. And then second, I liked it better because by the time I was in high school two of my best friends worked there (one in shoes, the other in repairs). And then also I liked it because I bought my first pair of loafers at Dorn's (my favorite kind of shoe to this very day). And finally I liked Dorn's better than Buster Brown's, although this might be kind of a strange reason to like a shoe store . . . unless maybe I was developing some kind of a foot fetish or something (which of course I hadn't even heard of at the time) . . . *anyway,* I finally liked Dorn's Shoe Store because MaryLou, the love of my life, and the girl with the shrimp-colored prom dress, whose father just happened to own a Buick Roadmaster (remember her . . . *and that car?*) bought some gray, patent leather, really high, high-heeled shoes there (with one side of each shoe sort of "cut out") that made her look really sexy and older than just high school. (Tough sentence again.) At least I thought so. Only now that I think about it, she could have been wearing those things the night she made out with my buddy on the Seventh Hole of The Washertown Country Club golf course. Probably not though, since the ground on the golf course would have been pretty soft that time of year, and the heels would have probably got stuck in it . . . unless maybe she took them off for a while or something. But Jesus, I don't even want to think about what she might have taken off! Anyway, let's just go on to the next place. This is getting me really upset again. I mean, shit! She knew I'd hear about what she did. And guys like me aren't supposed to get screwed over by "ex" goddamn girlfriends just because you maybe do something to piss them off. I mean goddamnit, that hurt! In fact, if it weren't for her dad's two-tone, four-holed, wire-wheeled, white-walled, Dynaflow Roadmaster (with leather seats), I wouldn't even think about her anymore. Ever.

OK. Out of Dorn's, and we finally reach the west end of the south side of the Washertown Square (I hope you're not too tired or anything). Anyway, here we are in front of The Casper County Bank. Red brick, with round concrete columns. Not nearly as impressive looking as Washertown National, but then there wasn't nearly as much pigeon shit on the sidewalk either. As a matter of fact, The Casper County Bank wasn't a particularly inspiring building at all. I'm sure a person's money was just as safe there as it was at Washertown National though, and I have to say that the people at Casper County (at least it seemed like it to me) were friendlier. So anyway, even though the place didn't look so important, when I started making really big money (a combination of mowing, shoveling, and my paper route), I left Washertown National and went there (i.e. to Casper County). I had given up my thirty-two customer *Des Moine Register and Tribune* route (on South Sixth Avenue West, probably the most high tipping Christmas route of all), and had acquired a bigger one (paper route, although I *was* approaching adolescence) with *The Washertown Daily News* (First, Second, and Third Avenues . . . not as affluent, but OK). So, I transferred my entire account (that's right, *all* of it, probably maybe almost thirty dollars even) from Washertown National to Casper County. It was obviously not a good day for the folks at Washertown National, and I have no idea what my temporary withdrawal might have done to the stock market. I of course didn't know what the stock market was then, but I did know that at least Washertown National had suffered a pretty heavy hit.

Anyway, as I said a little a while ago, Washertown National kind of scared me every time I walked into the place, and so it was actually pretty easy to take advantage of my route change to also change bankers. As a matter of fact, it just seemed like the intelligent thing to do. At least at the time anyway. Actually Casper County, I thought (although as I just said, it was not a real impressive looking building), was more "up to date." For example, it had really thick, glass (with no frames around them), modern front doors, at least two or three years before they installed them at Washertown National. And I also had the feeling that they were really excited about getting my account. I mean, they could probably tell that I had a pretty important future ahead of me. And then of course, as I already told you (I think it was because the tops of the columns in front of Casper County were not very elaborate . . . maybe just Doric even), the front of the place had much less, if any, pigeon shit around it. It really doesn't matter though, since we don't need to go in. Just trust me, it was a nice place to do my banking, and I knew that if my account really grew, like even got to fifty dollars or more, it would be safe there. And that was a pretty good feeling for a little fifth grader in Washertown, Iowa to have.

Well, before we end this little tour of the Square (you have been very patient, and I hope you enjoyed seeing it as much as I enjoyed showing it), I need to talk just a little bit about the fourth, adjacent-to-the-square, corner store. Since I told you about the other three, it wouldn't be fair to leave this one out. And besides, it was an interesting enough place, although for entirely different reasons than the ones I had for telling you about The Orange Bar (always the best), Bigelow's (next best), and the mighty Thriftway (with the drug den in the basement). So anyway, this other corner place was a Victorian-looking, red brick building with a sort of turret over the entrance. It was a special kind of women's shop (only real different from the Mode O Day, if you can remember that place). Try as I will, however, I can't remember the name of it. Whatever. Being "all boy," and super curious about weird stuff sometimes, I remember sort of slowing down and kind of "hanging out" as I passed by (pretending to be preoccupied by something else), so I could stare at the lingerie (although I didn't know that nice word then) that was always displayed in the window. This window display was about as close as I was going to get to women's underwear for awhile, except of course for when I had had those somewhat early and "close calls" with Janey (and her gaping, but only slightly, bathrobe), and then the "behind the piano thing" with Joycie (with her dress pulled up . . . and panties pushed down). And then, as the years rolled on, there were to be a few experiences perhaps with JoAnne, Mary Lee, Barbie, Carol, another Carol, Jana, and of course Mary Lou. But those are other stories for another time.

Anyway, this place (the sort of Victorian-looking corner store with the turret) was kind of like an "adult shop" for little boys with wild imaginations. Of course I didn't know that then, and in no way did it remotely resemble the adult shops that would appear years later. Not that I would know a lot about those places, of course, i.e. the places with the 25 cent movie and video booths, and the dirty magazines (which made Gurdy's book rack look like it belonged in the children's reading room at the Washertown Public Library) and the "sex toys" (like dildos and things), and plastic blow up dolls, and all the other shit they might have. And besides, when I was little Washertown, and even Des Moines maybe (although I can't say for sure about Des Moines, since I didn't live there), would never have allowed those adult kinds of places. And certainly Washertown wouldn't have let one be right next to the Square. (If they had allowed this kind of store anywhere, it probably would have been next door to the Washer City Café . . . remember that place?). Anyway, when I was little, rubber dolls and things like that (this was of course before the plastic era), were just baby dolls that wet their pants when you poured water down them and stuff. (They usually just had a cute little puckered up mouth to kind of stick a toy baby bottle nipple in, and a real whole in their butt to let the water out.) You certainly didn't "blow them up" into big people or anything like that that. I mean Jesus! What some people do now is really sick.

But what I'm trying to say is (and I was like just maybe nine or ten when I would do my "slow walk" by this store) that not even in my wildest dreams (well, maybe in the *very* wildest . . . meaning the kind every pre-adolescent kid prays for) could I imagine seeing as many women's panties and brassieres (old word) and stuff, as I saw in that store window (the Victorian-looking store with the turret). I couldn't even figure out what some of it was for. I mean this place had to be a real house of pleasure. I thought anyway. Some things laced up; other things seemed to kind of roll down; and some stuff even had little straps and "hooks" of some kind dangling from it. And then most things were made of a kind of see-through material and were real frilly. I think it was supposed to look like it came from France or somewhere. And hard as it may be to believe, the place was thoughtful enough to change the displays for me on a fairly regular basis. I remember that because this "Little Shop of Pleasures" was on the same street as where I got my hair cut sometimes. (This was when I got older and had outlived the excitement of my first barbershop, the one with the gumball machine, smelly rose hair oil, and the occasional opportunity to sneak into the adjacent Rialto Theatre through the shared men's room . . . remember?) Anyway, our trip around the Washertown Square has ended. And maybe I should have just ended it at The Casper County Bank, but I somehow didn't want to leave this sort of crazy, turreted place out. Whatever. Hopefully, you should know your way around enough now so you can go back to any place you want to.

So go ahead then and spend some time hanging out. I mean it's a nice day, and there's no reason not to. If you do, be sure to take another look at some of the better and more colorful awnings (Sander's Grocery especially), and for sure go back to Bigelow's and Roswell's. (You might even go over to Buster Brown's Shoes and break their goddamn windows for me.) And don't forget to occasionally glance across the street at the Courthouse. The well-groomed lawn and the wooden benches can be very inviting on warm afternoons. And finally, do not, do *not* leave the Square without having at least one glass of fresh-pumped orange juice at The Orange Bar, or a cherry-vanilla phosphate at Powell's, or a "Dusty Road" sundae or "Rainbow" coke at Rollen's (and if Nancy is there tell her "hi" for me), or maybe even (if indeed you get back to Roswell's) a Green River. In fact, if you're up to it, have one of each, although it might make you feel a little bit icky. But it also might be worth it (and you can always go throw-up in the bathroom at the Courthouse). And by the way, don't forget that you can find Fleer's "Double Bubble" at the Orange Bar, *and* get a "grab-bag" when you're back at Roswell's. Whatever. Just do what makes you happy. That's what all these places are here for . . . all the stuff . . . all the stores . . . and all the just right "down home," downtown feeling. This, my friends—*all this*—is Washertown's Square. And what a place it is!

CHAPTER SEVEN

CHURCH

You might wonder why I would have a whole chapter just for church, but that would be because you were never a Methodist in Washertown in the 1940s. I mean church in Washertown, when I was little, was not just church. It was more like a big flannel blanket that hung down and then spread over the whole town. Well, maybe it wasn't *quite* like that (almost though); but I need to tell you more about it so you'll understand. Washertown's First Methodist Church was kind of like a second home. At least that's what it was for my mom and my dad and my brother (although not quite so much) and me, and for about six or seven hundred other pretty good (mostly anyway) people. And if it wasn't Washertown First Methodist, it was some other church for hundreds of other Washertown people. But anyway, church for me was Sunday School, Vacation Bible School (when I was *real* little), being bored out of my goddamn mind during Sunday sermons, paint jobs, pipe organs (one old and one new, the new one having been installed during a major renovation of the place), and even more stuff still. It was my dad's "Constructor's Class" (for adult couples), and Youth Fellowship (and not just any youth fellowship either, as I mentioned before, but The *First* Methodist Church Youth Fellowship, a.k.a. "MYF"). And church was pot-luck suppers (which had to do with food, not marijuana from the bowling alley), Mr. Gurdy's wife (the organist), Edith Marlow (the very best Sunday school teacher any little kid anywhere could have had . . . with Mr. Marks as a close second), Bobby Boson (a well-intentioned, devout, but real pain in the butt sort of kid), Santa Claus, God, and Jesus. Especially Jesus (Jesus of course sort of topped the list). He even had his picture in the hallway, knocking at a door. I think that's what he was doing anyway. *And* (although I've already told you most of this part), The First Methodist Church of Washertown was the only building in town that had a diaphragm for a dome, bad smells in the basement men's room (although some other churches might have had them too, but since I didn't go to them I can't really say), and pigeon shit all over the sidewalk. Actually, if you put all this stuff together (except maybe for the bad smells and pigeon shit), I guess Washertown's First Methodist Church was a pretty good place. Mostly anyway. In fact, so far in my book I've been a little bit hard on it. (But only just to kind of have some fun.)

In Vacation Bible School, when I was about four or five, I learned that Jesus loved me (whoever he, Jesus, really was . . . I had a hard time figuring that out then). But anyway, I was told that he loved me because it said so in the *Bible* (we even sang a song about it). The song went: "Jesus loves me/This I know/For the Bible tells me so." Something like that anyway. And then: "Little ones are we below/We are weak but He is strong," I think anyway. Whatever, I guess I figured that if we sang about it, it must be true. And just before we sang it (at least at Vacation Bible School), or maybe it was just *after* we sang it (it doesn't really matter), we had juice and crackers. And I thought that was pretty nice. Not always though, because sometimes the crackers were kind of soggy, and seemed to taste just a little too much maybe like the church basement smelled. But that was OK. Mostly they were pretty good, and sometimes even crisp. Vacation Bible School teachers also taught us that there is no free lunch. At least I think that's what they were shooting for. Anyway, we had to take a penny with us every day and put it in a little wicker basket that was for God or Jesus or someone. Not Santa Claus, I don't think. I guess it could have been though. Or maybe the minister just needed money. I don't know. (I do know that when I got older I found out that some people thought there were some kind of "funny" things going on with money sometimes.) Whatever. When you think about it though, our Vacation Bible School tax amounted to a lot of money. I mean the school lasted for almost two weeks, and about a hundred kids went to it; so that (at least the way I figured it) was like almost ten dollars that they took in (ten days times one-hundred pennies equals that much). I think that's right anyway.

We also learned in Vacation Bible School (we learned a lot, now that I think about it) that Jesus had a special job for each of us. Really. A job for *each one* of us. He wanted us to be sunbeams. No kidding. Sunbeams. We sang about that too: "Jesus wants me for a sunbeam/A sunbeam/A sunbeam/Jesus wants me for a sunbeam/To shine for evermore." Sounds kind of stupid now, but I think that was how it went. And that was OK. I mean I felt pretty good about being a sunbeam (although in a way it didn't make any sense, even to a kindygardner). It was better than being some of the other things you could be though. Like maybe a dumb shit, or a total loser, or a "pansy" or something. Or an asshole even (some of the big kids might have called us that). And besides, if it made the teachers happy to try to sing us into sunbeams, why not? In fact, remember when a long time ago I told you about a woman named Kate Smith who sang "When the Moon Comes Over the Mountain" (and "God Bless America") and everything? Well, I guess maybe our little song was kind of like that, only we were singing about sunbeams instead of moonbeams . . . and also Kate Smith wasn't there (she was probably still in Lake Placid). Or maybe it wasn't like that. Sort of though. Anyway, I'm just trying to help you understand more about sunbeams and the sort of shit we had to sing about. But this is beginning to feel just a little bit like one of those times (again) when I could get really off track, so let's just forget it.

Whatever. I remember I felt a lot better about the songs we sang during Vacation Bible School than I did about a really scary prayer we were taught to say at bedtime. It went: "Now I lay me down to sleep/I pray the Lord my soul to keep/If I should die before I wake/I pray the Lord my soul to take." Again, I think that's how it went anyway. *Well,* not only was that prayer grammatically awkward (although I of course didn't know that then . . . it just seemed hard to say), it absolutely scared the shit out of me. If I should *die* before I wake? *Die?* I mean holy shit! I was only five years old. I hadn't even had my love affair with Janey, or seen Joycie's "thing" yet, or even been to any of the cartoon shows at the Capitol Theatre. And I'm supposed to be thinking that I could die? I mean *Jesus Christ!* I'm sorry, but this is getting me really upset. Was I *really* supposed to think that

Jesus might let me die in my sleep or something? The guy who supposedly loved me and wanted me to be a goddamn sunbeam? Grandmas and Grandpas (and other old people, and criminals, and soldiers and stuff) die. Not five-year-olds. I mean, *Jesus!* By the way, I would have gotten really, really punished if I had actually said that out loud, and actually I didn't, at least not when I was little (and I try not to anymore now). I'm just trying to tell you how it still makes me feel when I think back about it. And this (when I learned that prayer) was about the same time I got Scarlet Fever too, and they (some Washertown health agency) literally nailed a quarantine sign on our front door, and then made us "fumigate" the whole goddamn house (with little "candle cans" of chemicals) after we (my brother who didn't like me had it too) got better. That's right . . . fucking fumigate the place! (I mean it made you feel like you had had the plague or something.) So I was thinking that dying was a possibility anyway, although my mom and dad kept telling us we would get well (and of course we did).

Anyway, as you can tell, prayers were tough on you in those days. And (although not that it matters), it was even worse for Catholics. I know, because some of my friends were Catholic, like Mike my masturbation teacher, and Marcia Stringfinger (if you remember them), and they told me they had scary prayers too. And Methodist kids (and other Protestant kids too I suppose) were also taught by their grown-ups that they (i.e. *Roman* Catholics) actually had to say prayers all the time, and even carry strands of little beads around with them (to help them remember the prayers, I guess), and that they would go to hell if they didn't do it (say prayers and carry the beads). Even the boys had to carry beads (how embarrassing is that?). First though, before they went to hell, they were forced to make a brief, sort of transitional stop in a place called "Purgalory" (or something like that). Now that I think about all this stuff again, it's probably no wonder I became kind of a borderline neurotic or something. I mean I actually believed all this shit (about Methodists *and* Catholics). Most kids of course probably didn't pay any attention to it. And if they did, I'll bet they didn't give a rat's ass. But not me. I believed it! It was as though I was kind of a big, soft, throbbing sponge with a head on it, soaking all this stuff up. Whatever. I could handle being a sunbeam. That was OK. Maybe even a worried sunbeam. But a *dead* one? I mean *Jesus!* (I guess I've been saying that a little bit too much here.) But who the hell would write a prayer like that? Anyway, we'd better just get on with some other church stuff (*good* stuff). This shit (the kids who didn't think about it were right) is making me sick! Before we do though, I might just remind you one more time that when I got big (i.e. after I went to grade school and junior high school and high school, and then to college and graduate school, and then became a psychologist and was married and everything), my friends used to call me a clinical *psychopath* instead of a clinical psychologist. (As I said a long time ago though, they always told me that they liked me a lot and were just kidding, knowing that I had such a good sense of humor.) But you know, the more I think about it there might have been some truth to what they said. And I've decided that if that's what I really was (did I already tell you this too?), meaning a clinical psychopath instead of a clinical psychologist, it probably all started when I was just little and had to go to bed at night thinking that I might die because of that goddamn fucking prayer. I mean who the hell . . . but anyway, on to some good stuff. (And I'll really try to clean up my language from here on.)

Edith Marlow. What a lady! She was as good as good gets, and she came to Sunday School about every third or fourth Sunday to tell us (kindygardners and first-graders, like me) stories about Jesus and God, and sometimes angels, and once in a while even someone else who was special. Like Moses maybe (the Jewish kid who was found floating face up in a basket that was stuck in some weeds or something. (I mentioned him before . . . way back in Chapter One). Anyway, on "story" Sundays we would all sit in front of Miss Marlow in our little red wooden chairs with arched backs (meaning the chair backs were arched, not ours . . . although I guess some kids may have kind of *rounded* backs) . . . anyway, the chairs had arched backs, and small, round "spokes" in them (it hurt if you leaned back too much), and we would sit in them and just sort of gaze up at her (Miss Marlow). For a long time, by the way, my friends and I thought Miss Marlow, Miss *Edith* Marlow, was a missionary, or maybe even Jesus' mother or something. The Catholics were always talking about her too though (i.e. Jesus' mother, not Edith Marlow), so I guess that might have confused me. But anyway, she (Edith Marlow) maybe *could* have been Jesus' mother. I mean she looked old enough. In fact, she looked kind of like a lady who was actually named Grandma Moses (really). Not Moses' grandma (the kid in the basket), but a different one (the Grandma Moses I learned about later, who painted pictures that looked kind of like a second grader's). But this mother and grandmother stuff is maybe getting sort of confusing, so if you're kind of mixed up don't worry about it. (It doesn't matter anyway.)

Whatever. So as not to get off the track, the Miss Edith Marlow, of The First Methodist Church of Washertown, was kind of (actually a lot) skinny, sort of maybe a little bit homely (although I don't mean to be unkind about it), and really, really little. She wore mostly black dresses, and schoolteacher lace-up shoes, and she both walked and stood kind of funny (like a shy first grader maybe). And, Miss Marlow always, *always* clasped her hands in front of her when she spoke, like they were stuck together, or maybe itched or something (or maybe she just didn't know what else to do with them). But believe me, there wasn't a time that she didn't have a good story to tell. And she knew just how to tell it too. I mean this lady was like some kind of totally inspired, Biblical talking machine! And, just like she always clasped her hands in front of her, she always, *always* smiled . . . with all her smile seeming to be aimed right towards *you*.

Sometimes when we listened to Edith Marlow stories, I remember thinking (at least I *think* I remember thinking this) that maybe the sort of peculiar way she stood meant that she actually really *was* a missionary (I mentioned up above that we sometimes thought she was special enough to be one). But I guess I don't really think so. I mean I think (and I know I'm using the word *think* a lot here) . . . anyway I think (there it is again) I had somehow gotten confused when I learned about missionaries in general, and then about the various "positions" they allegedly assumed (for different activities). The main one, by the way (i.e. the main "missionary position"), I learned later, a *lot* later . . . like a lot, lot, *lot* later, meant something entirely different (*really* entirely different), and wouldn't have had anything to do with Miss Marlow (I'm pretty sure anyway) and how she stood. But now that I keep thinking about it, I guess there could have been more than one missionary position. Like maybe there was one for when they (missionaries) stood up (like Miss Edith Marlow did) to tell stories, and one for when they (missionaries) lay down, to "do" something else (meaning "it," although I'm trying to be delicate about this). I guess I actually still don't think so though. Whatever. (This whole train of thought isn't going where it should . . . I mean why do I get this way sometimes?) And besides, now that I think about it even more than I just said I was thinking about it (more), I couldn't have known about any of this stuff anyway. As I said up above, I didn't even learn about the missionary position thing until I was a lot, lot older. And when I was sitting in my little red chair (arched back and spindles), and listening to those stories (i.e. the Miss Edith Marlow stories), and I already said this up above too, only even further up above, I was just in first grade. Man . . . there really *must* be something wrong with me. I mean it even occurred to me to delete this whole goddamn paragraph. But it must be saying something . . .

Anyway, Miss Marlow was probably just self-conscious or something. That's it. She stood that way because she was self-conscious. But maybe not, since she was such a good storyteller. Whatever. Miss Marlow, as I sort of suggested before when I mentioned the idea that she could have been Jesus' mother or something, looked as though she was about a hundred and seventy years old. But that was probably just because we were only five or six. As I said though, she was pretty old. That's for sure. But one more thing, and then I'll go on with some other church stuff. Not only could that lady tell really good stories; she also was as loyal, and faithful, and devoted to what she thought as anyone could possibly be. So you can believe that it's for sure that Jesus loved *her.* He would have had to be crazy not to. And you could almost tell that he did (and also that she kind of knew it) by the kindness and the shared love that shone from her eyes. In fact, I'll bet that Edith Marlow, when she was little anyway, may have been Jesus' brightest and most favorite sunbeam. So anyway, just remember that Miss Edith Marlow, and Edith Marlow Sundays, were absolutely wonderful! And when she died, you can bet that she went straight to heaven. No need for extra prayers or a trip to "Purgalory" for that lady! Just straight to heaven.

Believe it or not (Mr. Ripley), but when I first remember going to Sunday worship services (always at 11 a.m. of course, which everyone knew was God's appointed hour), the minister at Washertown's First

Methodist Church actually wore a black, "swallow-tail" coat and striped trousers. No kidding. That's what he wore! Swear to God. He strutted around, greeted people, and preached his sermons in that outfit. I guess he must have thought he was pretty important, or maybe that God liked formal wear or something. I don't know. What I *do* know, however, is that he had to have looked pretty stupid to a lot of people ("dumb as shit" to junior and senior highschoolers). As a little person, I just thought he looked strange. (If I had been a few years older, like in junior high maybe, I would have probably concluded that he was simply a real "dick.") But I suspect that most of the Washertown Methodists (*First* Methodists) just thought of him as extremely vain. Or perhaps even nuts. Anyway, even though I was only five or six, or maybe seven years old, I kind of doubted that Jesus was much impressed by this sort of thing. I mean Jesus liked the Edith Marlows of the world, not the "fancy pants" guys. At least that's what I thought.

Furthermore ("cross my heart and point to God" this is no lie), I forgot to tell you that this gentleman also wore *spats!* That's right, he finished off his swallow tail coat and striped pants with spats. Gray spats, to be precise. I'm telling you, the guy was really weird. But then maybe he wasn't. I mean times change and everything. And also, we had a guy in the choir who (for the big Sunday morning solo) often sang a song about Jesus having "his eye on a sparrow" (I think it was a sparrow anyway . . . maybe a robin . . . I don't know). So then maybe that meant that having a preacher who wore a swallow-tail coat in a church that had pigeon shit all over the sidewalk sort of made sense after all. (Like maybe he was trying to develop some kind of a bird theme or something, just to sort of tie everything together.) But I don't think so. Not really. The guy was just nuts. And a dick. (Which now that I said that sounds maybe a little bit harsh, and kind of tasteless even . . . I mean "nuts and a dick" for a minister?) I mean a Catholic could probably go to hell for saying things like that about a priest. So then there probably *is* something wrong with me (but we've already gone into that). Anyway, eventually "Spat Man" encouraged the construction of a great big education building, over-extended the church budget by doing so, and left town before the bills came in—tails, striped pants, spats, and all. I'm not sure, but I think that at least some of the folks at Washertown's First

Methodist Church had hoped to throw a big going away party for him (although it didn't happen), featuring a picture of him standing on the front steps, right next to one of the Ionic columns from which the pigeons shit. (Shat?) But let's not try too hard here; the word was *shit*. ("Shat" for an Episcopalian perhaps, but just plain shit for the Methodists.) I mean being one at the time (i.e. a Methodist), I can tell you that when a pigeon shits, it just shits. Anyway, "Spat man" left, the bishop appointed a new guy, things seemed to settle down some, and the church eventually paid its bills. But (and to use yet another expression . . . and carry out *my* current theme), "enough of this shit.".

When I was a little bit but not a lot older, The First Methodist Church sanctuary was remodeled and completely redecorated. *Before* the remodeling, everyone had to sit and look up at a veritable (big word) sea of singing heads, all with their mouths open real wide (especially the people who took it too seriously or thought they maybe were really good or something). To tell you the truth, they kind of looked like Mississippi Catfish heads look, if you've ever seen one of those things. And they always seemed to be looking right at you. Regardless of where you were sitting. Anyway, all these singing heads belonged to The First Methodist Church choir. They sat in an elevated loft, and were supposed to open their mouths *real* wide when they sang, to make them look joyful and stuff. At least I think that was why. Unless of course it was a sad song (like for a funeral or something), and then they weren't supposed to look so good. Some of them could look pretty sad too. Even during the happy songs. Pitifully sad even. Almost (but not quite) enough to actually make you sort of feel sorry for them. At least that's what I thought. But I'm sort of going into too much detail I think. Whatever. On both sides of the singing choir heads, sort of like a frame for them, were lots of organ pipes; but I'll tell you more about the pipes later.

Anyway, below "The First Methodist Church Catfish Choir of the Singing Heads of Jesus Christ Our Lord and Savior" (and the organ pipes)—if you like that name, I'll keep using it—and on a really high platform in the very center (although maybe just a little to the left for some reason), were three tall (sort of musty-smelling, if you got too close), black, cracked, beat-up-looking leather pastor's chairs. Not that anyone went around sniffing them, but you could tell they were musty by just thinking about them. They looked like they should have been in a funeral home somewhere. At least that was my opinion. And I remember that where the cracks were the chairs looked kind of brown-like, instead of black, and just a little bit hairy; probably, I guess maybe, because the leather that they were made of was so thick. The chair in the middle was just a little bit higher than the other two, and that, of course, was the one in which "Spat Man" ("Reverend Spats and Stripes Forever") sat. Too bad it didn't have a Doric column behind it. What was funny (at least I thought so), although I'm sure it never occurred to him, was that his chair looked just like an "electric chair," the kind I had seen pictures of from the State Penitentiary. Anyway, it sure wasn't very inviting looking, I can tell you that.

Front and center on the platform that was under the loft with "The First Methodist Church Catfish Choir of the Singing Heads of Jesus Christ Our Lord and Savior" (I like it) was the pulpit, a dark-stained (mahogany, I think), wide and thick and pretty ugly-looking wooden speaker's stand. That was what Shithead ("Spat Man") stood behind when he preached, which meant that for at least the sermon part of the service you didn't have to look at his ridiculous goddamn outfit. He could have even "played with himself" behind that thing, and you wouldn't have even known it. I mean that's how big it was (meaning the pulpit). But I don't think he did. Although maybe. I mean, "stranger things have happened" (as another expression goes). But again, I just don't know. I guess I kind of wanted to believe that he would have thought he shouldn't do that though, at least not there (maybe when he was little he even took the same sex course I had experienced at YMCA camp). But anyway, I can still remember one of his sermons, because part of it was kind of arousing. At least I thought so . . . but then we know about my sometimes sort of twisted view of things, don't we?

Whatever. The sermon was all about some people from two little Bible towns called Sodom and Gomorrah (which for a long time I thought was just one place called "Sorghum-n-Amore," since Shithead ("Reverend Spats and Stripes Forever," "Spat Man," or whatever) had a tendency to kind of run his words together (and I probably wasn't listening real hard either). Whatever. What he said was that the people who lived there (in "Sorghum-n-Amore") got turned into blocks of salt (maybe like tall cowlicks or something . . . I'm not sure) for doing stuff like playing with themselves, and with each other even. He didn't put it quite that way, but that's what he meant. Anyway, he made it all sound pretty sick and threatening and everything. (None of it ever made much sense to me, but that's the way he saw it.) Cowlicks, by the way, if you have forgotten (I told you about them when we were in the back part of Hoague's Grocery Store), were blocks of salt that farmers put in their fields for cows to lick on, although I don't know why, meaning I don't know why the farmers put them there *or* why the cows liked to lick them. I don't think it had anything to do with "Sorghum-and-Amore" though. Unless maybe just kind of symbolically or something (remember my literature course in college . . . the one about Freud and sex, and that was taught by the wacko, chain-smoking, nail-biting teacher?).

Anyway, I for some reason thought that the sermon was strangely arousing. A little bit at least, but mostly I guess because of what I imagined, not because of what he really said. But later, when I was getting bigger (and older), I figured out that those people (he called them "Sorghumites") really *were* doing some sort of kinky stuff. But maybe not. I mean some of it might not have been "your cup of tea" (another kind of odd expression I thought), but then it says in the *Bible* (I think anyway) that you're not supposed to judge other people. And if you couple that with another saying in the *Bible,* the one about loving your neighbor and everything (although maybe not in some ways), you kind of get a different view. Maybe. I don't know. And anyway, as I said a long time ago, I might be a lot of things, but I'm not a theologian. Besides, this discussion is getting out of control (again). *And,* I suspect I might have been just a little bit too hard on the minister. (Like probably a lot too hard.) But sometimes I just can't help but to get carried away with some people. Whatever. I mean the guy was strange.

Well, so much for the *old* First Methodist sanctuary (solos and sermons included). After the remodeling job, and "Spat Man's, etc." departure, "The First Methodist Church Catfish Choir of the Singing Heads of Our Lord and Savior Jesus Christ" was split in half and moved to the sides (and down to ground level). Now what people looked at (where the singing heads had been before) were two big panels of white, gold-flecked "radio cloth" (so-named, I learned later, because it allowed sound to filter through). Each panel was about thirty feet high and ten feet wide, and included little squares and strips of wood latticework in front of it. And now all the wood was light walnut (the dark wood from the old sanctuary was history, except for the pews, which were still mahogany . . . probably because they couldn't afford to by new ones). Anyway, as I just said, the singing heads, or "choirheads," or whatever you want to call them (I realize that the now official name is somewhat lengthy) had been moved to the sides, so now they just looked at each other, and we, the worshipers, looked straight ahead at this sparkly radio cloth and the other wooden cutout stuff. The radio cloth, by the way, hid the pipes of a brand new pipe organ! The pipes from the old organ, as I told you already, had been exposed, and stood quite proudly (it seemed to me anyway) on each side of the choirheads. I only thought about this later (perhaps again because of my college course with the wacko nail biter), but maybe the reason they hid the new pipes was because some of the First Methodists had problems with the church exposing its pipes the way they had before. Especially their big ones (meaning the big pipes), which rose straight up, sort of like a vast forest of giant metal phalluses or something (again drawing from my literature class). I don't think so though. Covering the pipes was probably just part of the new, "modern" design. And besides, I really don't want to get carried away and off track again.

Anyway (and this is a really big "anyway"), the main focal point of the remodeling job (I've kind of been trying to generate some excitement and "lead up" to this), I mean *the* most important part of the whole project, had to do with a thirty foot high and five foot wide swath of thick, dark maroon velvet that hung down right in the middle of the two panels of white, gold-flecked radio cloth. *And* (and this "and" is even bigger than the "anyway" was before), the very, very, *very* most important part, more important than everything else put together, was that in front of the maroon velvet drape (that hung between the white, gold-flecked radio cloth . . . that "hung in the house that Jack built" . . . only kidding about the Jack part) there had been placed a twenty foot tall (ten feet wide at the "cross bar"), carved wooden cross—an *ornately* carved, twenty foot tall (ten feet wide at the "cross bar"), carved wooden cross! (Light walnut, with some of the carved stuff having been painted.) This cross (trust me) was nothing, *nothing* like "The Old Rugged Cross" that "The First Methodist Church Catfish Choir of the Singing Heads of Our Lord and Savior Jesus Christ" sometimes sang about. (I don't know if the design committee thought about that or not.) But I mean this thing (i.e. the cross) had religious symbols carved all over it (especially fish and grapes and lots of other "viney" kinds of stuff). All carved (and painted) right into and on it! *However* (and this "however," believe it or not, is even bigger than the "anyway" and the "and" I used up above . . . really), there is yet one more thing to tell you about this cross (although I almost wish I didn't have to). But here it comes, nevertheless. The whole thing (and this is no lie . . . "swear to God"), the *whole* cross, all twenty feet of it (and the ten foot "cross bar"), was outlined with red and blue tubes of neon! No shit! It really was. *Neon!* And you could "mix" the red tubes and the blue tubes to get purple.

To be honest though, and remember I always said I would be, the neon wasn't as bad as it sounds, since it (the neon tubing) didn't actually show. At least not like a beer or restaurant sign or anything like that. That's because the tubes were actually placed *behind* the edges of the cross, thereby allowing the twenty foot tall (ten feet wide at the "cross bar") cross to just kind of "glow," real strange-like, as the neon colors sort of mysteriously "emanated" from behind the cross onto the maroon velvet behind it (i.e. the velvet that hung between the side panels of white, gold-flecked radio cloth). So it wasn't *really* bad. At least I guess it wasn't. But it wasn't really *good* either. The lighting was controlled, by the way, with a rheostat that was out in the hallway (a pretty fancy device), so you could keep the red and blue separate, mix it to get purple (as I already said), turn it down or up ("down" gave it a kind of real soft, shadowy look, and "up" sometimes too much of a "commercially" look), or do anything else you could figure out.

Anyway, regardless of what you might think of this twenty foot tall (ten feet wide at the "cross bar"), carved, light walnut (some parts painted), neon cross (and in truth, it did sort of "work" with the rest of the décor), I can tell you for sure however that it certainly did *not* look like the kind of cross anyone would have been crucified on. In fact, had you tried to crucify anyone on the new Washertown First Methodist Church cross, the death would probably have had to be attributed to electrocution. And just think (although I guess you don't have to) of how "The Apostle's Creed" would have to go if Jesus had actually died on that thing: "Born of the Virgin Mary, Suffered under Pontius Pilate, Was *electrocuted*, died, and was buried," and so on, (*and*, they may even have added "at The First Methodist Church in Washertown, Iowa, home of 'The First Methodist Church Catfish Choir of the Singing Heads of Our Lord and Savior Jesus Christ'"). Yeah . . . I know . . . I'll probably really burn in hell for that one. And can you imagine some people (extremists) choosing to wear little silver electric chairs rather than crosses on their neck chains? I mean even *I* think that's sick (although you have to admit there is a strange although sort of twisted logic to it). But forget it; it never happened. And thank God I'm not Catholic; I would have been jerked back and forth between "Purgalory" and hell forever and ever. And it still might happen (even though I was Protestant, Methodist, a good little boy in general, and bought my mom an "Uncle Sam" vase with a flower hole in the top of it). I mean I'm actually even sorry I got into this. So moving right along . . .

The new church organ was somewhat of a separate issue, although it was part of the overall remodeling that took place at First Methodist, Washertown. And it was a big one too (both the organ *and* the issue). As you might suspect, a special committee, a *very* special committee, had been appropriately appointed (the committee itself might even have thought *anointed*), and had worked tirelessly to select the perfect instrument (considering of course the amount of money it had) for the music part of the "new" sanctuary. The old organ had been less than reliable, and often sounded pretty much like a box of whistles from an old theatre or maybe even circus organ, although I'm not sure very many people were particularly aware of that. The *new* organ, however, was to be just short of majestic (relatively speaking): three manuals (keyboards) rather than two (like the old one had); a "tremulo" (the device that makes the sound sort of "quiver") that quivered so much it could make you weep in your pew; and reed and trumpet "stops" ("stops" are what produce the various sounds of the organ) too numerous to name. So anyway, the new organ was indeed, as they say, "one big instrument." Unfortunately, however, it was better chosen than received. So let me tell you what happened. It's a pretty good story.

As I think I may have already told you (but I'm not totally sure), Mrs. Gurdy, the wife of Mr. Gurdy of Gurdy's Rexall Drug Store fame (never forget the rubber drawer, dirty books, and Kotex boxes), and the mother of one of my grade school to high school (i.e. "on again, off again") girlfriends, had played the organ at Washertown's First Methodist Church for years. Lots of years. And Mrs. Gurdy was really good at playing hymns and pretty preludes (a little alliteration there . . . remember I did that in a chapter a long time ago?). Anyway, Mrs. Gurdy was really good at things like "Softly and Tenderly Jesus is Calling" and stuff like that. I mean this woman knew her audience, and the First Methodist choirheads and the other people who liked to sing a lot loved her. In fact, her organ playing probably included most of the same sounds and selections that were soothing the souls of Methodists all across America (more alliteration . . . did you get it?). Maybe soothing people in Europe even, although I don't think they had many (Methodists) in Europe. Anyway, nothing was too harsh. And nothing too noisy. Just "sweet Jesus music," with various accompaniments to vocal solos that could make your eyes cloud over.

However, and here's where the trouble began, it seems as though certain people of "considerable taste" (different anyway) and musical "sophistication" (self-proclaimed at least) thought that the new organ just might call for a new organist. Quite frankly, they thought Mrs. Gurdy was simply not using the new reeds, trumpets, and "mixtures" to their satisfaction. Of course those very same stops (sounds) created only "noise" to the ears of the majority of the First Methodist audience, unsophisticated as they may have been. That, at the time however, didn't seem to matter. Consequently, Mrs. Gurdy was "out," and a Mr. Rantler (that's right, *Mr.,* and from Des Moines no less) was "in," or "on the bench," as one might say. (Actually I just made that "on the bench" part up.)

Whatever, Mr. Rantler knew (and used) those reeds and trumpets and "screamy" mixtures with absolute abandon. I can tell you that. And he knew his Bach and Buxtehude too (considered by the "select group" of course to be *real* church music . . . and it is). Furthermore, Mr. Rantler also knew the impact of using "Full Organ" (that meant playing it as loud as it would get) when he played the morning postlude (meaning the piece after the service). Therein however, and unfortunately, lay a different problem. I mean, how could Washertown's First Methodists start to talk to each other (immediately after the last prayer and the Benediction) while Mr. Rantler had the goddamn organ going full blast? (The idea of actually listening to the postlude would never of course had occurred to most of them.) Consequently, whereas years later it would take the Israelis only six *days* to win a war, it took Mr. Rantler only about six postludes (Full Organ), before the great majority of Washertown's First Methodist Church worshippers (woe to the "select people") longed for sweet Jesus to call them again . . . "softly and tenderly" (*very* softly and *extremely* tenderly) . . . back to the good old days of Mrs. Gurdy's "normal" church music. Therefore, before Mr. Rantler knew what hit him, he was back in the big city (i.e. Des Moines), and Mrs. Gurdy was back on the bench!

And that meant, of course, that peace had once again been restored (except for those music lovers of "considerable taste"). "Tremulo Exceleth Trumpet!" was immediately engraved on a plaque and placed somewhere behind the white and gold-flecked radio cloth (behind which, as I already told you, were the very organ pipes in dispute), and the good people of Washertown's First Methodist Church could proceed onward, as in "Onward Christian Soldiers," in their worship of God. Something like that anyway. Years later, I suspect, when the present organ would eventually meet the fate of the old, a new and of course "select" committee would probably wonder about the hardly used trumpets and "screamy goddamn mixtures" of the once mighty, three manual organ they were about to replace. But that was for the future committee people to ponder. For now, things were again, and clearly, "as they should be." Not only were the ordinary folks happy, but probably Jesus was as well. And Washertown's First Methodist Church was going to be just fine. The new organ would be played "right" (just as all organs should be). The maroon drape (with the white, gold-flecked radio cloth on the sides) would hang properly. The twenty foot tall (and ten feet wide at the "cross bar") carved wooden (walnut, with some parts painted) cross would stand in a stalwart, if somewhat ornate, manner. The red, blue, and purple (if "mixed" right) neon tubes would glow (softly). And "The First Methodist Church Catfish Choir of the Singing Heads of Our Lord and Savior Jesus Christ" would continue to sing (mouths opened wide, but beautifully). The pigeon shit, of course, would still be out on the sidewalk, but even that seemed to be an "all right" part of what was truly the essence (restored) of Washertown's First Methodist Church.

Another thing about church was a kid named Bobby Boson. He didn't like me very much, and I didn't like him. It always seemed to me that he thought he was more religious than most people, like "holier" and everything. At least that's what I thought, and so did my buddies. I don't mean to be hard on him though, and now that I look back I suppose he was just trying to be a really good person. And anyway, there was reason to believe that Bobby had reached his state of perceived holiness somewhat naturally, since his dad was the superintendent of the First Methodist Church Sunday School. And also, because when Bobby and his sister would get into a fight, his mother would calm them down by singing hymns from her kitchen window (my mother told me that once). That's the difference, I guess. When my brother (who tried to murder me with a wooden spoon, as you may recall . . . missing my "soft spot" only by a hair . . . ha ha) and I fought, we just got our butts kicked (our expression, not our mother's), or got sent to our rooms or something. It's for sure we didn't hear any hymns.

Anyway, I guess what happened was that as life went on Bobby got holy, whereas my brother and I just got hell, which again was our way of saying it, not our mom's. (In truth, our parents were actually very fair and quite restrained in their discipline.) Whatever, Bobby Boson (wouldn't you know) was eventually elected (or appointed maybe) president of The Methodist Youth Fellowship (that's *The* Methodist Youth Fellowship, a.k.a. MYF), and in one of his more public prayers (my friends and I referred to them as "pubic" prayers), like right in front of the whole goddamn group and everything, he prayed that God would somehow help us (my friends and me) correct our sinful ways (which I took to mean stop doing some of the shit we liked to do). I think he thought we were "feeling up" our girlfriends and stuff. And actually of course we were, although "and stuff" wasn't happening very much (at least not to me). Anyway, that prayer did it, and my friends and I quit Youth Fellowship and found other things to do on Sunday nights. Bobby Boson (again, wouldn't you know) went on to become a Methodist minister (really); whereas my friends and I just went on feeling up our girlfriends . . . and praying we might get to go farther . . . and if not, praying to have more wet dreams.

One other but really pretty special thing about First Methodist Church that I should tell you about was Christmas. (I'll tell you about Christmas in *all* of Washertown in little while.) But what an event it was at First Methodist Church! Right in the middle of the chancel (on the platform beneath the choirheads), and on God's side of the communion rail that circled the very front (this was before the remodeling project), was placed a great big (although some years kind of ugly-looking) Christmas tree. It was always a really fat tree, but also the kind of tree that was often sort of ruined by big empty places (holes) and some pretty scraggly-looking branches. But that was just part of what sometimes made it ugly. The rest of what made it ugly (but in a supposedly "meaningful" way) was "man (or children) made," meaning that the church believed that this magnificent tree was to be for everyone (and indeed it was), and thus it was to be adorned (a pretty fancy word for what actually happened to it) with every kind of member-made "ornament" imaginable. Most of these ornaments were made out of colored "construction" paper by sloppy Sunday school kids (we made "chains" of glued and looped-together pieces of the paper), and placed on the tree where we thought they would look just right. After all, it was Jesus' birthday, so things were supposed to look pretty good. And to tell you the truth, when I was really, *really* little anyway, that big, fat (with some holes in it) and sometimes wobbly tree seemed to be truly magical. And then of course, in addition to the tree, The First Methodist Church chancel provided (we thought anyway) the grandest setting one could ever imagine for the Christmas Eve pageant. Maybe grander even than Radio City Music Hall in New York City or something (although we wouldn't have had any way to know that). Whatever. It was for sure just as good (and maybe better) than anything in Des Moines.

Anyway, I was chosen (for the pageant), which is to say *forced,* to be a shepherd, and I had to wear a ratty-looking, goddamn "gunny sack" for a costume. Bobby Boson (of course) got to be a wise man and wear an old, but really important-looking, shiny satin bathrobe (I think it was blue). I can't remember who the other two wise men were. Probably girls dressed up like boys or something. Shit! It had been only about a month earlier that Ronnie Stith had been chosen to be the king in our grade school play about Columbus and Pocahontas and all that stuff. *He* got to wear a *purple* satin bathrobe (along with a goddamn cardboard crown). And I didn't get chosen for even anything! Nothing. Like not even an Indian or anything. I mean Jesus! How much rejection and suffering and humiliation and other shit is a fourth grader supposed to take anyway? I mean it was just awful. I didn't even want to go to school any longer. In fact I felt like going under the Overhead Bridge (a bridge that arched over the railroad tracks a few blocks from Washertown Elementary) and just living with the bums (tramps), and maybe even smoking old cigarette butts with them and eating canned beans and everything. And maybe even let a fucking train run over me or something. Well . . . I probably didn't feel *that* bad. Anyway (and to get back on track . . . not the train track, but the "what I'm talking about" track), part of the problem I think (at school anyway) was that our librarian, Mrs. Clubb, did the choosing for the play, and she never liked me very much. Well, I didn't like her either. Even before she didn't choose me. As a matter of fact, although I probably would have been afraid to say it then, I thought she was a real bitch. And so did some of my buddies too. A big fat bitch even! At least that's what I thought.

Whatever. Together with the Christmas wise man thing, and the Columbus crap, these were the kinds of experiences that I think might have kind of contributed to the problems I sometimes had with my mind wandering off the subject and everything—these two experiences *and* the broken water glass episode (remember my starring role playing the water glasses in second grade?), *and* probably thinking too much about what I'd like to do to my pretty fourth grade homeroom teacher, *and* feeling bad and guilty and everything because I had hit one of my really good friends in the head with a baseball bat one day (pretty hard too) when my parents were on vacation (although it was an accident), *and* dropping the goddamn baton in the fucking track meet, *and* having to wear that pussy pink suit for the goddamn Maypole dance. Anyway, all these things probably didn't help any either. I mean it just seemed that my mind was being constantly assaulted by something. I thought anyway. (I don't know why this stuff just seems to tumble right back on me sometimes.) Like now. But I'm not going to let it get to me. Not me. I mean it's too close to the end (meaning the end of what I'm telling you about, not like the end of the whole goddamn world or anything). People who talked about that kind of shit (the end of the world), at least when I was little, were mostly Jehovah's Witnesses anyway. And everyone knew they were fucking nuts. (There's that word again . . . twice in one paragraph, and once in the paragraph just before it even.) This time I really am sorry that I said it though . . . especially since it's Christmas at First Methodist Church and everything. So I guess I "better watch out" for sure. I mean if Santa Claus really *is* coming to town (and I still sort of believed that he was), I don't want him to be too pissed off at me.

But anyway, when people want to talk about things like that, meaning the end of the world and "Army Gettum," and other shit like that (I think those are the words they used . . . meaning "Army Gettum" are the words, not "and shit"), they really are crazy. And I'm not. Well sometimes maybe. But not much. *Anyway* (I need to settle down here . . . like whoa!), before I completely do though (i.e. settle down), I want you to know that I used to think that if he (I'm back to Bobby Boson again) hadn't been too big (like in second grade maybe), the church pageant planners would probably have had him be baby Jesus. (Although I would probably still have been a goddamn shepherd in a gunnysack.) As it was however, he would have looked pretty stupid with his two scrawny-looking legs hanging over the makeshift crib they used (year after year after year), instead of having a big pile of hay like in the real *Bible*. Actually, Bobby Boson probably would have made a really good Joseph though (the guy who was Jesus' dad, only not in the "real" way, since he and Jesus' mother, Mary the virgin as they called her, hadn't really "done it" yet). At least that's what it said in the *Bible* again. The Mary and Joseph thing, by the way, was another really hard-to-understand story that we were taught in Sunday School. I guess there was just something about Bible people. I mean like virgins having babies, and blocks of salt that used to be people, and oceans coming apart in the middle, and floods, and dead Egyptians all over the place and a lot of other shit. Anyway (again, to kind of get back on track), I'll bet being baby Jesus would have made Bobby Boson feel pretty happy. I mean not very many people get to be Jesus. However, none of this changes the fact that I had to be a skinny shepherd boy in an itchy gunnysack. Come to think about it though, that's what the Bible guy named David was (i.e. just a shepherd). Remember him . . . the kid with the slingshot who kicked Goliath's butt? (Goliath was a giant, in case you don't know that.) Actually, he didn't just kick his butt; he killed the son-of-a-bitch! So maybe being "a boy in a bag" wasn't so bad after all. But I think I need to pull myself together again.

Whatever. Most of this crap doesn't really matter, meaning who got to be what in the Christmas play (and the trouble I had for a few minutes there with my mind), since all this pageantry was soon to be eclipsed by the final and really, *really* big event anyway. Here's how it worked. After the nativity play (pageant) was over, all the "sacred" stuff would be cleared away. I mean like the old baby Jesus doll (which should have been replaced ten years before), and the fake palm tree, and the crib and everything. Anyway, it would all be carried off the platform by people (the "crew") who sort of hurried around picking up stuff, as if hurrying would make it look like they weren't really doing it. And then while all that was happening, we of the "holy cast" scrambled to the hallway to shed our gunny sacks or satin bathrobes (damn . . . I really did want to wear one of those things), and then returned to the sanctuary to join our families. And then, *then* (and "you better *really* watch out" this time) . . . *then*, from one of the side doors of the "right in the middle of the chancel" choirhead loft, far, far above the ugly, black cracked leather pastor's chairs, would tumble Santa Claus, complete with the jingling of sleigh bells, a big bag full of candy and toys, some really loud "Ho! Ho! Ho's," and an absolutely wild rendition of "Jingle Bells" on the old First Methodist Church pipe organ, played (of course) by Mrs. Gurdy (at her very best)!

Jesus Christ! It was Jesus' birthday! Talk about "up on the house top." I mean holy shit; the place absolutely exploded! (Sorry about some of my words again, but I don't know how else to say it.) I mean had Methodism reached its zenith or what (meaning, I learned later, a really high point)? But anyway, regardless of what else was going on, or what some people might have thought, it was in fact Christmas at First Methodist Church in Washertown! And in its perhaps pretty plain and probably simple way (and sort of tasteless even), it was the most wonderful kind of Christmas in the whole world (well . . . at least for kids in Washertown and Casper County it was). "Wonderfuller" even (good word, don't you think?) than being set free in the toy department at Younker's Department Store in Des Moines (well . . . maybe anyway). So "Happy Birthday Jesus!" And "Merry Christmas everyone!" Be sure to take your ribbon candy home with you (the "filled" kind too), and your present from Santa Claus. But bundle up before you go outside (it's really cold), and then try to go right to bed when you get home (impossible as it may be). Santa's not done with you yet! Oh, and by the way *don't* destroy the mood by saying that goddamn "Now I lay me down to sleep" prayer. Jesus will understand. Trust me.

CHAPTER EIGHT

CHRISTMAS IN WASHERTOWN
OR
IT JUST DOESN'T GET ANY BETTER
THAN THIS!

C hristmas was not only special at Washertown's First Methodist Church; Christmas was special all over Washertown. *Everywhere!* It was almost as though you lived inside one of those beautiful and "mysterious-to-a-little-boy," shiny glass snow-domes that maybe had a Santa Claus and his reindeer in it ("up on a house top" somewhere). Or maybe a little cottage (with its own chimney and a curl of smoke), with lots of tiny and "slopey" pine trees around it. Or maybe even a chapel (with stained glass windows and a real "pointy" steeple). And when you were *real* little, regardless of what was in it (honest, it didn't matter), it seemed as though you could kind of like just float around in there and go anywhere you wanted to. (Really . . . I'm not kidding either.) And *then*, when someone really nice turned it upside down for you (like maybe your mom, or your grandma, or someone else pretty special), you could actually sort of just fly it seemed, amidst all the really beautiful and sparkly snowflake flecks that were coming down everywhere. Anyway, that's how special Christmas in Washertown was!

I mean I think even the Washertown "nothings" thought that Christmas in Washertown was special. (The "nothings," as you may recall from way back at the beginning of everything I've been telling you, were the folks who weren't Catholics, or Protestants, or Jews, or Jehovah's Witnesses, or *anything* . . . like not even Mormons or the "square" people.) So what I'm trying to say is that although some people maybe didn't believe in Christmas in the *religious* way (meaning they didn't really and truly believe all that stuff about Mary the virgin, or her "sort of" husband Joseph, or the baby Jesus, or maybe even believe that there was a manger and shepherds and lambs and a donkey and the star and the wise men and everything), I know they believed in it (i.e. in Christmas in Washertown) in a *real* way. They had to. It was all around them! As a matter of fact, Christmas in Washertown was so wonderful and "all around you" that it's one of the very reasons that I said in great big letters, and right on the cover of this whole book, that Washertown was a masterpiece. I mean look at it again. It says, *WASHERTOWN: AN AMERICAN MASTERPIECE!* (It can't get any bigger or better than that.) And because it was so wonderful, and also because of how excited I can still get about it, I decided there was no better way to end what I've been telling you about, meaning *Where It All Began* and *How I Got To Be This Way* (I said the part about "where it all began" and "how I got to be this way" on the cover too, only as I just now showed you, in not such big letters) . . . *anyway,* I have decided that there is no better way to end my time with you than to let you know how totally good and grand and everything Christmas in Washington was. It's kind of like my wanting to give you a really special present that I've been saving up for. You know, the kind you can cherish forever (or at least for a long time anyway). Like my mom's "Uncle Sam" head maybe (well . . . sort of). Whatever. I hope you like it.

As I said then, Christmas at church was special; but Christmas in Washertown itself was even better. It made you feel excited all over, and everyday. I mean a Washertown Christmas was not only like living in a sparkly snow-dome; it could also almost (sometimes anyway) be like getting an over-sized and totally treasure-laden "grab-bag" from Roswell's. Like one that maybe had a real diamond ring in it, or a shiny new silver dollar, or maybe a little rolled-up picture of Lana Turner, or someone else really beautiful. And then of course (underline "of course") there was Washertown's world-renowned (at least it should have been anyway), absolutely grand, fantastic, and truly glorious and everything "Courthouse of The Ten Thousand Lights." (The "Ten Thousand Lights" part is something I just made up myself; it's not an official "saying" or anything).

In a very real sense though, "The Courthouse of The Ten Thousand Lights" (maybe ten *million* even) was pretty much the anchor of Washertown'a entire Christmas celebration, and it lighted up, almost as if by magic, every evening at about five o'clock. I mean it just sort of suddenly "came on" and was there. And when it did (come on), it was so, and I mean sooo beautiful (especially as the night got darker and darker, and if it was snowing and everything), that it was sometimes hard to believe it was even real. But then other times I actually thought that maybe *it*, i.e. "The Courthouse of The Ten Thousand Lights," was what was *really* real, and *everything else* wasn't! And not only that, but it was being "what was real" right there in the middle of Washertown! Like a spaceship had landed or something. Of course you'd have to be in Washertown in December to actually see and understand all this (or the very last week in November); but that's OK. Don't worry. I'll just assume that that's when it is (meaning December). Unfortunately though (but just a little bit unfortunate . . . not enough to spoil anything), I have to tell you (since you'd notice anyway) that the Courthouse, in addition to the ten thousand lights, had about ten thousand other things, i.e. "decorations," stuck to or hanging from it also, some of which it just *might* have been better off without. Maybe not though. It's hard to tell. Whatever. It's not that important. It was the whole effect that mattered. And the whole effect was absolutely fantastic!

So anyway, every year, on the very first night after Thanksgiving, the entire building was transformed into one gigantic, sky-high, faux-stone (and, as I kind of said before, faux just about everything else) "Christmas tree." (I guess I just can't keep from calling it different things . . . it's still "The Courthouse of the Ten Thousand Lights;" it's just that now the lights have kind of like made it into a tree or sorts.) You'd have to be dead or maybe be being held captive in a dark hole with a lid on it or something not to see all this. I mean that faux stone (etc.) Casper County Courthouse "Miracle Building," "Christmas tree" (still "The Courthouse of The Ten Thousand Lights") was visible for twenty miles around (maybe two hundred even)! Well, about ten anyway. Whatever. People who saw it from way far away probably thought it was some kind of transcendent (big word), shimmering, "finale of all finales" (sort of like how you feel sometimes at a really important symphony concert or something . . . only this time you're looking instead of listening). Probably not though . . . I get carried away sometimes. But maybe then it was like the "crème de la crème" of all Christmas places (although of course I wouldn't even have known what "crème de la crème" meant when I was little . . . or "finale of all finales," as far as that goes). Anyway, before I tell you more about "The Courthouse of the Ten Thousand Million Lights" itself (this paragraph and the last one are just meant to be sort of a "tease"), I want to give you a better feel for Washertown's December holiday season in general. It will add even more to the excitement of what's to come, and I don't want you to miss *any* of it. OK?

December in Washertown (and everywhere in Iowa) was mostly pretty cold. Sometimes it was *really* cold; and once in awhile it was just plain "scrunch up your shoulders, keep your face under your scarf, and try not to breathe in too much" cold. (Mostly though the "scrunch up" cold didn't come until January.) The one neat thing about those *really* cold days, however (at least to a little person), was that you could actually see your breath. And that seemed pretty strange, especially when you were real, *real* little. I mean it was kind of like you were a tiny little dragon or something. At least that's what I thought. But anyway, as you probably know, in Iowa the dark of the night comes increasingly early in December. Too early, it seemed to me. Sometimes in fact, to tell you the very, *very* truth, even kind of "scary" early. At least I thought. But of course I "scared" pretty easily sometimes. It was also true though (and this is the part I want you to really understand) that by dark time in December the Washertown air (and just about everything else) was literally saturated with a somewhat hard to describe, but pretty easy to feel, sense of peace and well-being. (It's the "peace and well-being" that was important.) So that made the dark nights not as bad as they could have been. And speaking of holidays, and peace, and "beginning to get" dark nights and everything, Thanksgiving of course had pretty much set the tone; you know, with snow (sometimes), and turkey, and drumsticks, and stuff like that (kind of like the "Over the river and through the woods" kinds of things that every gradeschooler sang about). But still it was the actual coming of Christmas that really, *really* made things special. Also though (to tell the whole story), you could sometimes get a sort of "dready" feeling at this time of the year too. At least if you weren't careful you could. "Dready" was the feeling you got if you let yourself think about the heavy snows, the long cold nights (with no "Courthouse of The Ten

Thousand Lights" anymore), slushy streets, and dead, abandoned Christmas trees that would fill so much a part of January (and, as far as the snow went, February, and March, *and* even into April). If you were smart though, you just thought about Christmas.

Anyway (I'm really determined to stay on track here), a few lines ago I started to tell you about the December air in Washertown. By late afternoon (just before it began to get dark and the peace and well-being feelings started to sort of well up in you), the air was also filled (most days anyway) with really, really *damp* but kind of nice smells, one of the best of them being the "too-often-too-faint," but sometimes pretty heavy (depending on where you were of course) scent of fresh pine. The best places to smell it were in front of Santen's Grocery, The Thriftway Super Market, or The Washertown Seed and Feed Store (which I mentioned was a good Christmas tree, and therefore "piney" place, a long time ago). Those were the stores where the merchants stacked the biggest piles of freshly cut pine branches ("greens") right on the sidewalk, and then leaned most of their Christmas trees right up against the fronts of the buildings.

It was really fun, by the way (at least I thought so), to get extra close and sort of stick your face right into the trees; that way you could really, *really* smell the pine, and even get some of the sticky sap and stuff stuck to your face and fingers if you wanted to (and I did). It also seemed to me that when you did that (i.e. stuck your face right into the Christmas tree branches) you could sometimes get the feeling (really) that every one of those beautiful green trees was wishing real hard (maybe pleading even) to get chosen by just the right family. Kind of like the strays at the dog pound maybe. In fact (if you remember some of the early stuff I told you about me), you won't be surprised to know that I also actually worried sometimes that a few of the trees (the kind of "straggly" ones, or maybe the crooked or somehow damaged ones) might not get chosen at all. By anyone. And that would be heart pretty breaking (if you were one of them anyway). At least if you asked me it would be. I know what you're thinking though: you're thinking that most people would say that Christmas trees don't have any feelings. But I'm not so sure. I'm really not. And it would be pretty sad if you were a Christmas tree and had been standing out on a cold sidewalk for several days, and then ended up an orphan. Especially when Christmas Eve came. I mean think about it; first you get chopped down, then they take you out of the forest, and then you end up all alone. An orphan. A tree orphan. Anyway (I guess "sentimental me" is maybe getting a little bit carried away here), just remember that if you want to (and I often did), you can actually sort of press your whole self right into a tree and get your face and fingers all sticky with the sap from the "leaky" branches. And as I said, I liked that. And maybe they (the trees) did too. I know that it convinced me even more that those trees were really alive (and trying as hard as they could to say something). It also let me take the pine smell (and some of the sticky stuff) home with me. Sometimes even I would intentionally wipe some sap on my jacket cuffs, although my mom didn't like it very much when I did.

And then of course, in addition to all the pine, Washertown in December often had that wonderful and welcoming (almost warm it seemed) smell that frequently wafted over the town from lots of real, wood-burning fireplaces. But also (you can ignore this part if you want to), there was sometimes (but not too often) the not so pleasant and kind of metal-like smell of lingering smoke from the foundry that fueled Washertown's factories. And then finally, along with the not good factory smell (I guess I should tell you everything), were these other and not very pleasant exhaust smells that once in a while visibly and curiously drifted out of someone's tailpipe (curious in the eyes of a little boy anyway). But the factory smell was never very strong, and the exhaust smells weren't very heavy (after all, this was Washertown in the 1940s, when there weren't very many cars anyway), so no one complained much. So putting it all together then, this is kind of what downtown Washertown smelled like in December: mostly fresh and sort of "coldish," kind of damp and pretty piney, sometimes fireplace smoky, and once in a while just a little bit not very good. But right now, *right this very minute*, I want you to add to the mix an extra measure more of the fresh, damp, "friendly" smells (especially the pine one), wipe the wet and lonely snowflake or two from your cheek (is a real storm on the way?), and then breathe in. *Real* slow. And *real* deep. Wow! Is that nice or what? But enough (for now) of the air smells.

December in Washertown was also red enameled kettles hanging on red enameled chains from red enameled metal stands. Kind of like big, swinging steel birdcages or something. And they were *really* red too. And shiny (although you could also see from the dents and stuff that they had been repainted a lot of times). "Chinese red," I think they called it, although the people who placed them there didn't have anything to do with China. At least I don't think they did. And it was for sure that the people who stood by them ringing their bells didn't look Chinese. They were all Americans (and in more ways than one). In fact, each of these kettles was attended all day and even into the evening by a uniformed Salvation Army Lady (or sometimes man, but usually not), ringing a loud and "clangy" brass bell, hoping to hear the familiar, dull, clinking sound of coins being dropped into the pot, or, rare as it was in the 1940s, thanking God for the muffled sound of a dollar bill being stuffed through the little slot in the middle of the kettle. The lids of the kettles, by the way, sloped in and sort of downward, just in case you were careless when you tossed your coins in, I guess anyway. And the "ladies of the kettles" (to distinguish themselves from the chains and pots, and take no chance of going unnoticed) wore plain, black uniforms and big bonnets (also black) that had *really* big red bows on them. The men (when they were there) wore uniforms also, with officer's hats (kind of like military or police hats), only with really wide red and gold bands that had brass buttons attached to the ends.

On special days, volunteers from the Washertown Chamber of Commerce and the Rotary or Kiwanis clubs would ring the bells. And Washertown was small enough, and the volunteers smart enough, that it made you feel pretty guilty if you didn't contribute on those days (they were really good at making you think they knew who you were, even if they didn't). As a little kid, if you didn't put anything in the pot you always kind of thought they might tell your dad, or maybe your grandparents, or even the principal of your school or someone. Or God Himself even. Some kids got pretty good at just looking the other way (you know, like they were thinking real hard about some stuff), but if I didn't put something in the kettle, like at least a nickel or something (which was a lot of money when you were a little boy in the 1940s), I would feel kind of bad. But what else is new. As you've noticed a lot by now, I always seemed to feel bad, or sorry for, or guilty about something . . . or someone (even, as I said up above, about straggly and maybe soon-to-be orphaned Christmas trees). On some days, by the way, and on Saturday nights especially (that's when the Washertown stores stayed open in the 1940s . . . although

I think I already told you that), and on *every* night for the whole last week before Christmas, all this putting money in the pots would be accompanied by the really loud Salvation Army Band.

This "big brass band" (and it really was, too . . . big in sound anyway) was always strategically placed on a busy corner, and often in front of Walgreen's, since lots of moviegoers walked by there. Sometimes though the band was on the corner by the dingy old Score Board, since that was closer to where the Salvation Army Building was. But what a band! It had a big, "boomy" base drum, the *really* loud kind that would sometimes sort of "roar" in your head, rumble in your chest, and even make your whole insides shake. And the drum had a shiny brass cymbal nailed to the top of it that the drummer would crash the other half of the cymbal onto (almost making you kind of nuts in the head sometimes). And then there were always two or three guys playing polished-up brass instruments (usually two trumpets and a tuba). So anyway, if you think real hard about it, and then try to feel the damp and cold of the night again, and then look up and see all the snow flakes floating in the light of the lamp posts and everything, you can almost kind of get yourself into a real "sentimentally" sort of mood. And maybe almost cry even. In fact, I'll bet right now you can hear that band playing "Oh Come All Ye Faithful!" (Hear it?) Or maybe "Joy To The World!" (Hear that?) Or "Silent Night, Holy Night." (*That* one will get you if anything does.) Anyway, I know *I* can hear it . . . kind of anyway. To tell you the truth though, it's making me sort of sad-feeling. Maybe like *I* could cry too. That's OK though. (Whew!) They just switched to their super happy, really snappy, bell-jangling, trumpets-blasting, cymbals-crashing rendition of "Jingle Bells." (And I didn't mean to leave the tuba out: "Oom Pah Pah . . . Oom Pah Pah—"Jingle Bells . . . Jingle Bells.") Wow! It can really be exciting.

OK. The stage is set, and here we go. This is what I promised you (your very special "present"). Day is done. Night is falling. The air is just right, with a cold (but not too) sort of freshness. The "just right" dampness of December, along with the scent of fresh-cut pine (and just a little, *little* bit of smoke smell) enfolds everything and everyone. But get ready; the lights are just now coming on. *There!* It's happened. All at once, it's happened! And towering, and I do mean *towering,* over *all* of Washertown (and the surrounding kingdom of Casper County), *bigger* than anything anywhere (in the whole world even), *brighter* than the stars in the sky and the sparkle from the decorated store windows (although some of them are pretty bright), *better* even than the magic of Younker's Toyland (forget about Penney's and Montgomery Ward's), and *more exciting* (although that's pretty hard to imagine) than the spirit of anticipation that already fills everyone's heart (at least when you are real little), is the Casper County Courthouse, arrayed, indeed *ablaze,* in all its Christmas splendor. Washertown's sky-high, "Courthouse of the Ten Thousand Lights," super-spectacular, and everything else you can say, "Christmas tree"! Absolutely awesome, and in the truest sense of the word (although, as honesty requires, perhaps in a way just a little bit *awful* too).

But forget the parenthetical part. "The Courthouse of the Ten Thousand Lights" is totally, *totally* glorious . . . a kind of monstrous (but in a good way), and magnificent (in a "bigger than big" way), conglomeration of all, *all* the following parts: the ten thousand many-colored lights; one bloated, plastic Santa Clause (with reindeer and sleigh); four huge, yellow, lighted (neon) Christian crosses; eight over-sized, red, white, and blue stars (also neon); a few red and white striped candy canes; at least four "Merry Christmas" signs (right . . . neon); two "Noel" and two "Peace" signs (if you were thinking *neon,* you're right again); a Mary the virgin statue (plastic); a "down and out" Joseph statue (also plastic); and a big baby Jesus doll (in worn-out, chipped plaster, or maybe plastic . . . I can't remember which). And of course there are a million (maybe even more) artificial candles (all of them made of shaped and painted cardboard or plastic . . . again I can't remember for sure), with white (or sometimes yellowy-orange) bulbs, and fake "drip lines" on them. Oh (how could I forget?) . . . and on the lawn (in addition to the *primary* nativity players, and the bloated, plastic Santa Clause, with his reindeer and sleigh) there are (all in plastic, I think, or perhaps worn, chipped plaster, like the baby Jesus doll) three wise men, three shepherds, three sheep, one manger, and (I think anyway) a donkey. And there you have it. *There* you have it! So this, my friends, *this* is the Casper County Courthouse (the last week of November and all of December) of Washertown, Iowa: "The Courthouse of the Ten Thousand Lights." It's Christmastime in Washertown! And the place is simply, but *preciously* (although perhaps just a *little bit* pretentious in its presentation), "my" town, "your" town, *our* town beautiful!

And then (it just gets better and better, and you should enjoy the details), all ten thousand lights (Edison-style bulbs) that adorn "The Courthouse of the Ten Thousand Lights" are actually strung on (and sort of hang from) miles and miles (at least it seemed like it when I was just little) of highly insulated electrical cords. And the bulbs themselves are of *every* color you can possibly imagine (more colors even than in the two-tiered, "big size" box of "Crayolas"), with only a few burned out ones (a hint of reality, I guess). And all these strands of light are strung from (not really . . . but they seem to be) the tip of the flagpole on the very, very top (like almost clear to heaven even) of that peculiarly shaped Courthouse dome, gracefully descending towards the welcoming winter wonderland of the sacred city (town) of Washertown below. They (the "ropes of light," as I liked to call them) swoop first from the flagpole to the cornices and corners of the square, flat roof of the building itself, and then keep swooping, again with never-ending grace, all the way out to the lamp posts which stand guard at the outer edges of the snow-covered (when it was at its holiday best) Courthouse lawn. I mean it is sooo beautiful you just can't believe it. All "swoopy," and glittery, and magical and everything. Sort of like a big, square, storybook circus tent, only ten hundred thousand times better. Or maybe twenty hundred thousand times. And at the very, very, *very* top of everything (the part I just mentioned that was almost sticking up into heaven), all the lights are white. Every one. I think maybe that's supposed to make it look more like a big bright star or something (especially when you're a long way away from it). And believe it or not, but this is really true (swear to God), if you were up on a hilltop you could see the lights of Washertown's Casper County Courthouse "Electrical Palace of Heavenly Glory" (I made up the "Electrical Palace of Heavenly Glory" part just now) all the way to Des Moines (well . . . as I kind of said once before, at least all the way to Fairfax).

But back now, and up (once more). Fly with me this time. Like Superman. OK? I mean really *fly*. (It's not that hard to imagine.) So then it's "Up, up and away!" "Is it bird?" ask some people below. "Is it a plane?" Nope. It's just Superman and the two of us reflecting the incredible glitter and glow of the Washertown Iowa Casper County Courthouse "Electrical Palace of Heavenly Glory" (it *is* a nice name, don't you think?). Only now we're kind of looking down on it, and also flying around it at a pretty good clip (this way we can take in even more detail). So anyway, from each of the "sides" of the dome (the dome sides are kind of flat-like) . . . from *each* side (and I'm not exaggerating either), shine the huge (and I mean *huge* . . . like twenty-five feet tall maybe) yellow crosses, each one made from lots of tubes, *neon* tubes, set side by side and framed with aluminum-like metal. That's right. There's not just one, but *four* of these things . . . a cross for each direction I guess, north, south, east, and west. (These "neonified" crosses are in such peculiarly strange taste, by the way, that they are actually, or pretty much anyway, almost OK.)

Then, from each and every window of "The Electrical Palace of Heavenly Glory" (or "The Courthouse of the Ten Thousand Lights," if you prefer), I mean from *every* window, glow tapered groups of five to ten of the plastic candles I told you about (the ones with the white or yellowy-orange light bulbs for flames and the glued on fake candle drippings going down the sides of them). Are they ever pretty! Just like candles in a cathedral, only I'll bet these are even nicer maybe. Of course Washertown didn't have any cathedrals, as I said a long time ago (when I was telling you about Roswell's jukebox); but if it did have, i.e. if Washertown did have cathedrals with candles in them, they still couldn't be any more beautiful than "The Electrical Palace of Heavenly Glory." So slow down a little and look. But then start to fly up again. (Are you with me?). On the corners of the building, but in from the sides just a little bit and on the top edge (just below the cornice), are the over-sized neon stars (neon was big in those days), two on each corner (meaning one for each side of the corner). This might be getting kind of confusing though (maybe because we're flying around too fast), so I'll try to settle down a little, and maybe you can too. I mean we can just glide for a while. Anyway, there are eight big stars, but only most of them (before I said *all* of them . . . I had forgotten) are red, or white, or blue. Two or three, I just noticed, are green for some reason. I guess it's just hard to remember everything (although I would have sworn they were all red, white, and blue). Oh well.

Keep flying, and stay close to me now, since everywhere, absolutely *everywhere* it seems, there are even more ropes, i.e. strands of lights. Some are going right down the edges of the building, and others are swinging kind of "criss-cross" around it. Kind of like the whole building is supposed to be wrapped up like the world's biggest Christmas present, only better. And fancier. And then, *then* there are gigantic, serpentine (although I didn't know that word when I was little) twists of evergreen branches (I think they call them "garlands") that are strung just like the lights, and going in just about the same number of directions too. Up and down and across and around, kind of "drapey-like" (or "swoopy," as I said before). It's hard to believe how pretty all this stuff is. I mean even though I can see everything with my very own little boy eyes (blue), I still can't quite believe how absolutely beautiful it is!

But there's even more! Above all four of the main doors of that Courthouse, one on each side (keep flying, but circle around real slowly now), on a kind of balcony-like place (where maybe some really important person like the mayor or a state senator or the governor of the whole state even might give a speech from), stand great big, *real* (nothing artificial about these beauties) Christmas trees, decorated like at home (only not as carefully). And then (and we might as well land now . . . but take it easy, the ground is really hard this time of the year), out on the lawn (i.e. the lawn of "The Electrical Palace of Heavenly Glory") is the one really huge (and bloated) Santa Clause statue (puffy plastic), with lights in it that cause it to kind of glow from the inside out, making Santa look even fatter and more jolly (and unfortunately I suppose more likely to develop diabetes) than he might otherwise have looked. And you can tell that that big Santa Claus is making people (especially little people) really happy. Unless maybe you're a big "Screw" or something ("Screw" was that "for a while anyway" not very nice person in a story about Christmas that was written by Mr. Charles Dickens, another good writer . . . but you probably already know that). Or was it "Scrooge?" Anyway, and to just sort of "round this out" (no pun intended), Washertown's own fat, plastic Santa has parked his reindeer and sleigh and everything here too. Right on The Casper County Courthouse "Electrical Palace of Heavenly Glory" lawn!

Finally, and so as not to leave anything out (especially this part, since *this* is what Christmas is supposed to be all about in the first place), on the Courthouse lawn, and pretty close but not right next to the diabetic Santa Claus (fortunately), there is the Nativity Scene (mostly plastic, but as I said before, part of it could have been plaster . . . and the more I think about it, it probably was . . . at least I think for sure the baby Jesus was). Anyway, there are Mary the virgin, and Joseph, her kind of "down on his luck" husband (who was not really Jesus' dad), and the big baby Jesus. And by the way, I don't mean to say that Jesus was a "big baby," like a crybaby or anything like that, but only that (as I also sort of said a long time ago) baby Jesus's always seemed to me to be bigger than they should have been. Like out of proportion to everyone else. Especially if you notice how kind of little Mary the virgin seems to be in most of her pictures, and then think about having to have him (the big Jesus) yourself (providing you're a girl of course) . . . meaning having to give birth to him and everything. That, as "they" say, could *really* have been a stretch.

Whatever. The nativity scene also has (of course) the shepherds, and the wise men, and the sheep (three of each, as I said before), and one donkey (as I also already said), and as far as I can remember maybe even a cow and some straw too. There may even be a star stuck up on a stick somewhere so as to look like the "star of the East," which of course is also part of the story. But I'm not seeing any sticks or stars right now, except of course the big neon ones (stars) on "The Electrical Palace of Heavenly Glory" itself. When you get older, by the way, you learn that the wise men didn't actually come to see Jesus and everyone until later (did you know that?). Whatever. I guess the Washertown Chamber of Commerce didn't, but since they were the ones who worked so hard to put this whole thing together (along with all the "stringers" and the "twisters" and the light bulb "screwer-inners"), no one was about to say anything. Anyway, all this Christmas stuff at "The Courthouse of the Ten Thousand Lights/Electrical Palace of Heavenly Glory" is really something. And for the most part (but not always), it's even more exciting than Santa Claus bounding out of the choir loft door on Christmas Eve at Washertown's First Methodist Church (and the home of the acclaimed Washertown Methodist Church "Catfish Choir of the Singing Heads of Our Lord and Savior Jesus Christ").

Finally (once more I almost forgot), and this then really is all I have to tell you, clear up high (again on all four sides) are the other neon signs: two saying, "Noel," and the other two, "Peace." How's *that* for being really nice? And then lower (for "balance," I guess), over each of the four doors (just beneath the Christmas trees I already told you about), are neon signs (this time in *script*, no less) that say, or I guess I should say proclaim, *"MERRY CHRISTMAS!"* OK? So now, holding all these words in your heart (and I really want you to do this), lightly "dust" the Nativity people (and Santa Claus), and all the lights, and the crosses, and the garlands of pine, and the signs saying "Merry Christmas," "Noel," and "Peace," with the purest and whitest and very most "sparkliest" snow you can imagine—the almost spiritual kind of snow, the kind that sometimes seems to emanate and fall from heaven itself (kind of like "the quality of mercy" that Shakespeare wrote about in *The Merchant of Venice* maybe). And then, having done so, i.e. having snow-dusted everything, and especially if you're just a little person, you shall find that you have indeed become a very real part of a very special time, in a truly magical place! And I do mean real. And special. And magical. "Realer," and "specialer," and "magicaler" than anything in the whole world. More special even, and more magical (well . . . at least in the winter anyway), than Washertown's emerald-cut, emerald-green swimming pool (code name *MPP*), with its high flying, and tremendously proud, big flappy flag!

So, dear friends, such was Christmas time in Washertown. And Christmas at the famed "Courthouse of the Ten Thousand Lights/ Electrical Palace of Heavenly Glory." And for me, the shy, four or five-year-old, blonde-haired, blue-eyed little boy (whose hair everyone always wanted to touch), it all meant that somehow it just had to be a truly glorious Christmas *everywhere*. For *everyone*. Therefore, to make sure we keep this all in perspective, and to remember it the way it is really supposed to be remembered, there is yet one more thing I want you to know. Think once more about all the beauty we have just experienced, and the signs that read "Merry Christmas," "Noel," and "Peace." And then let me ask you, "Do you think that there were shepherds 'abiding in the fields' that lay around Washertown? *Real* shepherds? Shepherds who were 'keeping watch over their flock by night'"? Well, there were! I want you to know that. They were there. The shepherds were there, in those very hills. I know. "And do you think 'the angel of the Lord came upon them, and the glory of the Lord shone round them'? A *real* angel"? Well, the angel did come to them. And glory did shine around them. "Do you think that 'suddenly there was with the angel a multitude of the heavenly host praising God'? And do you believe that they were saying, 'Glory to God in the highest, and on earth peace, good will toward men'"? Well, a multitude did appear. And yes, they did indeed speak those words. I can still hear them. Really.

And then of course, and finally (to get back to the center of Washertown and our story), there was this one bright and beautiful star in the sky . . . in the *eastern* sky (which meant that it might actually have appeared to lean a little toward the neighboring college town of Grinnell). But anyway, it was shining down right over where the baby Jesus lay, all decked out in his plaster or plastic swaddling clothes (whatever "swaddling" meant . . . I was never quite sure), asleep on the Casper County Courthouse lawn—the lawn of "The Courthouse of the Ten Thousand Lights/Electrical Palace of Heavenly Glory." Yes, my friends, the star was really there. And *He* was there too. Jesus was there! I know it . . . I just know it. You see, I may have been only four or five years old, but I was there too . . . .

So, you know what? I'd like to send you a Christmas card for you to keep. Hopefully (and hope is a pretty important thing to have) you will save it and read it every year, since I usually don't like to send cards very much. I like to get them though. It's just that I never think the ones I send back look very nice or something. I think they do when I buy them, but then (maybe it's just my handwriting) they don't. Anyway, here it is (your card). I hope you like it. If I could draw, it would have a picture of the "you know what" ("Ten Thousand Lights . . . Palace of Glory," etc.) on it.

+

Behold the multi-colored jewel in the center of this most h
of all cities (well, towns anyway). But *holy,* nevertheless
for me, and holy for all people, little or big, who kn
to believe in sacred things and special places.
Night." "Holy Night." A Washertown "just right n
"All is calm" (at least for now), and "All is
bright). I mean those lights on the "Court
Thousand Lights/Electrical Palace of
really something. But anyway (and I
from *my* heart to *yours,* from Wash
Christmas to all . . . And to all

oly
. Holy
ow how
o "Silent
ight." "Where
bright" (really
house of the Ten
eavenly Glory" are
really do mean this),
ertown to you . . . "Merry
a good night!"

CONCLUSION

Well, there you have it. Washertown, Iowa, U.S.A. Wonderful, *wondrous*, Midwestern Washertown: "where it all began," and "how I got to be this way." And both "where" and "how," I have concluded, and hope you have too, were really pretty good. In fact, because they were so good, I like to think that there are similar Washertowns for little boys and girls to grow up in today, only maybe Washertowns without some of the anxieties and the bigotry (self-induced as much of the anxiety might have been, and unintentional as was much of the bigotry). As I told you before though, Washertown was probably just about the way it had to be. The 1940s were very different times, and although not perfect, Washertown (and the 1940s) were indeed special. And genuinely, singularly, nurturing.

For those readers who remember some of the happenings from, or are themselves remembered in this book of many stories, forgive me if because of my occasional exaggerations, lapses of memory, possible (although unintended) indiscretions, or "mind problems" I have offended you. The truth is (Argentina), "I never left you." I loved you too much to do that (most of you anyway), as well as Washertown itself. For those of you who have enjoyed my account of Washertown, my personal (and maybe somewhat quirky) reminiscences regarding this treasured little town, I am happy to have pleased and amused you. And once more, I ask that you forgive some of the language (and perhaps a few of the "rougher" passages as well).

And so, dear Washertown, I must bid you goodbye. A "fond farewell" to yesteryear (although that might sound just a little too sentimental). Anyway, I truly thank those of you who were part of my early years of growth and development (I think that's what it was), both for the privilege of being able to "begin" *with* you, and for "how I got to be this way" *because* of you (well, to a certain extent anyway). You might like to know, that there are still times when I wonder if there is something wrong with my mind. But now that my writing this American masterpiece has afforded me the opportunity to reflect on so many different situations, and hopefully gain some clarity, I suspect that any mental difficulties I may yet have are "livable," and are simply (at least in part anyway) the unfortunate but inevitable result of my having had too many cherry-vanilla phosphates at Powell's, or one too many "Green Rivers" at Roswell's, or perhaps even one (or maybe even two) too many "Rainbow cokes" at Nollen's Drug Store (with Nancy). Maybe. In all fairness, however, I probably should also say that as I grew older several six-packs of Schlitz, Bud, or Miller High Life (and some cheaper stuff too . . . although it, the cheap shit, always kind of made me sick) *and*, as the years wore on even further, a few too many Manhattans, Martinis, and Dewars (scotch, and with a "twist") may have contributed somewhat to my mental issues also. But maybe not. It's hard to tell.

Also, just "to set the record straight" (as goes one more expression), my tendency to once in a while get a little bit carried away, or maybe off track, or strange or something, could also be, as I explained many, many pages ago, that the damage my brother so mercilessly and cruelly inflicted on me when he so unexpectedly and savagely attacked me with that gigantic wooden spoon (as I myself of course lay helplessly, vulnerably, and therefore pitiably in my wicker baby buggy . . . although I still think he missed my "soft spot") . . . *anyway* (and to just plain start that sentence over), when the asshole hit me with the goddamn spoon it may have been more serious than we originally thought. OK? Or perhaps (the possibilities are beginning to seem endless), and to date the origin of these "mental issues" several years later, I may have remained too fixated on my early love affair with Janey (I mean that "just slightly open" pink chenille robe was *so* soft). Or, it might even be that I never quite recovered from the shock and humiliation of having thrown up at the Masonic Temple dance and having had diarrhea and everything. I mean who really knows?

But now that I keep thinking about it, another possibility might be (and then I promise to try to "wrap this up") that I experience this occasional mind shit because I never quite got over the fact that all my dogs died (to say nothing of the absolute trauma I had to have experienced when my chameleon hanged itself). I mean although I know that "life isn't always fair," and that "it somehow has to go on," and that one has to learn to just "buck up and take it" and everything, those early and premature deaths were just goddamn awful! Including, as I just noted, the chameleon's; although as I explained to you before his untimely death was the result of his own decision (and it *was* hard to feel terribly attached to a skinny little lizard I had only known for six hours). But anyway, how would *you* like to wake up to find a new little friend just dangling there at the end of a string with a safety pin on it? And now that I've been reflecting on one suicide, I'm starting to remember my friend, the imperially slim Richard Cory again, and what happened to him. I mean Jesus! It just never seems to stop. (It's starting to happen again though, isn't it?) OK . . . and this can be like kind of both a review and a "lesson" for you. As I told you before, I have learned that all I have to do to bring myself under control (or try to **anyway**) is to just stop and focus, and then think about things like "into **every** life a little rain must fall," and although "it's always darkest **before** the dawn," if you maybe can just "look for the silver lining," **and then** *do something,* for God's sake, everything will be OK. I know; **it sounds** like a lot of bullshit, but sometimes it works.

So anyway, painful as it is for a little boy **from Washertown** (shy, blonde hair, blue eyes, adorable to almost **pretty, and** nearly perfect, etc.) to say goodbye, I must. The hard part is **that** to actually say it means that something really special has indeed ended—although never in my own mind or heart will it *really* end. Nevertheless, and however reluctantly, I borrow yet another expression, this one from Porky Pig of "Loony Tunes" fame (never forget the wonderful cartoon shows on those special Saturday mornings at the Capitol Theatre), and say, "Th-th-th-that's all, folks!" Which of course takes me right back to kindygarden and those goddamn air raid sirens and scary blackouts and shit. *And,* to all the f-f-f-fucking (sorry) people who made f-f-f-fun of me just because I, like P-P-P-Porky P-P-P-Pig, st-st-st-

stuttered. Shit! But that's OK (at least now it is anyway). It was all part of growing up in Washertown—"where it all began," and "how I got to be this way." Whatever. Having said all this, and to borrow one final expression, it is "with fear and trepidation" (although not as much as I used to have) that "Now I lay me down to sleep . . . ." Good night, dear friends. And thank you.

ADDENDUM

As I was finishing *WASHERTOWN: AN AMERICAN MASTERPIECE!* "Washertown" itself was undergoing what would undoubtedly be the most notable change, and challenge, in its entire history. Having recently "gone home," however, I was pleased to see so much that was familiar, to feel so much that was still good, and to sense the growing confidence for a bright future. It is my sincere hope that the Washertown of tomorrow can somehow, but in a manner appropriate to the present times, be a place that is as special to others as the Washertown of yesteryear was to me. A masterpiece endures forever. Remember that.

Love,
Ernie

Printed in the United States
205329BV00001BB/36/P